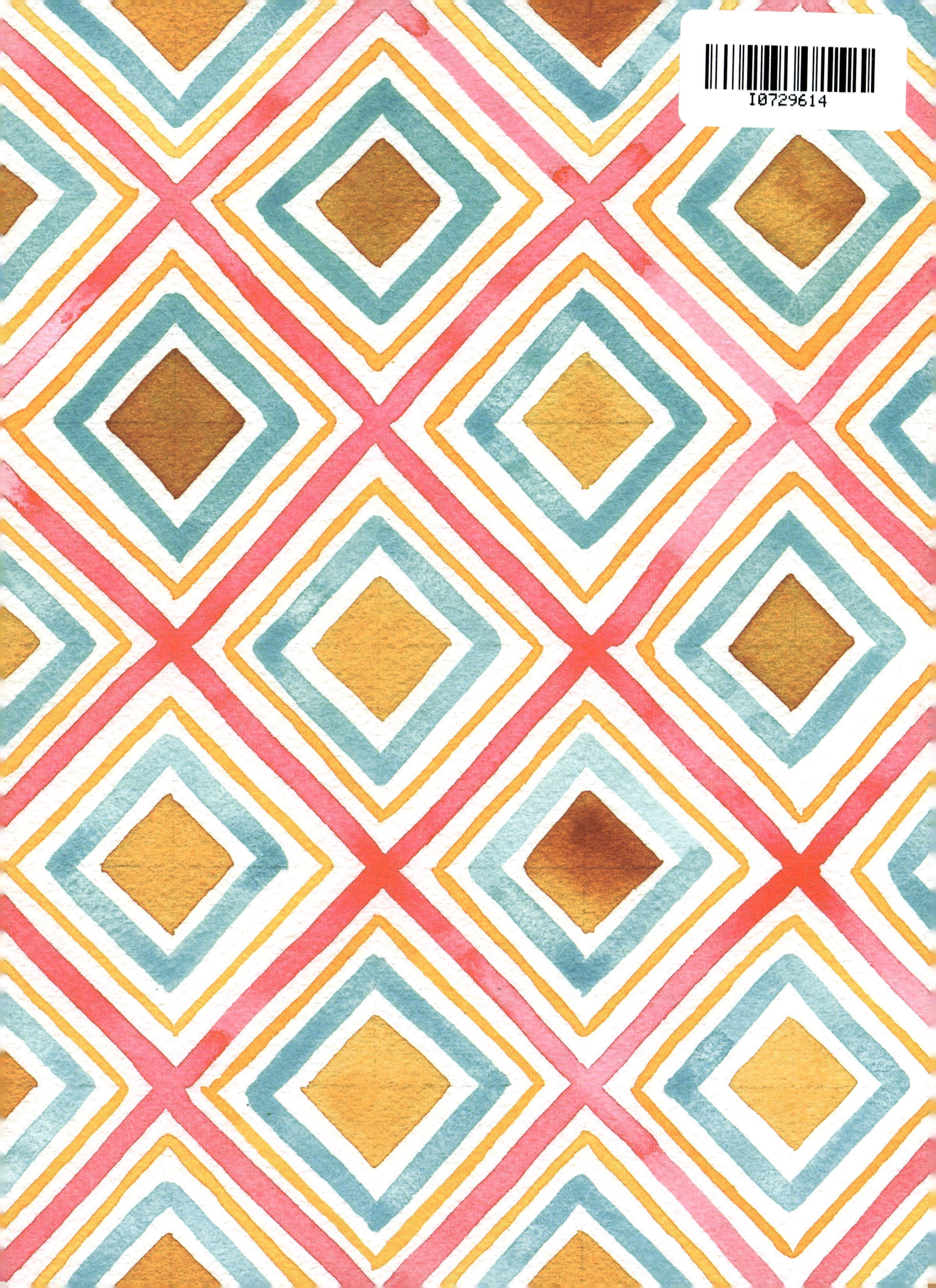
I0729614

Modern
Watercolor
Workshop

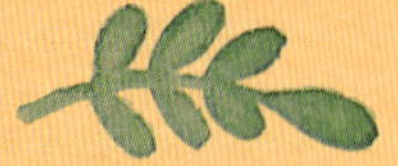

DEDICATION

To my mom, Suchitra, for giving me a childhood in which I was
always surrounded by art, art supplies, and art classes at home
and could see her paint and teach her students.

To my father, Deepak, for always providing us the best of things
during school days. I feel grateful and blessed that he took me
around as a kid to all the art competitions that were held in the city.

To my daughter, Mehr, who is the biggest cheerleader of my work
and a constant source of positive energy, the sun in my universe.

To my husband, Swapneel, for always keeping me grounded
and for being a silent supporter of my dreams.

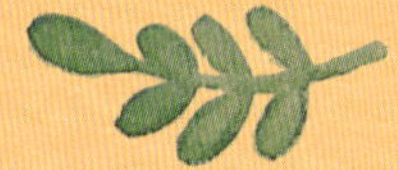

Modern Watercolor Workshop © 2024 by Pooja Kenjale-Umrani and
Better Day Books, an imprint of Schiffer Publishing, Ltd.

Publisher: Peg Couch
Book Designer: Michael Douglas
Editor: Colleen Dorsey
Photographer: Pooja Kenjale-Umrani

Library of Congress Control Number: 2024934344

ISBN: 978-0-7643-6859-2
Printed in China
10 9 8 7 6 5 4 3 2

Published by Better Day Books, an imprint of Schiffer Publishing, Ltd.

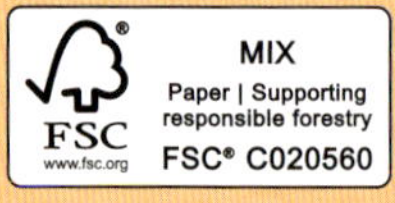

Better Day Books
Email: hello@betterdaybooks.com
Web: www.betterdaybooks.com
Visit us on Instagram!
 @better_day_books

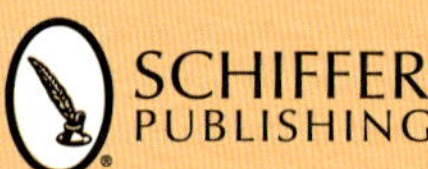

Schiffer Publishing
4880 Lower Valley Road
Atglen, PA 19310
Phone: 610-593-1777
Fax: 610-593-2002
Email: info@schifferbooks.com
Web: www.schifferbooks.com

For our complete selection of fine books on this and related subjects,
please visit our website at www.betterdaybooks.com. You may also write
for a free catalog.

Better Day Books titles are available at special discounts for bulk
purchases for sales promotions or premiums. Special editions, including
personalized covers, corporate imprints, and excerpts, can be created
in large quantities for special needs. For more information, contact the
publisher.

Modern **Watercolor** Workshop

A Calm & Creative Approach

Learn to Paint Geometric
Shapes, Floral Designs &
Other Repeat Patterns

POOJA KENJALE-UMRANI

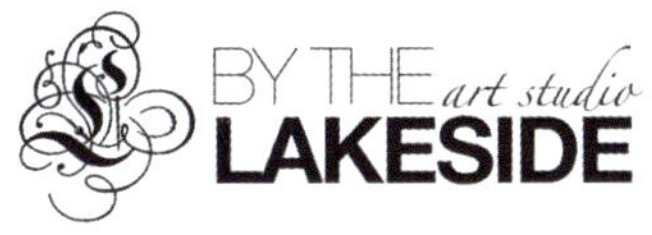

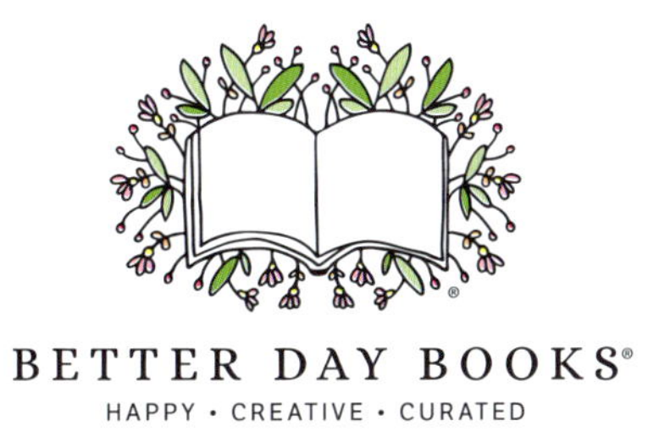

Contents

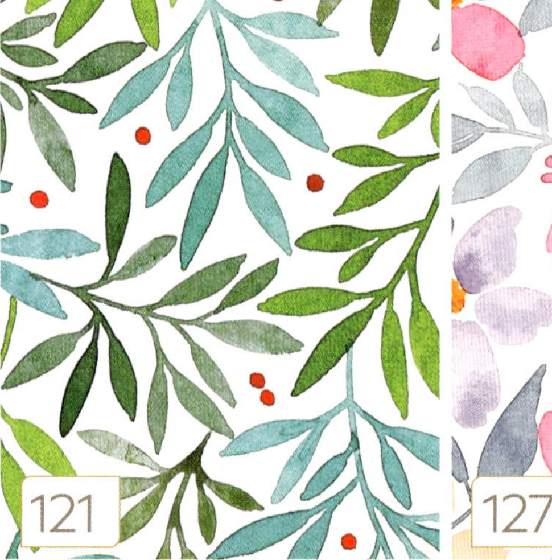

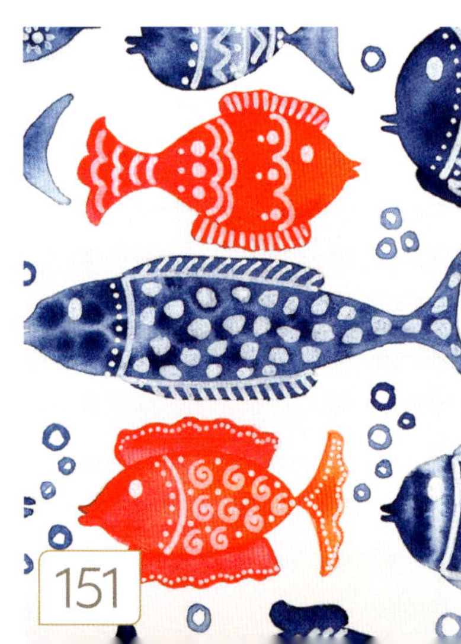

Let's Paint Patterns!

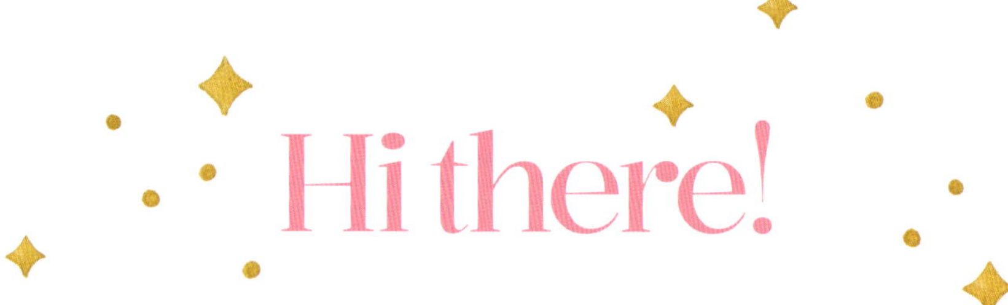

Hi there!

*Thank you so much for choosing this book.
I am so glad that you and I are going to paint together.*

You have this book in your hands because you either are in love with watercolors already or are ready to fall in love with them. Either way, I can't wait to see you dive in and create pieces that will nourish your soul and fill you up with immense joy and satisfaction. I am excited for you!

I still remember the day I painted with watercolors for the very first time. I bought a cheap $5 watercolor pancake palette from a hobby store along with a random sketchbook and a paintbrush. I began painting flowers every day—but not very successfully. Part of me wanted to stop, but I just kept coming back to my failed attempts. Then I started reading about watercolors on blogs, watching YouTube videos, and continuing to paint daily. I slowly started understanding my supplies better, practiced even more, and learned about water control after making countless puddles on my paper. Things really started to fall into place for me after almost a year. Looking back, I cannot point to one specific piece I painted that made me decide to take up painting professionally; rather, I saw a smooth transition from worse to bad to okay to better to good. I credit the success of my journey to just one thing: showing up daily with consistent practice.

I want you to grab hold of the opportunities you have today for learning watercolors. Make the utmost use of every resource available to you and learn the smart way—including with this book! And if on any day you feel like giving up, simply put your supplies down and come back to your art the next day.

To give you a jump start in your watercolor journey, through this book, I offer everything I have learned about watercolors thus far so that you have all the essentials here in one place. Each chapter has been written with dedication and sincerity and was designed to foster learning in a step-by-step manner while revealing lots of tips and tricks along the way.

As you paint with me, pay attention to how you feel; I want you to feel relaxed and positive every time you sit down to paint. Some projects may feel too easy, while others may be a bit challenging. Each of us is at a different point in our skill development, and I want you to accept where you are today. That will make learning a lot more fun and enriching.

I wish you all the best in your watercolor journey!

Keep creating,

Pooja Kenjale-Umrani

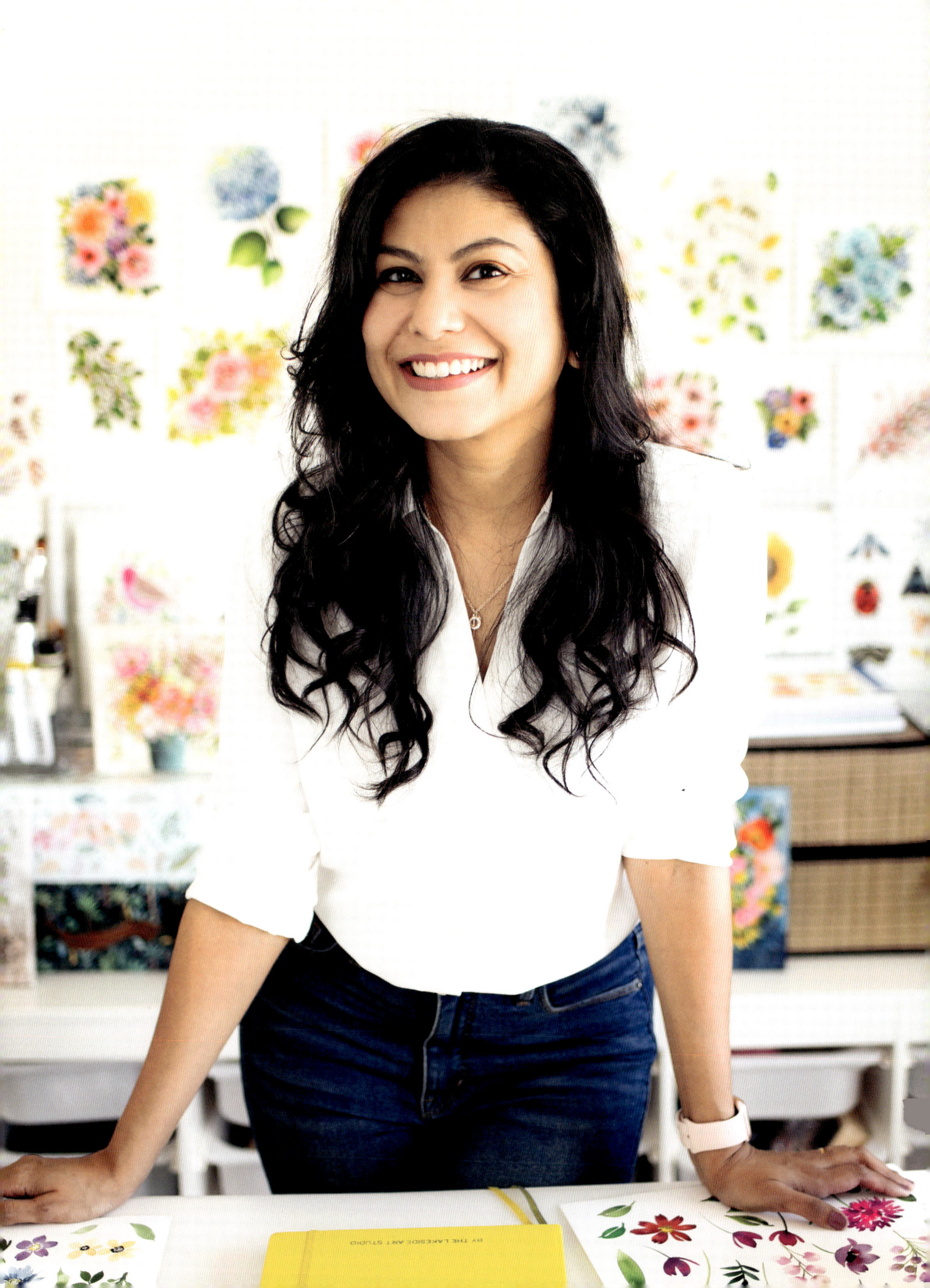
BY THE LAKESIDE ART STUDIO

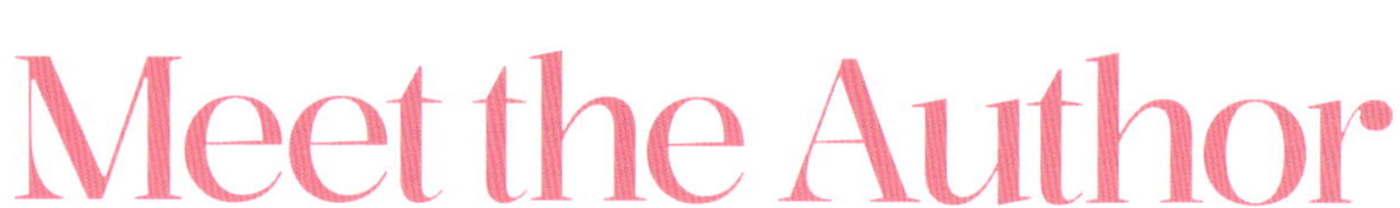

Meet the Author

We sat down with Pooja to learn a little more about her and her painting journey. Join us!

Tell us a bit about yourself.

Hi, I'm Pooja. I currently live in North America, but I am originally from Pune, India, which is where I consider home. I have a bachelor's degree in software engineering and a master's degree in information management, but here I am, pursuing art as my career for the rest of my life. Well, they say better late than never! I love being surrounded by nature and my family, and my favorite place to be is at my desk, which is where I feel closest to my art and connected to all my ideas and creations.

How did you learn to connect with art in your life?

I took up art at a very young age because of my mother. She was always painting and conducting art classes at home during the '90s, so I was constantly exposed to oil pastels, acrylics, glass painting, knitting, tie-dying, crocheting, and more. I would use her leftover supplies and try my hand at everything. Later, a wonderful art teacher in middle school, Ms. Pathak, was very encouraging and motivated me to participate in drawing examinations, which gave me a solid technical foundation in art. Despite all this, I took a long hiatus from making art while I was finishing my education. Then, in 2016, I stumbled upon watercolors and gave them a go—more detail about this on page 6!

How did you develop your personal design style?

To be honest, I am still developing my design style; I have a couple different styles and can adapt to different forms of art easily. I am most confident when painting watercolor florals, but in this book, you will see me showcasing an altogether different style of pattern work that came out quite organically. I was thrilled to write a book on this topic. I love to dabble in different styles, and I feel it is completely okay to have diversity in your art portfolio!

What other creative pursuits do you enjoy?

I absolutely love making candles; before I took up art professionally, I was making and selling candles as a side hustle! More recently, I have been finding solace in nurturing plants; it is my dream to one day have a vegetable garden of my own.

What advice can you give readers who want to spend more time on creative pursuits?

I believe that having a creative outlet can help you find peace in your everyday life and transform your personality for the better. No matter how busy life gets, always make the time to do something that rejuvenates you. If you think your creative pursuit can become your profession, then work toward it bit by bit and slowly and steadily increase the number of hours you devote to it.

What is your favorite item to paint? Where do you find inspiration?

I remain forever in love with flowers. They were one of the very first things I painted with watercolors, and I am still hooked on them. I find inspiration in photographs, plant nurseries, and even the little flower section at my local grocery store! There is inspiration everywhere.

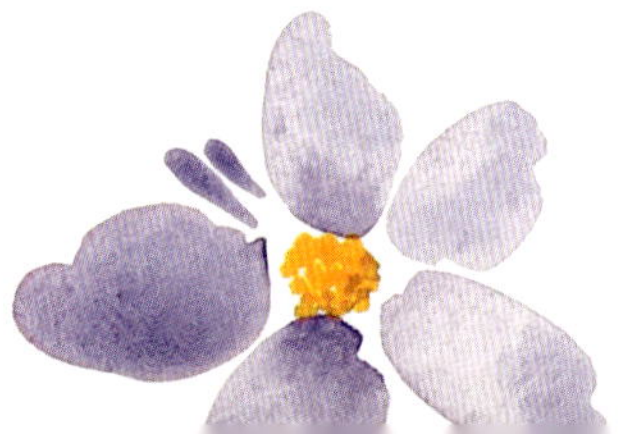

What's a perfect day for you?

A perfect day for me is to wake up early and finish work before 4 p.m., fit in a short workout, spend time with my family, and read a few pages of a good book before heading to bed. Yes, a day spent in the most efficient and productive manner is a perfect day for me— but I promise, I am not boring!

What is your favorite beverage and music to enjoy while painting?

My favorite beverage and the one that I look forward to every day is the afternoon ginger chai made graciously by my husband. I absolutely love listening to relaxing jazz music; I will play it all day long at a low volume in the background while painting (or even now as I type this out!). Cheerful and upbeat jazz rhythms lift my spirits and provide me a much-needed boost of energy in the morning.

What is your advice to a beginner artist?

Four things! First, practice makes progress— every brushstroke counts! Second, be patient and accept the outcome; not everything you paint has to be beautiful. Third, show up daily no matter what, especially as you start your watercolor journey. And fourth, remain open to new ideas, evolve, and always keep learning.

What do you hope readers will get from this book?

I hope they will find watercolors to be a relaxing medium and make it their creative pursuit for many years to come. And I also hope this book will help them paint other watercolor subjects, not just patterns!

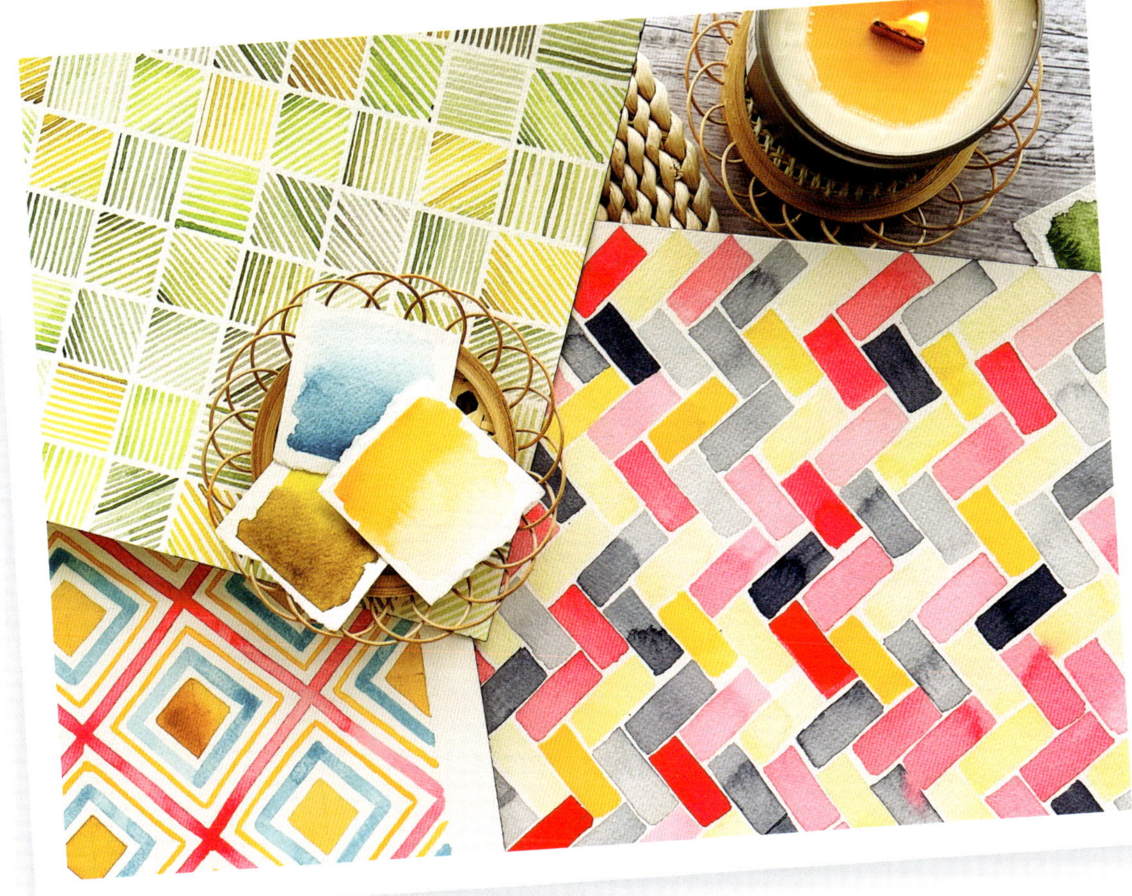

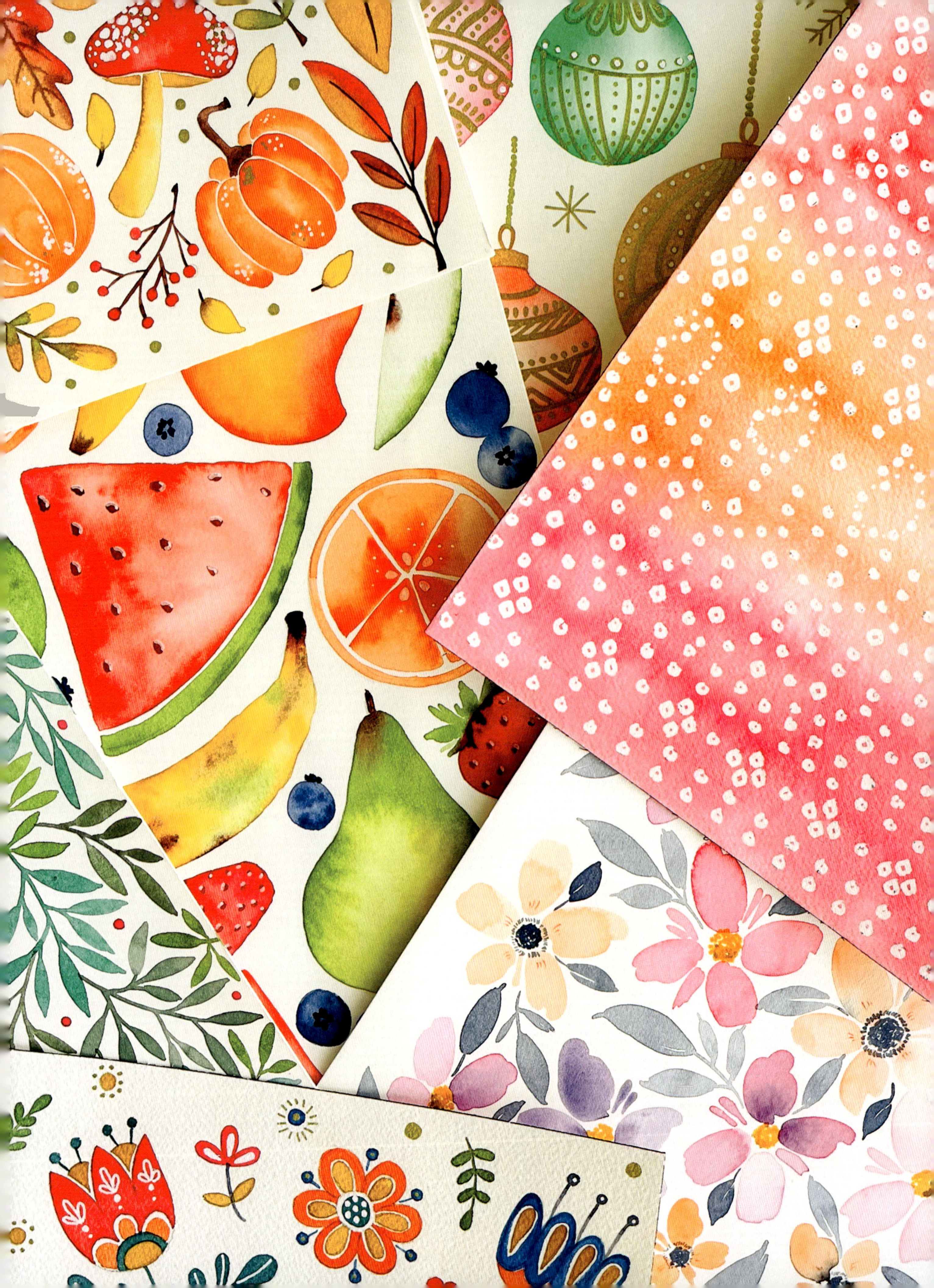

Why Watercolors?

Before we answer that big question—which will take a few pages!—let's talk about what watercolors are. Watercolors are a medium in which pure pigments mixed with gum arabic as a water-soluble binder are used to create lightweight, transparent, luminous, and beautifully layered pieces of artwork. Being able to control the color intensity through various paint-to-water ratios and using the white of the paper to show transparency and depth are some of the particular features that make watercolors special. Watercolors are designed to blend, bleed, and create happy accidents, and they work for painting landscapes, florals, portraits, and anything else you could ever want to paint.

Beyond the technical, there are many reasons why watercolors are so satisfying and several ways in which they can serve different purposes for you as a budding artist and creative. Let's dig a little deeper.

Letting go of control

Watercolors are a free-flowing, fluid medium that require you to at least somewhat let go of control as you allow the paint to flow on the wet surface of the paper. Unlike with denser mediums such as gouache, acrylics, or oils, with watercolor you don't move the paints around precisely where you want them—instead, you help them move. There is much less of a "surprise" element in these other mediums (though that does not mean that these mediums are less enjoyable!). Watercolors can also be reactivated after drying as many times as you want—and, because you don't know exactly how the paint will dry on the paper, you can enjoy seeing what beautiful effects bloom!

A therapeutic experience

Working with watercolors, in my experience, helps to quiet the brain, which more often than not is thinking about so many different things at the same time. As you become engrossed in mixing your paints and laying them down onto paper, you will notice that your mind becomes almost silent, not preoccupied about a single thing happening around you. When you make watercolors into a regular habit, you may find that sitting down to paint puts you quickly into a state of flow—a state in which you are united with your brush and your paper, a state in which you mix your paints with an effortless ease. When you achieve this natural rhythm that feeds your soul, I call the feeling "watercolor therapy." You may not feel it with every painting session, but I guarantee you'll experience it and enjoy its benefits.

Learning to fail as part of the process

When you first start working with watercolors, you are going to struggle in one way or another. Maybe you'll struggle with mixing your paints, maybe you'll lack confidence in your brushstrokes, or maybe you'll simply doubt yourself, wondering if what you are painting will be good enough or whether you will ever feel the "watercolor therapy" effect. Each of these struggles is part of the watercolor learning process, but none of them is permanent!

It can be difficult to keep going when you look at your own failed attempts, but I don't want you to judge yourself. Don't focus on labeling something a "bad painting"; rather, consider it an outcome that you wish had not occurred. Learn from the errors you made, the ones you can control and fix. Then put that painting aside and move on. Try not to shy away from the outcomes that don't match your expectations. Be glad that you made those mistakes, because you surely taught yourself at least one lesson that will make you better at watercolors tomorrow.

If you continue to practice and stick to a consistent painting routine, you will soon see the results not just in the quality of your painting but in the increased therapeutic feelings you enjoy while painting. You will feel comfortable and relaxed, and mistakes won't stop you from finishing a painting. Every fresh attempt will only make you better and prepare you for the next session.

So, why patterns?

I chose to use patterns to teach watercolors through this book because patterns truly allow you to slow down, set your own pace, and concentrate on your own work. Patterns are not focused on a final, concrete, rigid outcome the way that painting specific, realistic subjects such as flowers or a landscape might be. Instead, patterns provide a repetitive process not pinned to a real-life model that you might otherwise constantly compare to. Plus, a pattern ends when you choose to end it—when YOU decide to stop painting, not when you've "successfully" created an image that imitates reality.

As you paint along with me throughout this book, I want you to slow down and take your time to paint each line, curve, and shape. By the end of every project, I hope that you have at least for a few moments experienced the slowness and meditativeness of the process.

Learning watercolor techniques through this book

As you can see, there is a big focus on slowing down and getting into a therapeutic flow while working through this book. However, that doesn't mean we won't be learning real and useful techniques that require some concentration and focus. The idea of this book is to learn the techniques, but to do so in a relaxing and repetitive manner. In every pattern, the repetitive nature of the design will build your confidence as you learn each technique. You'll build muscle memory in your wrist and hand that will smooth out your brushstrokes, and you'll learn intuitively how much water you need to have on the tip of your brush. With every pattern you work through, you will better understand the techniques and be able to answer your own questions and fix your own mistakes.

A Note About Colors

Real-life colors sometimes look a little different than colors printed in a book, especially if the real colors have super-bright or neon tones that don't translate well to print. Always refer to the exact color names provided in the materials list for each project.

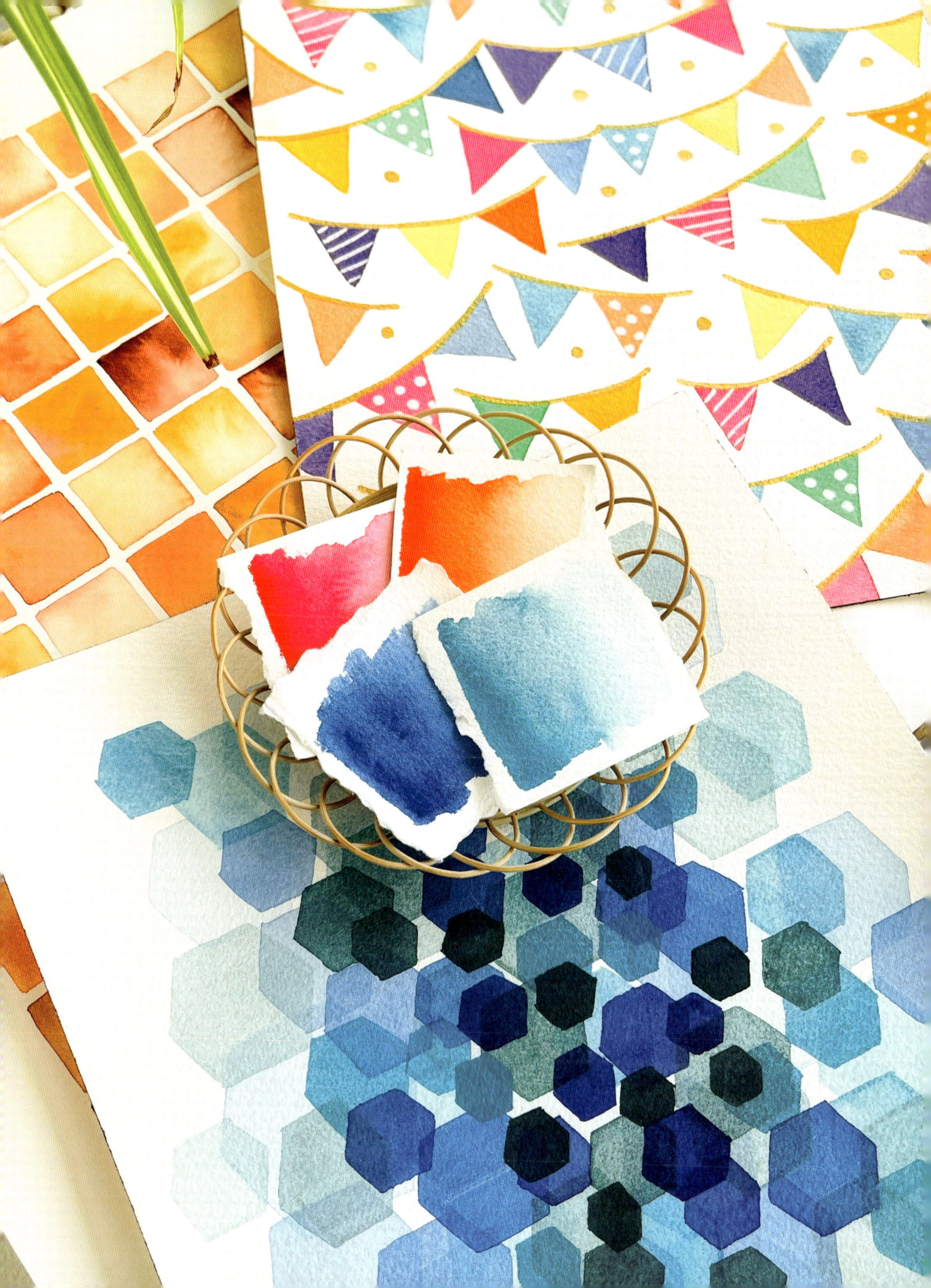

What's Inside This Book?

The projects

In this book, you will learn to paint 21 unique step-by-step patterns that will help you master your watercolor techniques in different ways. The projects are fun, relaxing, and designed to allow your creativity to flow in a progressive manner.

The 21 projects are divided into seven themed sets of three, each including a mix of difficulty levels and teaching different skills. There are patterns that focus on geometric shapes, patterns inspired by countries and cultures, patterns that include abstract shapes, botanical shapes, or seasonal motifs, and more.

Each project includes color swatches of the paint colors used, a materials list, a step-by-step Let's Practice exercise to learn the relevant techniques and shapes for that project, and step-by-step instructions for painting the finished piece.

Watercolor linework patterns

Many of the 21 projects also include a linework "blueprint" for you to follow in the form of a reference sketch that serves as a guide for when you are ready to sketch out a full design before you start painting. You can also download bonus digital versions of seven of these linework patterns for free by visiting **www. betterdaybooks.com/modern-watercolor-workshop-pattern-download**. You can use these printable patterns simply as practice sheets, or to paint the final design right there on the pattern, or to trace or copy the pattern onto your own watercolor paper using pencil—it's up to you!

And so much more!

In the first section of the book, before the projects, you'll get a complete introduction to the tools and materials of watercolors, essential watercolor techniques, and color theory and mixing. If you've never touched a paintbrush or a watercolor palette before, don't worry—everything you need to know is here. If you've already dabbled in watercolors before, this material will serve as a refresher, a solid technical reference, and a source of tips and tricks.

7 themes with
3 skill levels to
build your skills!

The 21 projects are divided into seven sets of three. Each set includes three different difficulty levels: easy, medium, and challenging. For most projects (except for a few freehand projects), you'll learn how to create the baseline grid or sketch the elements before setting out to paint.

Set 1: CIRCLE PATTERNS

To start off, you'll learn patterns based on circles through freehand, pencil grid, and compass drawing approaches.

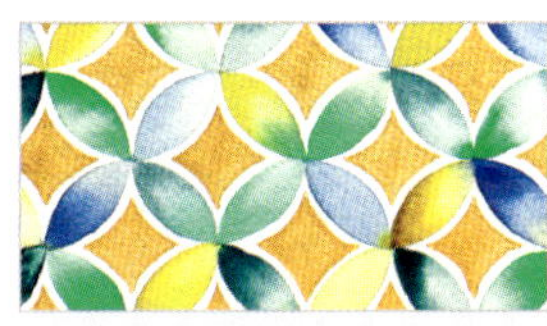

Set 2: LINE PATTERNS

In this section, you'll continue building your skills by learning to paint lines using three different brushes: a round brush, a filbert brush, and a flat brush.

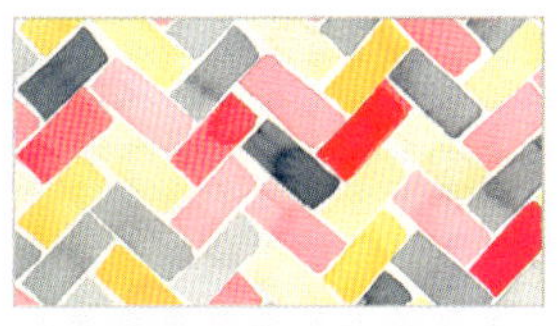

Set 3: GEOMETRIC PATTERNS

Let's explore some more shapes: squares, triangles, and hexagons! This section focuses on strengthening skills like brushstroke control.

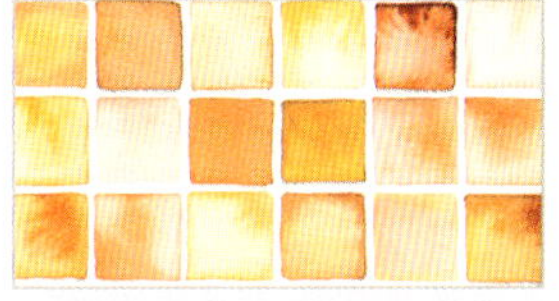

Set 4: GLOBAL PATTERNS

In this special section, you'll learn to paint traditional patterns that have been passed down through various cultures. We will explore patterns inspired by dying techniques from Japan, India, and Indonesia.

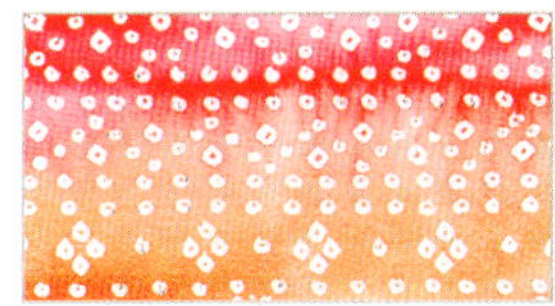

Set 5: BOTANICAL PATTERNS

With these patterns, you'll learn to get comfortable painting basic botanical shapes such as leaves and flowers.

Set 6: MOTIF PATTERNS

Any motif can become a pattern! In this section, you'll gain confidence painting motifs such as rainbows, stars, fish, and fruits.

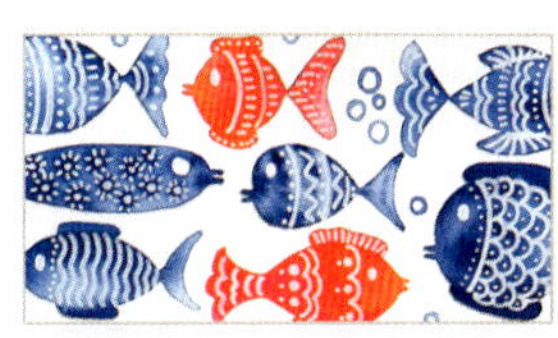

Set 7: SEASONAL PATTERNS

In the final section, we will paint some fun occasional and seasonal patterns for Valentine's Day, autumn, and Christmas.

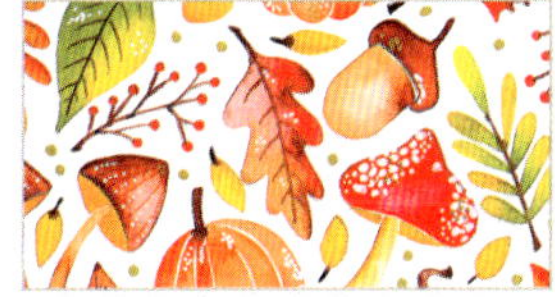

15

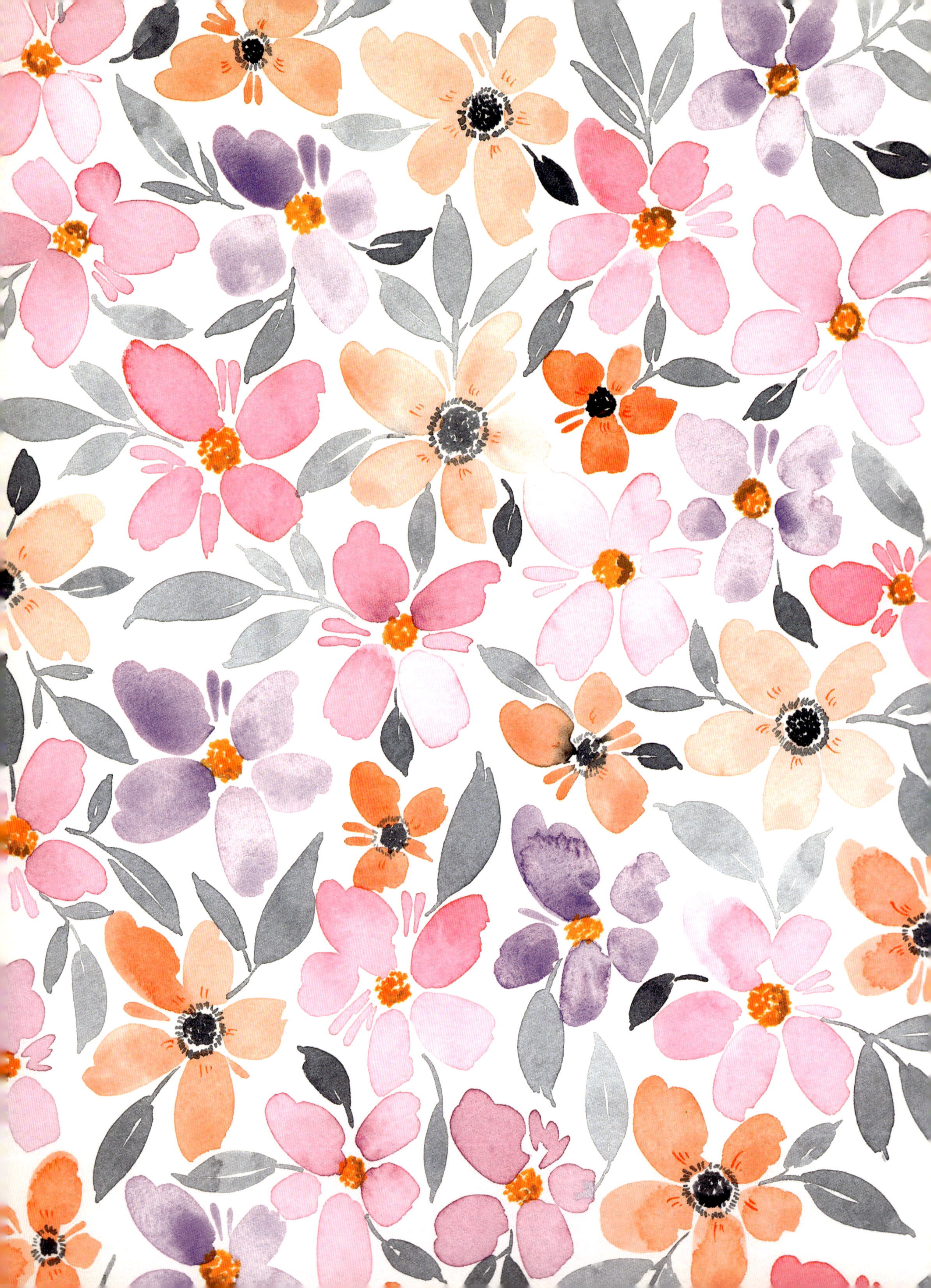

PART 1

Getting Started

Whether you're new to watercolors or already practiced, there is something in this chapter for you. We'll cover all the basic tools and supplies (along with my personal recommendations), discuss specific methods for holding the paintbrush, explore wet-on-dry and wet-on-wet techniques, and delve into color theory with the help of a color wheel. Take some time to learn along with me by reviewing this information before diving into the projects!

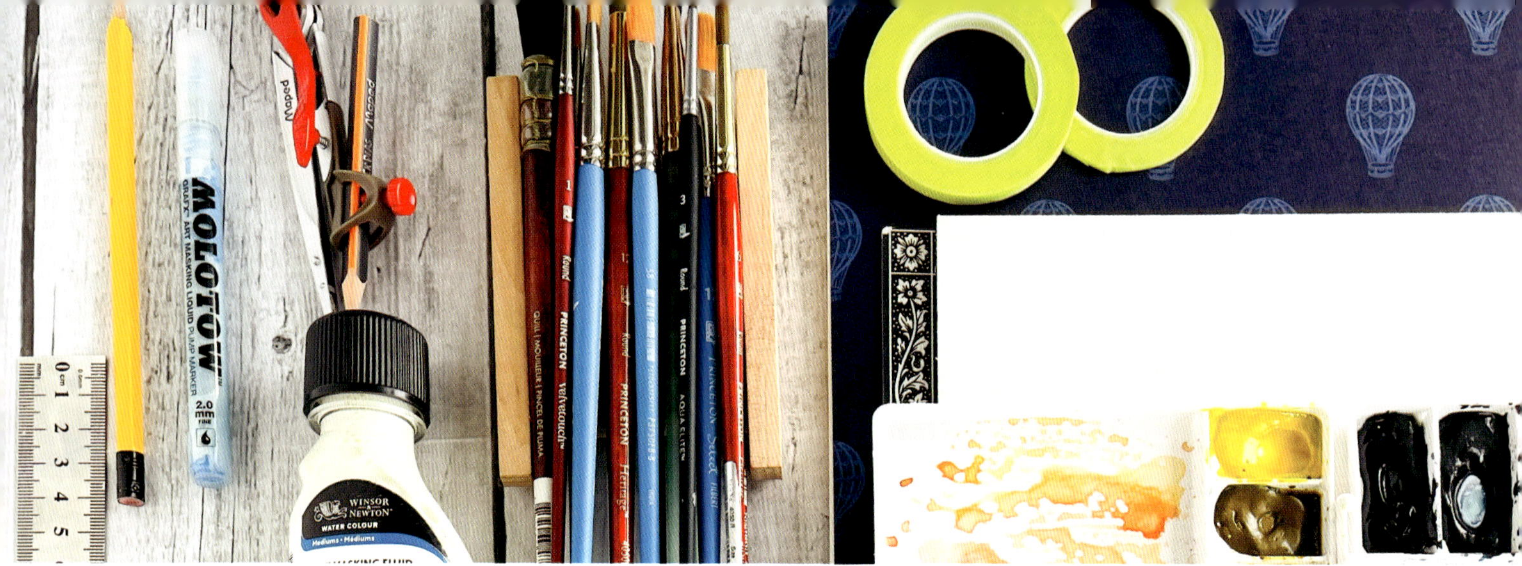

Tools and Supplies

Watercolor Paper

Watercolor paper comes in a variety of different forms depending on its texture, thickness, and composition. Whenever possible, use professional-quality watercolor paper that is **acid free, 100% cotton,** and **140 lb. in weight.** This kind of paper can handle lots of water and allows you to create different watercolor effects like wet-on-wet and wet-on-dry. It also gives a smooth gradient and even finish once the painting is dry. Watercolor paper comes in pads, glued paper blocks, sketchbooks, and as loose sheets.

Types of Paper

In terms of texture, there are three main types of watercolor paper available:

From left to right: cold-pressed, hot-pressed, and rough paper

Cold pressed: Cold-pressed paper has a light to medium texture, also called "tooth," which adds a desirable amount of texture when you paint on it. The soft grain gives an organic and natural look to a painting. The paint does not sit on the surface of the paper long before it is absorbed, but it still gives sufficient time for you to play around and mix colors on the paper. This is the most desirable and traditional paper texture used by most watercolor artists.

Hot pressed: Hot-pressed paper is smoother than cold-pressed paper. Artwork created on this paper has a beautifully soft, airy look to it. The paint flows smoothly on the paper, and if you were to glide your hand over it, you would instantly know that it is hot pressed. This paper works well for artists who like to paint fine details. It is the least absorbent paper of the three types. This means that watery paint can sit on the surface for a longer amount of time and may form pools of paint, making it trickier for beginners to work with.

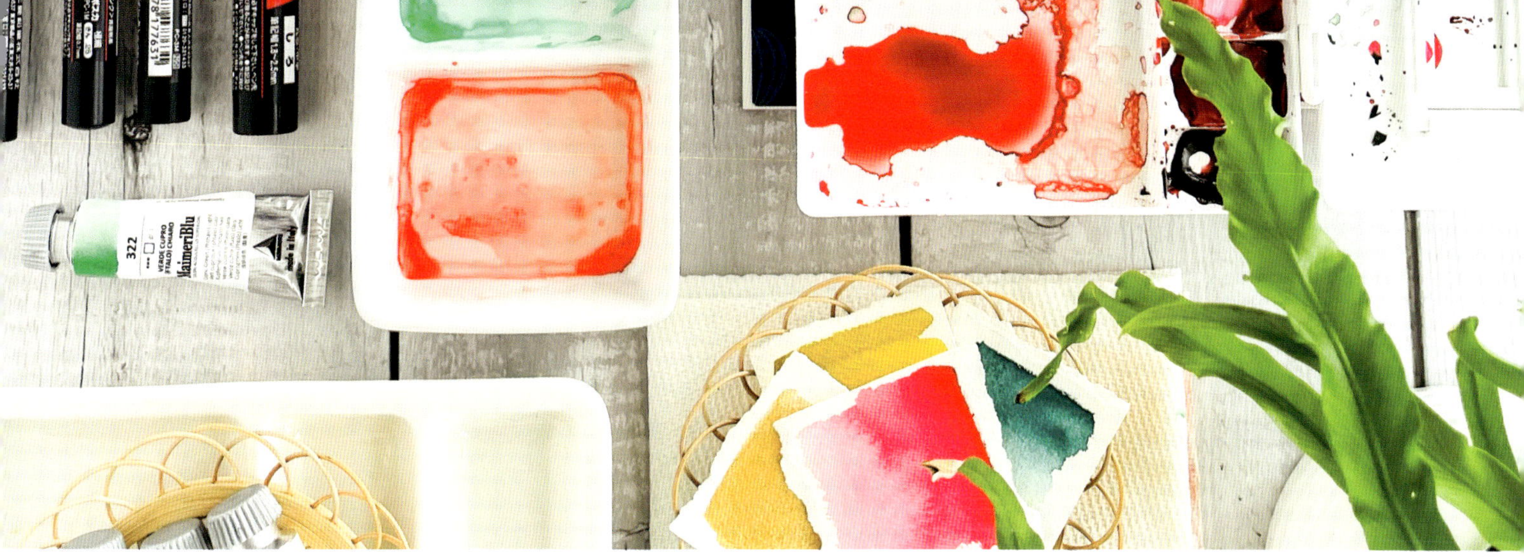

Rough: As its name suggests, this is the roughest watercolor paper you will find. It has significant ingrain texture, which means the paints will be given a sort of granulated effect. It is not suitable for doing detailed work, but it works well when there is a lot of color play on a larger scale. The rough texture can make brushstrokes look dry, and blending can require some effort.

Choose whatever paper suits your painting style. I typically use cold-pressed and hot-pressed paper. To create the projects in this book, I used the following two products: Arches cold-pressed paper block (100% cotton, 140 lb., 8" x 10" [20 x 25 cm]) and Canson Heritage hot-pressed paper pad (100% cotton, 140 lb., 8" x 10" [20 x 25 cm] and 11" x 14" [28 x 35 cm]).

Tips about Paper

Here are some tips regarding watercolor paper.

1 **Explore.** It is good to try a variety of paper from various brands with different textures, but always use the one that suits YOUR style. The paper that works for me may not work for you! Of course, you don't need to splurge on tons of different papers, but a fear of trying something new should not get in the way of your creativity.

2 **Don't waste.** If you purchase a particular brand of paper that you decide isn't suitable for your style after trying it out, find a different use for it. Use it for making swatch cards, holiday cards, or gift tags, or use it as scrap paper to test a new brush, mix color shades, or even just to warm up before a painting session.

3 **Buy as you need.** Don't hoard paper, even if you find good deals in the store. Watercolor paper does deteriorate with time, especially if it is stored in humid conditions, so having a huge collection won't do you much good.

4 **Be economical.** The most economical way of buying watercolor paper is to buy full-size sheets that you cut down to size yourself. I did this a lot in my early days of watercolor. This strategy also works well for my workshops because I like to provide 5–6 sheets of paper for students to practice on.

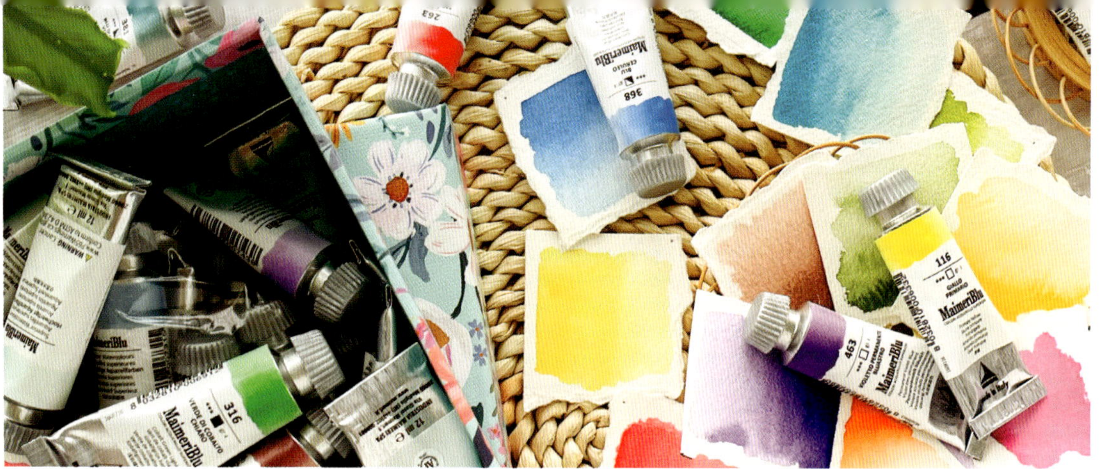

Watercolor Paints

Student-Grade versus Professional-Grade Watercolors

Just like paper, there are a variety of watercolor paints available on the market. The most common way to divide watercolors is into student-grade and professional-grade products. Student-grade watercolors have less pigment in the binder, making them weak in saturation. Student-grade paints don't dilute very well and can create dull, muddy mixes. That said, not all student-grade paints are cheap in terms of quality. There are certain brands, like Winsor & Newton Cotman or Daler-Rowney Aquafine, that create exceptional student-grade watercolors. I absolutely recommended you start with these if you are a beginner or tight on budget.

Professional-grade watercolors, on the other hand, have a higher pigment ratio in the binder and are highly concentrated and pigmented. Just a small dot of paint dilutes to create a vibrant and strong wash of color. For this reason, using good-quality professional-grade watercolors can pay off in the long run. Once you feel confident and have put in enough daily practice, you can start investing in professional-grade paints if you like.

I don't recommend buying a huge set when you are just starting out. Try to buy individual professional-grade tubes from one or two brands. You can start with a basic yellow, a couple of blues, a red, a couple of greens, a fresh pink, and a gray or brown. This is a solid base to grow from.

Packaging Formats

Professional watercolors come in three main forms of packaging: tubes, pans, and liquid. I personally love to squeeze the paste-like paints from tubes out into plastic palettes that have wells and let them dry overnight, ready to be used the next day. You simply wet the wells before you begin painting so that just a small amount of paint dilutes easily when mixed with water. Tubes can last for months or years.

Ready-to-use professional watercolor pans in solid, dry cake format are available too. Most brands sell these as sets as well as individual pans.

Liquid watercolors are almost like ink or dye and are extremely vibrant and saturated. They are free-flowing in consistency and come in bottles with a pipette and dropper-like cap. However, liquid watercolors are not lightfast, which means that paintings made using them can fade over time. This makes them most suitable for watercolor work that will be scanned and used digitally to create prints and surface design patterns.

I have used a variety of different brands of watercolors, and the ones that I end up using the most are Industria Maimeri Blu professional-grade watercolors. This is the brand that I have used throughout the book—check out the full palette on page 43.

Watercolor Brushes

I use synthetic-bristled brushes for all my watercolor work. There are a variety of brush shapes, but the most common brushes used by all artists are round brushes.

Instead of buying multiple small round brushes, I suggest that you purchase a medium to large-sized round brush that has a beautiful point. This way, you can paint larger areas with the belly of the brush and paint fine details using the point of the brush. **A size 6 or 8 round brush with a fine point** is quite versatile and will serve you well for painting the florals and patterns in this book. You can also add two or three small round brushes in sizes 1, 2, and 4 to your collection to work on finer details.

Other than round brushes, in this book we will also use **filbert** and **flat** brushes in a couple of projects. These two brushes are great for creating certain types of strokes, and it is a useful skill to be able to paint with them.

If you work with medium to large-sized paintings, you may want slightly larger brushes, like a round mop or quill brush, and some flat brushes for washes.

To create the projects in this book, I used brushes from Princeton Brush Co., particularly their Heritage, Neptune, and Velvetouch series; they are my go-to brushes that I have been using for many years.

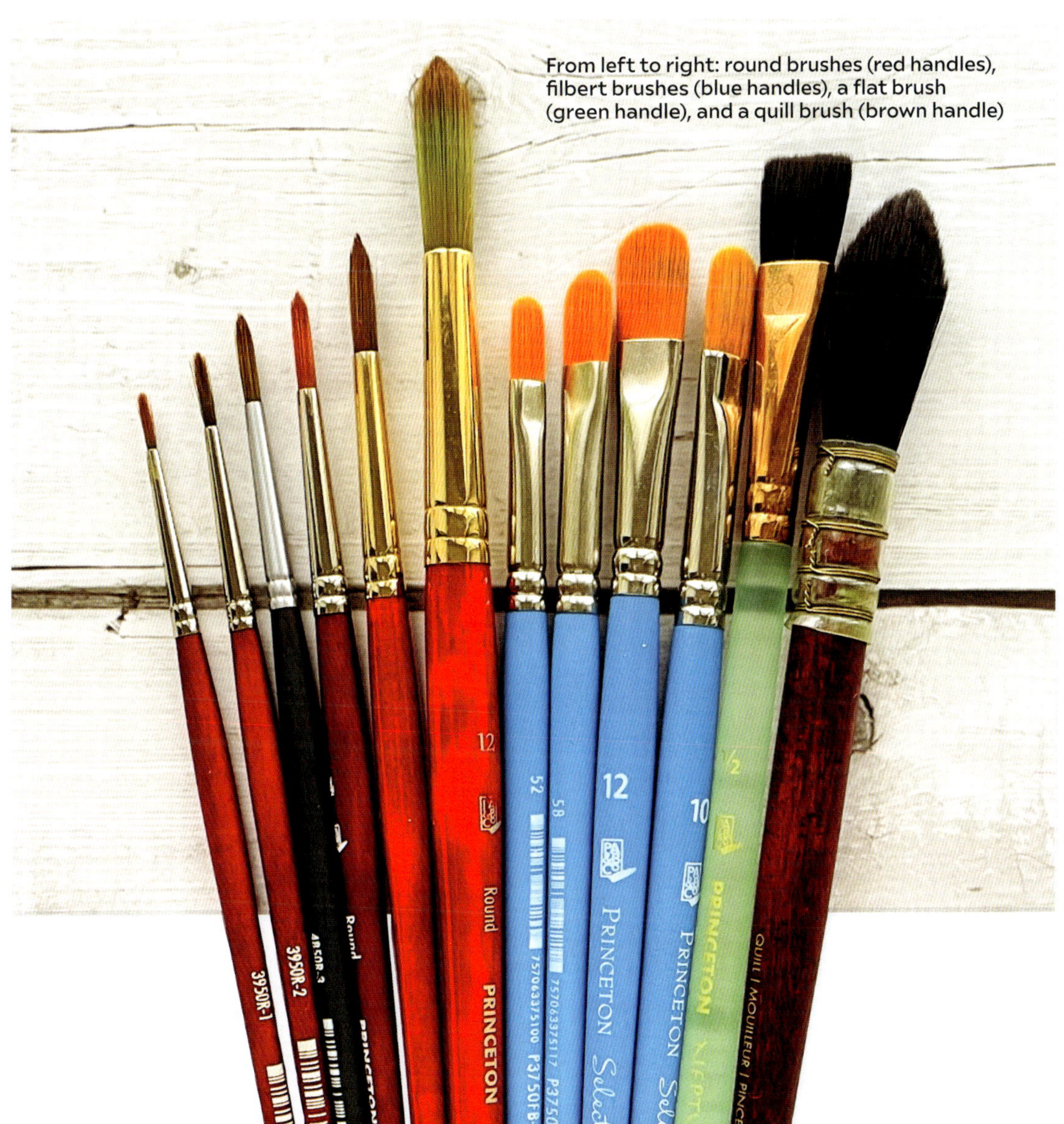

From left to right: round brushes (red handles), filbert brushes (blue handles), a flat brush (green handle), and a quill brush (brown handle)

Water for Rinsing Paints and Brushes

You might be wondering what there is to say about simply using a cup of water to wet paints and rinse brushes . . . but here's a bit of backstory to explain how important water is during painting.

When I first started painting with watercolors back in 2016, I would use just one cup of water to rinse my paints and brushes . . . After a few washes and some color mixing, the water would turn brown and muddy. I didn't realize that the muddy water (as a result of rinsing reds, greens, blues, pinks, and browns in the same cup) was affecting the soft pinks and bright yellows. My subjects would turn out inexplicably dull. After a lot of trial, error, and research, I realized it was the muddy water that was affecting the transparency, saturation, and brightness of my work!

Ever since then, I always use at least two cups of water for rinsing: one cup just for the blues and greens and another for the reds and pinks. If I have browns, grays, and purples in play too, I use three cups! Make sure the cups you are using are clear so that you can see how clean or dirty the water is and change it when needed.

I also recommend keeping a separate cup of clean water just for dipping into when applying water washes for wet-on-wet techniques.

There's nothing worse than ruining a potentially great painting with something that could be avoided so easily, right? These details about water are worth taking the care to get right.

My Secrets for Brush Care

Every time you are done using your brushes for the day, clean them one last time using clean tap water instead of the same cup of water that you were using while painting. After washing them, lay them flat on the desk. Recently, I also started using The Master's Brush Cleaner and Preserver, and it works great, especially on hard, dry brushes— so if you paint every day, consider trying it out!

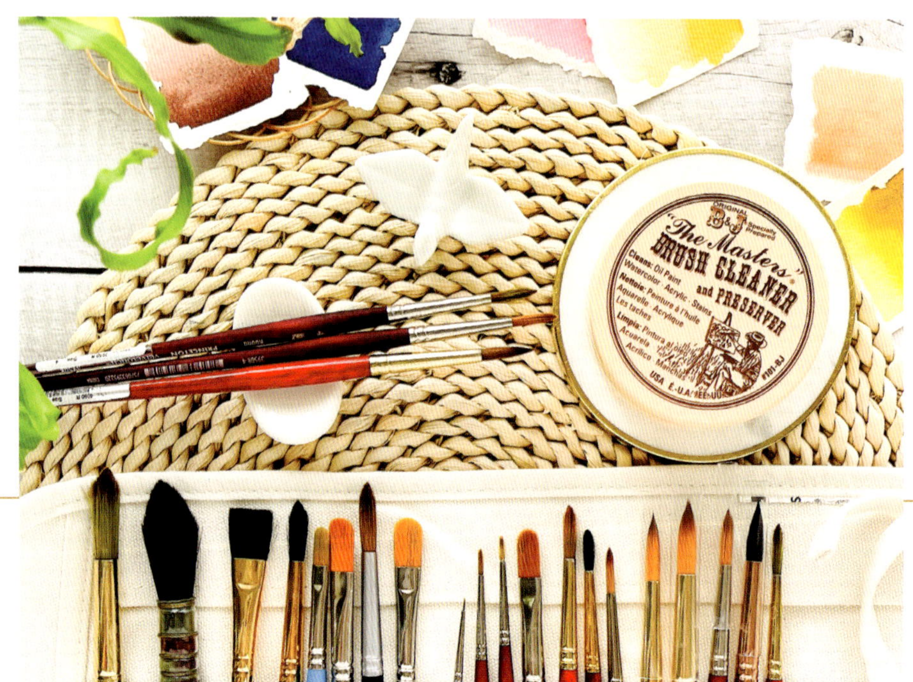

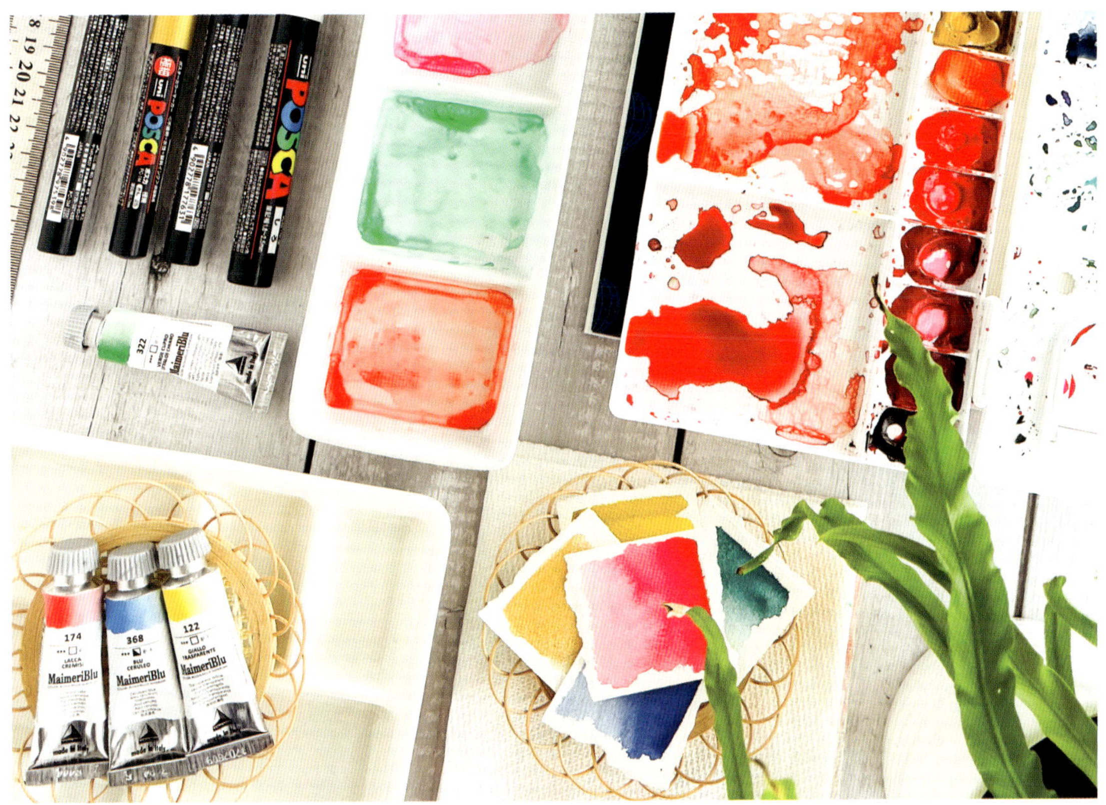

Miscellaneous Other Supplies

Paint palettes: If you use watercolor tubes, I recommend using plastic palettes with wells that allow you to squeeze your paints into the wells and organize the colors to your liking. These are often handy folding palettes with 20 or so small wells and four or so larger mixing areas, and you can shut them closed when not in use. I absolutely love these! If you need extra room to mix more paints, add ceramic palettes with sections to your collection. White dinner plates work just fine too!

Paper towel or a soft cloth: You'll need this to wipe down or dab your wet brushes on after rinsing.

Sketching supplies: Keep a pencil, eraser, compass, and ruler handy for sketching and creating grids.

Gold and white paint pens or markers: A few projects in this book call for these, but they are optional. They make adding final white or metallic details a breeze. You can use white gouache as a substitute for white markers and yellow ochre watercolor as a substitute for gold markers.

Masking tape: We will explore how to use masking tape in a couple of the projects. You don't need to buy a specific brand or product—just make sure you choose a product that is designed for use with paper. I suggest having it in a couple of different widths. We will also use masking tape to tape down the paper when doing heavy washes, such as in the Shibori Stripes and Indian Bandhani projects—you may need to do this if you are not using a glued paper block like I am.

Masking fluid: In addition to masking tape, we will also learn how to use masking fluid in a few projects. This is a great tool for adding lovely, detailed white spaces to your paintings. Masking fluids come in both bottle form and pen form.

Creating an Ideal Workspace

Always try to work in a room that inspires and motivates you. Here is a description of my workspace and what works for me—you may have different needs, though, so develop a space that works for you!

I am deeply motivated to paint by natural, bright light, so I placed my desk next to a big window that faces east. If it gets too sunny, I can shift the desk to allow bright but indirect soft light to hit it. My workspace is beautifully lit up between 10 am and 4 pm, which is my work period. I don't paint past 5 pm, as it affects the way I mix and see colors on the paper. If your desk placement options are limited, try to make sure you have enough bright lamps around you and that there are no dark shadows on your desk while you're painting.

Having a clutter-free desk matters a lot to me. I can't function well if all my art supplies are out on the desk. It hinders my ability to search for what I need at any given moment and adds mental clutter. Before I sit down to paint, I take out only the things I will need—everything else is packed away.

When I sit down to paint, I usually place all my palettes in front of me or on my right-hand side. Also on my right side are my water cups, paper towels, and brushes. My recording clamp is always on my left side so my hand doesn't block the view while painting.

Once I begin painting, I like to have soft, relaxing jazz music playing in the background. It instantly sets my mood and helps me to detach myself from any other work-related thoughts. In my opinion, quiet mornings are the best to begin a piece of work, when your mind is fresh and bubbling with ideas.

See what works best for you, and do everything you need to do to get into a creative mood to paint!

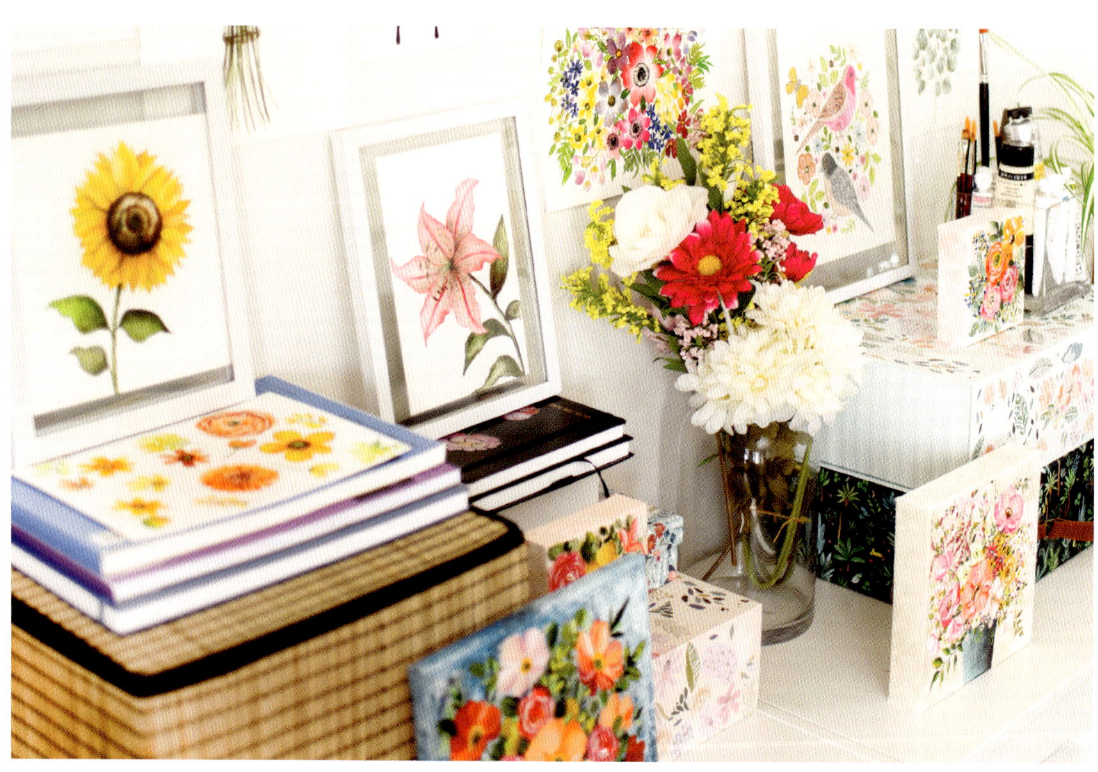

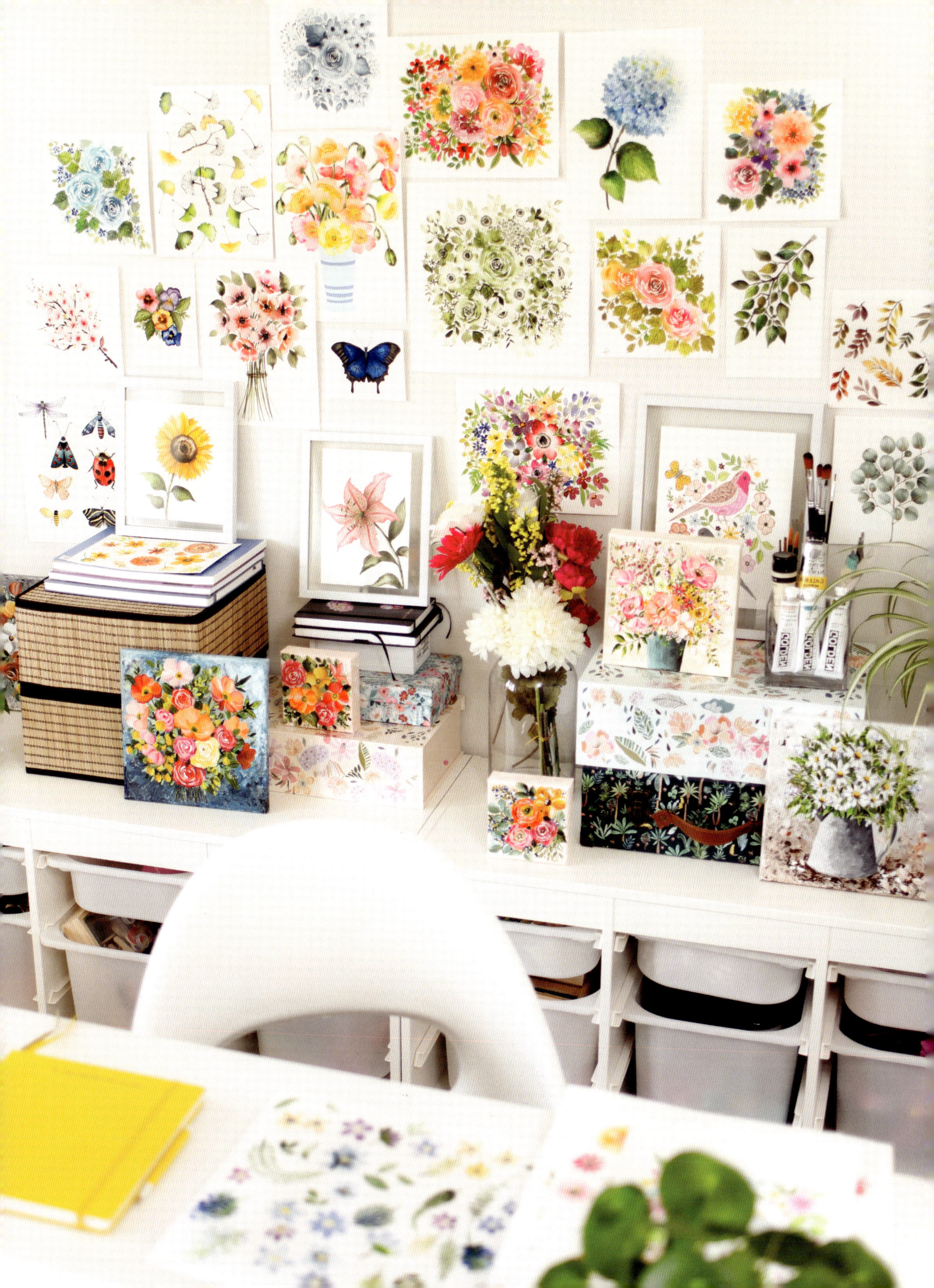

Watercolor Techniques

Holding the Paintbrush

Holding a pen or a pencil to write is very different from holding a brush to paint. There are a few different ways to hold brushes, and they are determined by the kind of brush you are holding and what you want to paint with that brush. Each of the methods detailed here is for reference when you are just starting out. Once you start painting regularly, you will get accustomed to your own way of holding brushes, so don't stress too much about it.

Before you begin painting, always warm up your wrist by rotating it clockwise and counterclockwise a few times.

Precision Work with Round Brushes

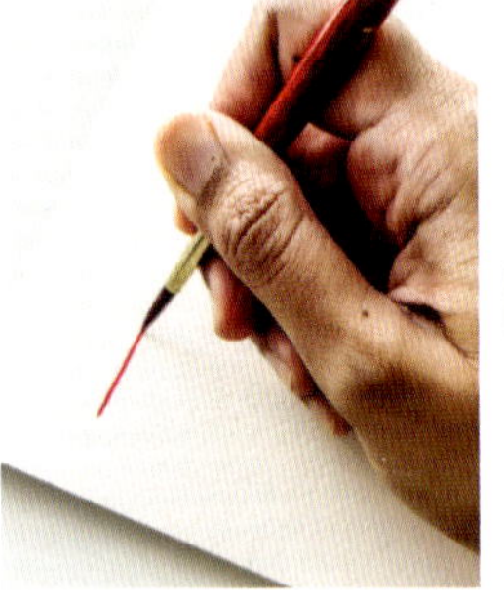
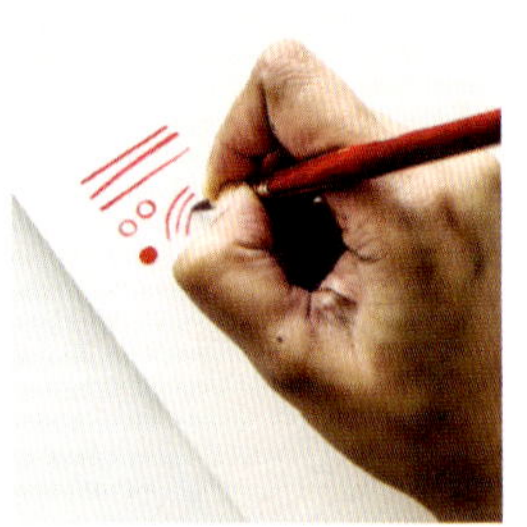

If you are painting thin, delicate lines, small rings or circular borders, outlines of any shape, small dots, or similar, hold a small-sized round brush almost at an upright angle or perpendicular to the paper. This allows you to use the tip of the bristles to get thin, controlled lines. Don't apply too much pressure on the brush. At all times, keep your wrist rested on the desk surface and not floating in the air without support.

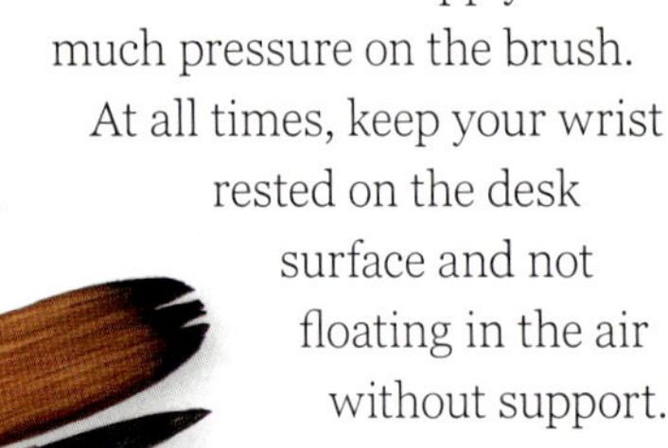

Filling Large Areas

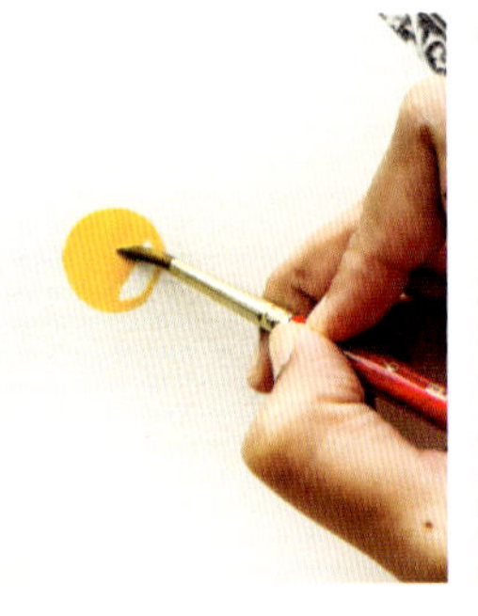
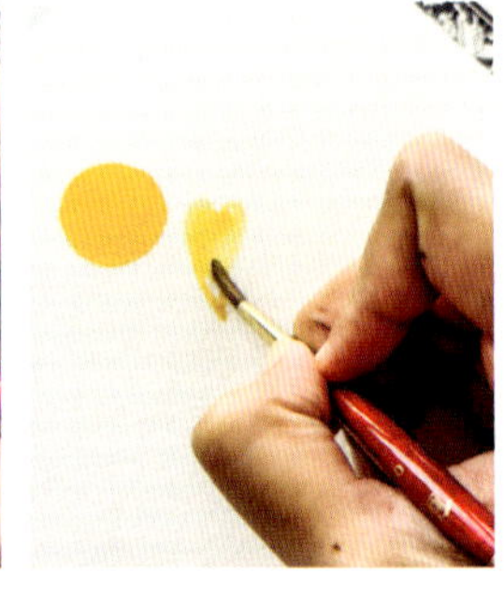

If you need to fill up geometric shapes such as circles, squares, or hexagons or realistic shapes such as fruits, florals, or pre-drawn motifs, use a medium to large-sized round brush (such as size 6, 8, 10, or 12) by holding it at a slight angle close to the paper. The angled position allows you to use the thick belly portion of the bristles to fill space quickly and efficiently. Rest your hand firmly on your work surface while filling small areas.

If you're covering a very large area, such as for a wash, and are using a really big brush, such as a size 16 round brush or a quill brush, you can hold the brush a bit closer to the end of the handle but still at the same angle as described above. For these large areas, though, you can lift your hand up off the paper if you need to.

Consistent Strokes with Flat and Filbert Brushes

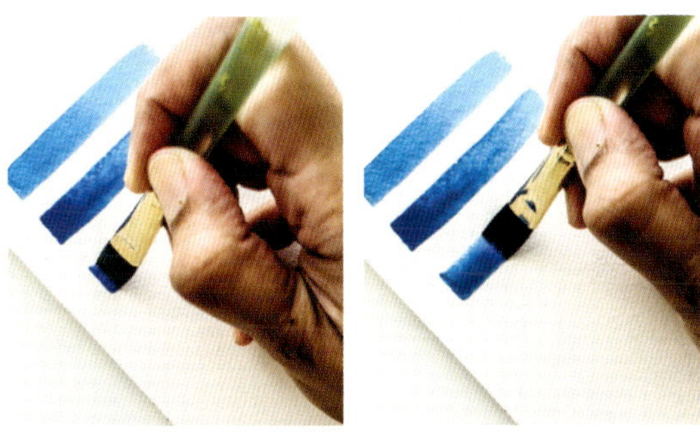

You need to hold a flat brush at an upright position when you commence the stroke, then slant it down a bit while dragging the stroke. Your hand should be just a bit in the air when you first place the brush tip and then rested on the paper while you paint the stroke. If you want to make a longer stroke, you may have to lift your wrist just a bit while you drag the stroke. Try painting a few short and long flat strokes and see if this works for you.

Tiny Details While Holding the Brush in the Air

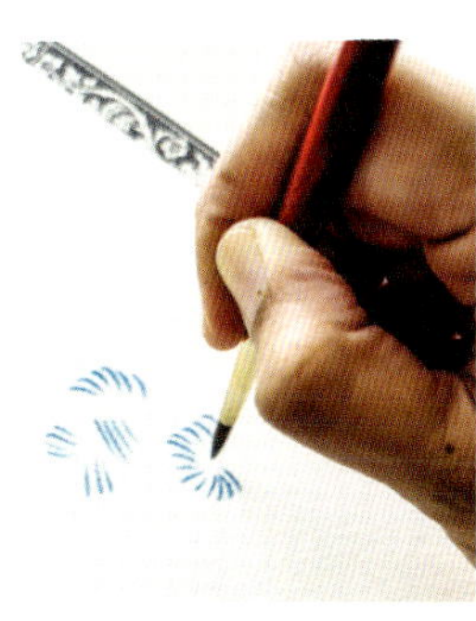

For very small, soft details or lightweight strokes such as the ones on flower petals or leaf veins, switch to a small round brush (such as a size 1) and make the strokes by holding your hand in the air so there is no pressure on the hand and you can achieve soft, featherlike, quick strokes. If you need to paint a delicate dotted texture, though, you should rest your hand on the paper as described in the first method on page 26.

27

Sample Brushstrokes

Shown here are some brushstrokes made using brushes of the various sizes and types used most frequently in the projects in this book.

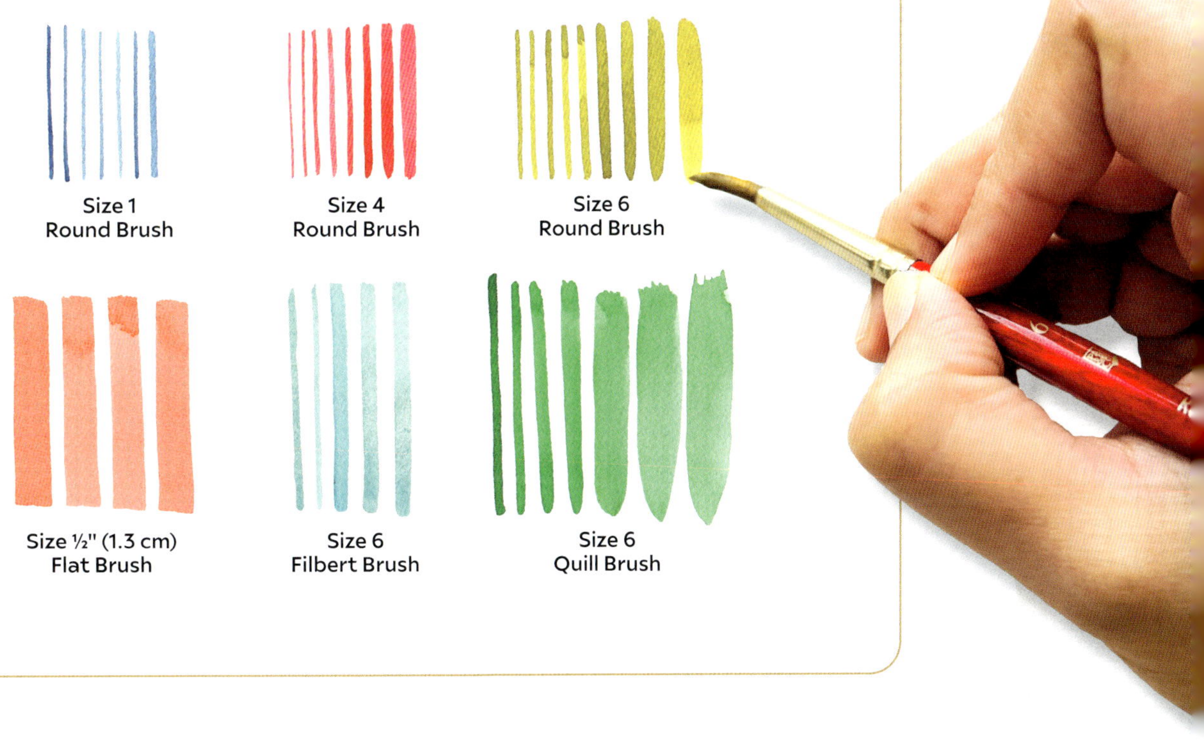

**Size 1
Round Brush**

**Size 4
Round Brush**

**Size 6
Round Brush**

**Size ½" (1.3 cm)
Flat Brush**

**Size 6
Filbert Brush**

**Size 6
Quill Brush**

The Two Key Watercolor Techniques

The two most common methods that you will use over and over again in watercolors are the wet-on-dry technique and the wet-on-wet technique. Both methods play an important role in achieving desirable effects in your watercolor paintings. Let's look at each in detail.

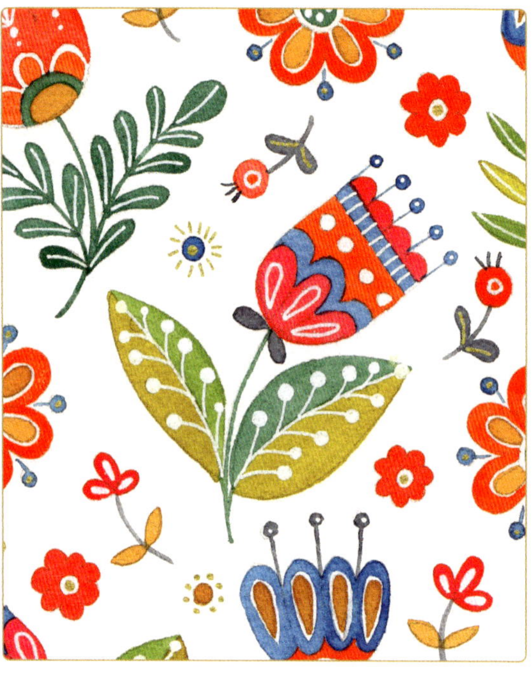

Wet-on-dry technique

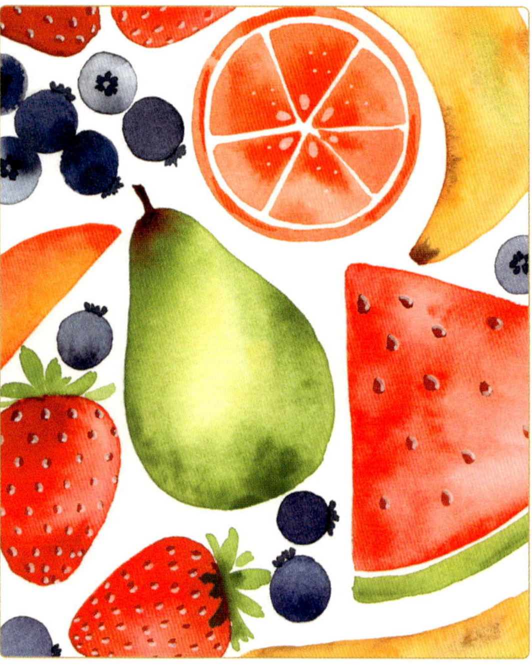

Wet-on-wet technique

Tip about Paper Sizes

If working on a full-size pattern in sizes such as 8" x 10" (20 x 25 cm) or A4 makes you nervous, don't worry. You can start as small as 4" x 6" (10 x 15 cm) and work your way up as you progress through the projects. I do encourage you to try to work with sizes like 8" x 10" (20 x 25 cm), 8" x 8" (20 x 20 cm), 10" x 10" (25 x 25 cm), or 9" x 12" (23 x 31 cm), though, because using paper of this size will give you the space to slow down and sink into the flow.

Wet-on-Dry Technique

In the wet-on-dry technique, paint is applied to a dry surface, which can either be the plain paper or a dry layer of paint.

When the technique is applied on dry layers of paint, you can achieve great, crisp color layering. For this approach, you begin with a layer of paint and wait for it to dry completely. Then, with wet paint, you add details on top of the dried layer. Because the first layer is completely dry, there is no blending between the layers.

Wet-on-Dry
Basic Practice Patch

Let's paint a quick practice patch to understand this technique better.

1 **Paint a yellow patch.** First, mix some yellow paint in your palette. Using a round brush, paint a small yellow patch. (This itself is an example 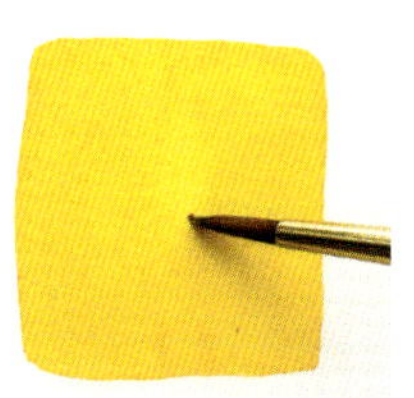 of wet-on-dry: applying wet paint to the dry surface of the paper.) While you are applying this paint on the paper, make sure that your brush is not too dry—you want enough water so that your brush moves smoothly and you can avoid dry brushstrokes. Allow this patch to dry completely—this is important!

2 **Add red details.** Now, mix some red paint with enough water so that the paint can move around on the palette. You don't want a runny, watery 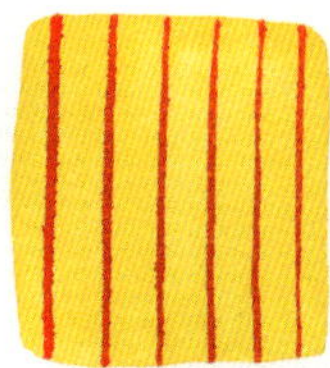 paint. Load your brush with this red color and start drawing vertical lines on the yellow layer using the tip of the brush. You will notice that the red paint doesn't bleed into the yellow. You can add clean red details this way.

Wet-on-Dry
Blended Practice Patch

You can also blend a color on top of an existing dry layer of paint. Try the following exercise.

1 **Paint a yellow patch.** Paint a small patch of yellow. Let it dry completely. 

2 **Add a red section.** Next, add a red paint area on top of the yellow patch. 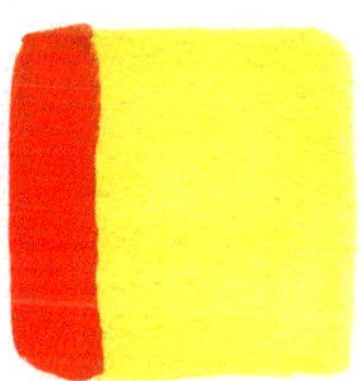

3 **Blend the red section.** Now rinse your brush to take off the red pigment. Dab the brush on a paper towel to remove excess water. Using the moist 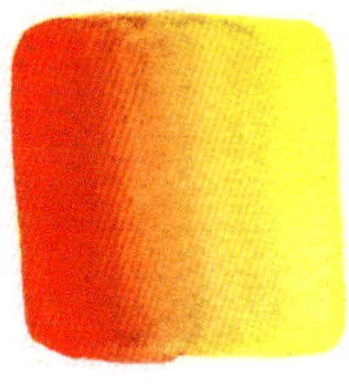 brush, blend the red paint into the dry yellow patch so that there is a smooth transition between the two layers.

Wet-on-Wet Technique

In the wet-on-wet technique, paint is applied to a wet surface, which can either be a wetted paper surface or a wet layer of paint.

Wet-on-Wet
Basic Practice Patch

Paint the following exercise along with me to understand the wet-on-wet technique better.

1 **Create the wet area.** Dip a medium round brush (such as a size 6) in clean water and ensure that the bristles of the brush are thoroughly wet.

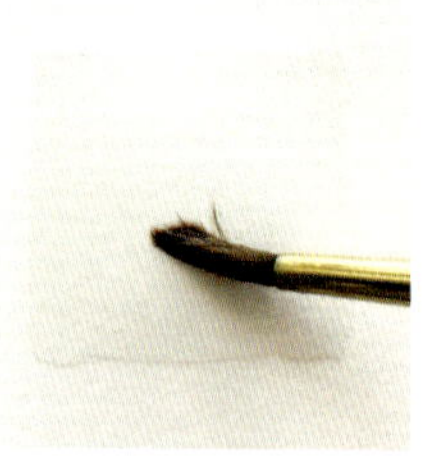

Glide your brush smoothly on watercolor paper to paint a small, not-so-perfect square patch. While you are gliding your brush, make sure that you are not forming a puddle of water—instead, be sure to even out the water so there is a consistent wet patch. Check that you have not left any dry spots by picking up and tilting the paper to see the shine of the water.

2 **Prep your paint.** Next, mix any color of your choice in your palette by mixing it with a little bit of water— just enough to move it around easily on the

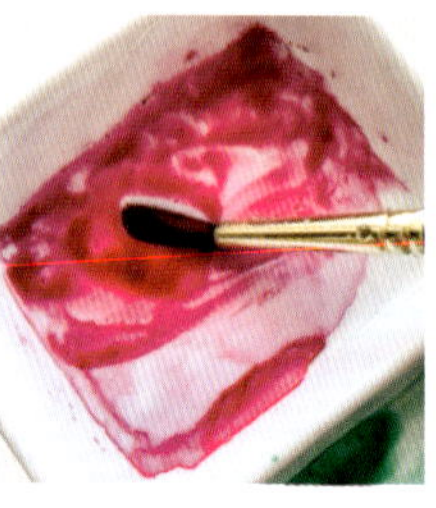

palette. Load your brush with the paint.

3 **Add dots of paint.** Start dotting your brush on the wet patch. You will see that the paint instantly starts to bleed across the wet surface, creating a soft, blurry look. Allow the result to dry without moving the paint around too much.

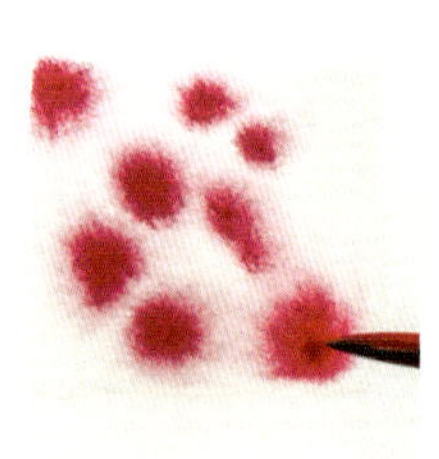

4 **The finished result.** Here is the result once dry. That's it—that's the essential secret of the wet-on-wet technique!

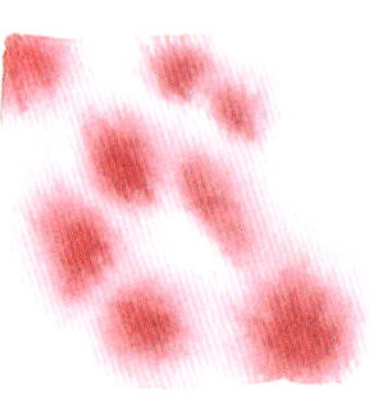

Fixing a Paint Puddle

If you happen to have a puddle of paint sitting someplace, you can use the lifting method to clean it up. One way is to use a paper towel to gently dab the wet area and soak up the excess paint. Alternatively, you can use a clean, moist brush: simply place the bristles of the brush on the paint puddle and they will soak up the excess.

Wet-on-Wet
Additional Practice Ideas

You can play around with the basic wet-on-wet technique in many different ways.

Try not wetting the paint. Apply paint onto the wet area without adding water to it. You will notice that the paint doesn't spread very much—compare this result to the basic technique explained on page 30.

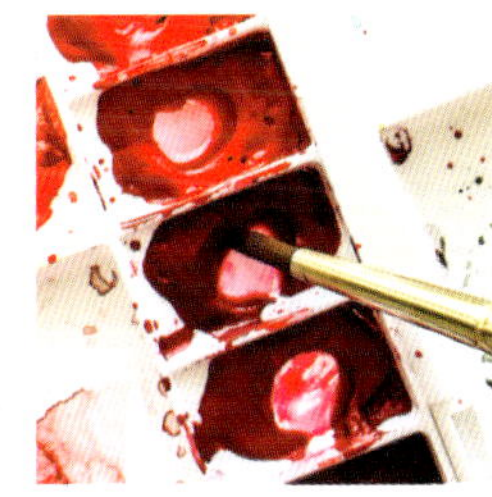
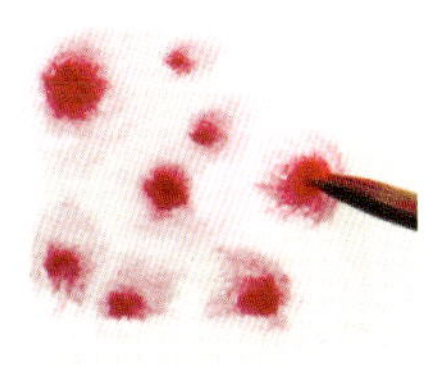
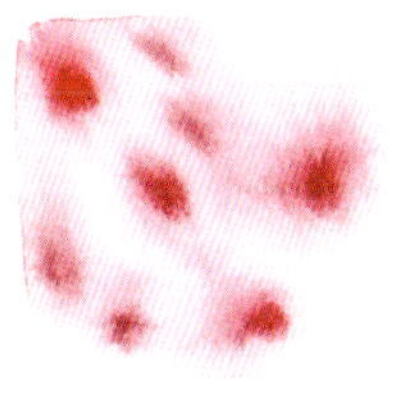

Try adding a lot of water to the paint. Add more water to the paint, and you will notice that the paint bleeds a lot faster and farther. The watery paint may also sit on the surface, forming a small puddle, which takes a longer amount of time to dry.

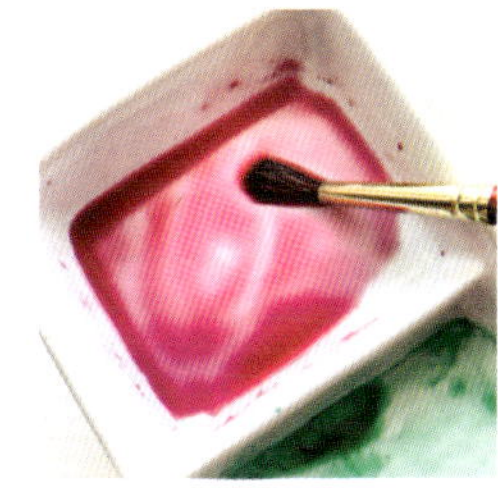
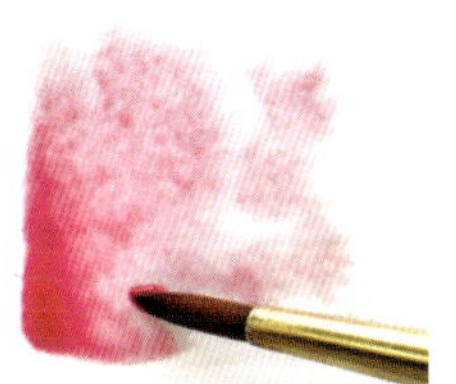

Use a colored wet area. Instead of using clean water for the initial wet patch, use a light wash of yellow paint, then drop in pink or red on the surface to see how the two colors bleed into each other organically.

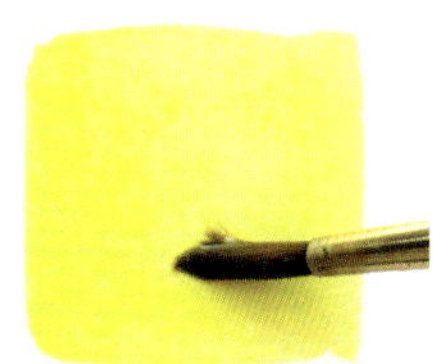
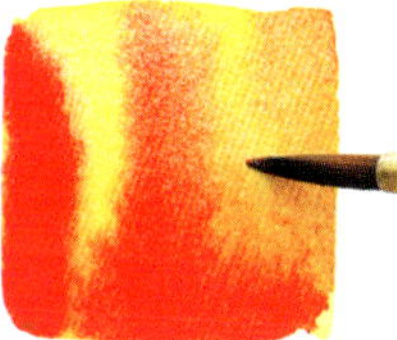

Blend two colors manually. As with the idea above, use a light wash of yellow paint for the initial wet patch, but instead of letting the second color bleed organically into the initial wet patch, blend the red paint with the yellow paint using a clean, moist brush to create a smooth transition.

Creating Watercolor Washes

Let's explore several different watercolor washes! A wash is essentially a medium to large color-filled area. If you are trying out large washes on loose sheets of watercolor paper, I recommend taping the paper down with masking tape so it doesn't buckle and distort from the heavy amount of water used. If you are using a glued paper block, then you won't need to worry about it. For now, though, we are simply experimenting with some small test patches, so you can proceed without any tape regardless!

Flat Wash

In this wash, just like how we painted color patches earlier, we will paint a small patch by applying the paint evenly all over the desired area. The area should not show dark and light patches—it should be smooth and consistent as shown here. The wash should also dry flat. You can try this using a medium-sized round brush or a flat brush. While applying the wash, it is okay to re-dip your brush into paint again if it feels dry halfway through. A flat wash can be done wet-on-dry or wet-on-wet, but if it is done wet-on-wet, you will have less control over how consistent the area looks as the paint interacts with the water on the page.

A simple flat wash

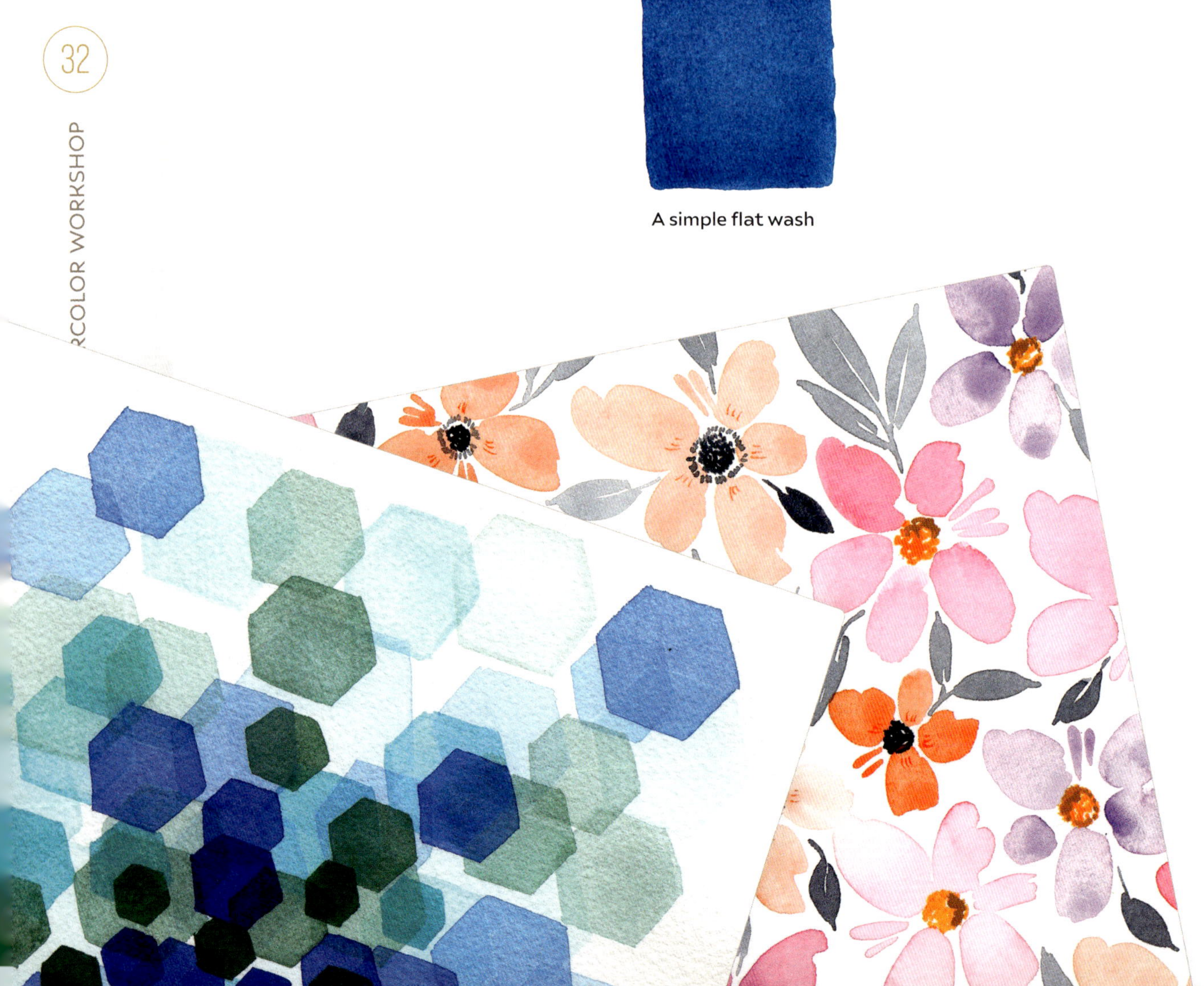

Gradient Wash

In a gradient wash, you typically go from dark to light. To try this wash, mix some blue paint in your palette without diluting it with too much water—you want a high pigment ratio. At the same time, it should be fluid enough to be applied as a wash. You may have to mix some extra paint to get the highest pigment level possible. You could call this a high-pigment "paint puddle" that will last you through the entire wash, especially if you want to paint a big area.

Gradient washes look a lot smoother with a clearer ombré effect if you apply a clear water wash beforehand and essentially create the wash using the wet-on-wet technique. The wet surface will make it easy to blend, removing hard edges between different paint applications and allowing you to create smooth transitions from dark to light or light to dark.

Experiment by trying a gradient wash on a dry surface as well as on a wet surface. Study both outcomes.

A wet-on-wet gradient wash

A wet-on-dry gradient wash

Gradient Wash Step by Step

1 **Choose your approach.** If you are doing a wet-on-wet gradient wash, apply an even layer of water to your desired wash area. If you are doing a wet-on-dry gradient wash, skip this step and proceed with step 2.

2 **Start with full color.** Load your brush with paint (premixed as explained in the first paragraph on this page) and start gliding your brush smoothly from left to right, applying the paint as you go. Keep dipping your brush in paint if you are painting a big patch and if your brush runs out of paint and water.

3 **Dilute little by little.** As you approach the midpoint of your wash area, dilute the paint little by little by dipping the brush tip in water, gliding it along the surface of the cup to take off excess pigment each time, and removing the excess water by dabbing the brush on a paper towel. Then pull down from the previous point, and, as you come down by gliding the brush on the paper, you should start to see a progression build from dark to light.

4 **Finish with pale color.** Once you reach the bottom of your wash area, the paint should be quite light, almost translucent, showing the paper underneath. If you see some extra water at the edge, mop off this excess with a moist or dry brush.

Variegated Wash

A variegated wash has two or more colors blended into each other. This kind of wash shows color gradation and transitional colors between the two "end" colors. Just like the gradient wash, you can try this wash on both wet and dry surfaces and compare the results.

A wet-on-wet variegated wash

A wet-on-dry variegated wash

Variegated Wash Step by Step

1 **Choose your approach.** If you are doing a wet-on-wet variegated wash, apply an even layer of water to your desired wash area. If you are doing a wet-on-dry variegated wash, skip this step and proceed with step 2.

2 **Prepare your paints.** Mix the two paints you wish to use in separate sections of the palette. I used Cerulean Blue and Permanent Yellow Lemon for the samples. Make sure both mixed paints are pigmented enough (see description in the first paragraph on page 33).

3 **Start with one color.** Starting from the top left corner of your wash area, begin laying down the first paint color by moving horizontally. Keep dipping your brush in the paint to ensure that your brush is loaded with paint at all times. You don't want dry streaks of paint.

4 **Introduce the second color.** As you reach midway along your wash area, introduce the second color. Lay it down and let it blend with the first color. You will see a variegated effect as the two colors blend into each other, creating a new color.

5 **Finish with the second color.** Glide the brush smoothly to come down and finish the wash using the second color. Mop off any extra beading at the bottom of the patch for a smooth finish.

A variegated wash used as the background of the Indian Bandhani project (see page 109)

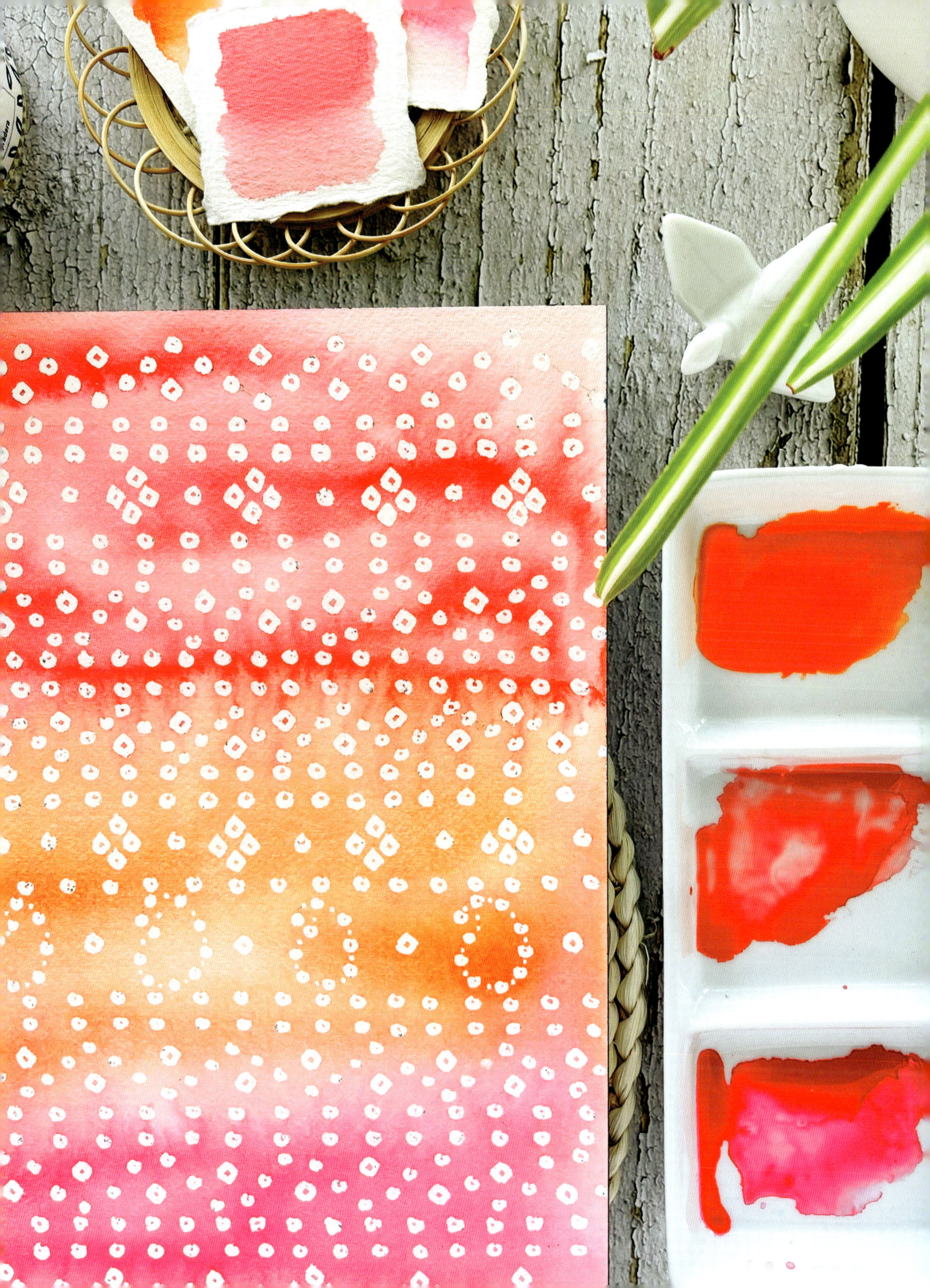

Color Theory

Color Theory Basics and Terms

Color theory is a simple topic if you look at from a perspective of simply mixing any colors to get a desired color palette. But it can also be a complex topic if you delve deeper to understand every aspect, such as why certain colors look good together or don't. Color theory, in a nutshell, is understanding the relationship between colors and how certain colors can be combined with each other in such a way as to affect the final mood of a painting or the place where it will be featured. For instance, bright, poppy colors can create an uplifting mood to make your subject the focal point in a room. Pastel, muted colors can evoke a feeling of calm and peace. A good mix of earthy colors can be used to create an organic piece to suit a moody, nature-inspired setting.

Why Study Color Theory?

There are several reasons you shouldn't skip over this section of the book!

Exploring and painting the color wheel at least once will give you a good knowledge of color proportions. Understanding color theory will help get you comfortable mixing your own custom colors. At that point, you will be able to mix colors to match real-world colors, which is a very important skill to develop to make your art pieces look a lot more organic and natural.

In addition, a basic understanding of how colors work with each other can improve your ability to effectively pair colors to create beautiful combinations that will evoke your intended emotions. Who doesn't wish for their paintings to express the intended feeling?

The Essential Vocabulary of Color Theory

Let's do a quick rundown of the basic terms and definitions you'll need when it comes to getting comfortable with color theory. You will often hear these words when artists are describing a piece of art or sharing their work process. It is good to understand these terms and keep them at the back of your mind, but don't get bogged down by trying to memorize all the technicalities. The more you paint, the more it will become easy to relate with these art terms.

A hue is simply a pure color.

Hue: A hue is what we more commonly call a color, such as red, green, yellow, or blue. A hue is color in its pure form without dilution or transformation.

Value: Value refers to the lightness of a color. We always paint using different values of colors to give dimension to our work. For instance, we don't necessarily always use red in its truest color or hue form. We may dilute it a bit with water or reduce the value to make it light in order to get color gradation. If you look at the color wheel on page 39, you will see two additional circles inside the main outer wheel. The outermost ring represents the main hue, the middle ring represents a mid value, and the innermost ring represents a light value. The mid and light values are achieved by adding water.

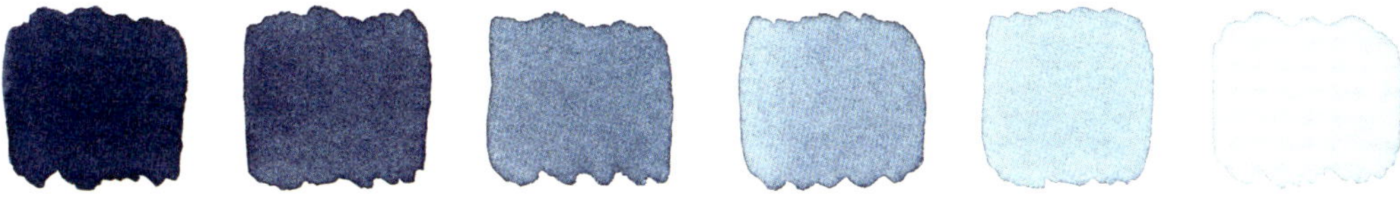

Value refers to the darkness or lightness of a color, such as this series of dark blues to light blues.

Intensity: The intensity of a color refers to the saturation level, or chroma, of that color. Bright colors, such as red, blue, yellow, orange, and pink, can be examples of saturated colors in their unaltered pure forms. Desaturated (or unsaturated) colors are lower in intensity, look duller, and veer more toward black or gray. You can reduce the saturation level of any hue in the following three ways: by adding more water to the color, by adding the color's complement to it to turn it into a duller shade closer to brown or black, or by adding gray or black to it. (For paints other than watercolors, you can add white to reduce saturation as well.) Tints, tones, and shades are all subtopics of intensity. Let's look at each of them more closely below.

If you add water to red, you lessen its intensity.

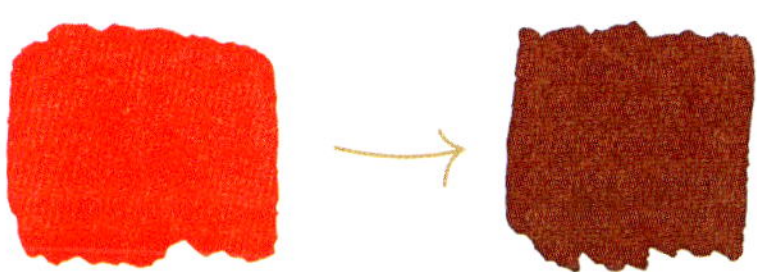

If you add green to red (green is red's complementary color), you lessen its intensity.

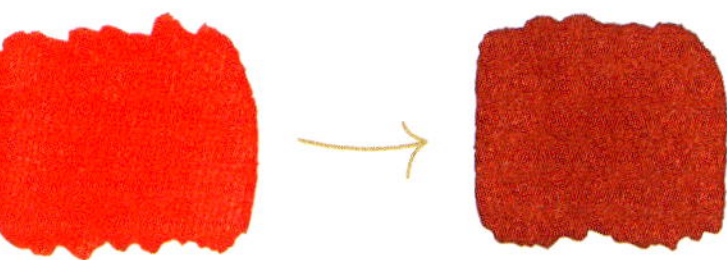

If you add gray or black to red, you lessen its intensity.

38

Tint: When you add white to any hue, you get a tint of that hue. The amount of white you add gives you different variations of the tints. However, we don't really use white watercolor to get tints in watercolor. Instead, we dilute with water, which allows the white paper to show more through the paint.

A tint is any hue mixed with white.

Tone: When you add gray to any hue, you get a tone of that hue. The amount of gray you add gives you different variations of the tones.

A tone is any hue mixed with gray.

Shade: When you add black to any hue, you get a shade of that hue. The amount of black you add gives you different variations of the shades.

A shade is any hue mixed with black.

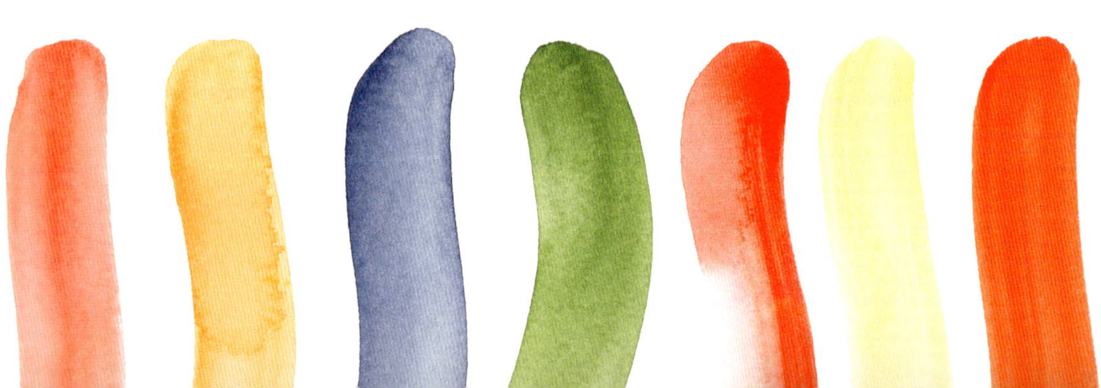

The Color Wheel

Now that you know a few terms related to colors, let's delve deeper into color theory with the help of a color wheel. The color wheel will help us start seeing color combinations and schemes as interesting possible palettes for your work.

Primary colors: These are colors that cannot be formed by mixing any other colors. All other colors are derived from the primary colors. The primary colors are red, yellow, and blue.

Secondary colors: These are colors that are formed by mixing equal parts of two primary colors. The secondary colors are orange (equal parts yellow + red), green (equal parts yellow + blue), and violet (equal parts blue + red).

Tertiary colors: These are colors derived by mixing one primary color and one secondary color. The tertiary colors on the color wheel are yellow-orange, red-orange, red-violet, blue-violet, blue-green, and yellow-green.

The color wheel also helps us to identify warm and cool colors. Every color is a member of either the warm or cool family. **Warm colors** include yellows, oranges, and reds, and **cool colors** include blues, greens, and violets.

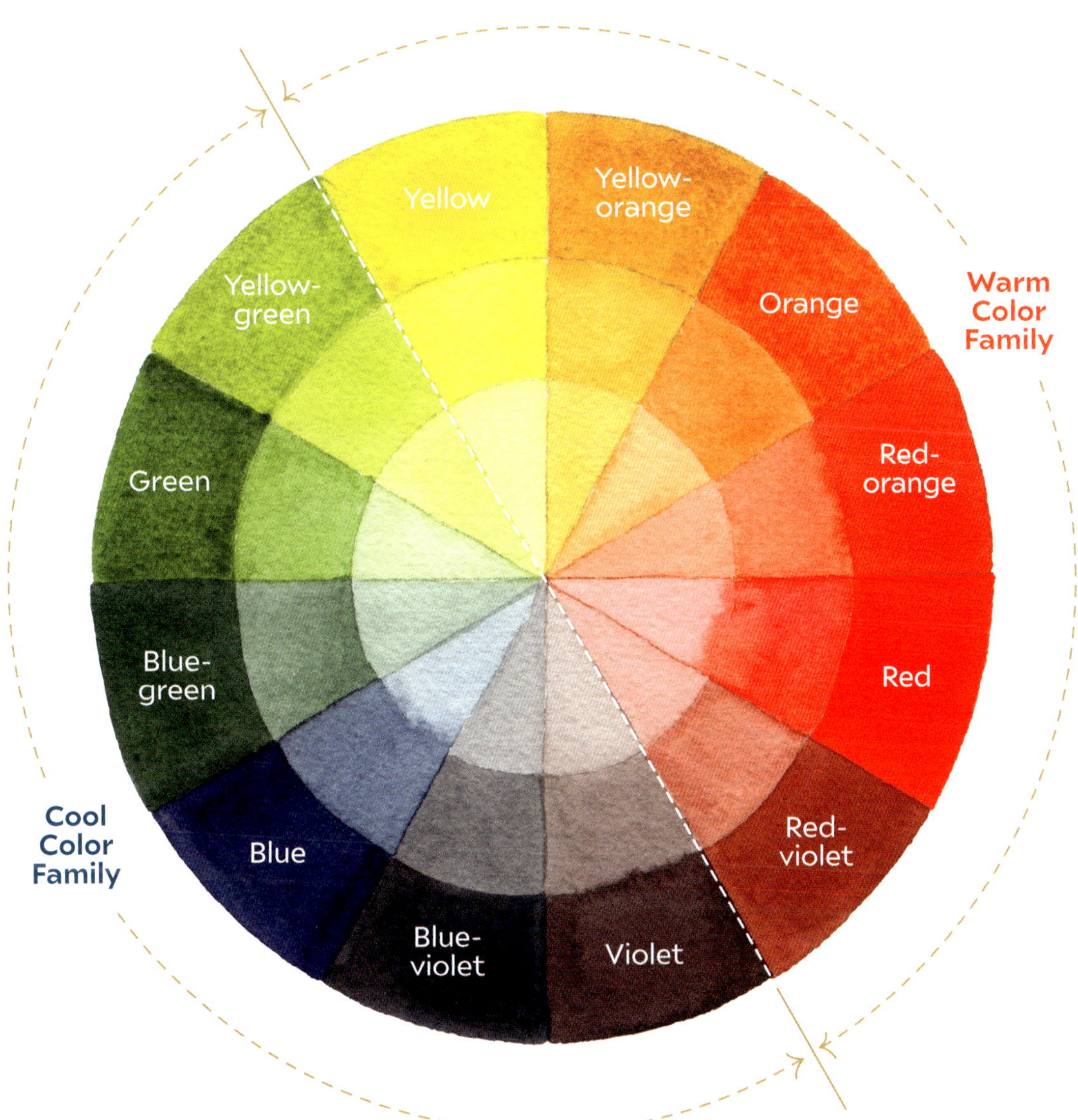

Color Schemes and Color Combinations

Now let's move on to the fun stuff! This is the most exciting part of color theory, where you can actually understand how colors look with one another. Color schemes can make or break a painting and are a big deciding factor in whether or not a viewer feels interested in or positive toward a piece of art.

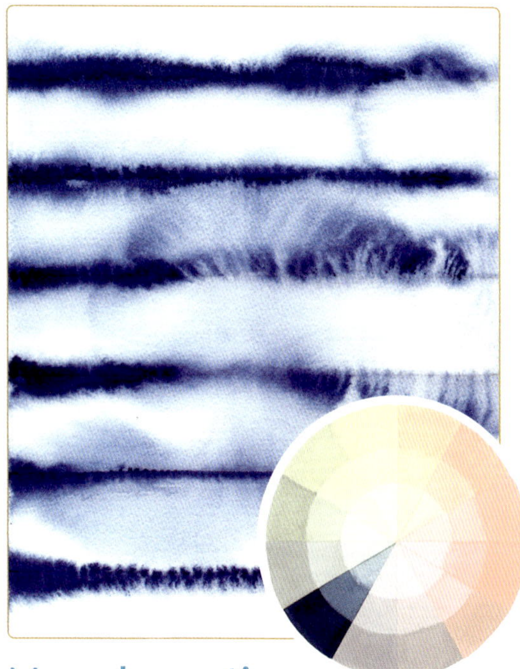

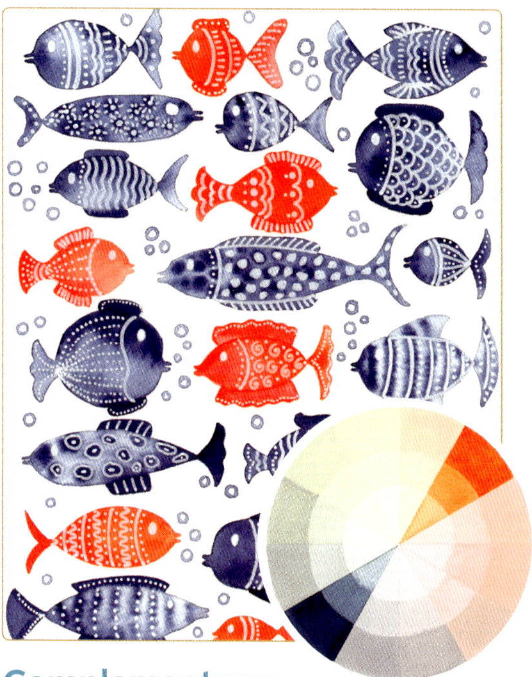

Monochromatic Color Scheme

This is the most easy-to-identify color scheme. Each hue on the color wheel can have a lot of variability in its value. We can create paintings using a single hue but in a wide range of values from light to dark. This is an easy color scheme to execute.

The perfect example of this color scheme is Shibori Stripes, in which a single blue is used to create the pattern.

Complementary Color Scheme

Any two colors that sit exactly opposite one another on the color wheel are known as complementary colors. If you look at the color wheel, you will be able to find complementary color pairs such as red and green, yellow and violet, and blue and orange.

A complementary color scheme produces quite vibrant pieces of art. If you look at nature, you will find complementary color schemes all around you: a red strawberry with green leaves, a yellow and violet pansy flower, etc.

A perfect example of this color scheme is Gone Fishing, in which blue is the dominant color, with orange adding a bright complementary contrast.

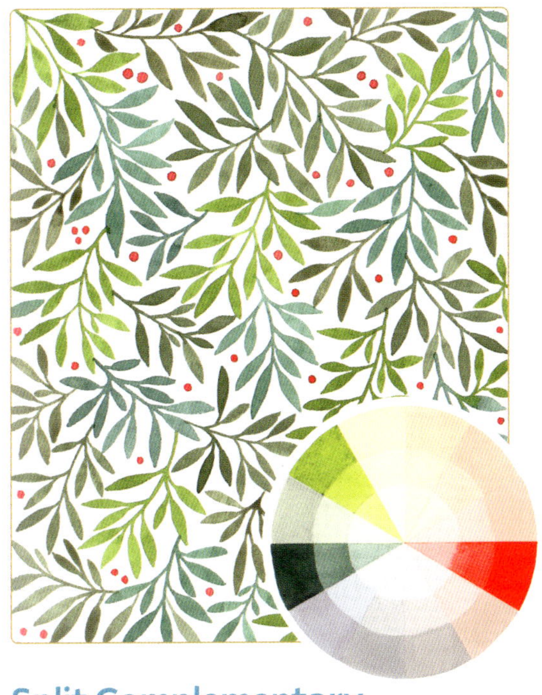

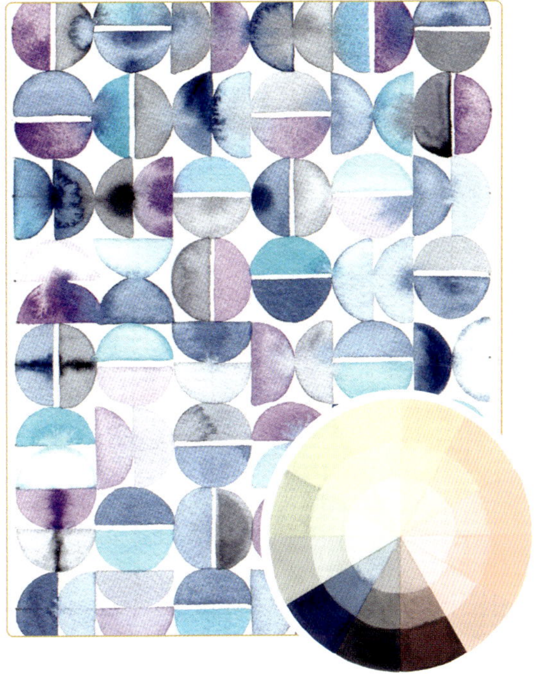

Split Complementary Color Scheme

A split complementary color scheme includes three colors: one color plus the two colors that are on either side of its complementary color on the wheel. For example, let's start with red as the first color. Red's complement is green, and the two colors on either side of green are yellow-green and blue-green. So, a split complementary color scheme including red consists of red, yellow-green, and blue-green.

Other examples include blue, yellow-orange, and red-orange, or violet, yellow-green, and yellow-orange. Can you look at the color wheel and find a few more examples of split complementary colors?

A close-enough example of this color scheme is Therapeutic Leaves, in which a reddish magenta, a yellow-green, and a blue-green combine to create a split complementary effect. In truth, you won't often find yourself using a color set that precisely matches a color scheme from the color wheel, but the general idea is to choose hues that are close to the color schemes to get palettes that look pleasing to the eye.

Analogous Color Scheme

Analogous colors are the ones that are sitting right next to each other on the color wheel. In an analogous color scheme, you can include as few as two colors and as many as five colors. If you take a look at the color wheel, you will see many possible analogous color groupings, such as orange, red-orange, and red; yellow and yellow-green; blue, blue-green, green, and yellow-green; or violet, red-violet, red, red-orange, and orange.

Some examples of this color scheme include Ethereal Half-Moons, which uses blue, blue-violet, and violet analogous colors and their values, as well as Honeycomb Hexagons, which uses blue and blue-green analogous colors and their values.

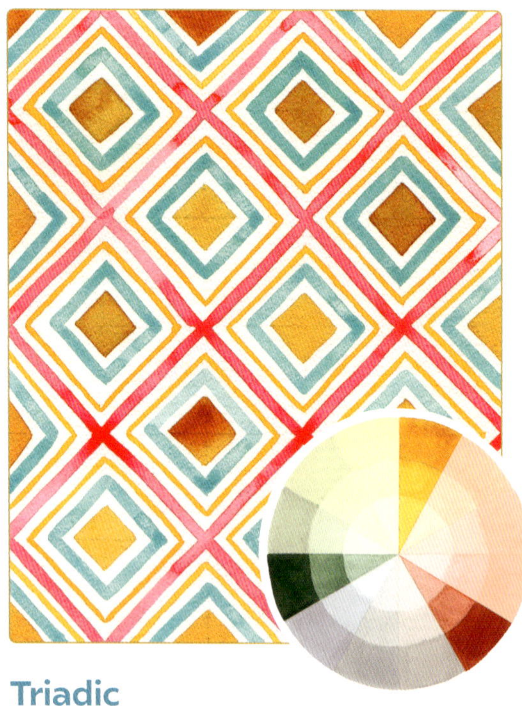

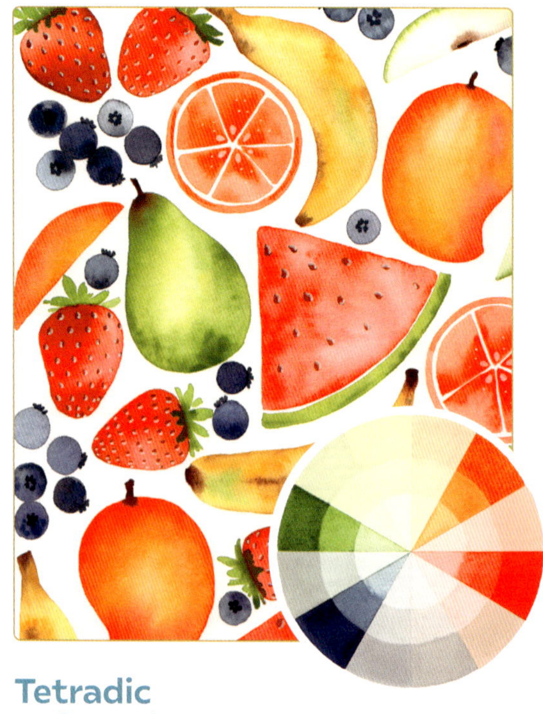

Triadic
Color Scheme

A triadic color scheme consists of three colors. Rather than including colors that sit next to or directly across from each other, triadic colors are equidistant or evenly spaced around the color wheel. If you draw imaginary lines to connect these colors, it forms a triangle. Two examples of this color scheme would be red, yellow, and blue, and green, orange, and violet. Can you find a few more triadic color sets on the color wheel?

Diamond Trellis is a good example of this color scheme, since it uses reddish pink, cadmium yellow, and a cool blue, which pretty much form a triadic color scheme on the wheel.

Tetradic
Color Scheme

A tetradic color scheme is created by selecting two sets of complementary colors. An example of this color scheme is green, red, blue, and orange. If you draw imaginary lines to connect these colors, it forms a rectangle.

Fruitful Finds could be an example of this color scheme because it predominantly features two sets of complementary colors for the fruits: orange and blue (for the mangoes, oranges, and blueberries) and red and green (for the strawberries and watermelons).

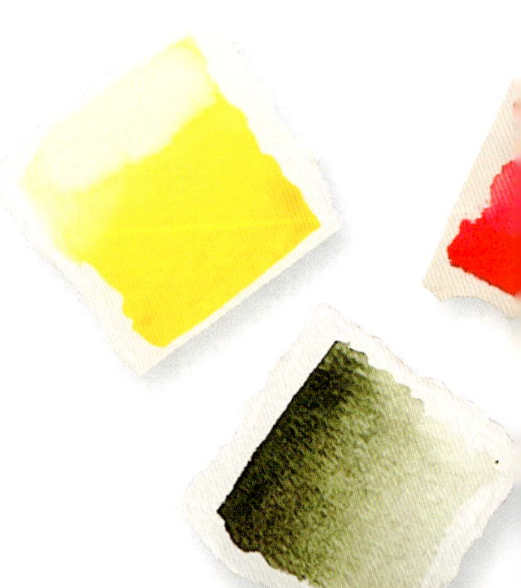

Our Easy Breezy Color Palette

Shown here is a swatch of every color used in this book. You can try to match each color roughly if you do not have an exact match—that is where your knowledge of color theory will come in handy! Use your color wheel sensibility to achieve the nearest possible color by mixing one or more colors that you have. Maybe you will create a unique color palette for your project that will pleasantly surprise you! Go with the flow and have fun mixing colors.

That said, there are numerous professional watercolor brands out there making beautiful, unique hues that are sometimes difficult to re-create by color mixing. Always think about what such hues might do for you before you make the leap to purchasing them. For example, I cannot really mix colors to match the vibrancy of Turquoise Cobalt, Rose Lake, Cupric Green, or Green Gold, so I invested in getting those exact tubes because they are useful to me.

The colors in this book's various color palettes represent my personal go-tos on a daily basis; I seldom need colors beyond these. (These particular colors are all Industria Maimeri Blu professional-grade watercolors.) As you practice watercolor, you will discover which colors speak to you and suit your body of work.

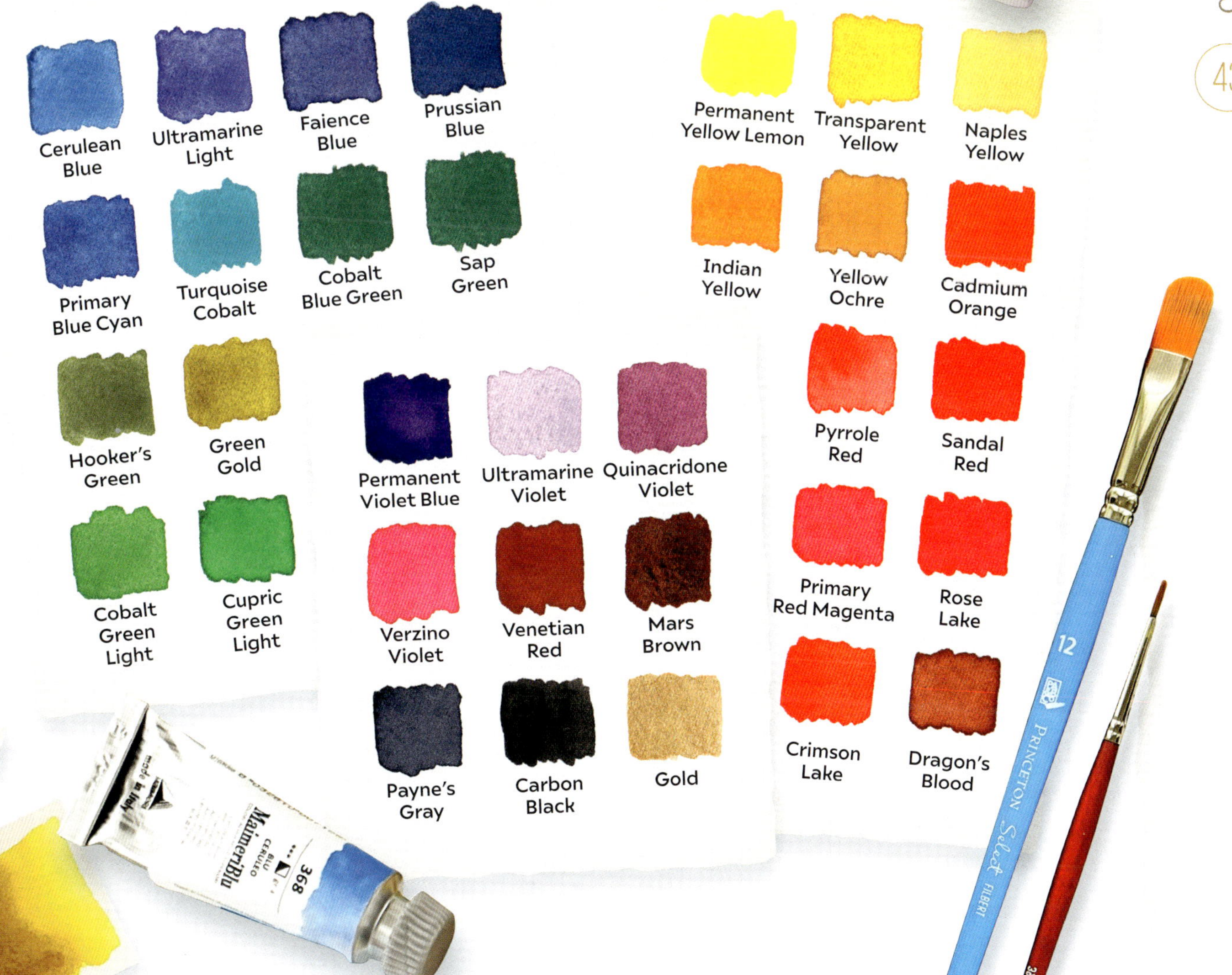

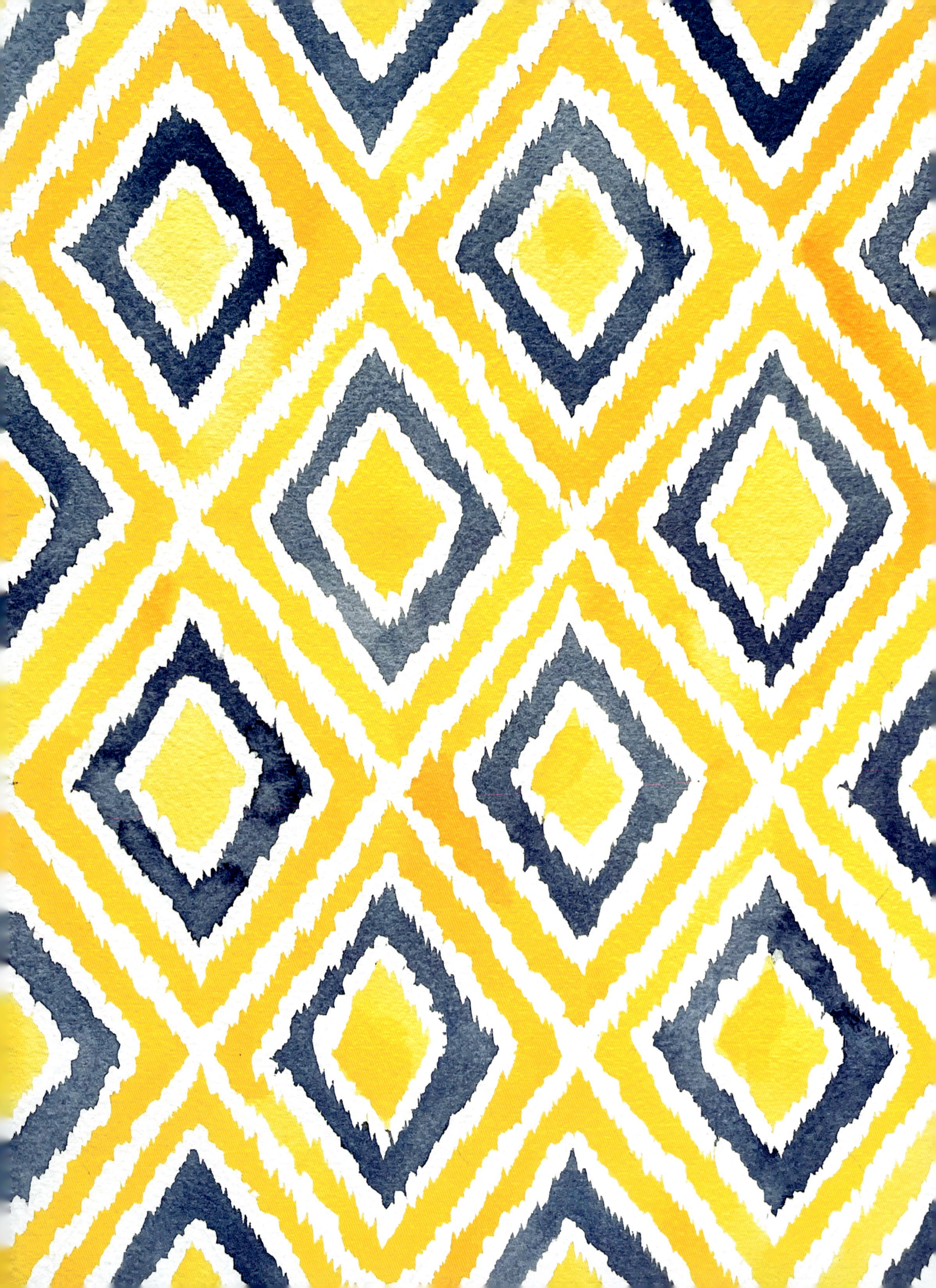

PART 2

Let's Paint Patterns!

A pattern in the world of art is any design in which lines, geometric shapes, hand-drawn shapes, and/or colors are repeated. Patterns can be symmetric or abstract, natural or man-made. You can find patterns in leaves, flowers, and seashells just as easily as in tiling, brickwork, and textiles. We will explore and learn via all sorts of different patterns through the projects in this book!

The 21 projects are divided into seven sets of three. Each set includes three different difficulty levels: easy, medium, and challenging. Go to page 15 to see a detailed description of the seven themes.

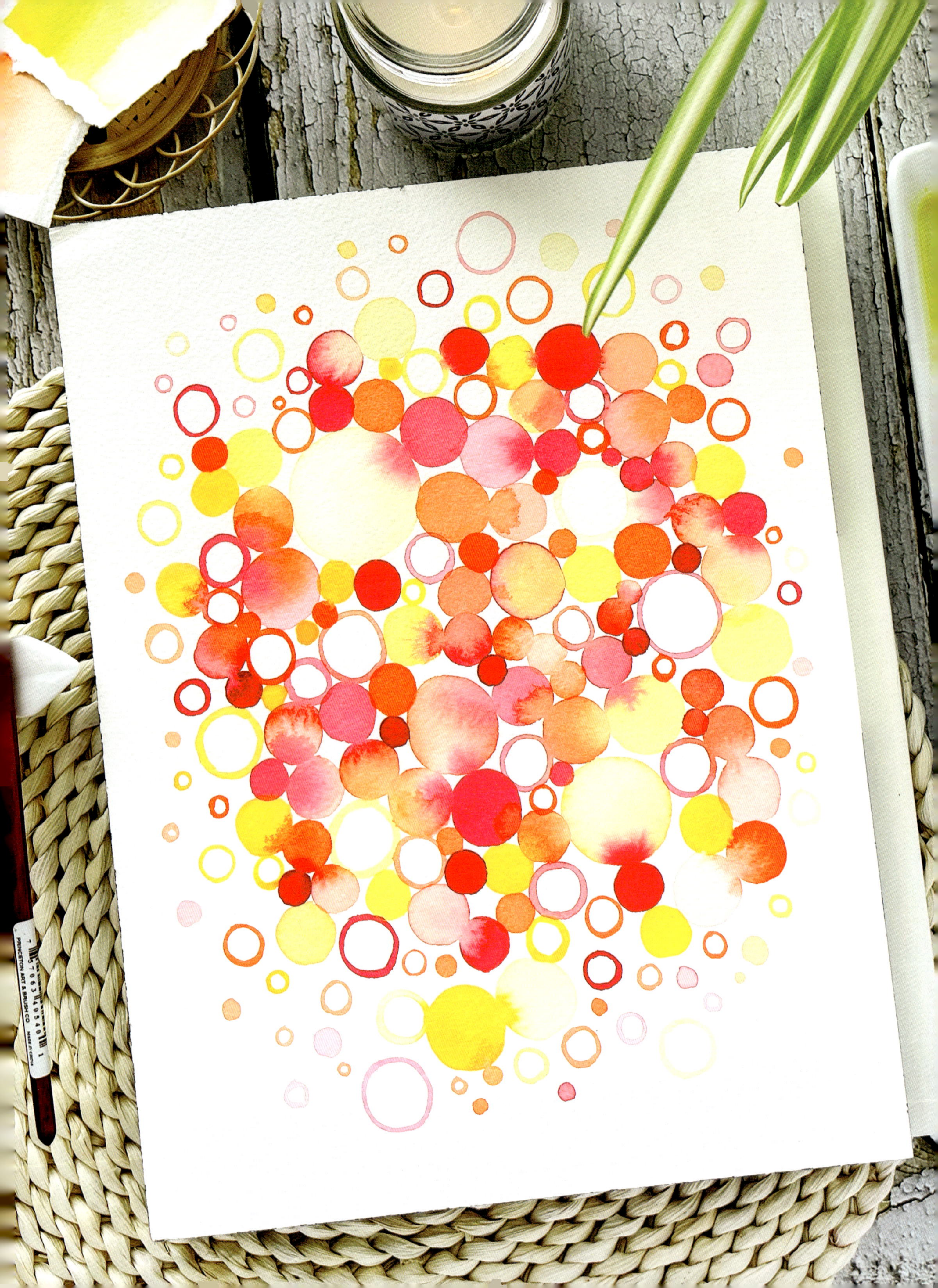

Playful Bubbles

This is an abstract pattern in which we will focus on drawing solid circles and rings of varying sizes using shades of three warm colors. The idea behind this pattern is to learn to paint circular shapes with a loose, tension-free hand. Painting circles in a repetitive manner will allow your wrist to develop strong muscle memory for drawing circular shapes without shaky hands. As you approach the end of painting this playful pattern, you will be a lot more confident and at ease while drawing solid circles and rings!

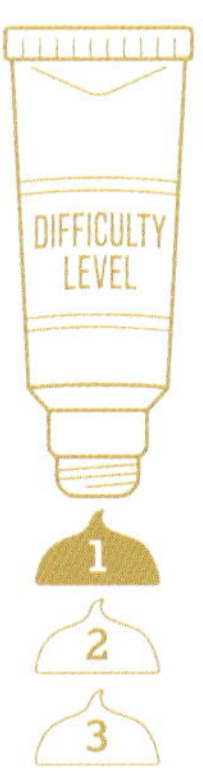

MATERIALS

BRUSH: Size 6 round brush with a good tip

PAPER: 8" x 10" (20 x 25 cm), cold pressed; or use a smaller size, such as 8" x 8" (20 x 20 cm) or 5" x 7" (13 x 18 cm), if you are short on time

COLORS:

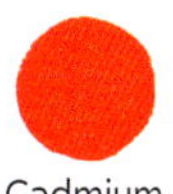
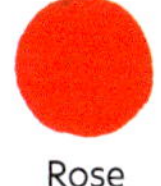
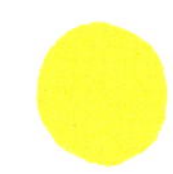

Cadmium Orange   Rose Lake   Permanent Yellow Lemon

TIP: This pattern will turn out well if you are able to bring out variation in the sizes of the circles and rings and mix enough gradients of colors using controlled amounts of water. Being able to use a wide spectrum of the same color will certainly add some depth to your pattern!

LET'S PRACTICE

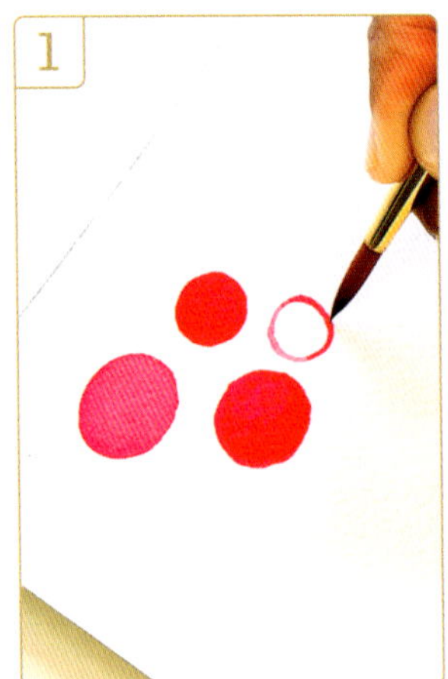

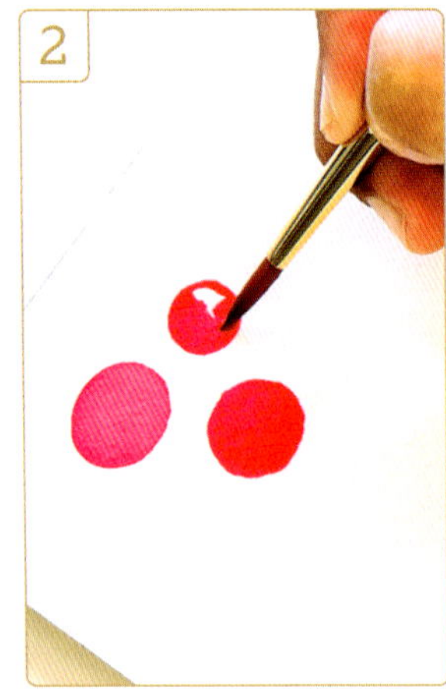

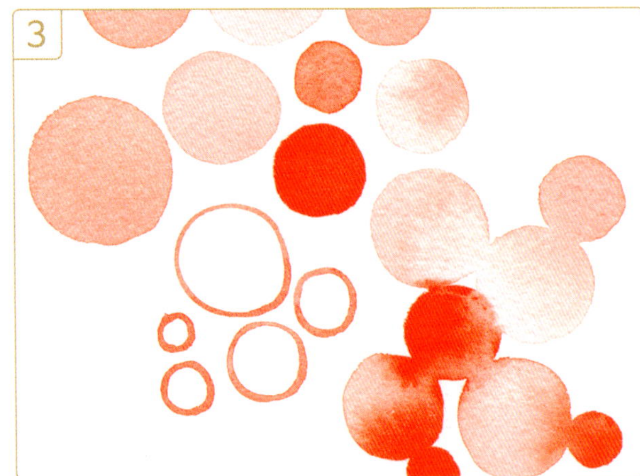

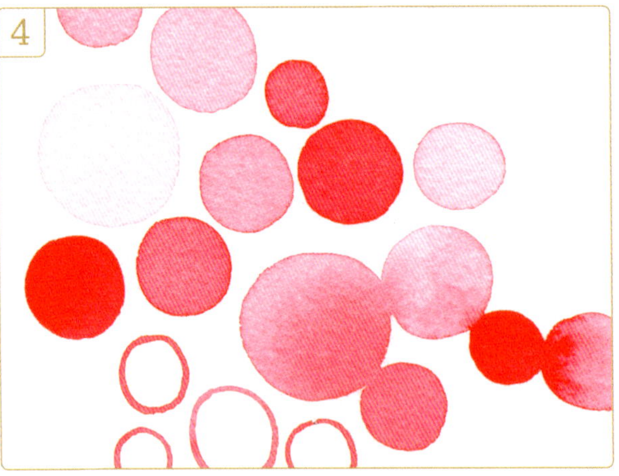

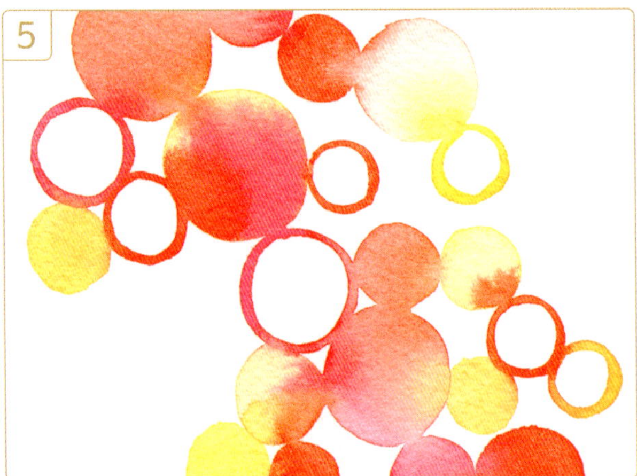

48

1 **Paint a ring.** Hold the brush slightly tilted or at an approximate right angle (80–85 degrees) to the paper. Rest your wrist firmly on the paper. Use the pointed tip of the brush to gently draw the ring. You want the stroke to be neither too thin nor too thick.

2 **Paint a solid circle.** Start by drawing a ring as explained above and then fill in the circle with the same paint. Once you get the hang of drawing a ring and a circle, we will go a step further and draw multiple rings and circles using all three colors.

3 **Practice in one color.** With Cadmium Orange, paint circles of different sizes and in at least 4–5 different shades (by adding more or less water). Keep some circles apart and make some touch each other. Observe the blending wherever there is contact.

4 **Practice in other colors.** Rinse your brush and move on to the next color, Rose Lake. Repeat step 3 with this color. Then rinse and repeat with the last color, Permanent Yellow Lemon. This will get you comfortable painting circles and mixing shades.

5 **Use all three colors at once.** Now paint circles and rings using all three colors and observe how the colors blend into one another.

Let's Relax

The Playful Bubbles abstract pattern is inspired by light, airy bubbles that blow with the summer breeze. Have you ever experienced how relaxing and calming the act of blowing bubbles is? I often do this activity with my daughter, and it instantly lifts my mood and calms me down as I see soft, translucent bubbles of varying sizes blowing away with the gentle breeze and disappearing into thin air as they quietly pop. It is as if all the worries in life vanish magically with each pop!

I want you to visualize bubbles as you begin painting this pattern using a mix of warm colors (the same ones used for the practice session). Don't forget to bring out the translucency of the bubbles as you mix lighter shades by adding more water to your paint. While you are in the process of painting this pattern, allow your mind to relax. Let go of your worries as you watch two circles slowly bleed into each other as they touch, thereby creating your own beautiful *pop* of a watercolor bubble. Sounds like a calming process, doesn't it? Let's begin.

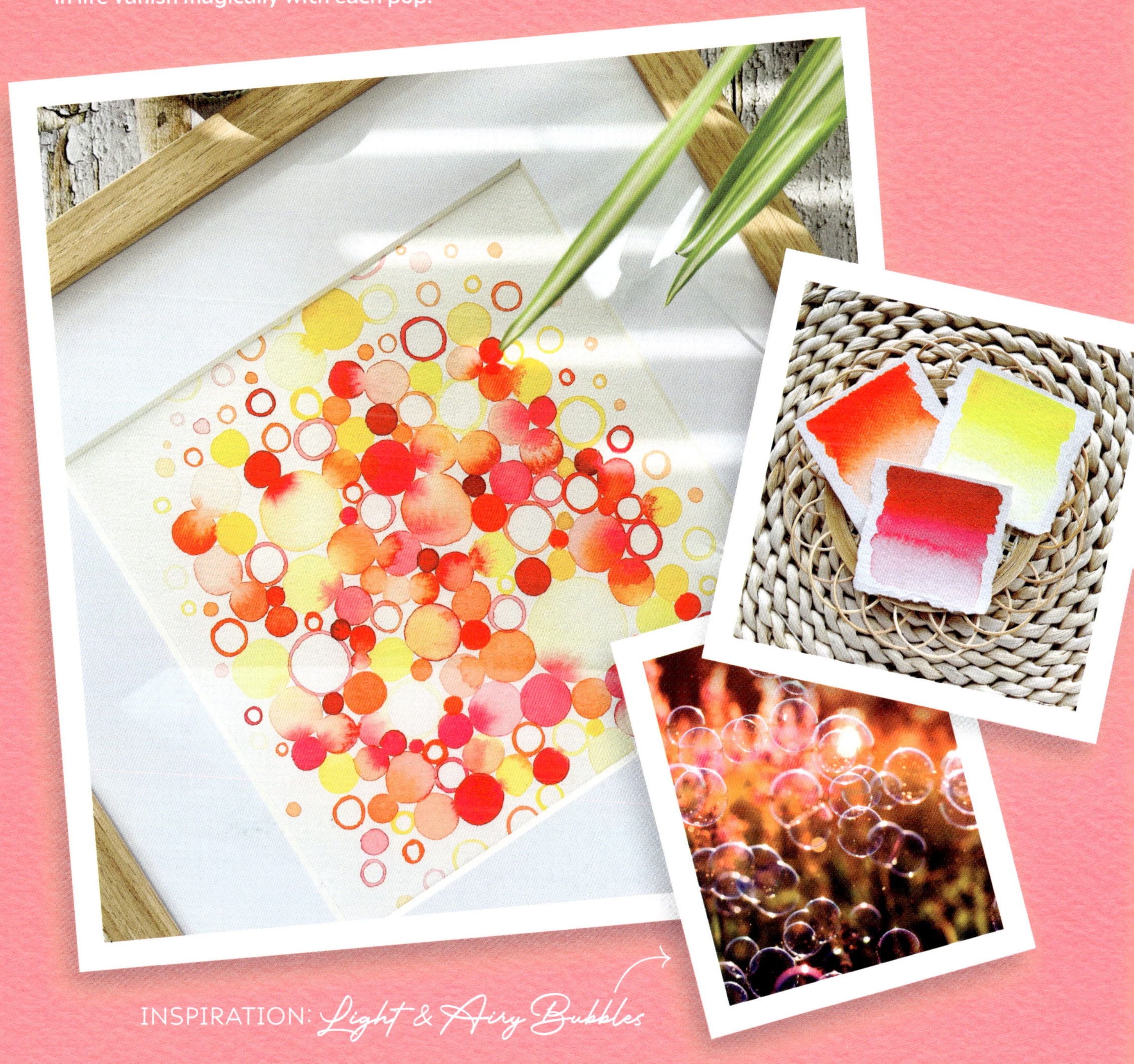

INSPIRATION: *Light & Airy Bubbles*

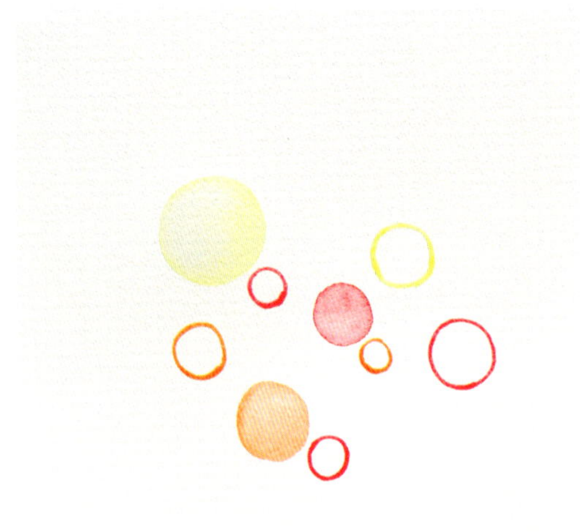

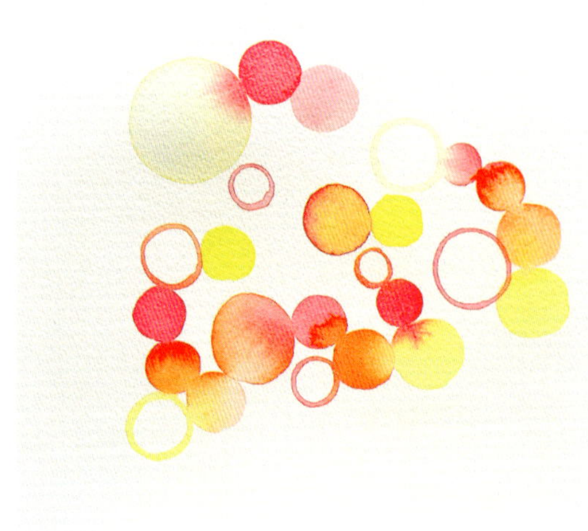

1 **Start in the center.** Mix light shades of the three colors. This pattern is made by working from the center out to the edge. Start painting using the three colors as shown, including a few small circles, a few big ones, and a couple of rings.

2 **Build up different shades.** While the first circles are still wet, paint a few more around them by touching them ever so slightly and letting the colors blend. Be intentional about your color choices. Think about the placement and use a shade of each color as you go.

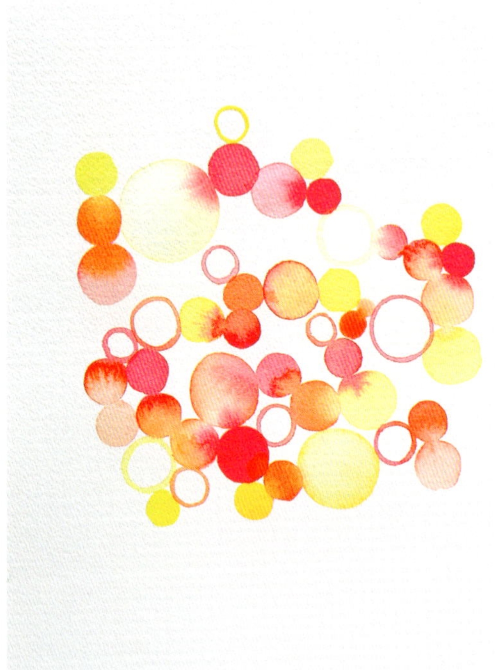

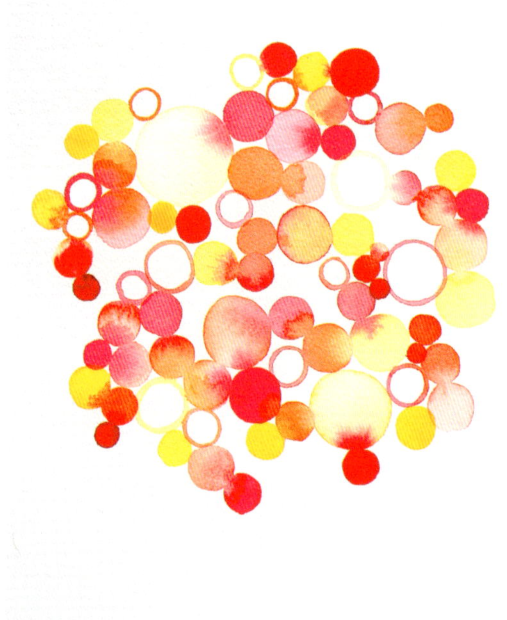

3 **Build up different sizes.** Keep an eye on how your page is filling up. If you have too many smaller circles, draw a few big ones, and vice versa. Don't be afraid to use darker values of the colors. You can always bring them down by adding water again.

4 **Fill in gaps.** Check if you have drawn circles in all sizes, then start filling in large gaps. Try to work your way outward. Continue to blend, and keep mixing shades as you need. Don't forget to rinse your brush between colors.

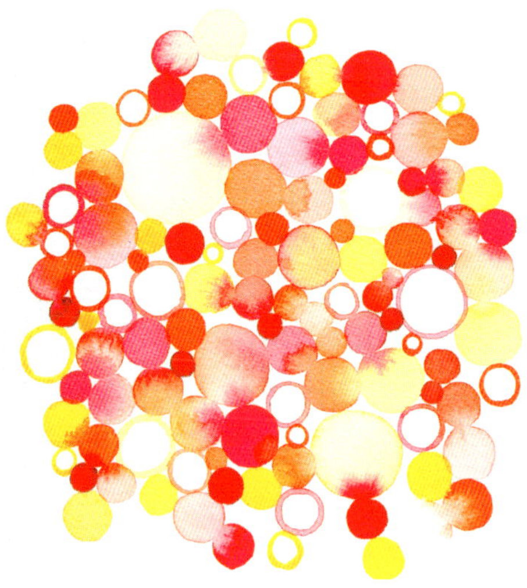

5 **Continue adding density.** Check if you are seeing enough light and dark contrast in your piece. Is there enough variation? If not, continue to add circles and rings to balance things out. Here I added a lot of smaller, tighter bubbles in the gaps.

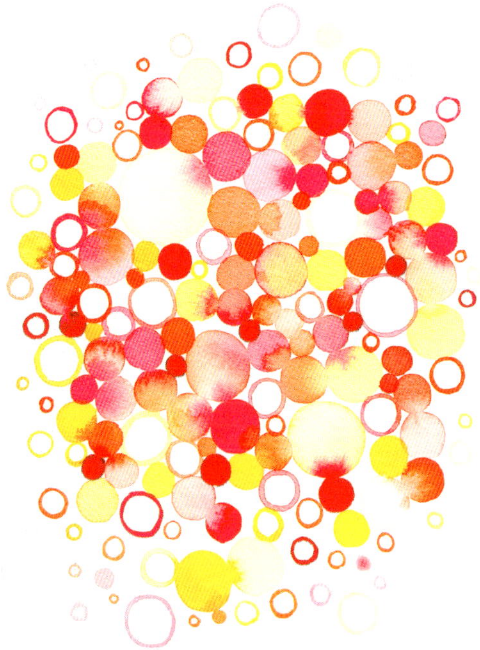

6 **Add outer rings.** As you approach the edge of the page, incorporate some separated rings and circles around the edges to depict bubbles that are floating away. These shouldn't touch. Include a few tiny rings to represent the tiniest bubbles.

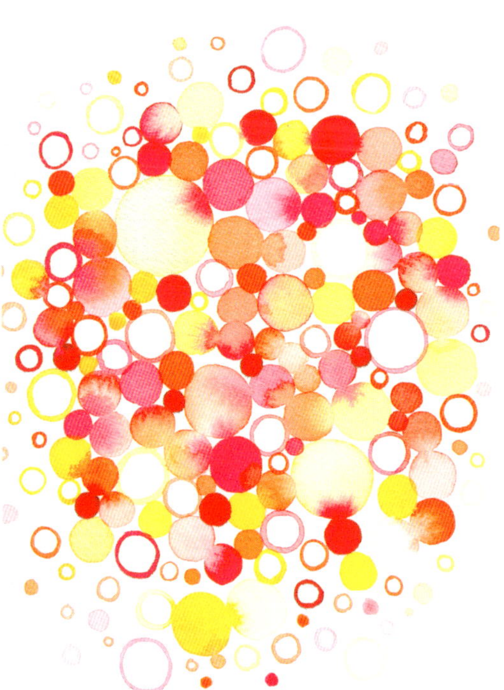

7 **Add outer circles.** Now pause to check if your pattern is nicely distributed. Add small, light, filled-in circles only if necessary. Fill any big gaps. If you think everything looks airy and balanced, consider your pattern complete!

Let's Paint

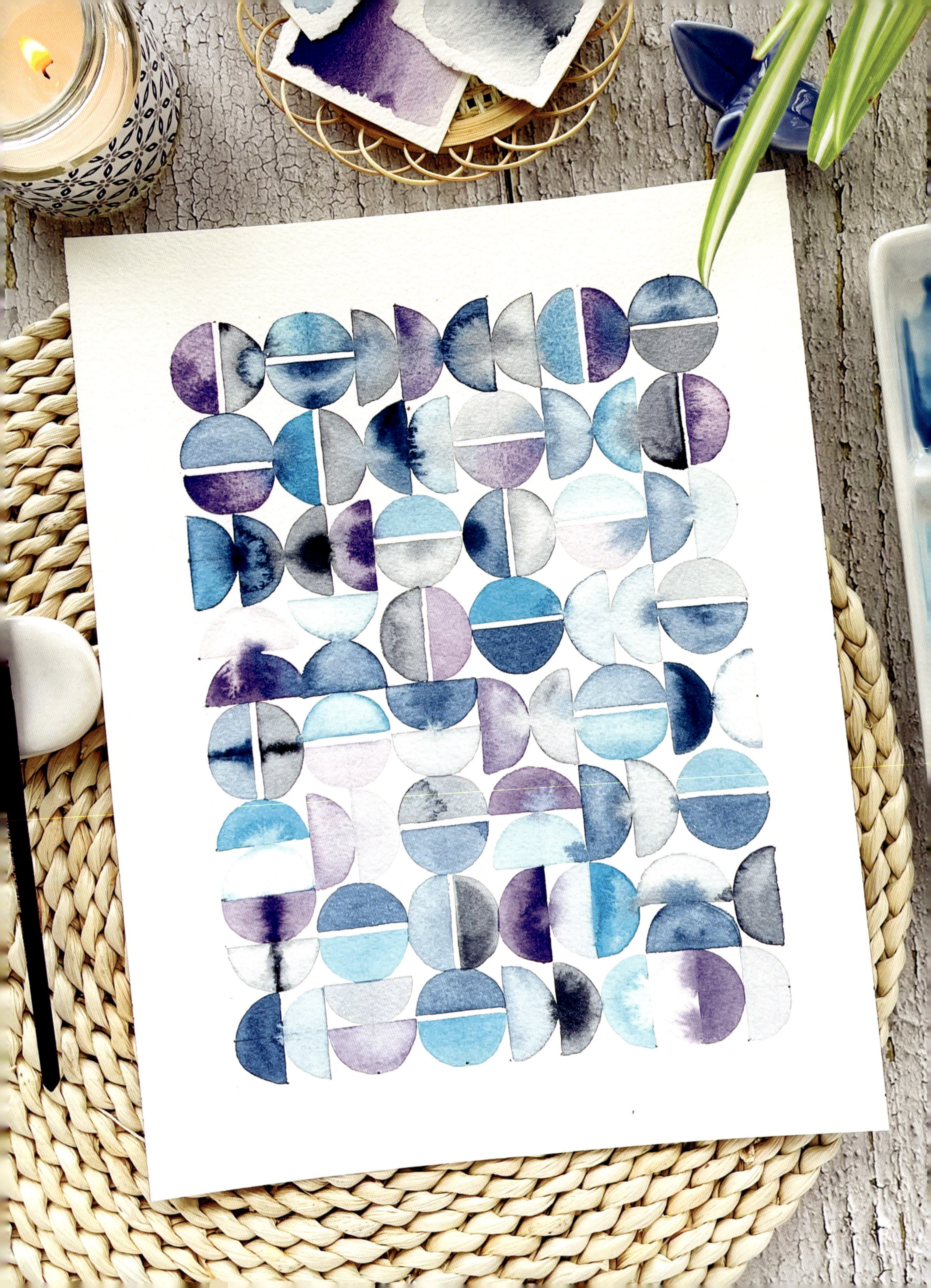

Ethereal Half-Moons

This is a highly structured pattern in that we will paint half-circles of a fixed size in a structured grid format. Unlike the previous pattern, in which you could vary sizing and playfully place the circles and rings, this pattern focuses more on brush control and an ability to draw symmetric half-circles of a consistent size. This project will help you paint in a slightly more geometric and calculated manner.

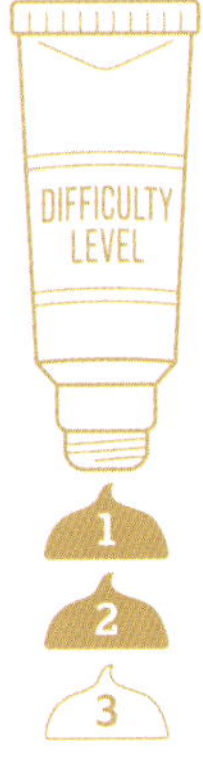

MATERIALS

BRUSH: Size 4 round brush with a fine tip

PAPER: 8" x 10" (20 x 25 cm), cold pressed; or use a smaller size, such as 8" x 8" (20 x 20 cm) or 5" x 7" (13 x 18 cm), if you are short on time

OTHER: Pencil; ruler; eraser

COLORS:

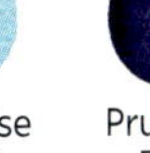
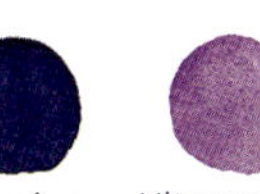

Turquoise Cobalt   Prussian Blue   Ultramarine Violet   Payne's Gray

TIP: This pattern uses a grid format to place the half-circles in a symmetric row and column structure. Spend a few minutes to draw the grid precisely as explained to make it a simple task to place the half-circles correctly during the painting process. Don't forget to lighten your pencil marks before you begin painting—you don't want harsh lines to show through the pattern later.

LET'S PRACTICE

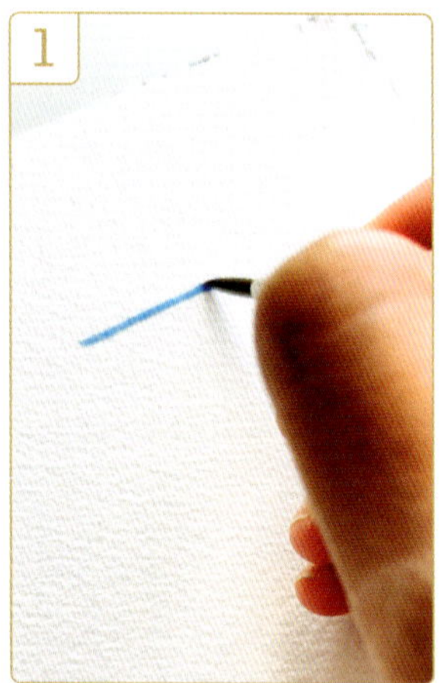 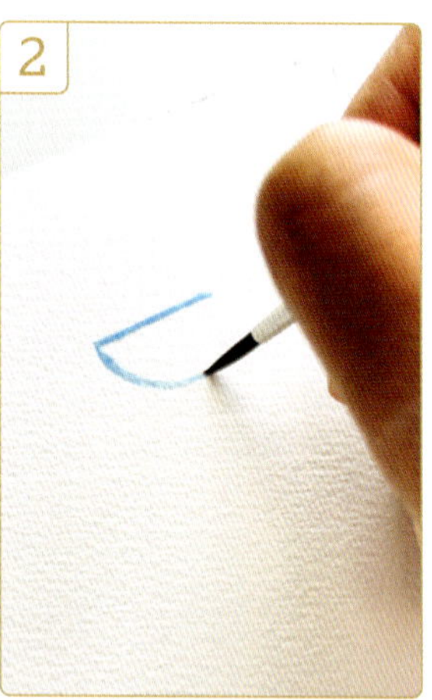 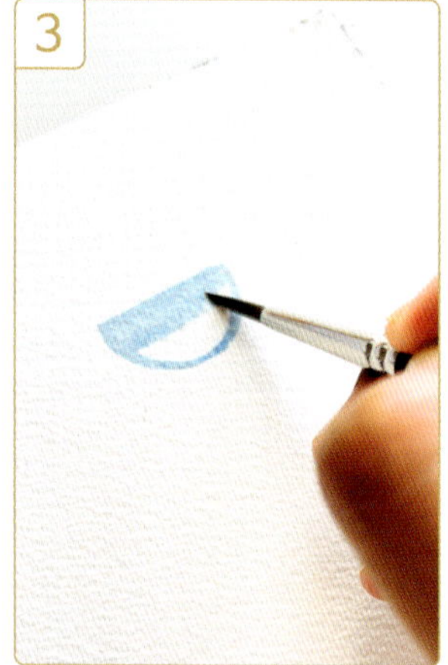 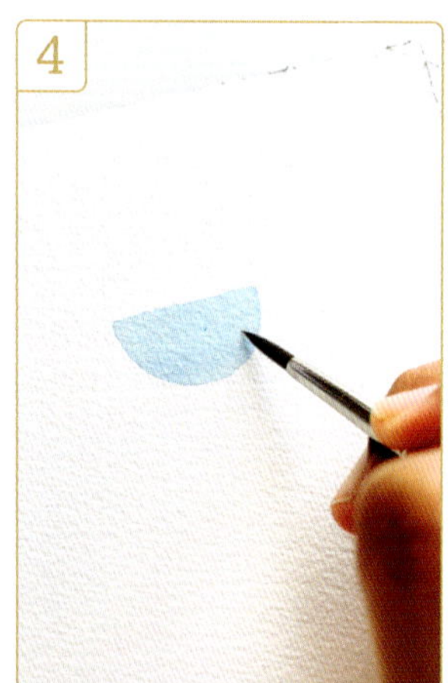

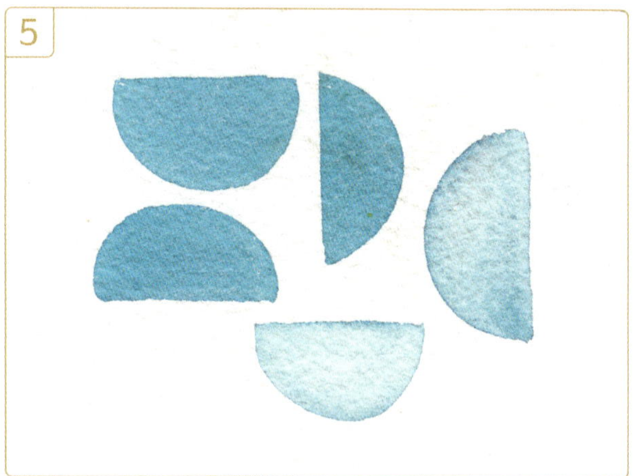 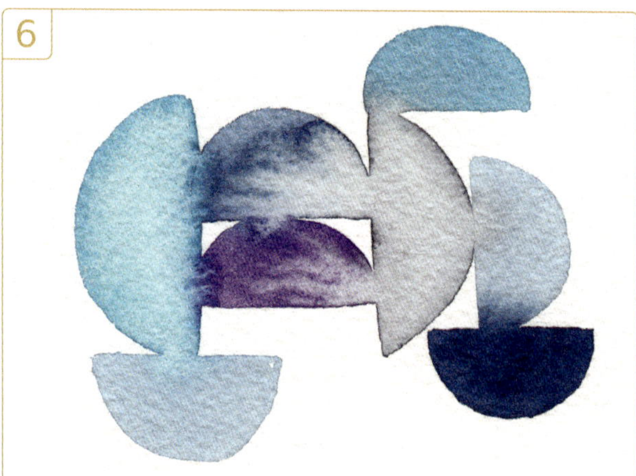

1 **Start the outline.** To begin painting a half-circle, hold the brush slightly tilted or at an approximate right angle (80–85 degrees) to the paper. Rest your wrist firmly on the paper. Using the pointed tip of the brush, draw a small horizontal line about 1" (2.5 cm) long.

2 **Finish the outline.** Apply gentle pressure and draw a downward curve touching the two ends of the line to form a half-circle.

3 **Fill the half-circle.** Once you have the outline ready, fill in the half-circle with a flat wash.

4 **Check.** Check your work to ensure that the half-circle is neither too flat nor too curved.

5 **Paint samples in each color.** Paint about 4–5 half-circles of a consistent size using various shades of one color. Draw both vertical and horizontal half-circles as shown. Repeat this exercise with all the colors in the palette to get comfortable with them.

6 **Paint samples in mixed colors.** Now switch to using all four colors and seeing how it works when they touch at certain points. Practice this freehand and watch how the colors blend into one another. Don't worry about symmetry during this warm-up!

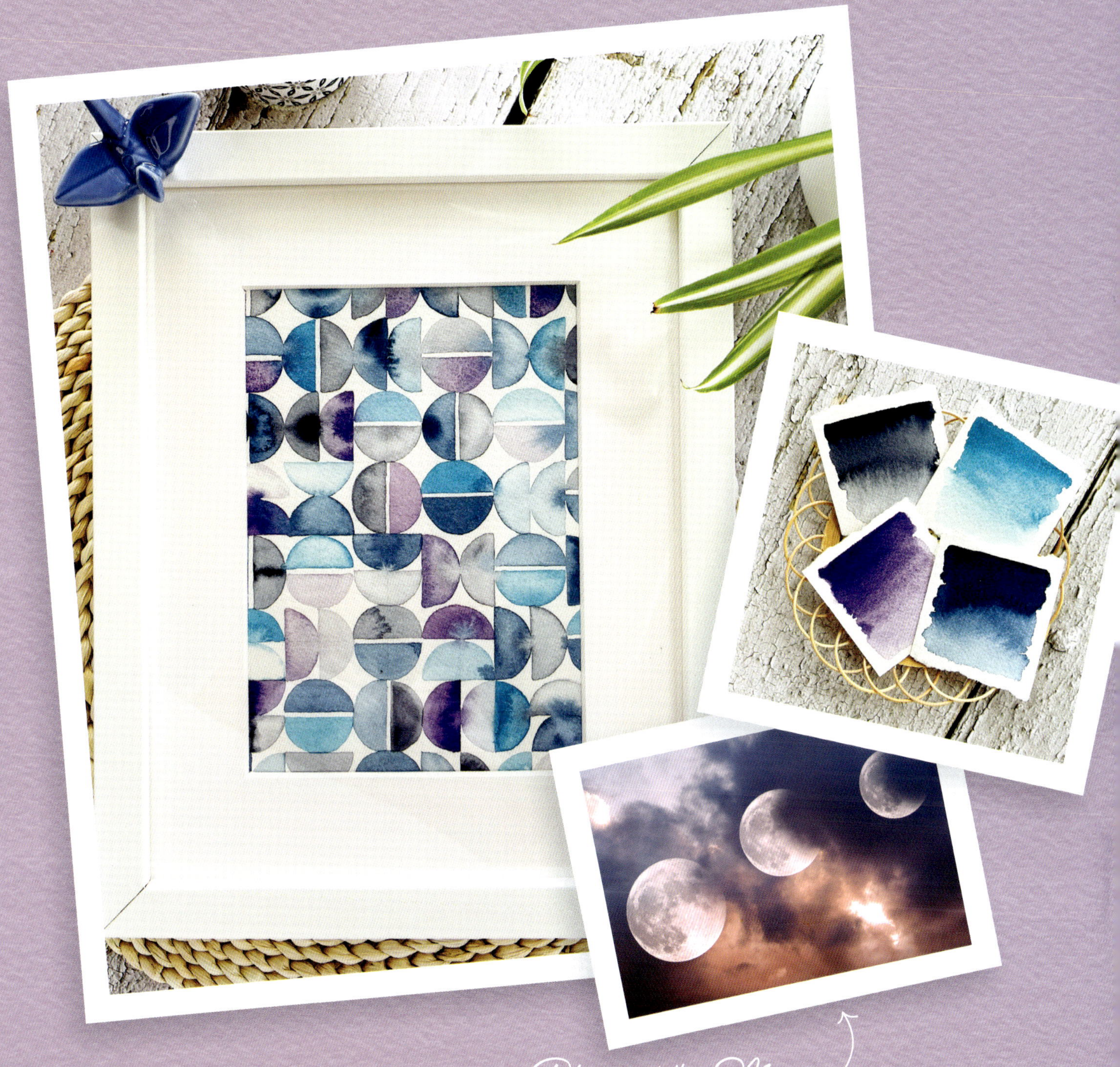

Let's Relax

This pattern is inspired by moon phases. Pictures of the moon and its phases have always fascinated me. The prominent texture on its surface, its ethereal colors, and the soft, violet night sky are the key elements that I wished to incorporate into this pattern. Before you jump into painting the main project, take a couple of minutes to get into a relaxed state and to bring some astral visualizations into your mind. As you paint, enjoy the unpredictable blending of colors that brings out unique textures and the intentional water blooms that allow the pattern to have an otherworldly, soft feel. The final overall pattern will look like a series of beautiful half-moons held together in a grid. Let's begin.

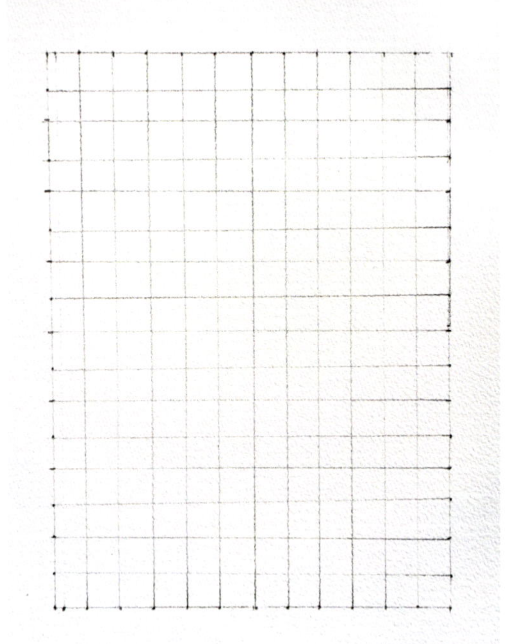

1 **Draw the grid.** With a ruler and pencil, draw a 6" x 8" (15.6 x 20.8 cm) rectangle grid of ½" (1.3 cm) squares. Then use an eraser to lighten the pencil lines so they won't show through the transparent colors to come. Finally, mix light shades of the four colors.

2 **Start painting half-circles.** Each half-circle will have a 1" (2.6 cm) diameter/flat side. Paint the first four half-circles with gaps as shown, then add two half-circles facing the same direction as shown, without gaps. As a rule, only include gaps when half-circles face each other to form a "complete" circle.

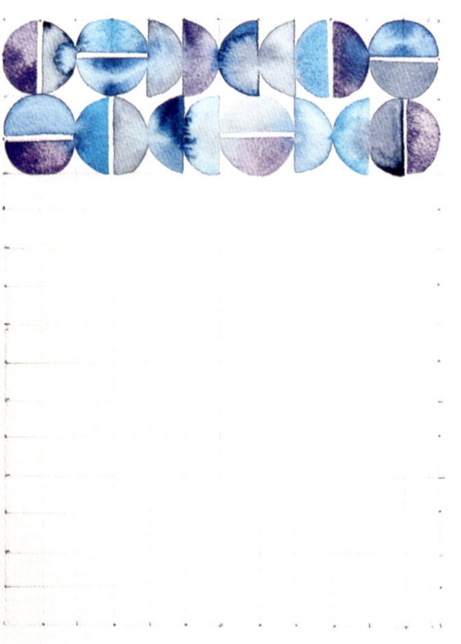

3 **Continue adding half-circles.** As you proceed, mix colors on the go and make good use of lighter and darker tones. Be sure to place the half-circles a bit differently every time to get good variety in the pattern. Allow the colors to effortlessly bleed into each other.

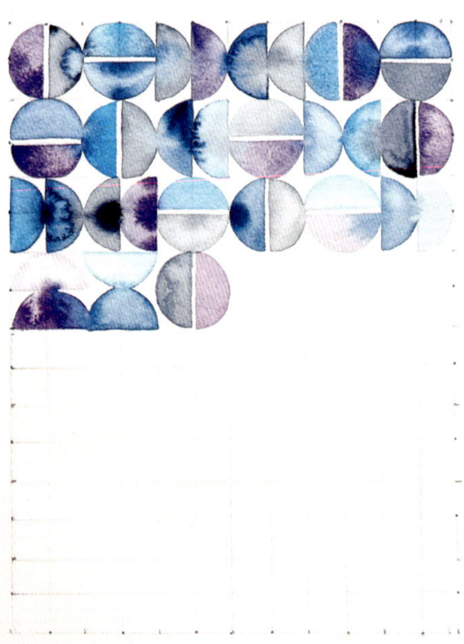

4 **Vary the direction you paint.** If you consistently paint left to right, you will see that by the time you are back to the beginning of the next row, the half-circles on the previous row have dried, so no bleeding will take place vertically. Paint column-wise if you want bleeding to happen vertically too.

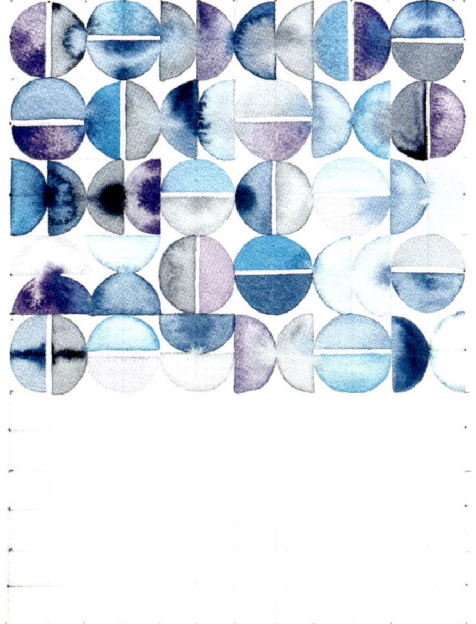

5 **Keep an eye on your paints.** As you work, make sure that the paints on your palette are not drying out or becoming too watery. Remember to rinse your brush between colors. Let the colors mix into each other on the paper, not on your palette.

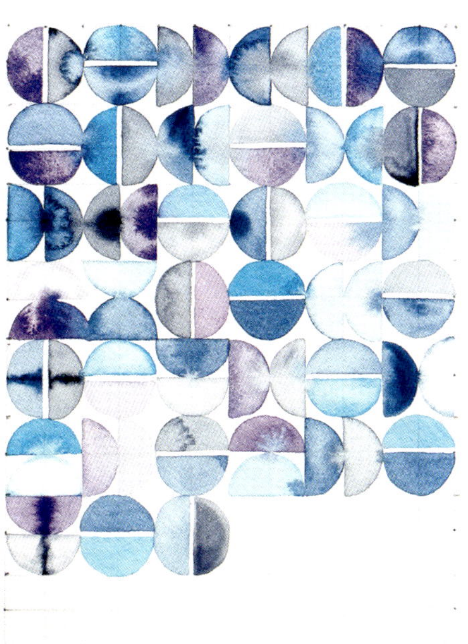

6 **Check your progress.** At this point, check if you are seeing enough depth in your pattern and have enough dark and light contrast. If not, continue to add half-circles that will balance out the overall look of the pattern.

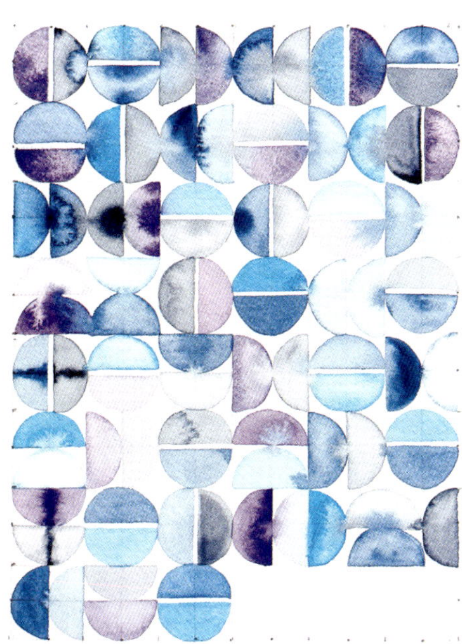

7 **Get in the zone.** Once more than half of your page has been filled, the painting process should start to feel meditative; hopefully you will be enjoying the flow without needing to pause and read from the book!

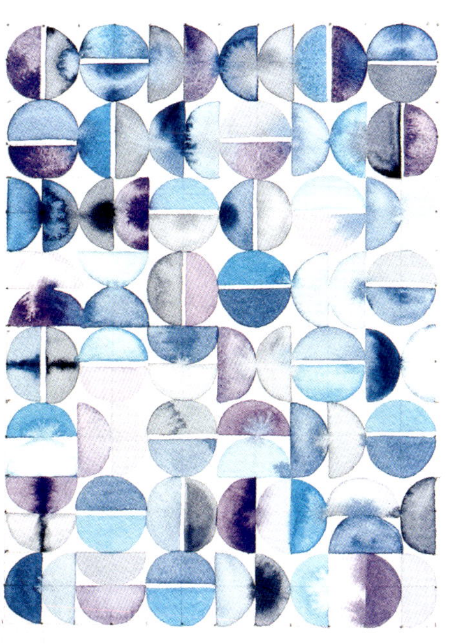

8 **Make final adjustments.** Once you finish, look over your work. This pattern largely depends on how well you placed the grid in the beginning, but you may be able to make final tweaks. Once the paint is dry, erase any exposed pencil lines.

Let's Paint

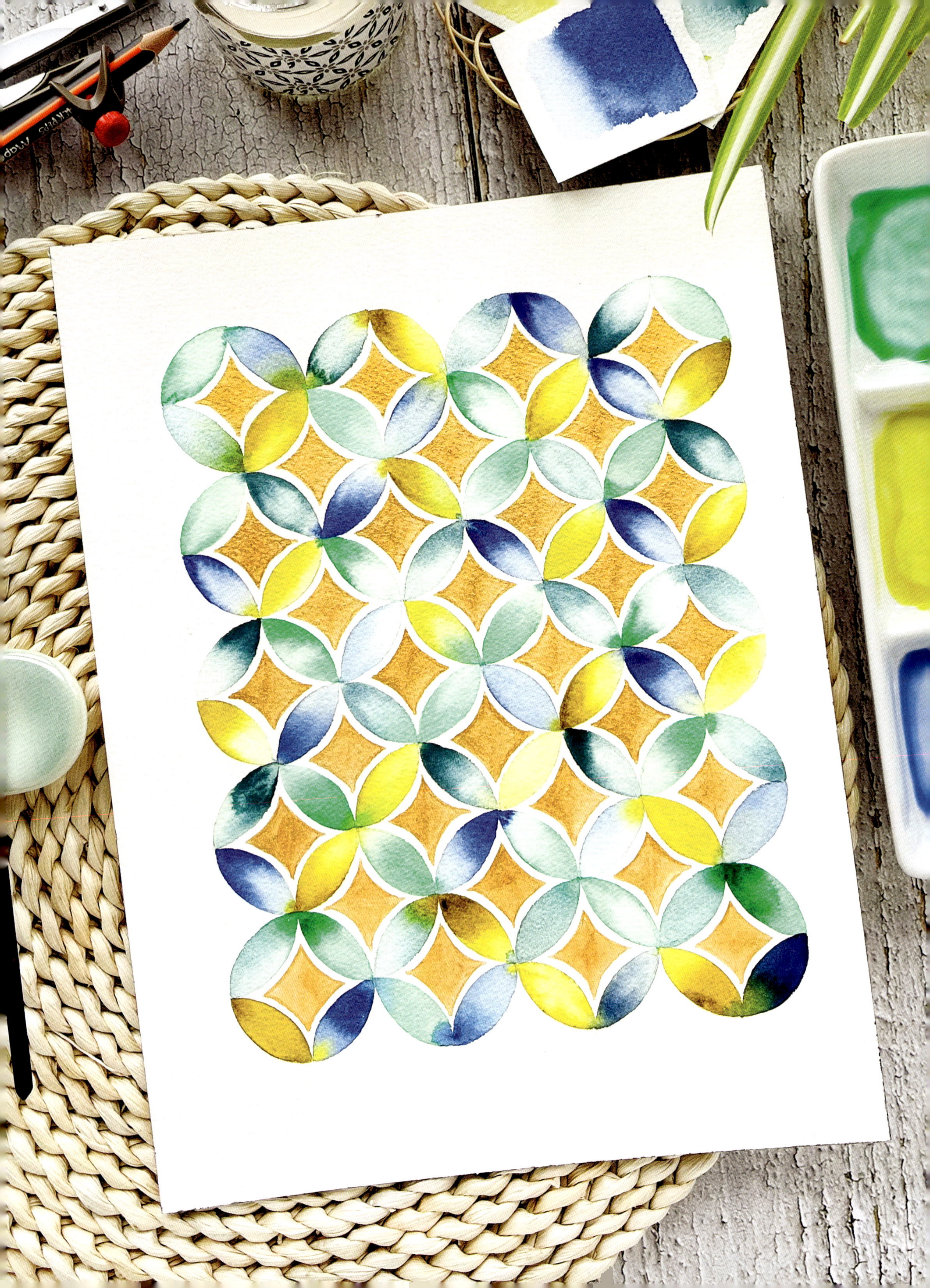

Shippo Tsunagi

We will now explore an advanced pattern that uses circles. This is a symmetric, geometric pattern that requires some solid pencil work to draw the grid and overlapping circles. It will take some time if you choose to paint on an 8" x 10" (20 x 25 cm) sheet like I did. In this pattern, we will be using a total of five colors, so it will require some effort to keep the paints wet at all times while you paint. By the end of this pattern, you will have the confidence to work with precision and understand how to place multiple colors strategically for the best effect.

MATERIALS

BRUSH: Size 4 round brush with a fine tip

PAPER: 8" x 10" (20 x 25 cm), cold pressed; or use a smaller size, such as 8" x 8" (20 x 20 cm) or 5" x 7" (13 x 18 cm), if you are short on time

OTHER: Drawing compass; pencil; ruler; eraser

COLORS:

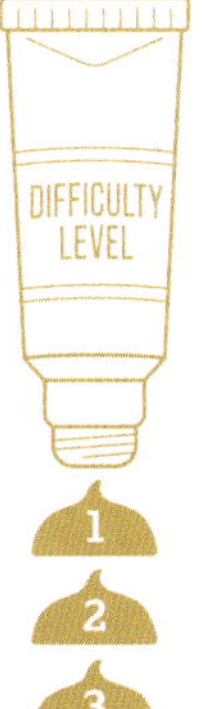

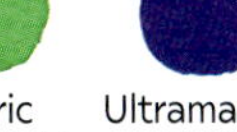

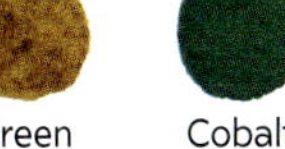

Cupric Green Light	Ultramarine Light	Green Gold	Cobalt Blue Green	Gold

TIP: Precision and patience are the secrets to this pattern! How this piece turns out will depend largely on how well you draw the grid and circles initially, so I suggest that you spend some time getting the geometric structure right. Once that is done, it is easy to paint in the shapes and bring out the lovely effect of this pattern.

LET'S PRACTICE

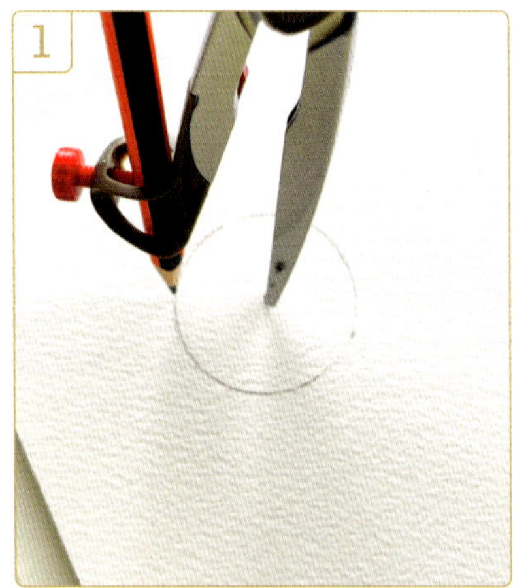 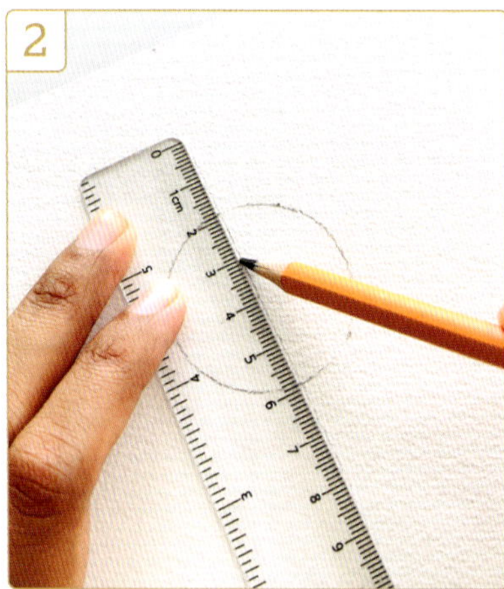 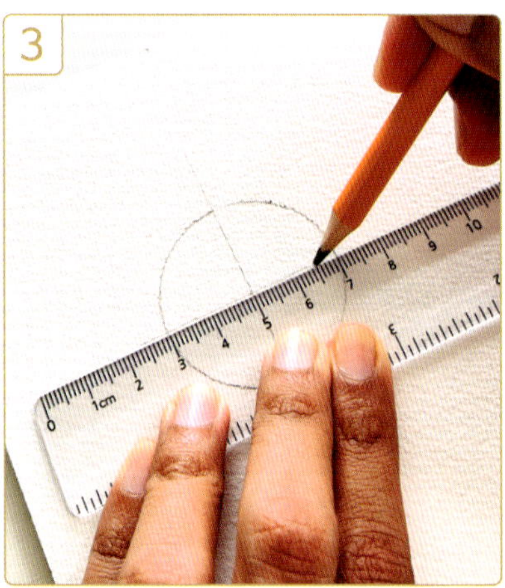

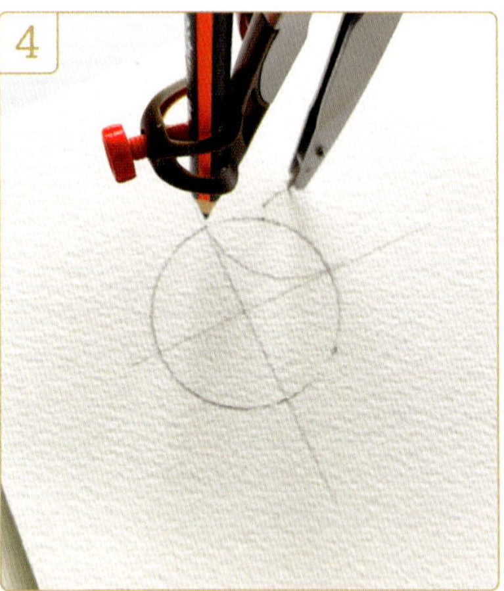 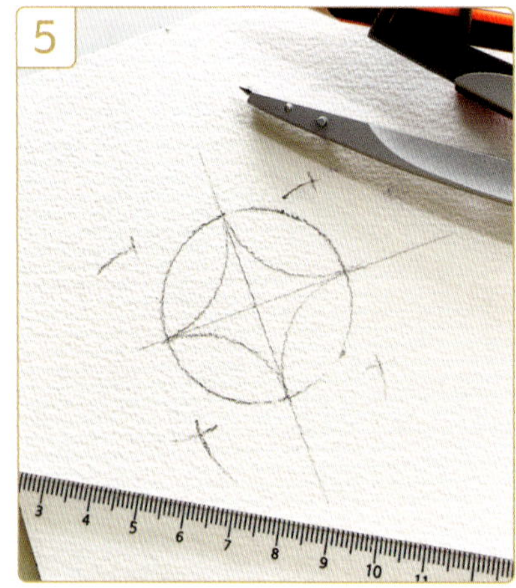 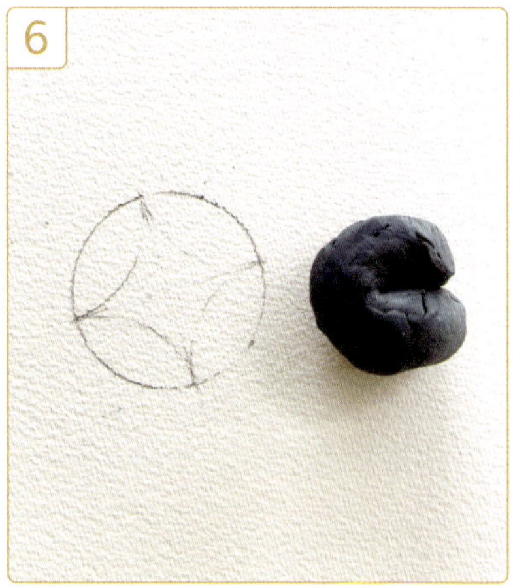

1 **Draw a circle.** Let's begin by drawing a circle that is 1½" (4 cm) in diameter—¾" (2 cm) in radius—using a compass.

2 **Divide the circle.** Use a ruler to draw the vertical diameter of the circle, dividing the circle vertically into two half-circles.

3 **Divide the circle again.** Use a ruler to draw the horizontal diameter of the circle that is perpendicular to the vertical diameter, dividing the circle into four quadrants.

4 **Draw the first arc.** Keeping the compass set to draw a 1½" (4 cm) diameter circle, use it to draw one arc in each circle quadrant such that each arc connects to two of the dividing lines around the circumference of the circle. Here the first arc is drawn.

5 **Draw the remaining arcs.** Repeat step 4 to draw the remaining three arcs as shown.

6 **Clean up the drawing.** Erase all the extra pencil lines so that only the main shape of the pattern is visible. Lighten the pencil marks of the main shape so that they will not be seen through the paint.

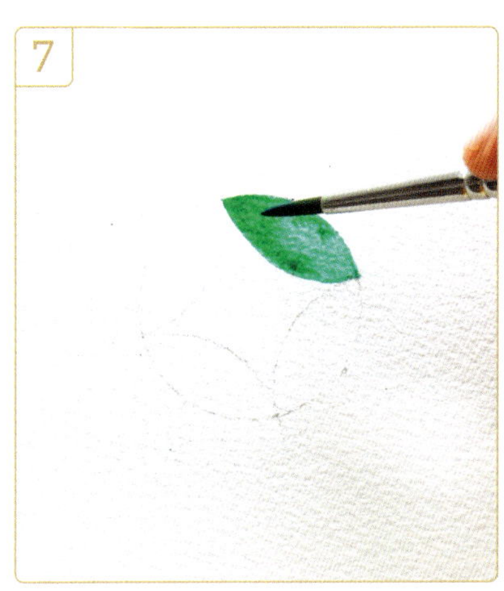

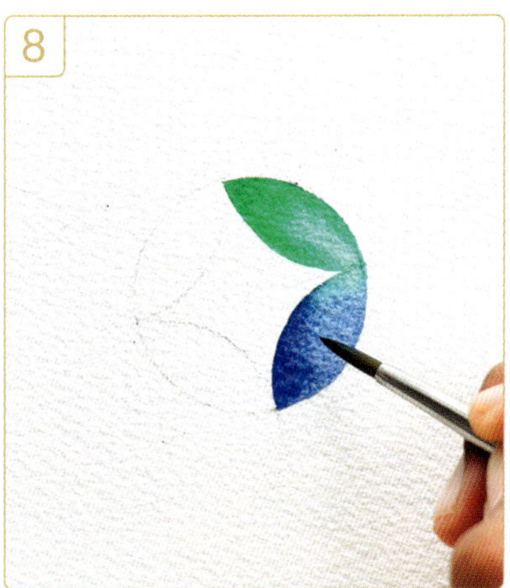

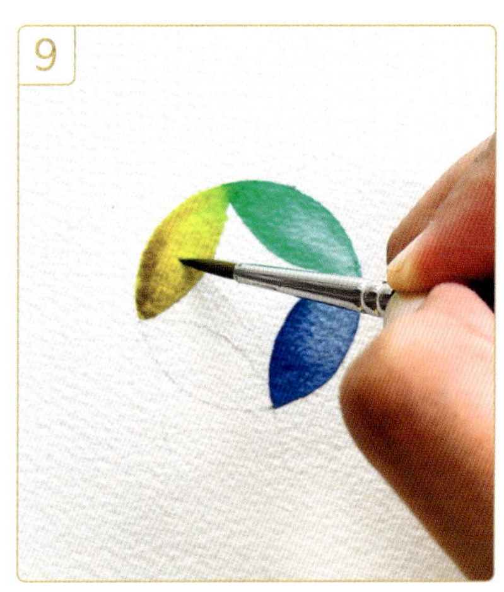

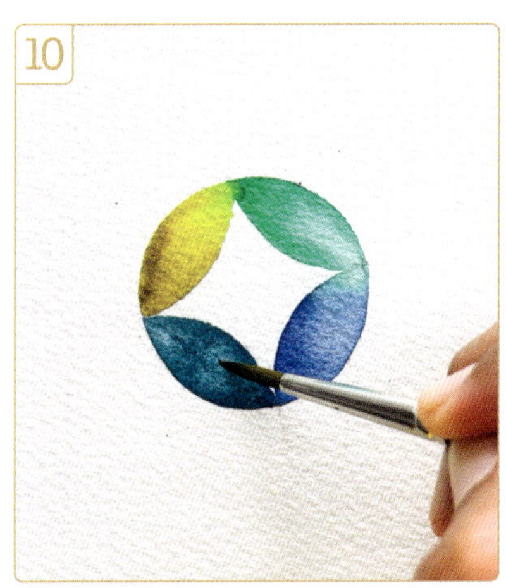

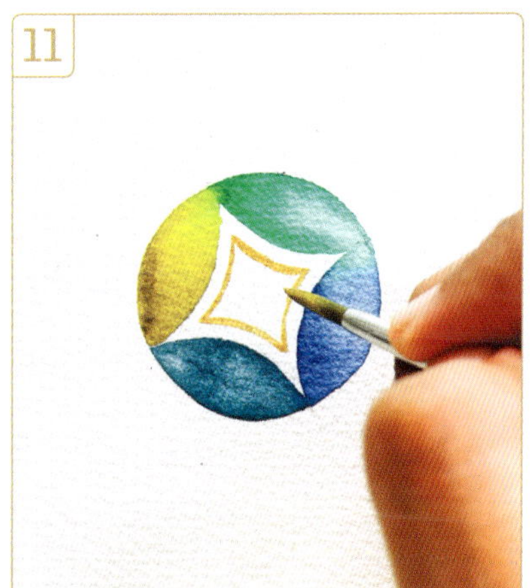

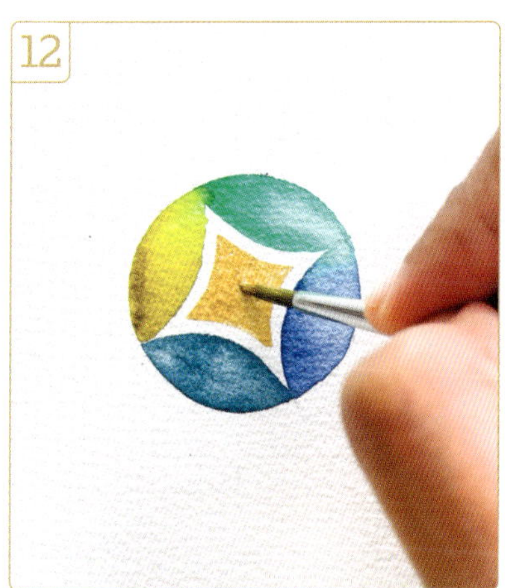

7 **Paint the first section.** With the paint color of your choice, paint the first petal-shaped section around the edge of the circle as shown.

8 **Paint the second section.** Rinse your brush, switch to a new color, and paint the next petal-shaped section. The wet paints will instantly bleed into each other at the point where the two adjacent petals touch each other.

9 **Paint the third section.** Rinse your brush, switch to a third color, and paint the petal-shaped section on the other side of the first section you painted.

10 **Paint the fourth section.** Rinse your brush, switch to a fourth color, and paint the final petal-shaped section. You can now see a diamond shape or a star being formed inside the main circle.

11 **Draw a diamond outline.** Using your gold paint, draw an inner diamond shape as shown, leaving a small white gap between it and the painted sections.

12 **Fill the diamond.** Carefully fill in the diamond shape with the gold color. This forms the foundational shape of the project pattern!

Let's Relax

This pattern is inspired by the traditional Japanese embroidery style called sashiko, which is a simple running stitch to form repeating or interlocking patterns. There are many different types of such sashiko patterns, and shippo tsunagi is one of them. Shippo tsunagi, which means "linked seven treasures," is a geometric design that encompasses four petals and a single circle. The circumferences of many circles overlap by a quarter, just like how we drew intersecting circles in every quadrant in the practice session. These circles flow symmetrically in all directions—that is, left, right, up, and down. Because of the endless continuity of the intersecting circles, this pattern symbolizes peace and happiness in Japanese tradition.

You can look at the pattern in different ways and perceive different meanings. To me, the center shape comes across as a shining star or a diamond, which I decided to paint in gold, and the intersecting circles form floral petals, which I painted in shades of blue and green. What comes to mind when you look at the piece? Let's begin.

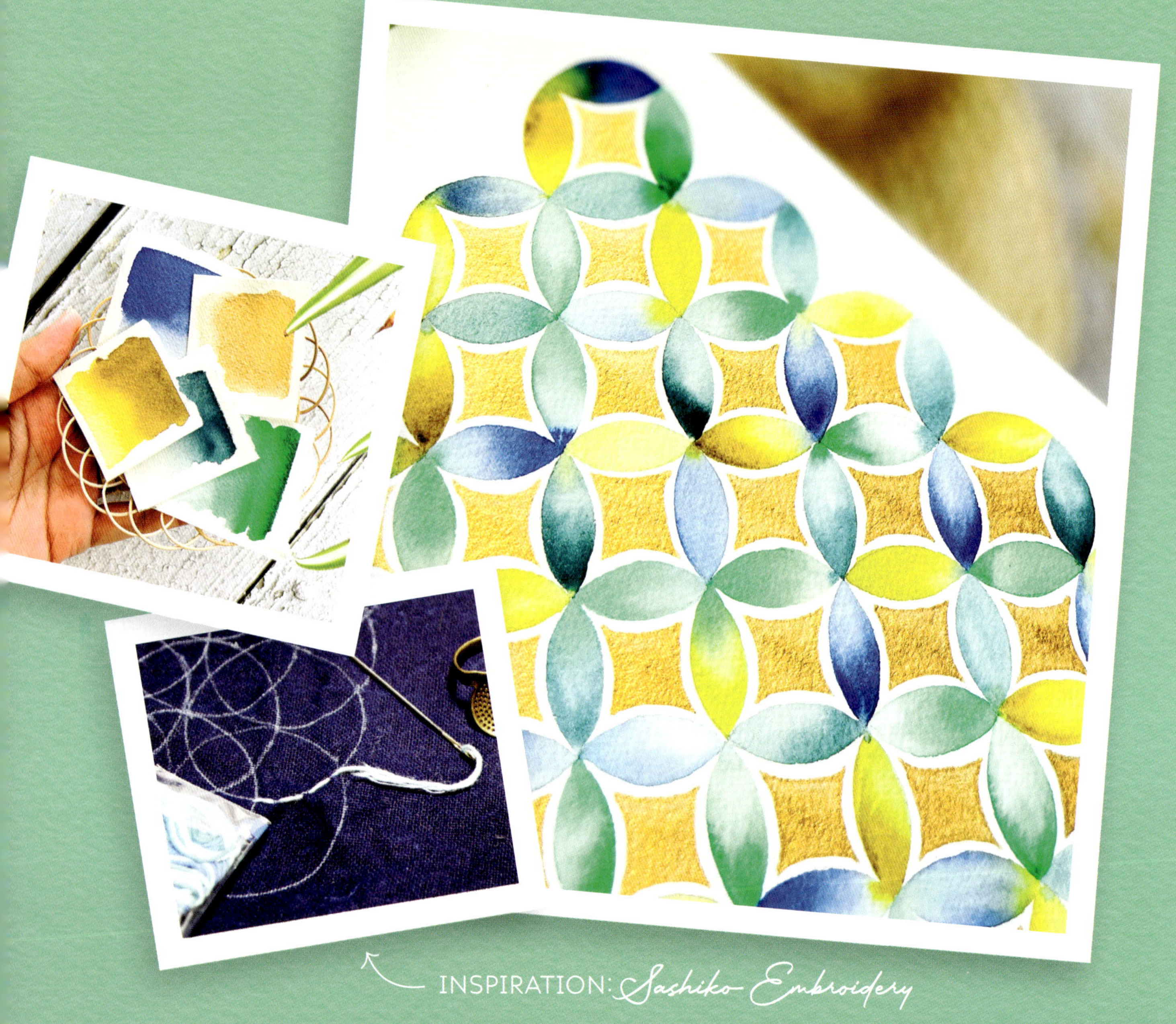

1 Draw the grid.

Draw a 6" x 8" (16 x 20 cm) rectangle (or adapt the size to your paper size). Mark each ¾" (2 cm) along all sides. Use the ruler to draw clean lines demarcating rows and columns as shown.

Set your compass to a circle radius of ¾" (2 cm), which will create circles 1½" (4 cm) in diameter. Start drawing circles, beginning from the top left corner of your grid. Place the compass on the middle intersection point of the first four squares and draw a circle.

Move to the next set of four squares and draw the second circle. Continue horizontally until you have filled the row with four circles total. Then go back to the left side and draw circles using the next set of four squares below the first row. Continue until you have filled the entire grid.

All the circles should be touching each other at their circumferences only at this point.

Now we need to draw the overlapping circles that will intersect the main circles that we already drew. To do this, go to the top left corner of the grid and draw a circle using the very top left corner point of the grid as its center. You will see that this circle will cut across the first circle in the top left quadrant, creating the first petal there.

Move over two squares to the right and use the point between the existing two circles as the center point to draw the next overlapping circle. This circle will intersect the two existing circles, forming two more petals. Continue this way to draw overlapping circles by always moving two squares across and two squares down.

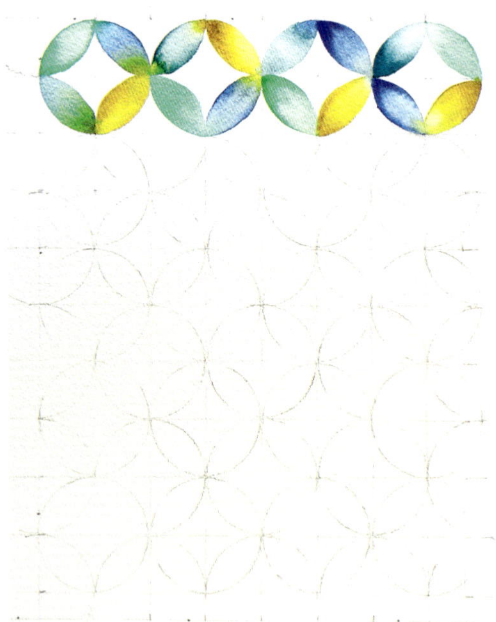

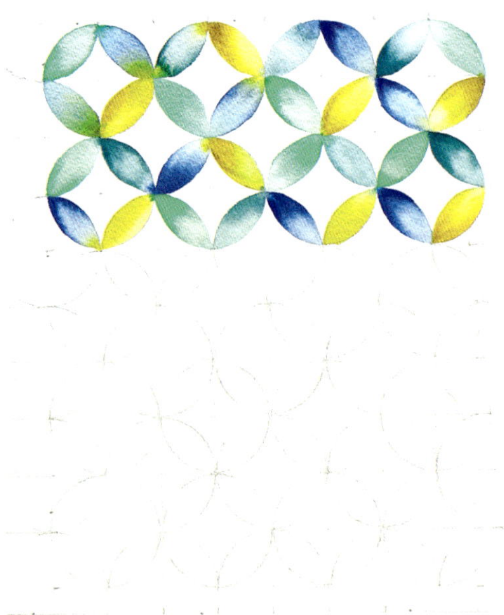

2 Paint the first row. Just like you painted the basic shape in the practice session, start placing the four main colors (not the gold) one by one in each of the four petals within every circle.

3 Paint the second row. As you proceed, start mixing colors on the go and make good use of light and dark tones. Try using soft colors next to darker ones and allow the colors to effortlessly bleed into each other.

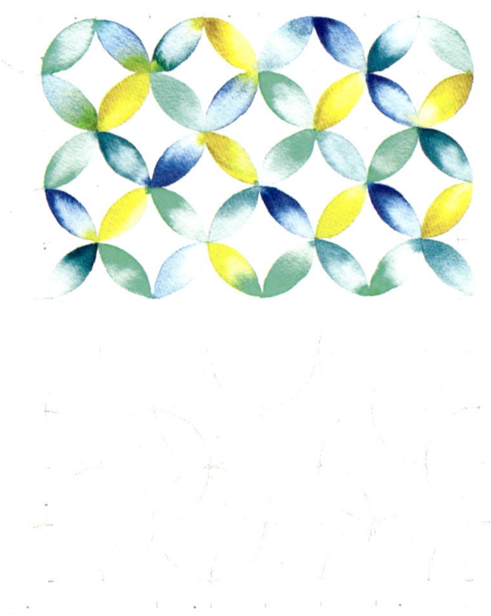

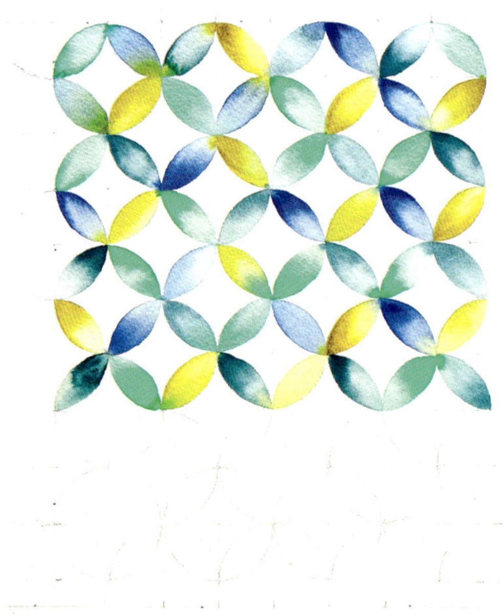

4 Continue with another row. Continue painting the petals one by one. You will start to feel comfortable using the four colors interchangeably and the pattern will slowly start to emerge. Don't forget to rinse your brush between colors!

5 Check your progress. At this point, check if you are seeing enough depth in your pattern and have enough dark and light contrast. Is there enough variation? Make sure to use the right amount of color saturation to bring out the vibrancy.

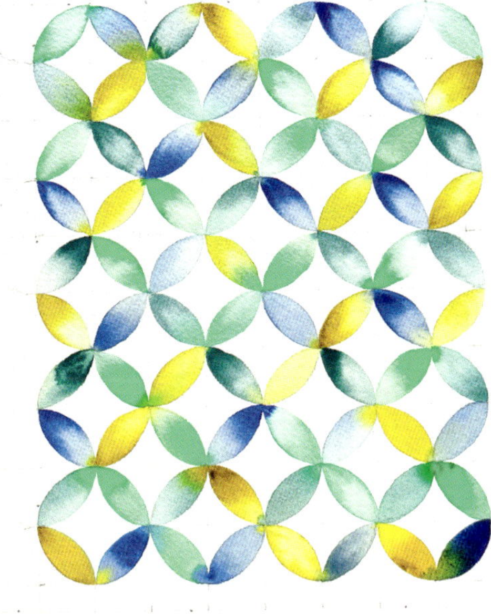

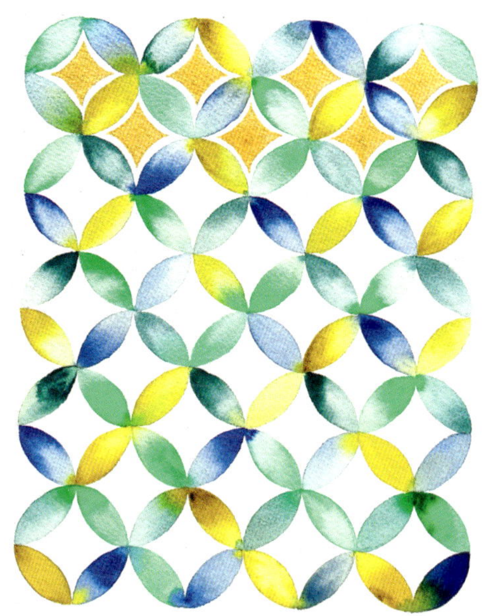

6 **Finish the main petal painting.** Continue painting until you've completed the grid and all the petals are painted. Allow the pattern to dry before proceeding to the gold diamonds.

7 **Start adding the gold diamonds.** Begin filling out the diamond shapes in the centers of the circles. Always paint the outline first, then fill it in. Try not to make the gold color too runny—keep it opaque and slightly creamy.

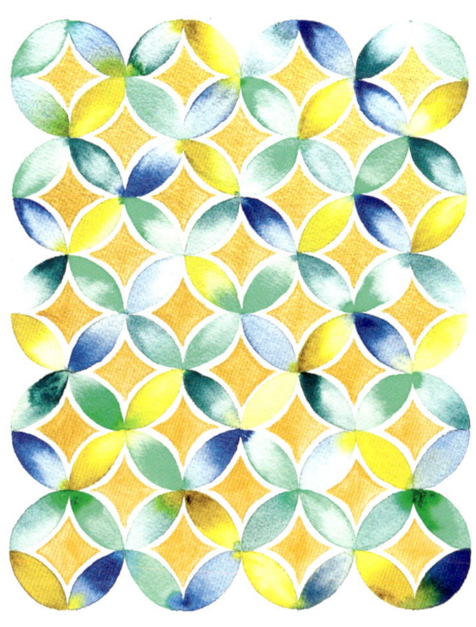

8 **Finish and adjust.** Continue to fill up the empty spots with the diamond shapes until you reach the end of the grid. Once you are done working with the gold color, appraise the result. Erase any pencil lines that are still visible.

Let's Paint

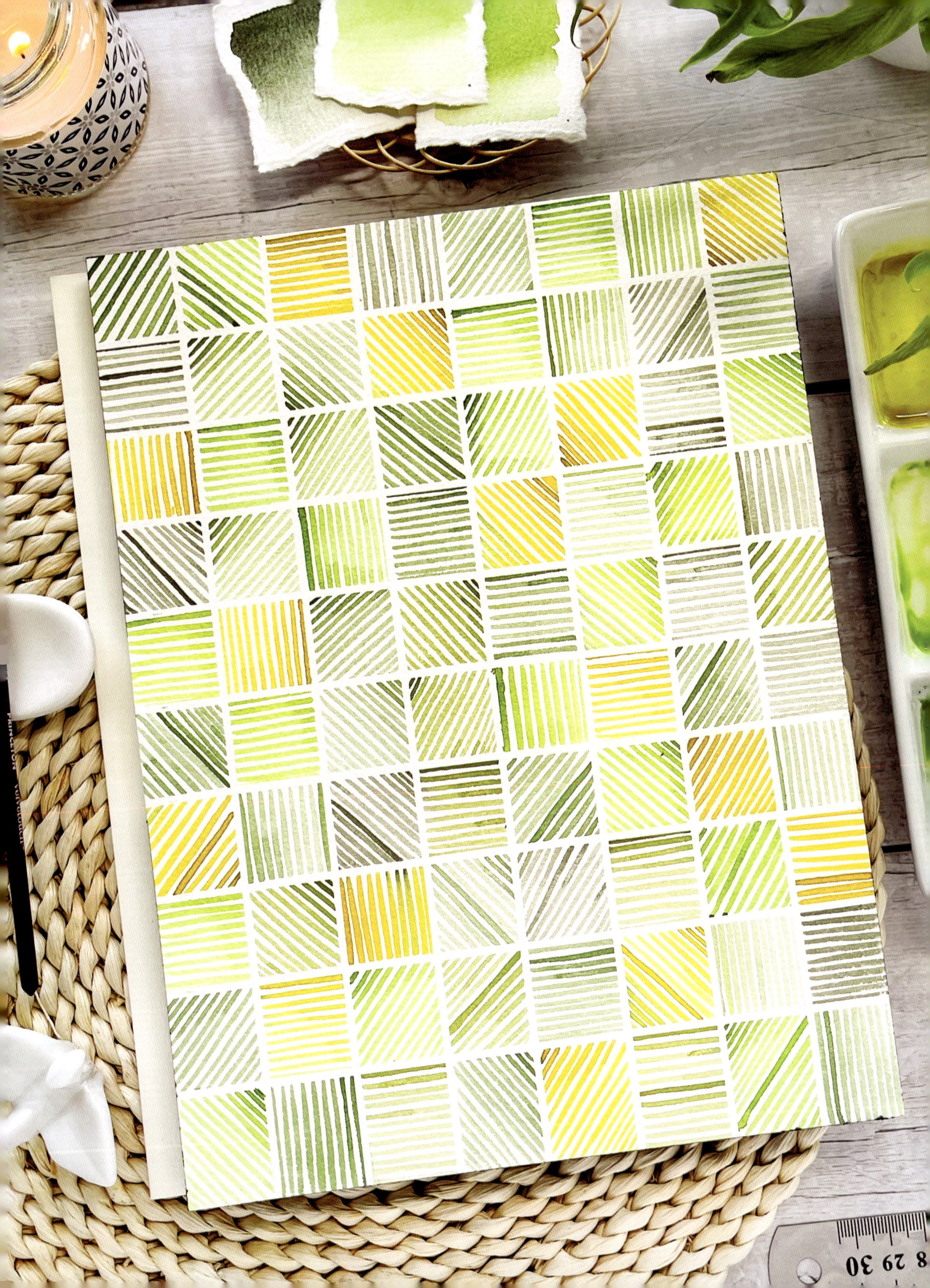

Fields from Above

Through this pattern, we will develop one of the most important skills to have while painting with watercolors: painting lines. This is a grid-based pattern in which each square will be filled with lines that are placed diagonally, horizontally, and vertically. If you are feeling creative, you could drop the grid and make abstract quadrilateral sections using a ruler and fill them up with lines that are placed in all directions. But to make this a beginner project, I chose to draw a grid. I also used masking tape to make this project; though optional, it helps to create a nice white gap between the grid lines and gives the whole pattern a sleek finish.

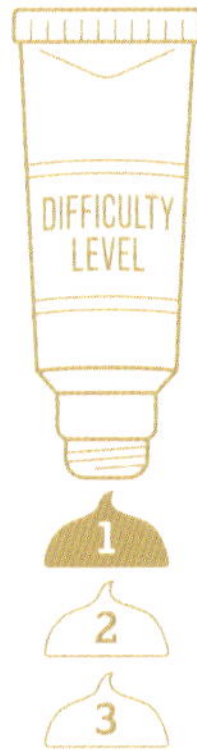

DIFFICULTY LEVEL

1
2
3

MATERIALS

BRUSH: Size 4 round brush with a fine tip

PAPER: 8" x 10" (20 x 25 cm), cold pressed; or use a smaller size, such as 8" x 8" (20 x 20 cm) or 5" x 7" (13 x 18 cm), if you are short on time

OTHER: Thin masking tape (I used 3 mm-wide tape—see Tip below)

COLORS:

 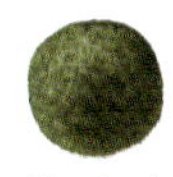 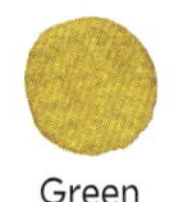  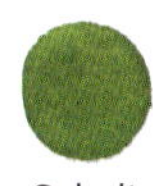

| Sap Green | Hooker's Green | Green Gold | Primary Yellow Lemon + Ultramarine Light | Cobalt Green Light + Yellow Ochre |

COLOR NOTE: You can use any shades of green for this project. Be sure to have a good mix by choosing a few bright greens and a few muted greens. This is a good exercise for mixing your own greens and seeing what you come up with!

TIP: When choosing a masking tape, use one that is the least wide possible. The pattern will look sparse and not so intricate if you use a wider tape. On the other hand, if you don't use masking tape, you can still leave approximate gaps between the grid squares or not leave any gaps at all; in that case, drawing a light grid will be helpful.

LET'S PRACTICE

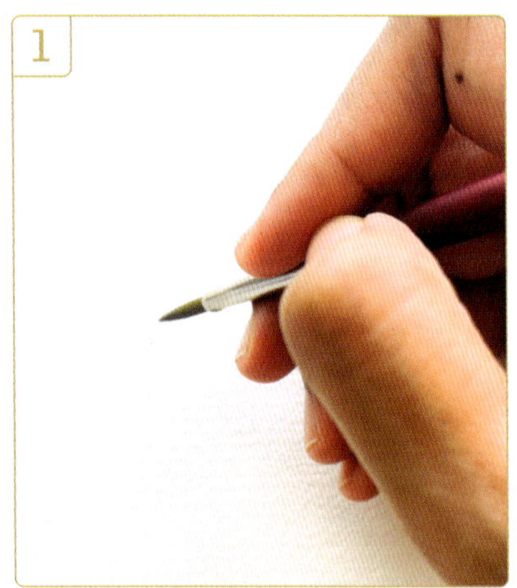

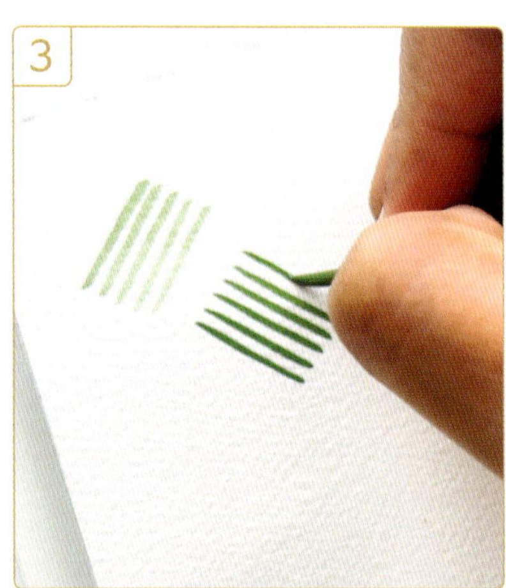

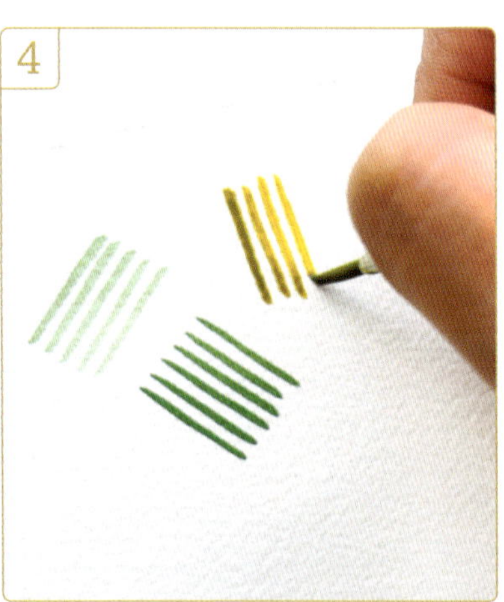

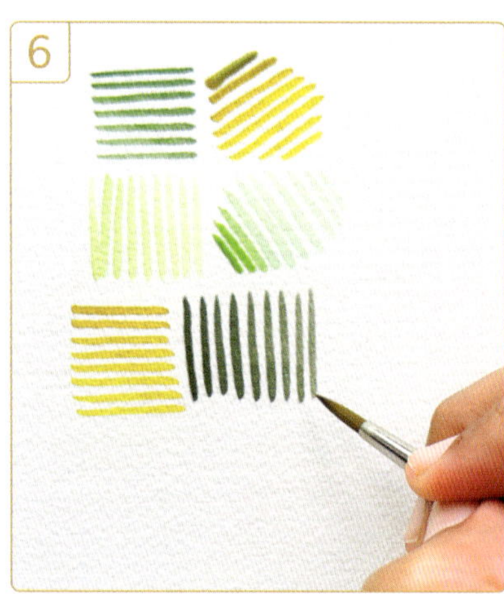

1 **Be conscious of your brush angle.** To draw lines that are thin and steady, hold your brush at an angle close to 90 degrees. This will help you to draw smooth and strong lines. Rest your wrist firmly to avoid shaky lines.

2 **Draw a few diagonal lines.** With your paper laid at an angle, start painting diagonal lines from left to right. Paint them close to each other and about 1" (2.5 cm) in length. Keep drawing lines in this direction until you feel comfortable.

3 **Switch direction.** Now draw lines in the opposite diagonal direction. Again, make sure your lines are somewhat uniform in length. Also try to maintain uniform distance between the lines.

4 **Draw some vertical lines.** Next draw vertical straight lines. I find it easier to draw straight lines if my paper is slightly angled. Keeping the paper straight while drawing vertical lines can be challenging. Try both ways and see what works for you.

5 **Draw some horizontal lines.** To paint straight horizontal lines, I find placing the paper straight while my hand is moving parallel from left to right helps me achieve stronger lines. Figure out what is comfortable for you.

6 **Practice with colors and closer placement.** Now focus on using the different shades of green you plan to use in your final piece. Place sets of lines close to each other and see how steadily you can draw the lines using the different shades.

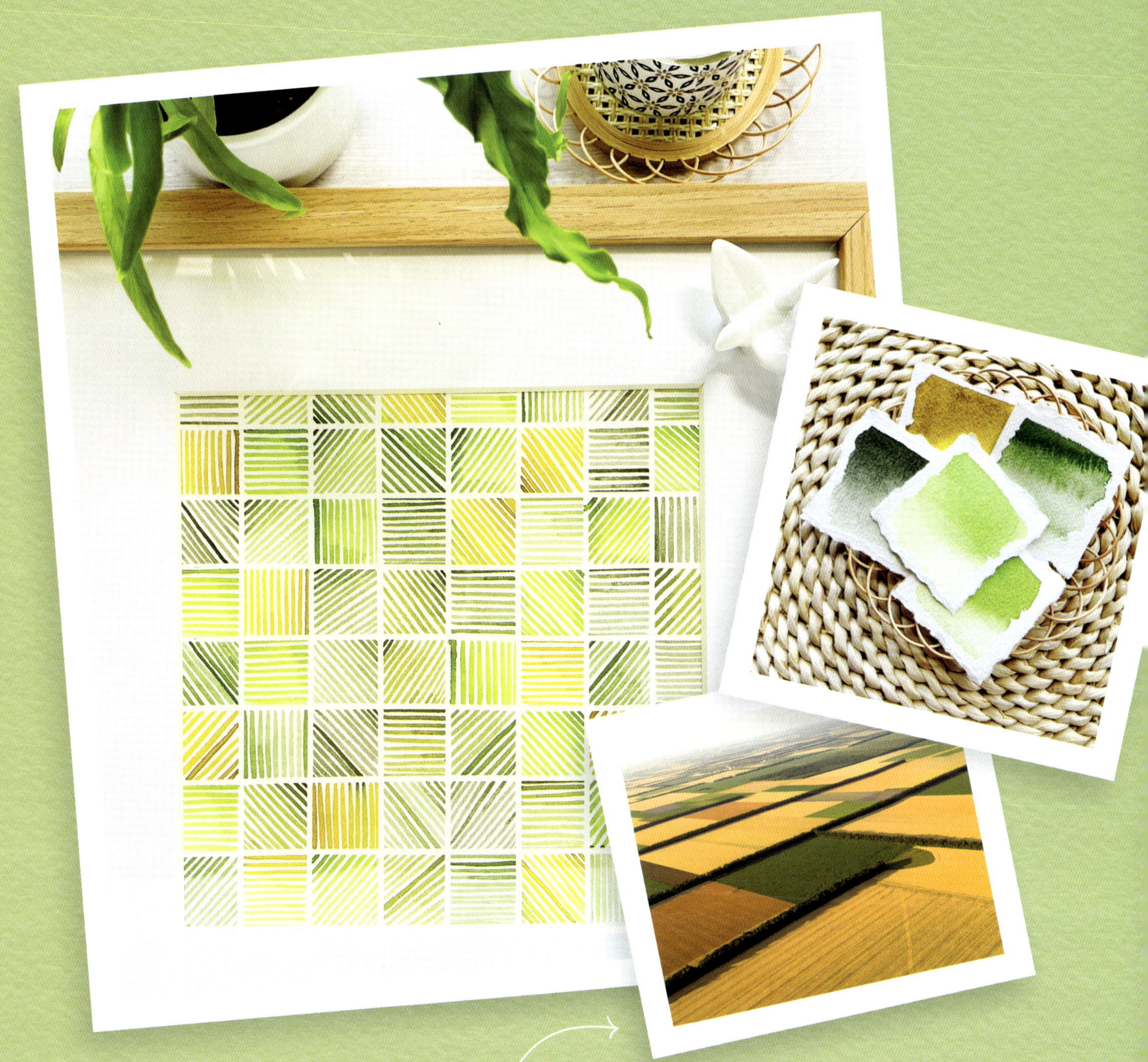

Let's Relax

This pattern is inspired by aerial shots of expansive agricultural fields, which look like a dense green patchwork when seen from above. Vast acres of lands covered in lush green crops, carefully plotted in rows and columns, are the main inspiration behind this design.

There is something about the color green that attracts my attention and calms my inner being. While I was mixing so many different shades of green for this pattern, I truly experienced calmness and a feeling of peace. The act of drawing steady lines over and over is also oddly satisfying! I hope you feel the same way as you engross yourself in mixing your own shades of green. What feelings do these shades evoke in you? Come, let's paint some green fields!

1 **Create the tape grid.** Make markings 1" (2.5 cm) apart across all sides of the paper. Place strips of thin masking tape horizontally, joining the markings on the sides, and then vertically, joining the markings on the top and bottom.

2 **Paint one row.** Start painting lines in each of the grid squares. Use a mix of diagonal, vertical, and horizontal lines and all your shades of green. You will see a cool gradient effect in the lines if you don't dip your brush in paint or water while drawing a set.

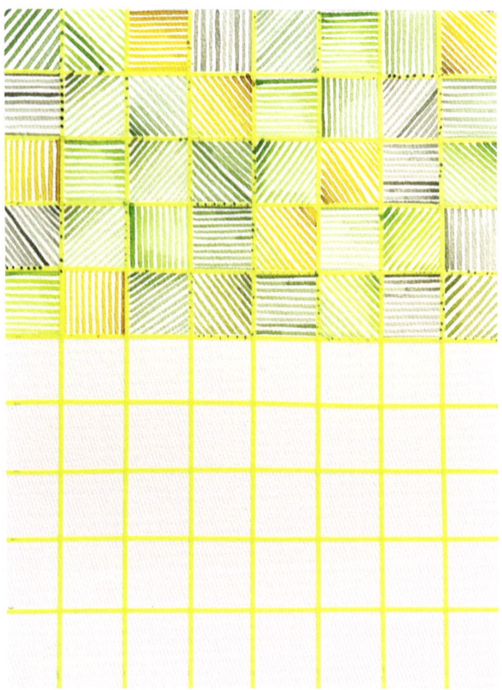

3 **Continue painting.** You can paint column-wise if you like, but row-wise felt easier to me. As you proceed, start mixing your greens on the go and making good use of light and dark tones. It is fine if your paint goes onto the tape— it will all be peeled off in the end.

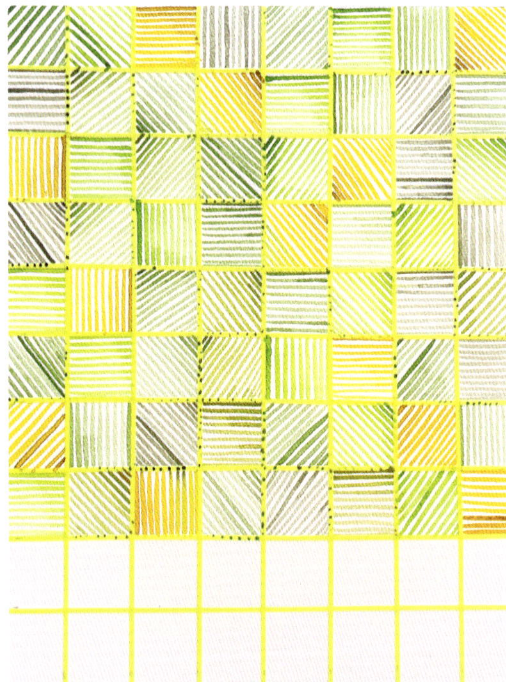

4 **Get into a groove.** Continue painting the lines in each of the squares; you will find a sweet meditative spot that will make the process feel smooth and effortless. Move your paper around to find the optimum angle while painting lines in all four directions.

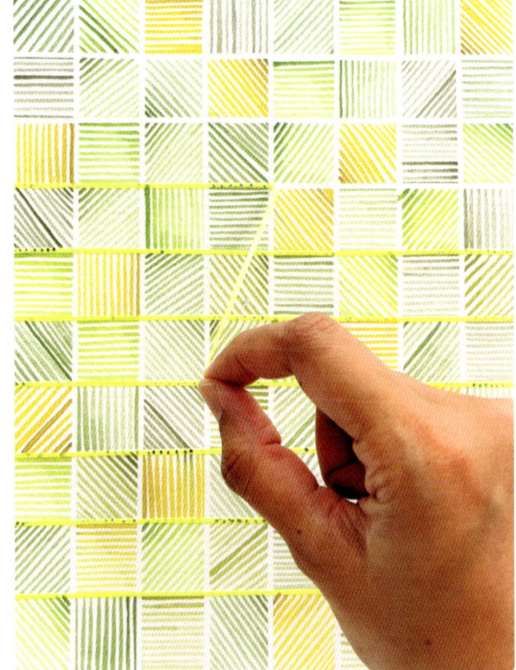

5 **Remove the tape.** Once the painting is done, make sure all the lines have dried completely. When you're ready to peel, start with the vertical pieces that were taped last. Be gentle and keep your fingers close to the paper to avoid tearing it.

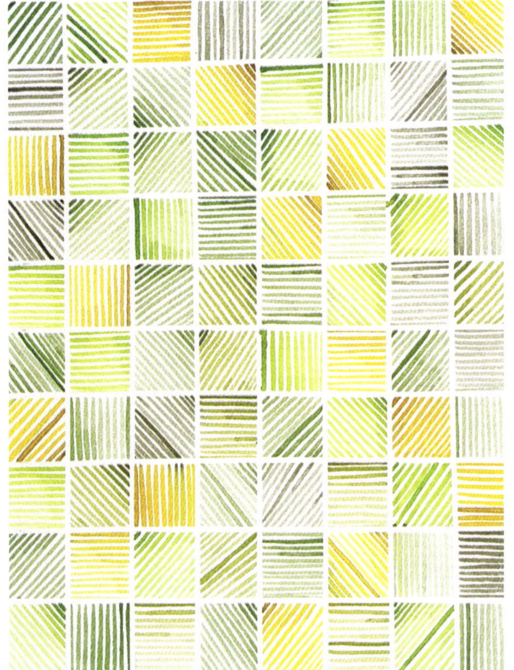

6 **Reveal the final pattern!** Finally, remove the horizontal pieces of tape. You will see beautiful, evenly spaced white gaps between the grid lines. The contrasting green lines will complement the white gaps and really elevate this simple concept.

Let's Paint

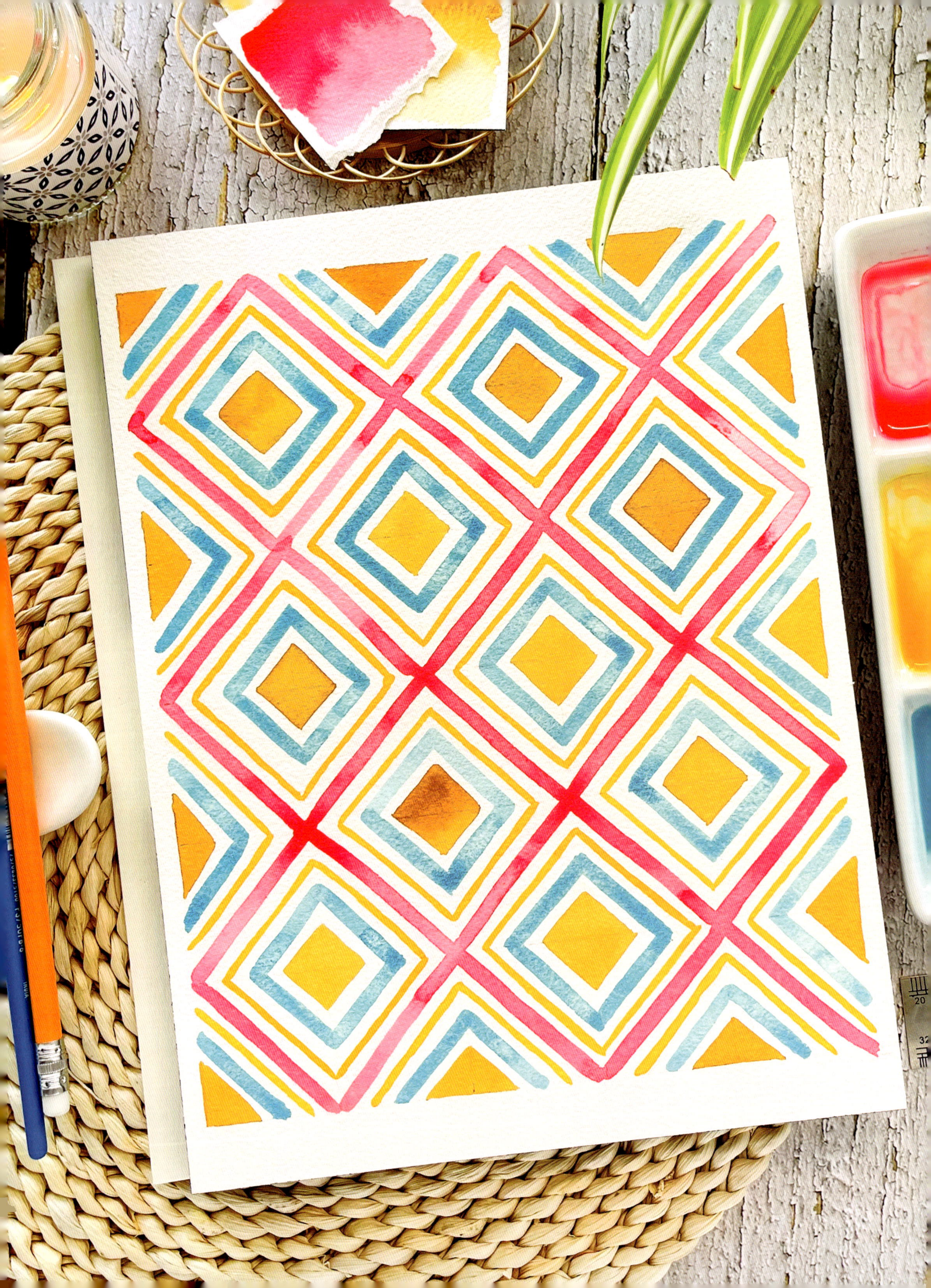

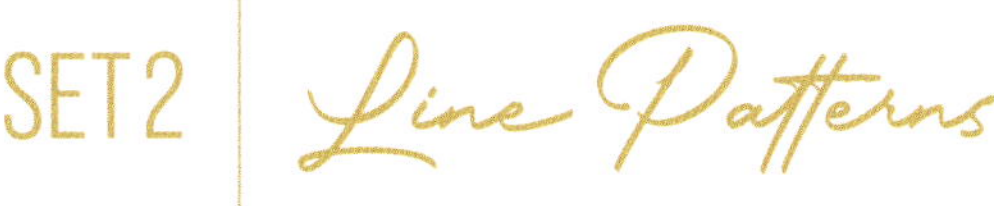

Diamond Trellis

This pattern focuses on the use of a filbert brush to draw lines. Filbert brushes are quite versatile and can be used to paint florals, leaves, and geometric shapes. The blunt tip of the brush helps you to paint thick and thin lines of uniform width, especially at the points where a line starts and ends. That is one reason why I like to paint medium-thick lines using a filbert brush. We will learn to use a filbert brush by holding it in two different ways. This is a symmetric pattern and requires a very basic grid structure.

73

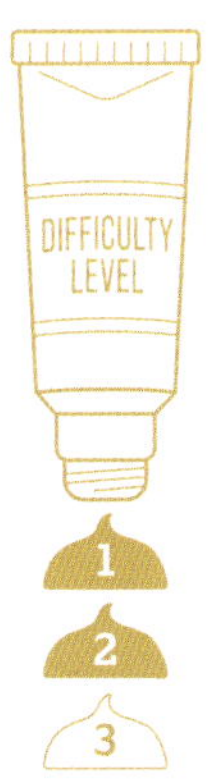

MATERIALS

BRUSH: Size 6 filbert brush

PAPER: 8" x 10" (20 x 25 cm), cold pressed; or use a smaller size, such as 8" x 8" (20 x 20 cm) or 5" x 7" (13 x 18 cm), if you are short on time

OTHER: Pencil; ruler; eraser

COLORS:

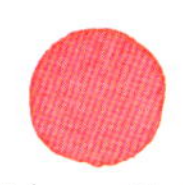
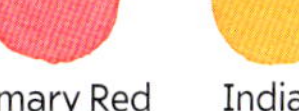
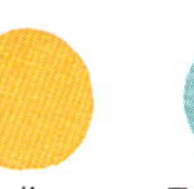
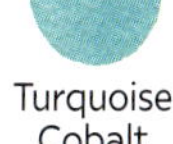

| Primary Red Magenta | Indian Yellow | Turquoise Cobalt | Yellow Ochre |

TIP: We will be working with one color at a time going from top to bottom as we paint this piece. Before you proceed to the next color layer, ensure that the previous colors—especially toward the bottom of the page— have dried, to avoid smudging when you place your hand on the paper to paint from the top again.

LET'S PRACTICE

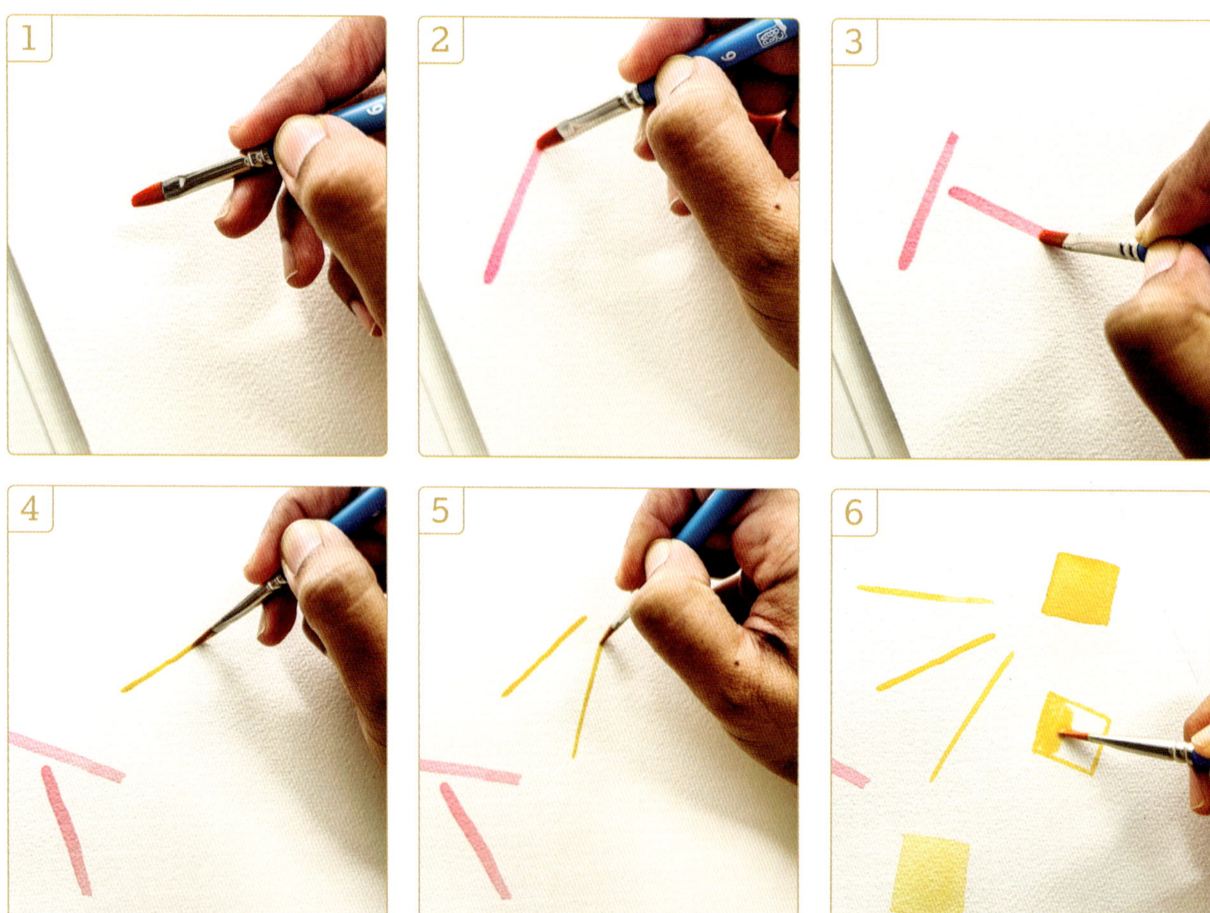

1 **Learn to hold the filbert brush.** Mix some paint in your palette that is fluid enough to draw lines. Practice holding the filbert brush correctly: hold the brush almost upright, perpendicular to the paper, so that the flat, blunt tip of the brush is touching the paper.

2 **Paint a line.** Carefully press the tip of the brush down and paint a straight but angled line going up. Don't forget to rest your wrist while painting the line. Lift the brush and your hand when you reach the desired line length.

3 **Continue practicing this form.** Still holding the brush correctly, draw a line coming down this time. Practice painting such lines going up and down a couple of times until you get the hang of holding the brush correctly.

4 **Switch the brush position.** Now you will learn to hold the filbert brush sideways so that you can use the sides of the bristles to paint a thinner line. Holding the brush sideways, paint a horizontal line going from left to right. It's much thinner.

5 **Continue practicing this form.** Paint a few more thin lines by holding the brush sideways. Keep practicing until you feel warmed up.

6 **Practice painting filled diamonds.** Using the side bristles, draw a small diamond shape. Fill in the diamond using the broad tip of the brush. Practice painting a few of these small diamonds with sides that are about 1" (2.5 cm) long.

Let's Relax

This pattern is inspired by the wooden lattice framework structures that are used in gardens to support the growth of climbing vines and creepers. Using diamond trellises really elevates the look of an outdoor garden space, and I have always loved this simple no-fuss pattern. We will use this framework, but make it a bit more artsy by layering the lattice using four colors. This is a good example of incorporating patterns from real-life structures into art to create something new. As you paint, imagine green and growing things weaving in and out of and climbing up this solid structure, building to a gloriously lush conclusion.

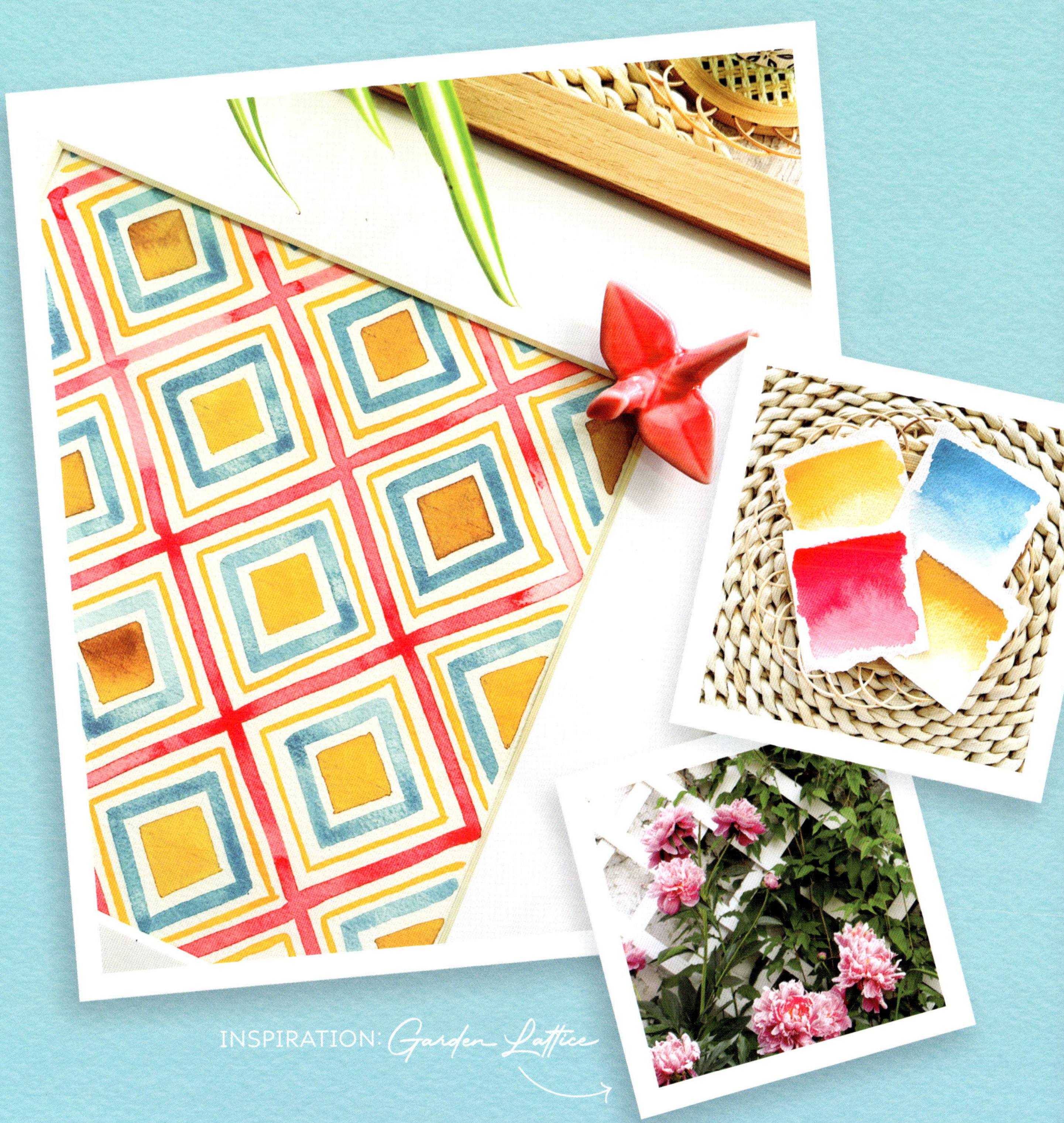

INSPIRATION: *Garden Lattice*

Let's Paint

76

1 **Create the grid.** Mix the four paints. Add enough water so that your filbert brush can glide smoothly to make a line without going dry at the end of the stroke. Create a basic grid of 1½" (3.8 cm) squares.

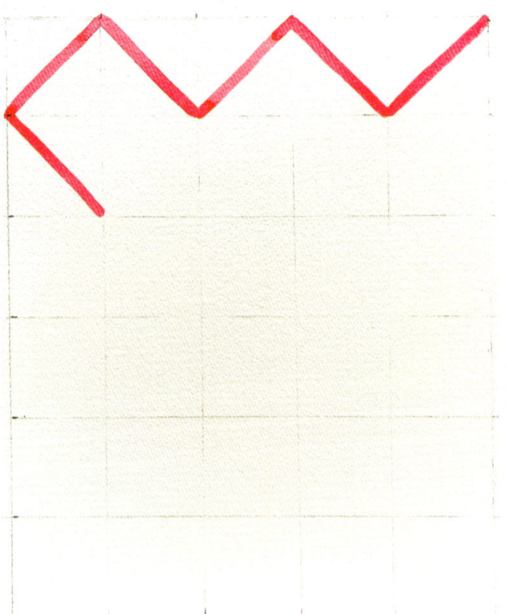

2 **Start with the pinkish red lines.** Using Primary Red Magenta, join two corners of the top left square with a diagonal line as shown. Proceed to the next square and join two corners with a diagonal line in the other direction as shown. Complete the first row like this, then mirror the lines for the second row.

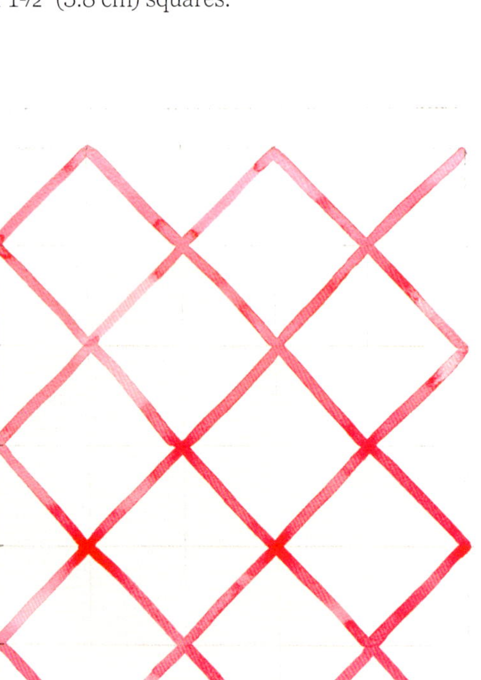

3 **Complete the pinkish red lines.** Finish painting all the diamonds row by row to establish the basic diamond trellis structure. You could also draw long diagonals that go edge to edge through many squares.

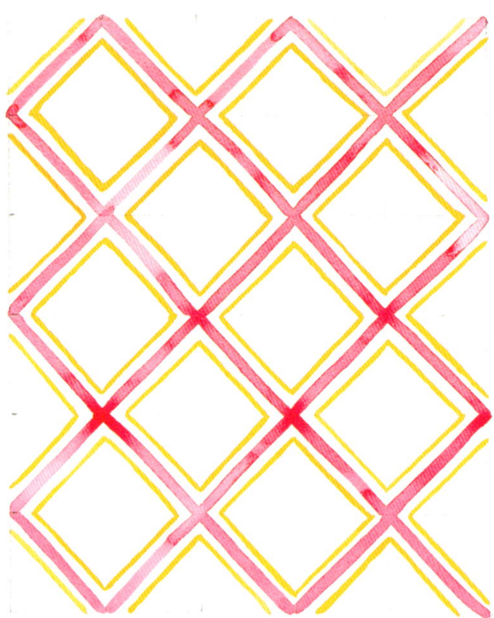

4 **Paint the yellow lines.** Once the previous layer is dry, use the side bristles of the filbert brush to draw Indian Yellow diamonds inside each of the pinkish red diamonds. Leave a small white gap between the two diamonds. Don't forget the half-diamonds around the edges.

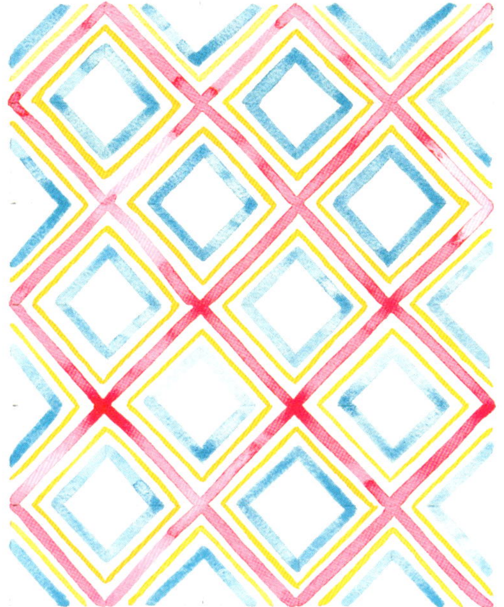

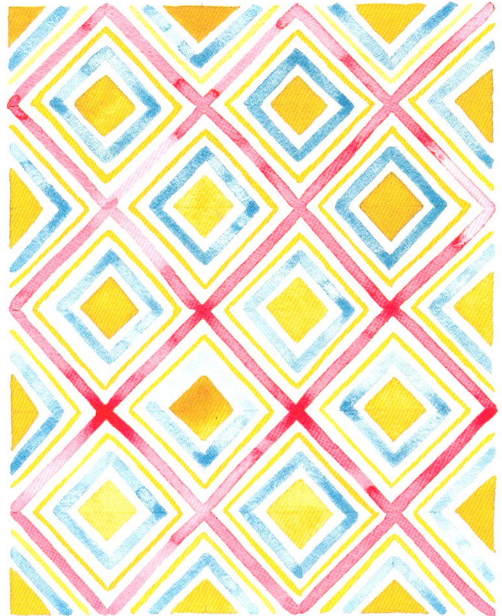

5 **Paint the blue lines.** Once the yellow layer is dry, use the third color, blue, to draw slightly smaller diamonds, this time using the flat tip of the brush. Leave a small white gap between the diamonds again.

6 **Paint the Yellow Ochre diamonds.** Ensure that the blue layer is dry. Using the side bristles of the brush, draw each Yellow Ochre diamond and fill it in, again leaving a white gap. Once this final layer has dried, erase any visible pencil lines.

Let's Paint

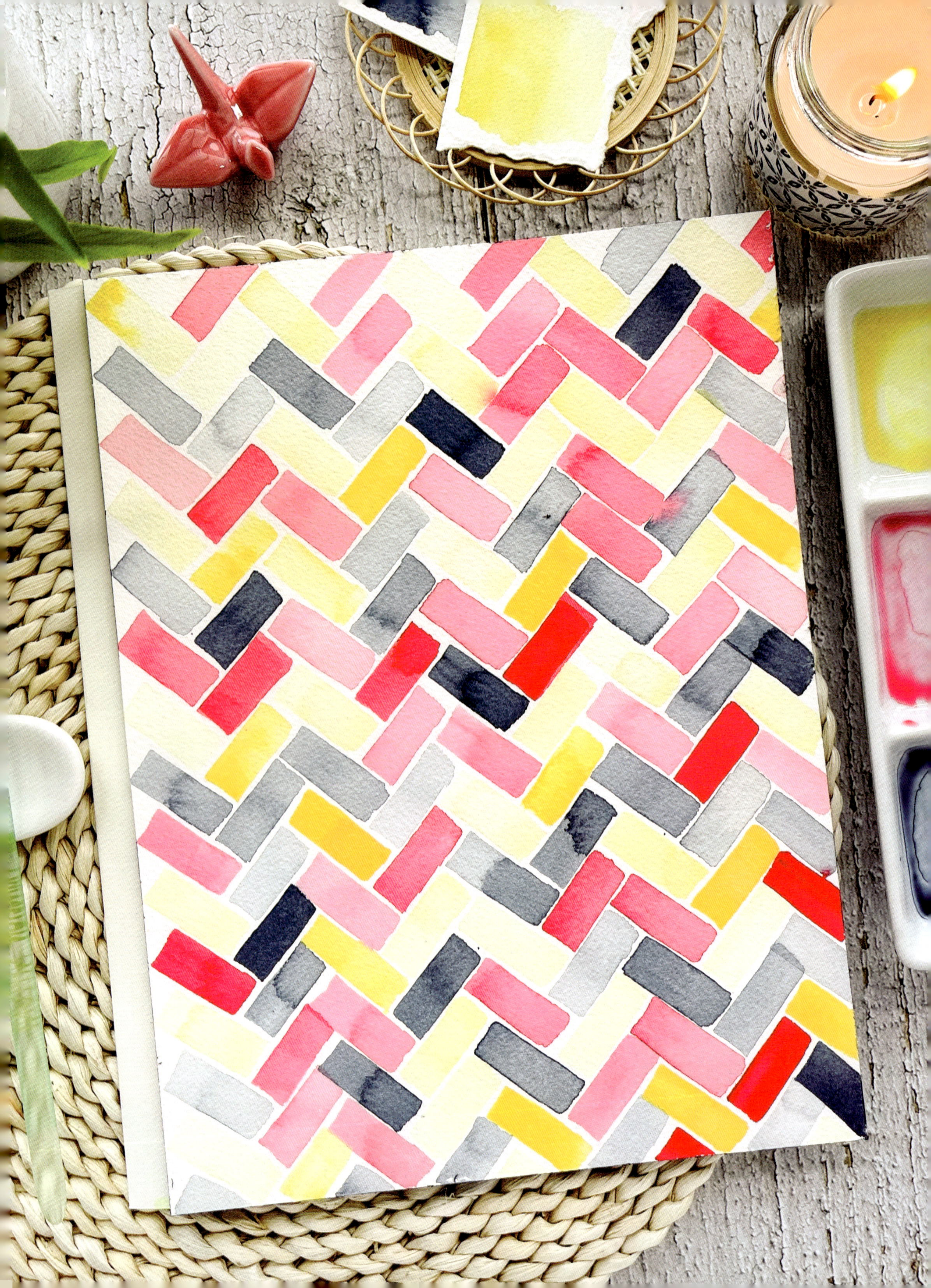

Timeless Herringbone

In this pattern, you will learn to work with flat brushes. Flat brushes are very useful for painting brushstrokes of a fixed width. We are going to paint a stacked herringbone pattern using a flat brush and explore the way this brush works. This is a symmetric pattern, but we are going to make it interesting and take it up a notch by using three colors to paint it instead of just one.

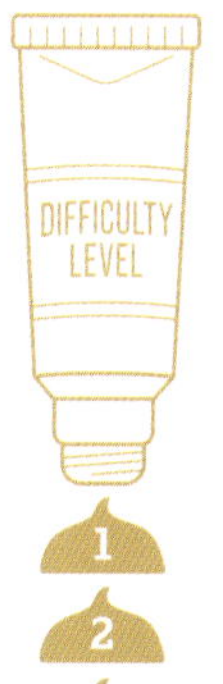

DIFFICULTY LEVEL

1

2

3

MATERIALS

BRUSH: Size ½" (1.3 cm) flat brush

PAPER: 8" x 10" (20 x 25 cm), cold pressed; or use a smaller size, such as 8" x 8" (20 x 20 cm) or 5" x 7" (13 x 18 cm), if you are short on time

COLORS:

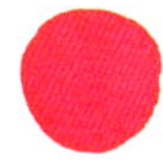

Rose Lake   Naples Yellow   Payne's Gray

TIP: This pattern is painted freehand, rather than using a grid or any pencil guidelines, which is what makes it a higher difficulty level. Be sure to go slowly and maintain steady lines while you work. You will make fewer mistakes if you mindfully place each stroke at the correct angle!

LET'S PRACTICE

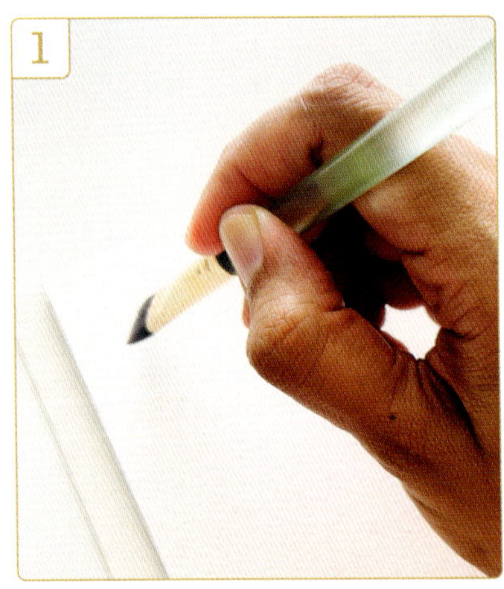

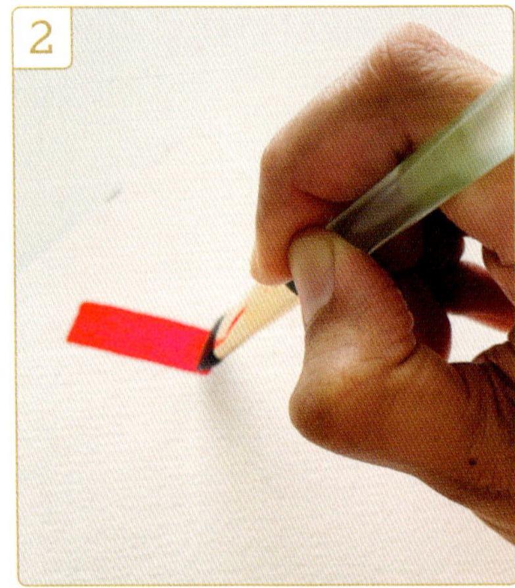

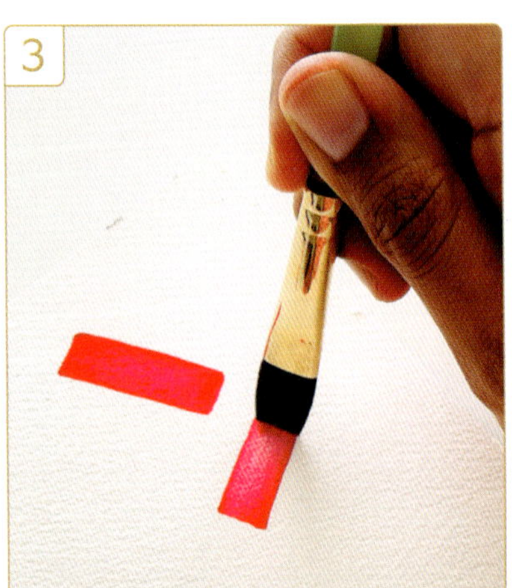

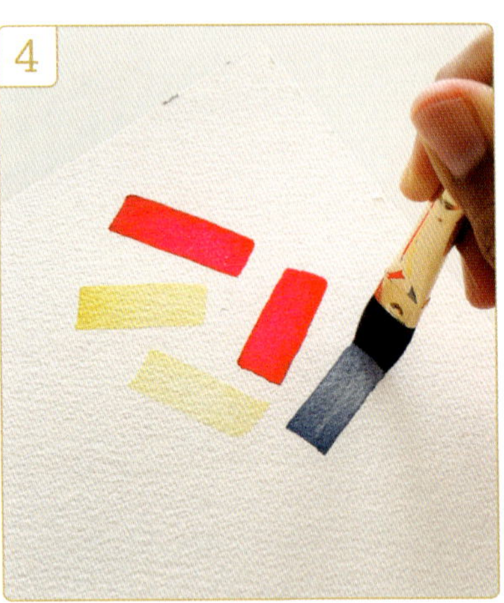

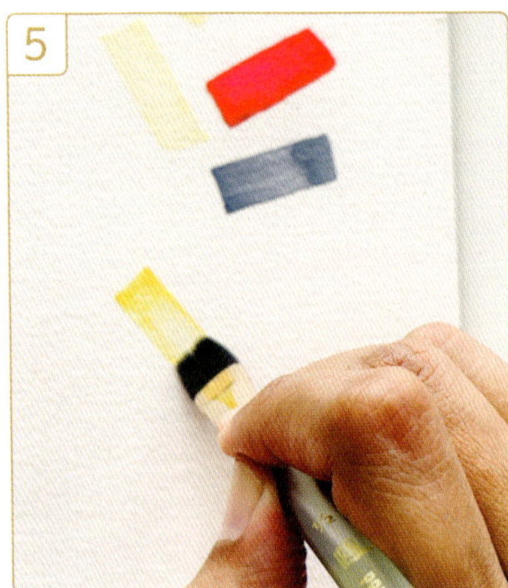

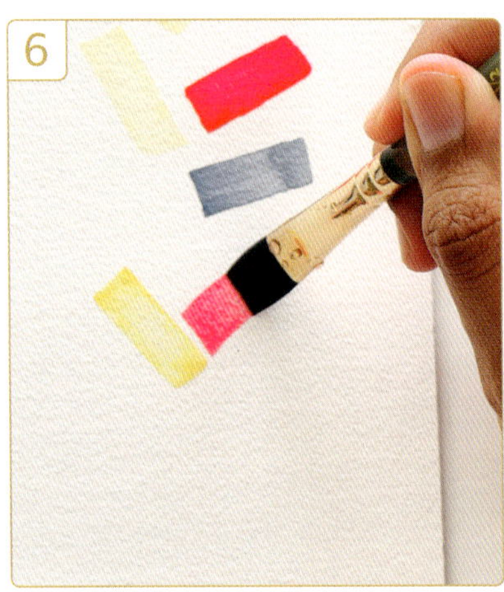

1 **Learn to hold the brush.** Hold the flat brush almost upright, perpendicular to the paper. If you hold it at an angle very close to the paper, you could get leftover marks as you lift it. Try holding the brush correctly and incorrectly to see the difference.

2 **Make your first test stroke.** Load your brush with paint, hold it correctly, and drag it down to make a mark. Lift the brush quickly and confidently to avoid creating extra marks—you want a crisp, flat end.

3 **Make a stroke at another angle.** Now try painting a different direction, from downward to upward. Hold the brush upright and drag it to create the stroke, cleanly lifting the brush to end the stroke.

4 **Continue practicing these strokes.** Paint a few more strokes going both upward and downward using the other two colors in the palette.

5 **Start working on the structure.** Rinse the brush and load it with the first color. Draw the first stroke, a little longer than 1" (2.5 cm), going up to down. Make sure that this stroke is at an angle, not parallel to the bottom edge of the paper.

6 **Place the second stroke.** Rinse the brush and load it with the second color. Position the brush so that it will form an L shape or is at a right angle to the previous brushstroke, then place the tip of the brush and draw the stroke going down to up.

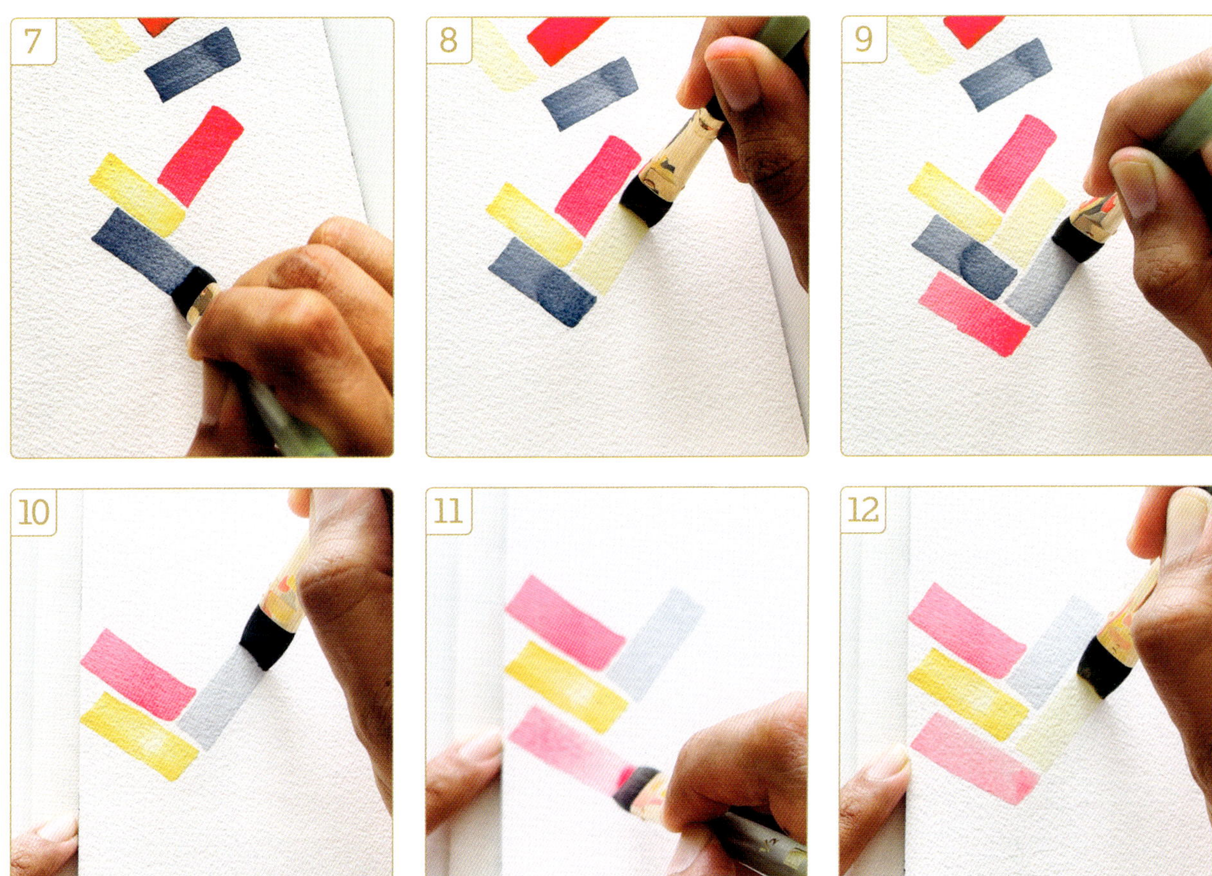

7 **Place the third stroke.** Rinse the brush and load it with the third color. The next stroke is next to and parallel with the first stroke but starts halfway along it. Paint the stroke, being careful to make it the same length.

8 **Place the fourth stroke.** Rinse the brush and load it with the first color again. You will cycle through the three colors throughout the pattern. Place a fourth stroke as shown.

9 **Place the fifth and sixth strokes.** Repeat the process once again to place two more flat brushstrokes. Practice the stroke placement like this in small chunks until you feel confident in your ability to place the strokes neatly.

10 **Practice along the paper edge.** If you place the first (leftmost) column correctly, the remaining parts of the pattern will come together easily. Start off near the very left edge of the paper, placing the brushstrokes right along this edge as shown.

11 **Use your finger as a reference.** Place your left index finger at the point where your brush should rest for the next stroke, as shown. Place your brush there, touching the left edge of the paper, and bring the next stroke down from there.

12 **Keep practicing.** As you can see, using the edge of the paper as a guideline helps to keep the first column straight and aligned. If you freehand it from the start, you may end up with a bit of a slant in your final piece. Try both ways to see the difference.

Let's Relax

A herringbone pattern is rather ubiquitous; you must have seen this pattern before on things like floor tiling, kitchen backsplashes, fabrics, pavement, wooden furniture, etc. I call this pattern timeless because of its simplicity and ability to add character to any object it is used on.

It is believed that this pattern got its name because of its resemblance to the bone structure of a herring fish. The zigzag, staggered tiles are quite appealing to the eye, and the pattern supposedly dates back to the ancient Roman era! There was no way I could have excluded this iconic pattern from the book. As you paint, imagine an expert craftsperson laying individual tiles or bricks carefully to form a tidy, attractive path. You will become this very same craftsperson through your painting!

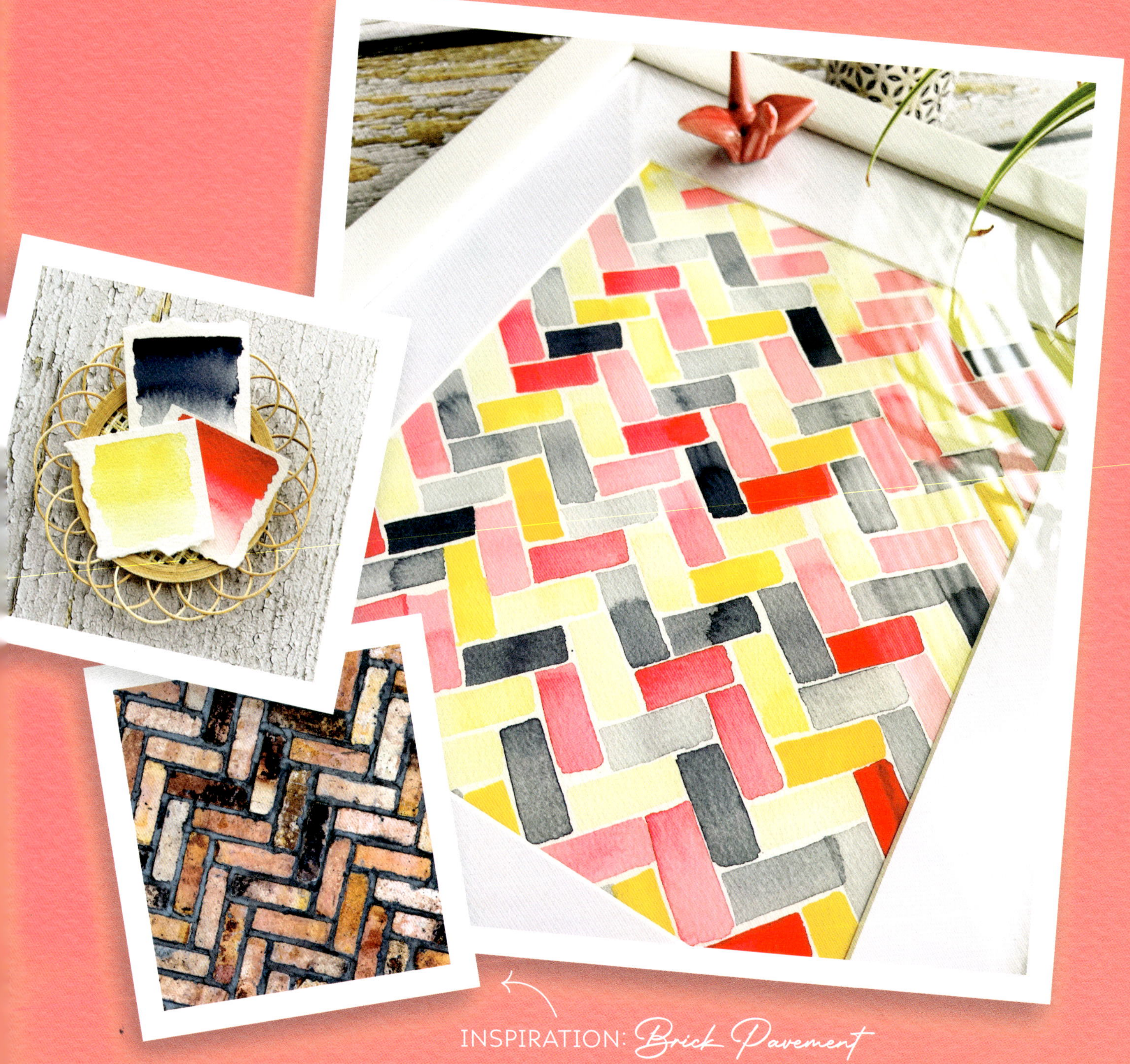

INSPIRATION: *Brick Pavement*

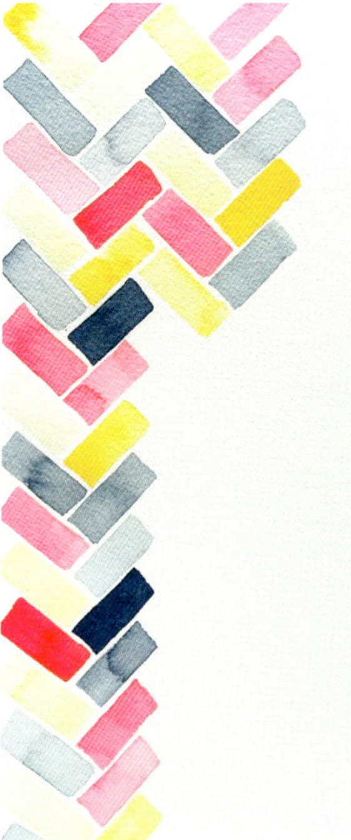

1 **Get a strong start.** Mix the three paints. Add enough water so that your flat brush can glide smoothly. Start from the top left. It's important to get these first few strokes right. Mindfully place each stroke.

2 **Start the second column.** Once you reach the bottom, move up to the top of the next column. Stack the strokes slowly and start coming down. Don't fret about minor imperfections—just continue maintaining the basic look of tiles.

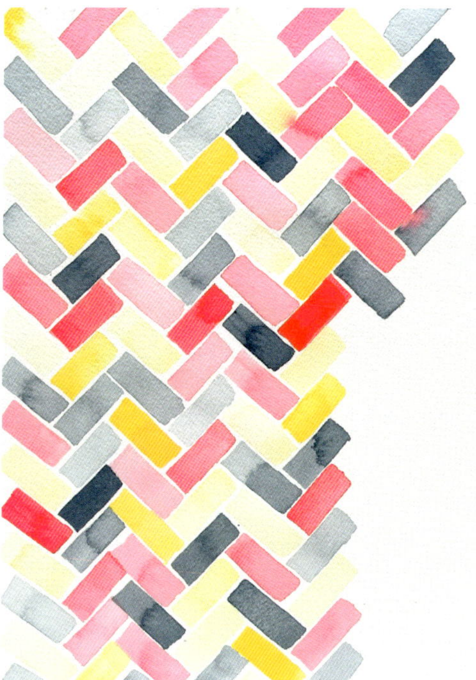

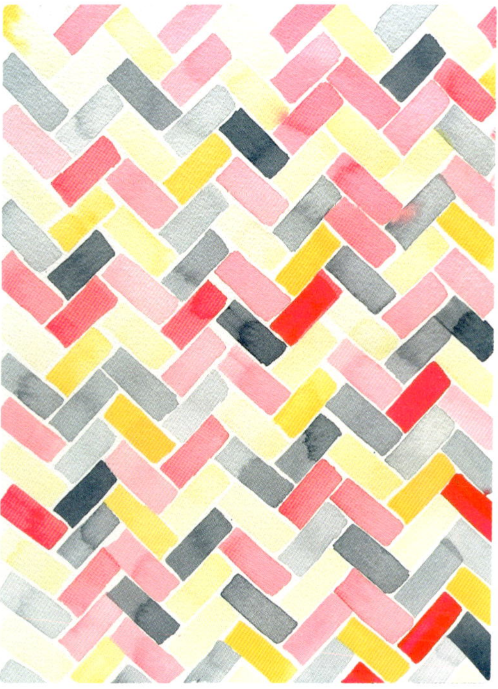

3 **Vary it up.** Continue painting, being sure to rinse your brush between colors. I have intentionally placed dark tiles of each color after every few light ones. This adds interest and movement. Re-mix your colors whenever they become too watery.

4 **Fill in the final partial column.** As you reach the end, you may have a small gap on the right side of the paper. Simply continue, letting your brushstrokes go off the edge of the page. Fill in any white spots along the left, top, or bottom if you like.

Let's Paint

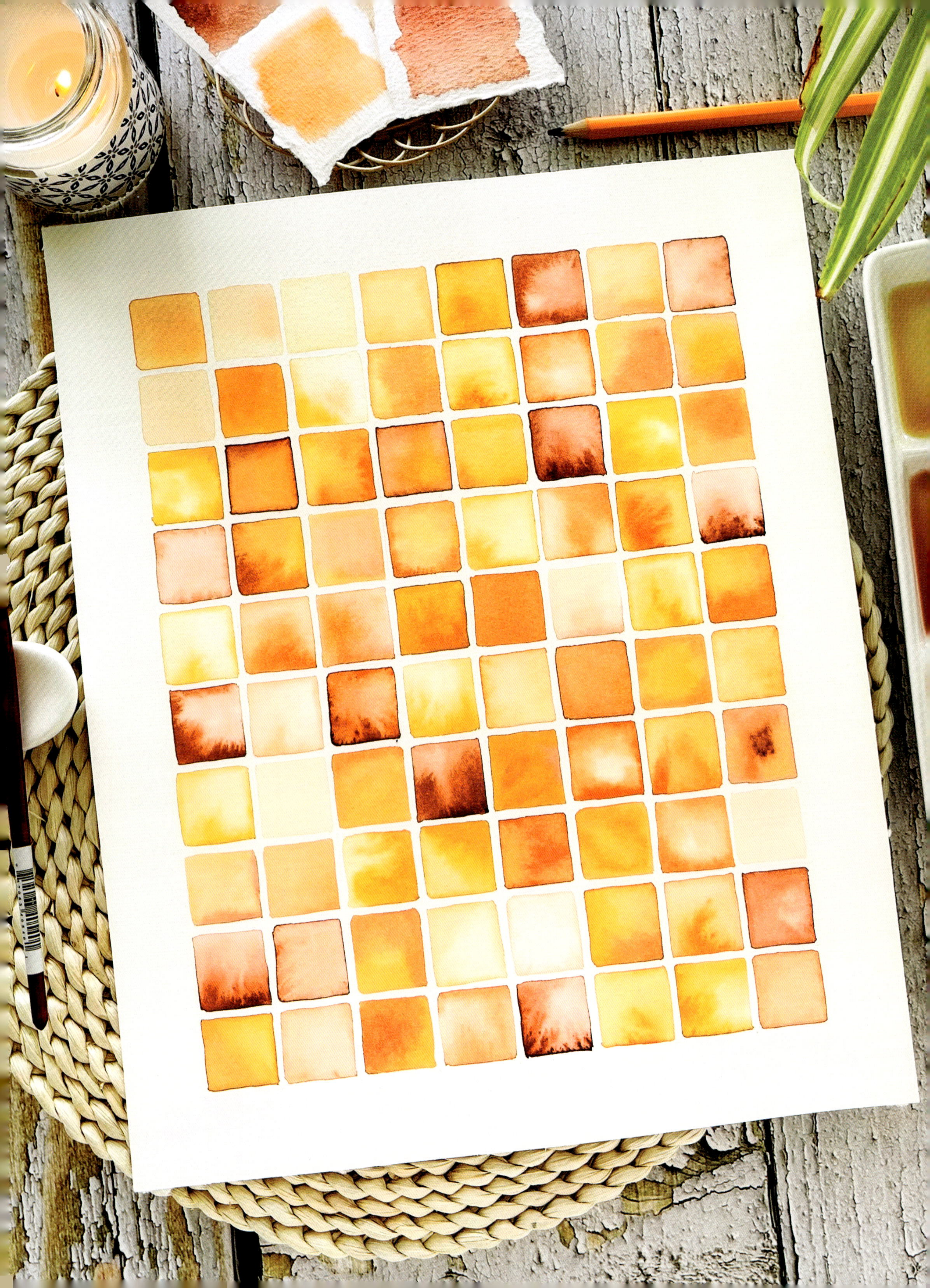

Baltic Amber Squares

This pattern will strengthen your ability to draw freehand squares and is a great way to practice the wet-on-wet technique. We will be placing squares in rows and columns using a basic grid structure. It is a simple pattern, but the use of wet-on-wet makes each square look unique and beautiful.

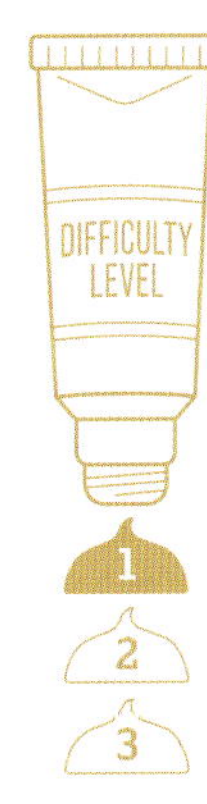

MATERIALS

BRUSH: Size 6 round brush

PAPER: 8" x 10" (20 x 25 cm), hot pressed; or use a smaller size, such as 8" x 8" (20 x 20 cm) or 5" x 7" (13 x 18 cm), if you are short on time

OTHER: Pencil; ruler; eraser

COLORS:

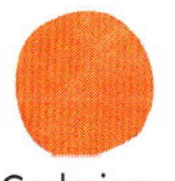 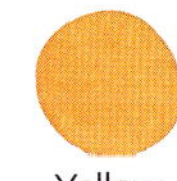 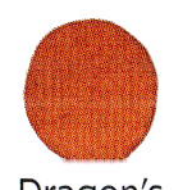 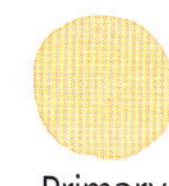

Cadmium Orange + Yellow Ochre + Venetian Red*

Yellow Ochre

Dragon's Blood*

Primary Yellow Lemon + Rose Lake*

***COLOR SUBSTITUTES:**

Cadmium Orange + Yellow Ochre + Venetian Red (any orangey brown of your choice)

Dragon's Blood (any brown of your choice)

Primary Yellow Lemon + Rose Lake (create a peachy shade using any yellow + pink)

TIP: We are using multiple colors, including brown, yellow ochre, primary yellow, pink, and orange, to derive different shades of amber. Before you start painting the final piece, mix at least four shades and keep them ready. Trying out swatches will help you to choose the right shades. This will also allow you to focus on the wet-on-wet technique and take away the stress of what to mix next.

LET'S PRACTICE

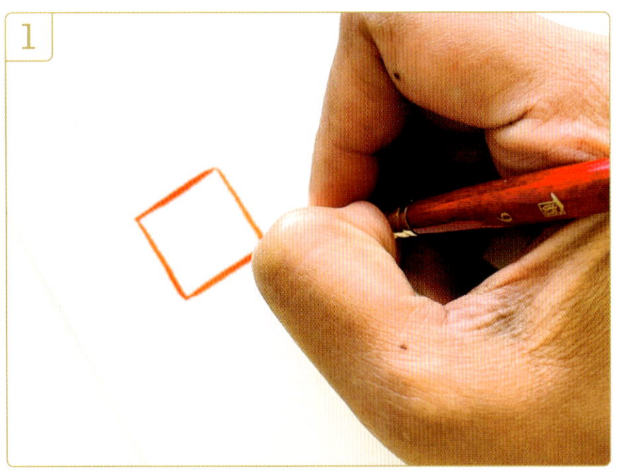

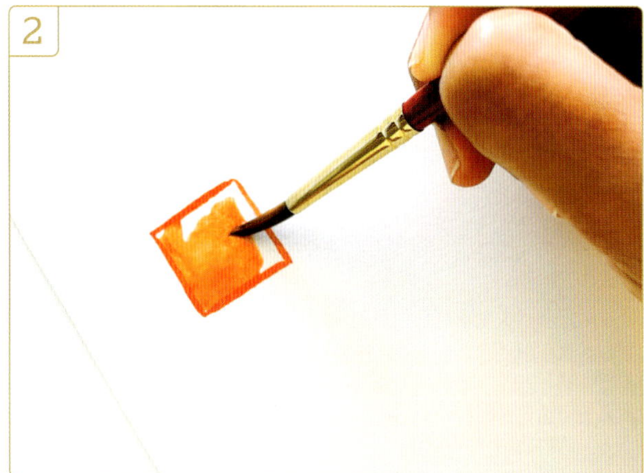

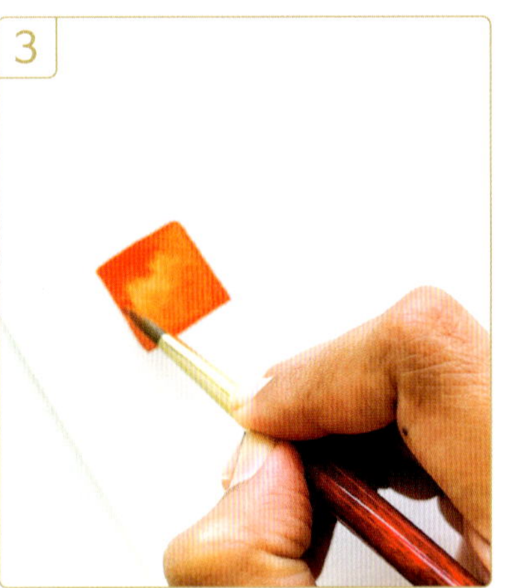

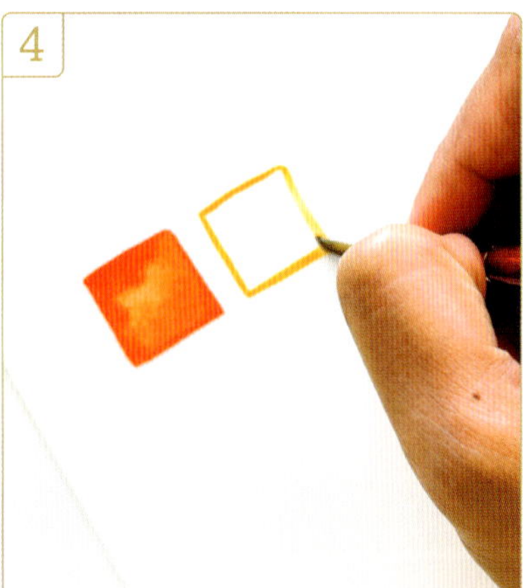

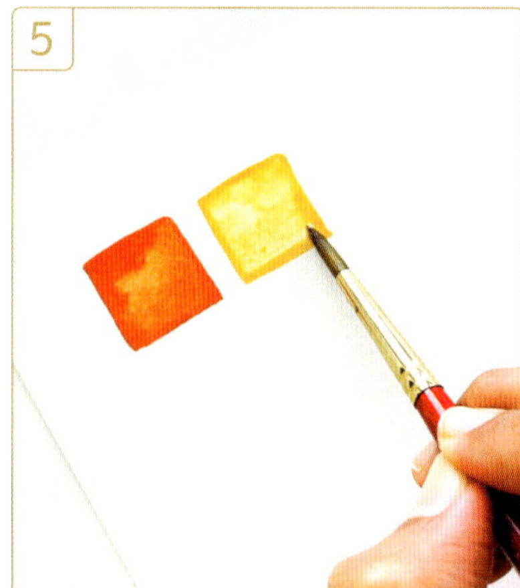

1 **Outline a square.** Mix some paint in your palette that is fluid enough to paint lines. Hold the brush almost upright, perpendicular to the paper, so that the tip of the brush is touching the paper. Now paint a small square with each side about 1" (2.5 cm) long.

2 **Fill the square with a wash.** Using a watery wash of the same color, fill in the square.

3 **Add darker paint.** Before the wash layer dries up, drop a darker mix of the same color into one corner of the square and allow it to blend organically into the watery wash. Don't glide your brush around too much.

4 **Test a second color.** Mix another shade. Paint a new 1" (2.5 cm) square.

5 **Add the wash.** Fill in the square with a light wash of the same color.

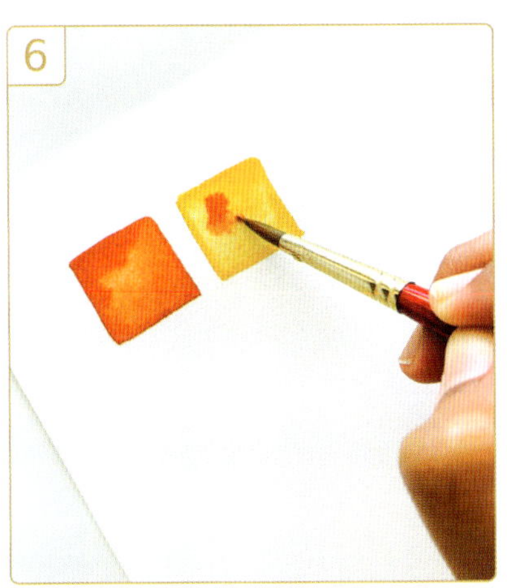

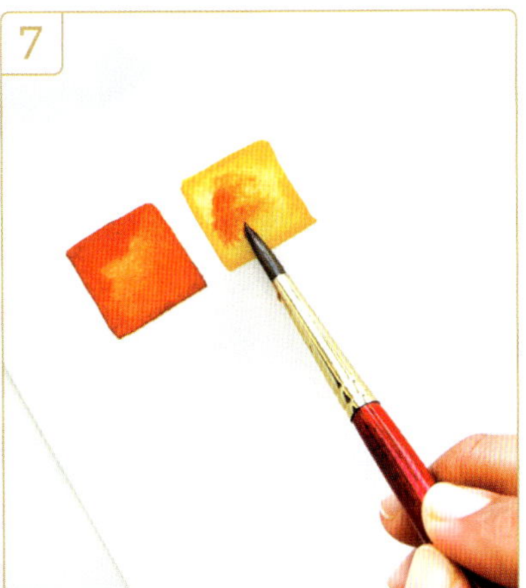

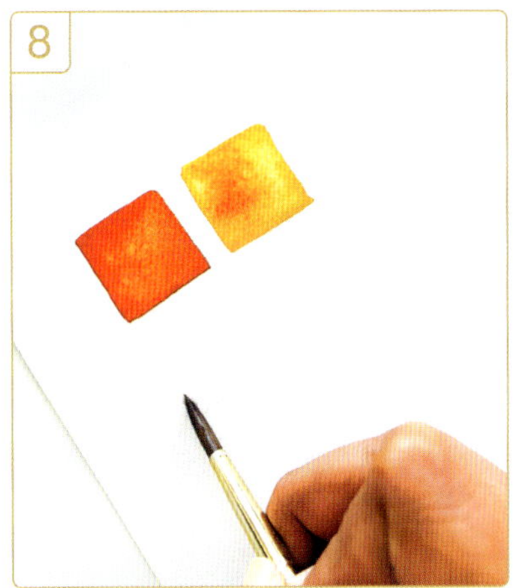

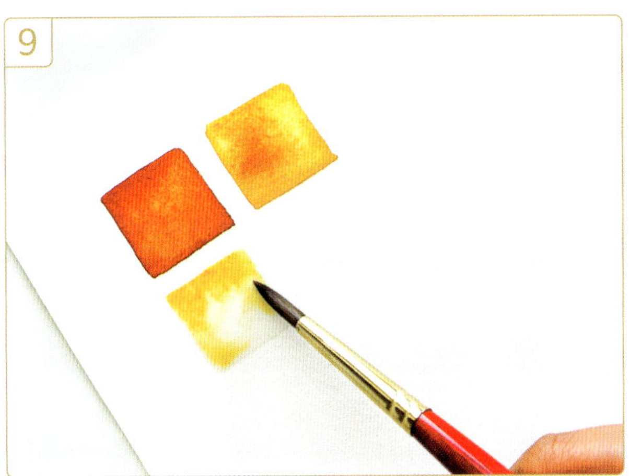

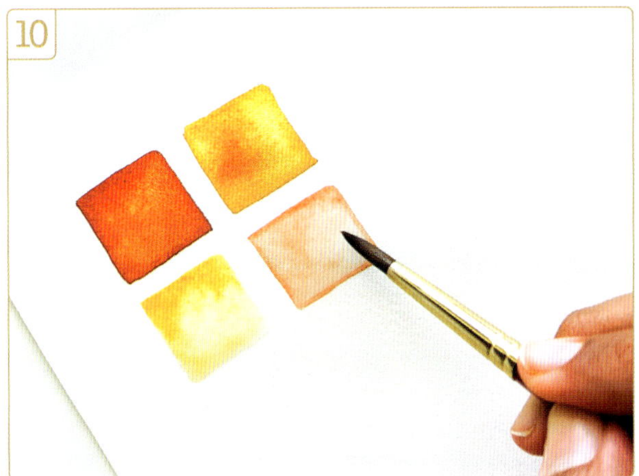

6 **Add a different darker color.** Take a darker mix of a different color and drop this shade on top of the wash layer. This way, you are using the wet-on-wet technique but with two completely different colors.

7 **Blend minimally.** Let the new color bleed into the existing color naturally. You can glide your brush ever so lightly around to help the colors blend into each other.

8 **Create a water square.** Rinse your brush clean and paint a square using clean water.

9 **Add color to the water square.** Take the next color and drop it onto the water square. You will see the color instantly start to spread on the clean layer of water, creating a nice, contained wet-on-wet effect. This is a great technique to achieve the lightest-possible squares.

10 **Keep practicing with different colors.** Explore and paint a variety of squares as explained in each of the previous steps. Paint a few dark ones, a few light ones, ones with multiple colors in them, and ones with just one color in them.

Let's Relax

This pattern is inspired by mysterious, transparent, and warm-toned Baltic amber, which comes in beautiful shades of yellow, orange, red, and earthy brown. Baltic amber is simply fossilized resin from ancient forests. This is a fun pattern in which you will enjoy mixing warm tones ranging from yellow to orange to brown. I absolutely loved painting these warm amber tones, and I hope you will enjoy the process of painting these imperfect, freehand squares too. Don't worry about perfection—just go with the flow. As you paint, imagine walking through an age-old forest filled with trees that are destined to become Baltic amber.

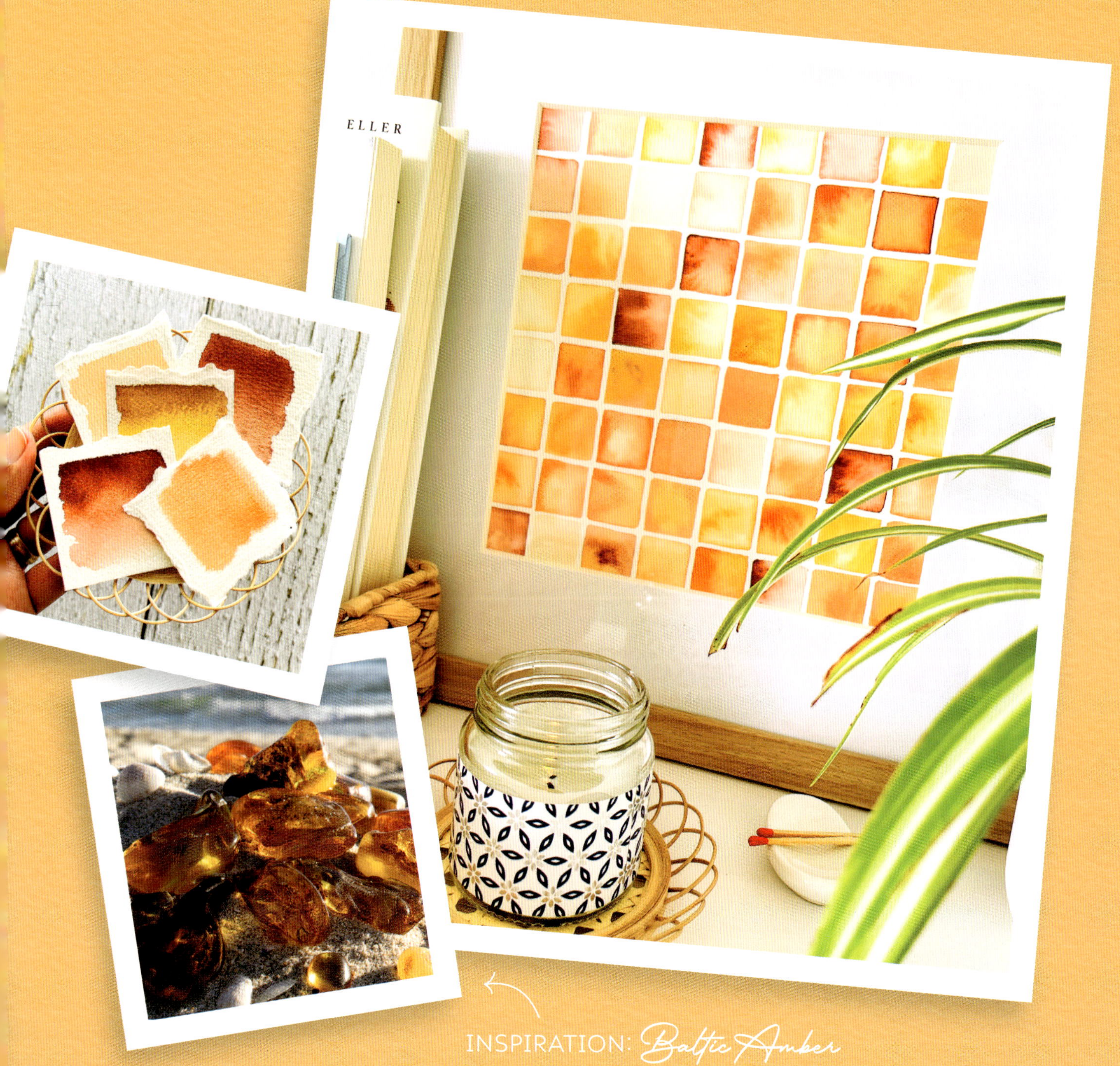

INSPIRATION: *Baltic Amber*

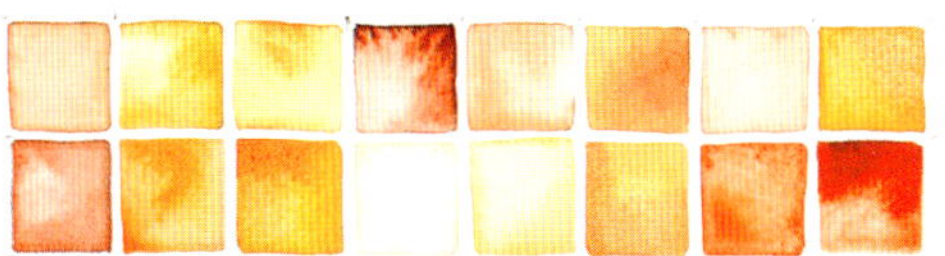

1 **Create the grid.** Mix the four paints and keep them ready in separate sections of the palette. Add enough water so that your brush can glide smoothly while painting the squares. Draw an 8" x 10" (20 x 25 cm) grid with 1" (2.5 cm) rows and columns.

2 **Start painting squares.** Using the wet-on-wet technique you learned in the practice session, start painting squares in varying shades. Make sure that the sides of the squares don't touch the grid lines. Aim for perfectly imperfect freehand squares!

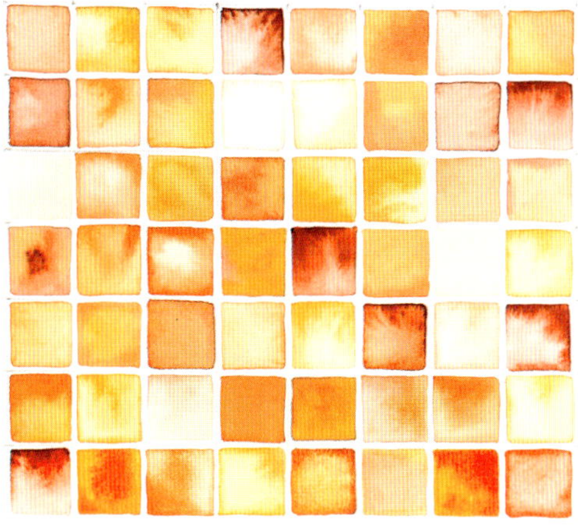

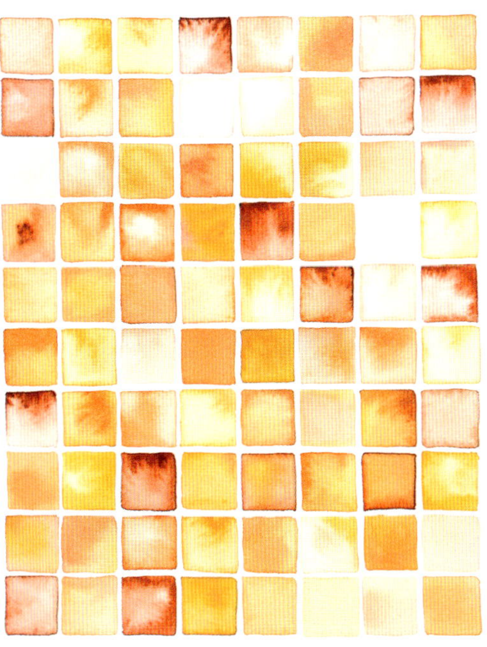

3 **Include a lot of variety.** Use an ample range of colors from light to dark and good mixes of yellow, orange, and brown. Try to create strong contrast by strategically placing light and dark squares as you paint squares in each row.

4 **Keep building the piece.** Using watery mixes will give you lovely bleeding effects. Layer multiple colors in one square and see how they blend into each other. Once everything dries, carefully erase the grid lines to reveal the completed pattern!

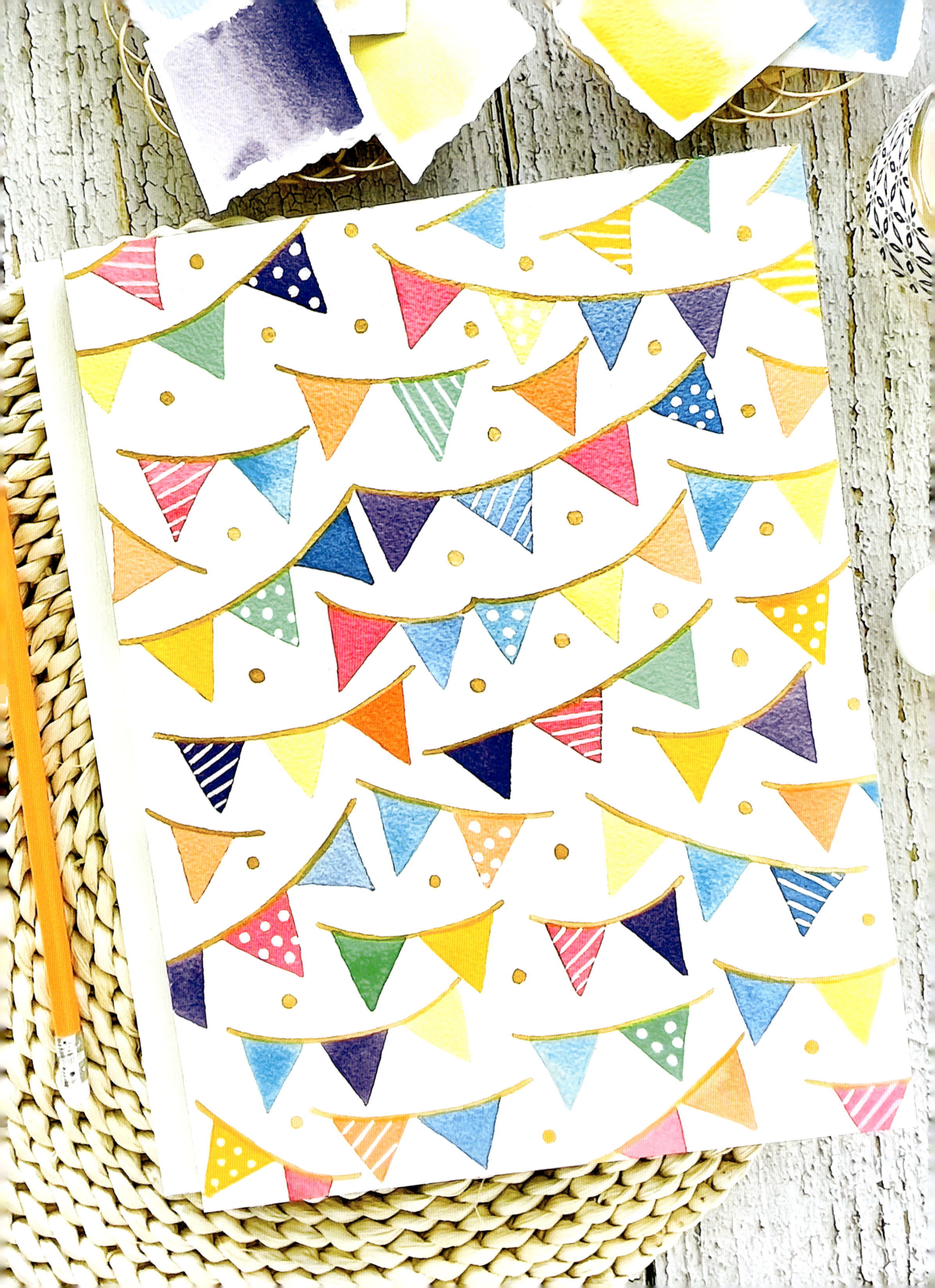

Birthday Bunting

For this pattern, we will explore the triangle shape in its simplest form and make a pattern that appears to be repeating but is actually irregular. We will also use some additional supplies, such as white gouache and gold watercolor, to elevate the look of the pattern. The final effect is full of birthday joy!

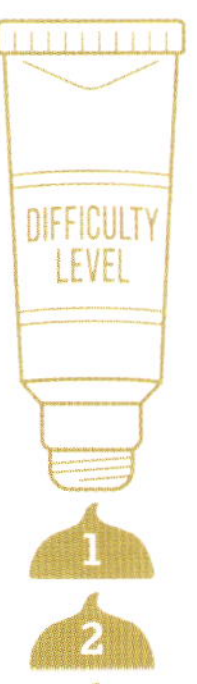

MATERIALS

BRUSHES: Size 6 round brush; size 3 round brush

PAPER: 8" x 10" (20 x 25 cm), cold pressed; or use a smaller size, such as 8" x 8" (20 x 20 cm) or 5" x 7" (13 x 18 cm), if you are short on time

OTHER: Pencil; white gouache (optional); gold watercolor (optional)

COLORS:

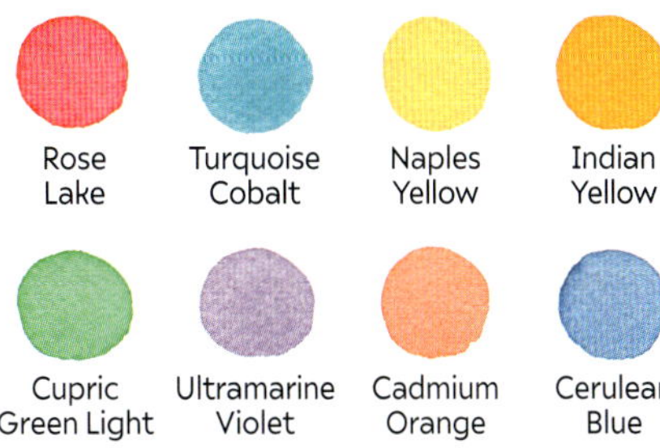

TIP: We are going all in with this pattern in terms of color! We will be using slightly lighter values of the colors—more on the pastel side. It is supposed to be a fun pattern, so don't worry too much about choosing a color palette. Just pick whatever sparks joy and go ahead. This pattern is a reminder to have fun while painting.

This project's pattern is available as a bonus digital download! See page 14.

LET'S PRACTICE

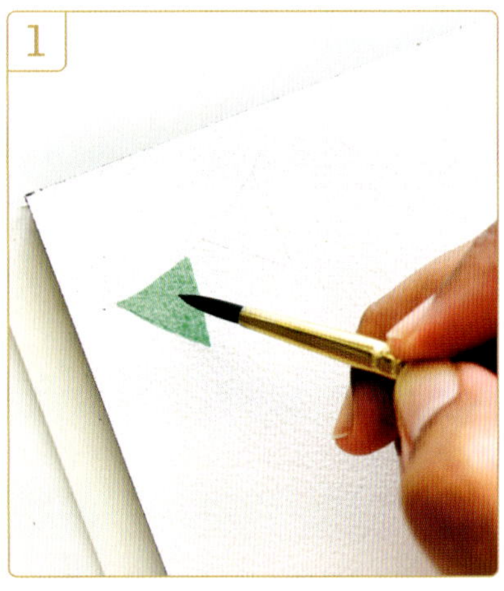

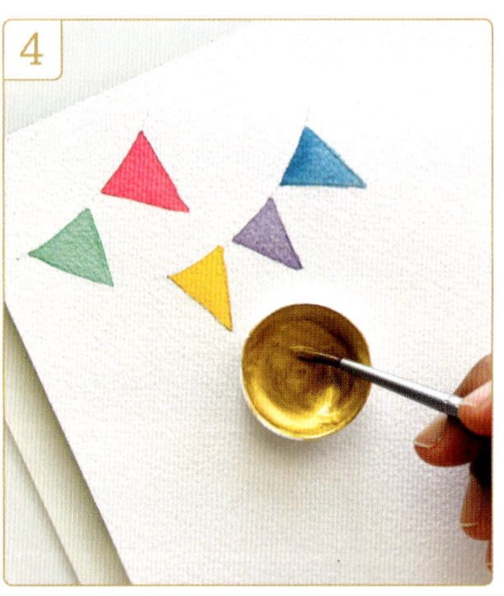

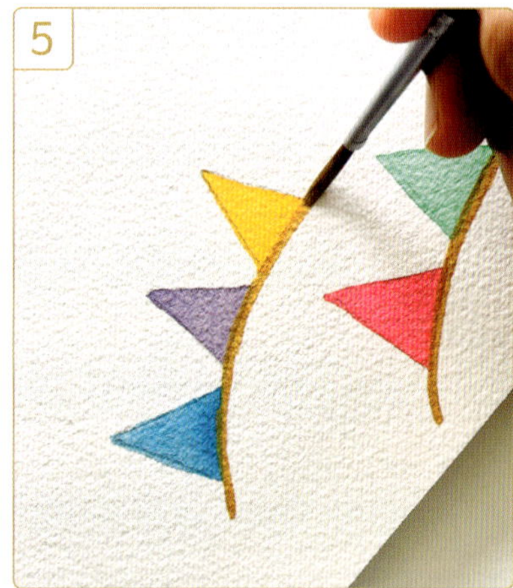

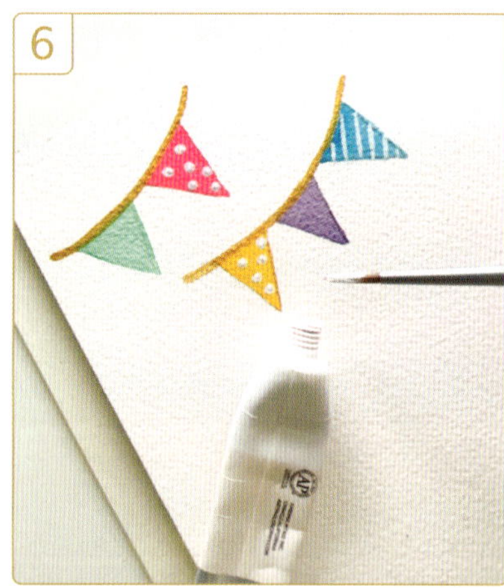

1 **Test the first color.** With a pencil, draw a small curve with two or three inverted triangles attached to it, keeping your pencil lines light. Mix all the paints you wish to use for the pattern. Then, using any color and your size 6 round brush, paint the first triangle using a mid-tone or lighter tone of that color by adding water to it. We want a bright yet soft pastel look.

2 **Test the second color.** Rinse your brush, then paint the next triangle using a contrasting color to the first triangle.

3 **Test several more colors.** Draw a fresh bunting string and use it to test three more colors.

4 **Prepare the gold paint.** Once the triangles are dry, it's time to paint the strings. Mix a thick, creamy gold watercolor paint. Don't dilute it too much. I mixed the paint in the pan itself and loaded my brush with it to get maximum color strength.

5 **Paint the strings.** Rotate the paper as desired to get a comfortable angle from which you can paint the strings using the gold shade. Use a size 3 round brush to paint them. Extend the strings slightly past the triangles on each side.

6 **Add the details.** Once everything is dry, use thick but creamy white gouache paint to draw some lines and polka dots on the triangles. Not every triangle needs these details—leave some plain.

Let's Relax

Are birthday parties ever complete without birthday bunting? For me, bunting is a classic decoration must-have, and I absolutely love the ample variety you can find, each bunting fitting the mood and theme of the party. For this piece, we are deriving our inspiration from classic colorful bunting with polka dots and stripes on it. I promise you will have tons of fun painting this simple and adorable pattern. You can practically feel each little flag flapping in the breeze!

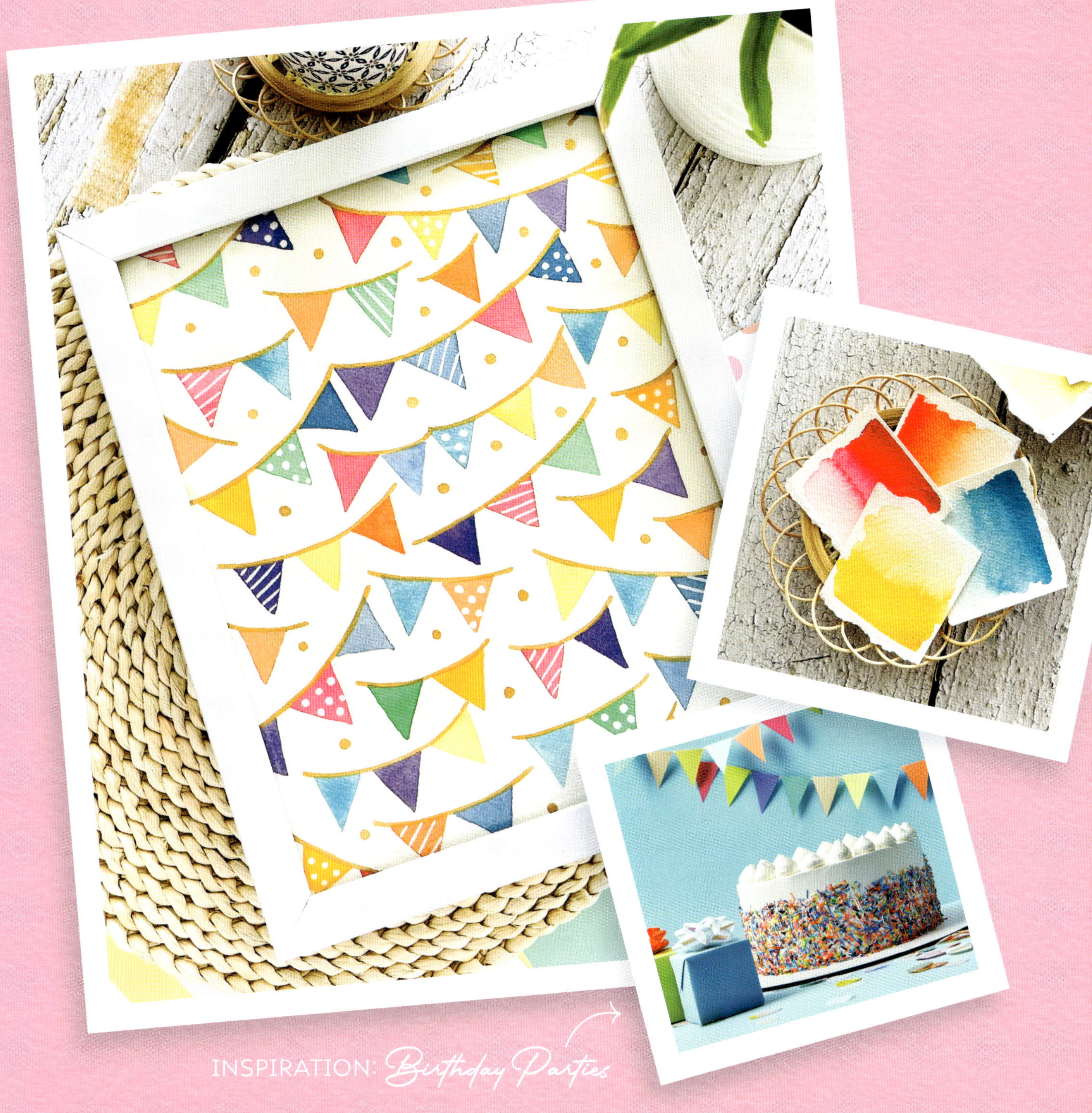

INSPIRATION: *Birthday Parties*

Let's Paint

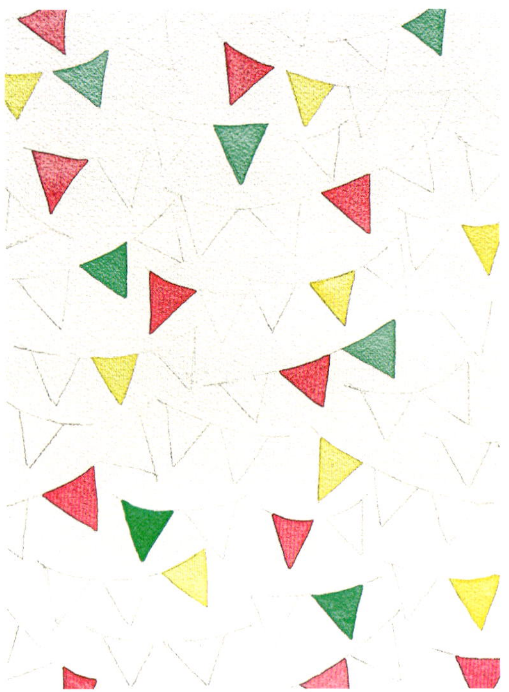

1 Paint the first few colors. You can either draw bunting strings and triangles yourself or download the linework provided and trace it onto your paper. Start by painting triangles using the first three colors of your palette. I chose pink, green, and yellow. Balance the color placement as you go.

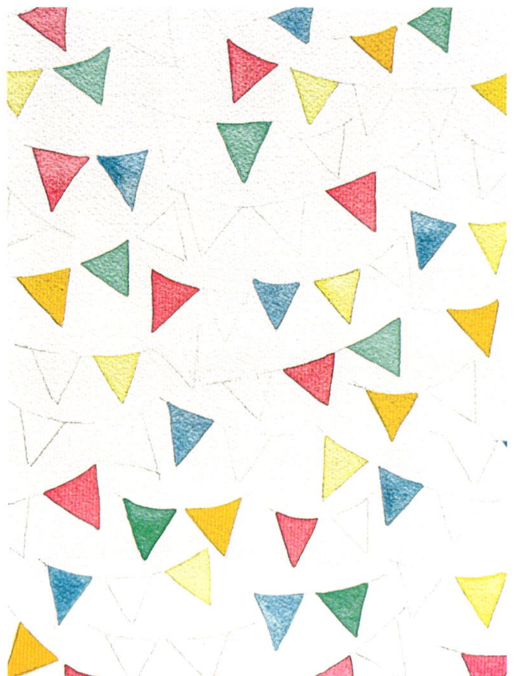

2 Add two more colors. Choose the next two colors and distribute them evenly across the page. Remember to use lighter values rather than dark tones. For this step, I chose Turquoise Cobalt and Indian Yellow.

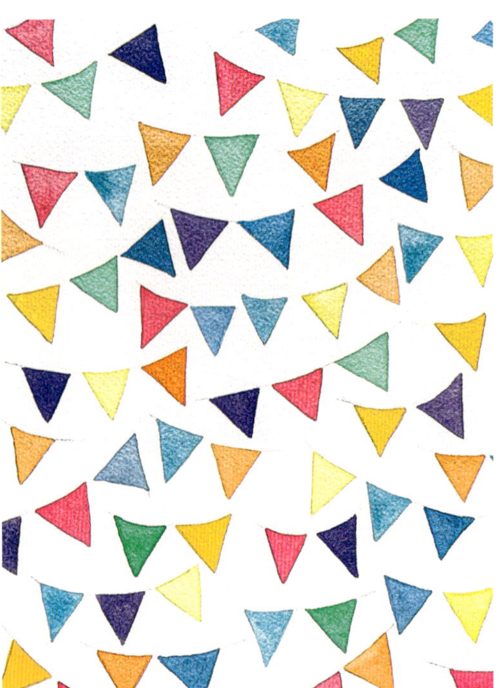

3 Add the final three colors. Use up your last three colors—in my case, orange, violet, and a darker shade of blue—to finish painting all the triangles.

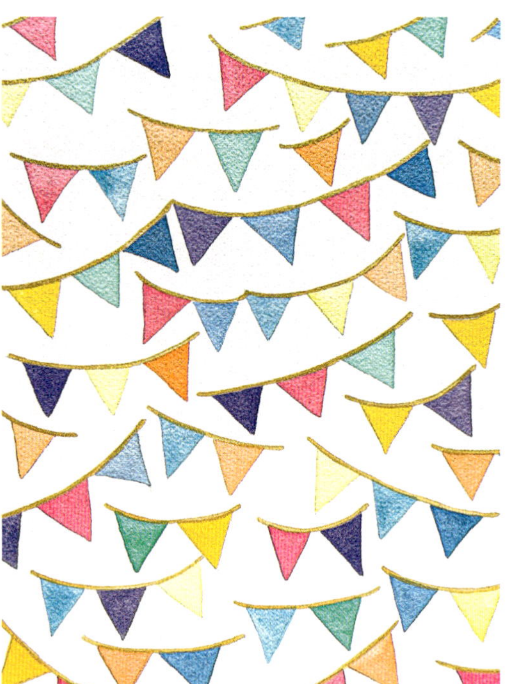

4 Paint the bunting strings. Wait for everything to dry. Then mix some creamy, opaque gold watercolor and carefully start painting the bunting strings one by one, starting from the top. Remember to use a size 3 round brush to get thin lines.

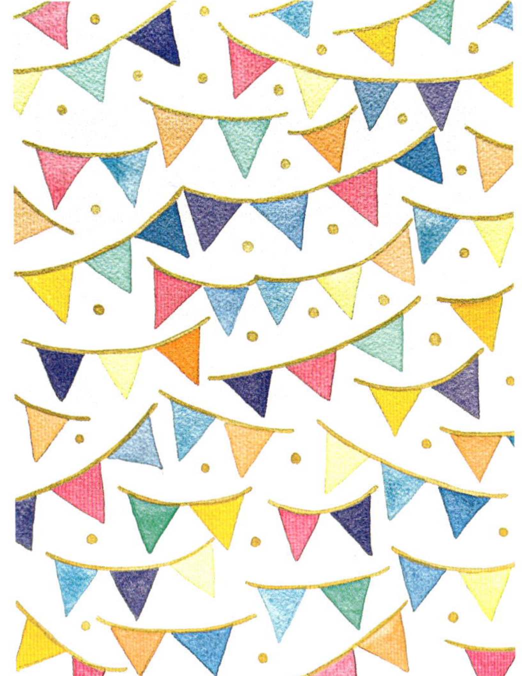

5 **Add decorative dots.** Wait for the gold strings to dry completely. Then paint small gold dots in the white gaps between the strings.

6 **Add the details.** Mix some creamy white gouache paint and place some polka dots and stripes on some of the triangles. Make sure to keep the composition balanced and to leave some triangles plain. Your birthday bunting pattern is ready!

Let's Paint

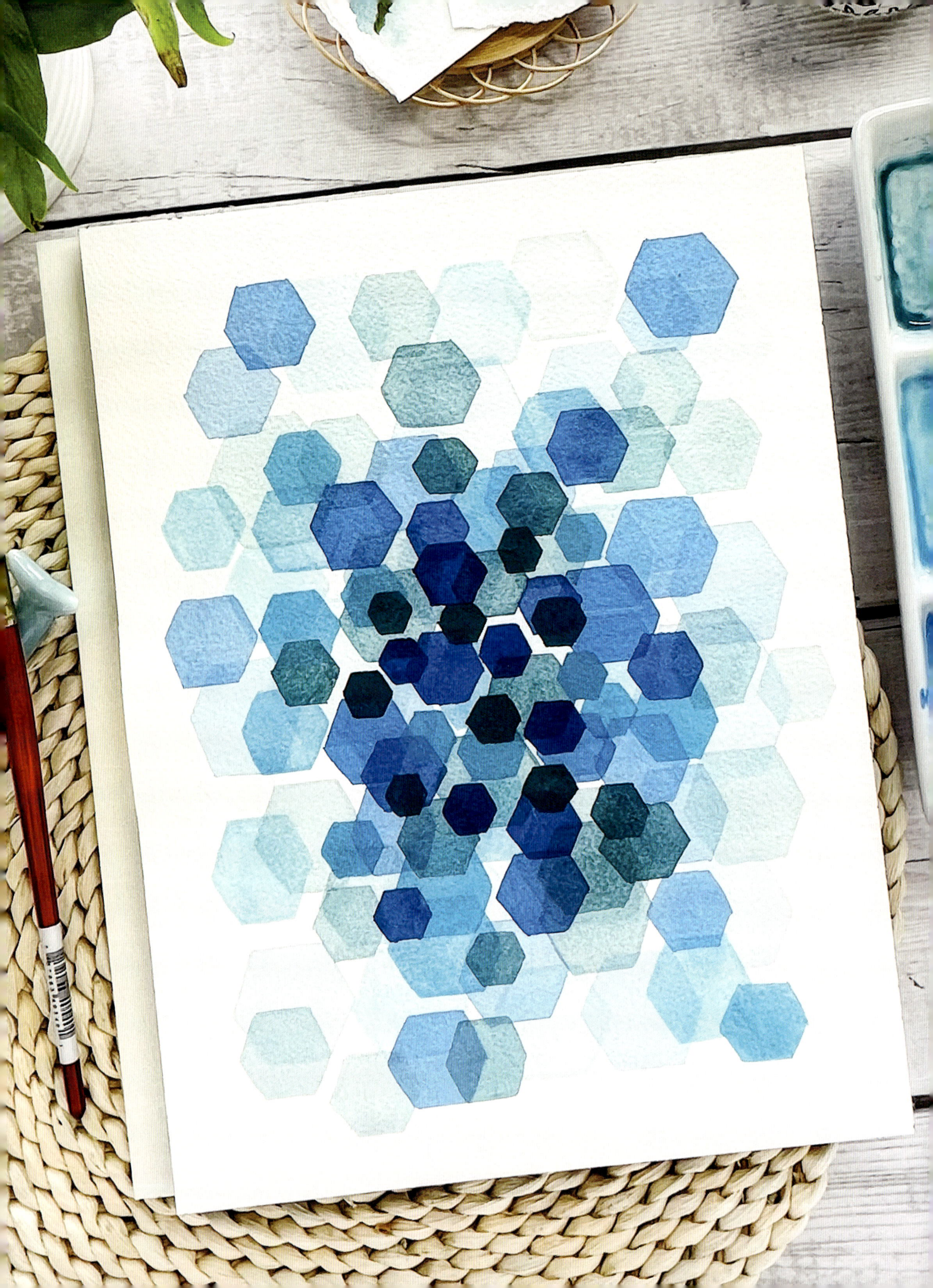

Honeycomb Hexagons

This pattern will strengthen your ability to draw freehand hexagons and to paint in layers using color gradation. We will paint overlapping hexagons of varying sizes to build a final piece in layers. I have chosen three shades of blue to paint this pattern in a cool color scheme. We will use gradient values of each of these colors, going from light to dark. The idea is to begin with the lightest shades and progress toward the "purest" pigment as we fill up the page.

97

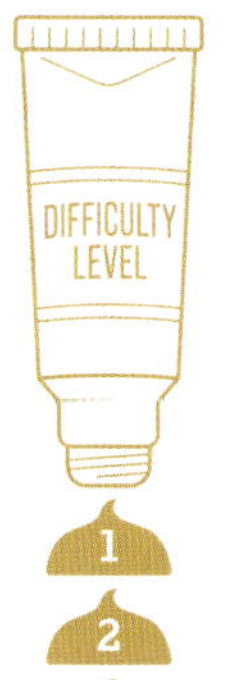

DIFFICULTY LEVEL

1

2

3

MATERIALS

BRUSH: Size 6 round brush

PAPER: 8" x 10" (20 x 25 cm), cold pressed; or use a smaller size, such as 8" x 8" (20 x 20 cm) or 5" x 7" (13 x 18 cm), if you are short on time

COLORS:

Primary Blue Cyan

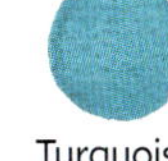

Turquoise Cobalt

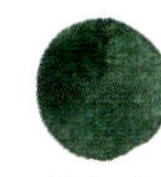

Cobalt Blue Green

TIP: The way you begin is very important for this pattern. Make sure you start out with the lightest possible wash for all three of your blues. This will ensure that there is translucency and depth in your pattern. Keep in mind that you need to end the pattern in the center of the page, so place your hexagons accordingly.

LET'S PRACTICE

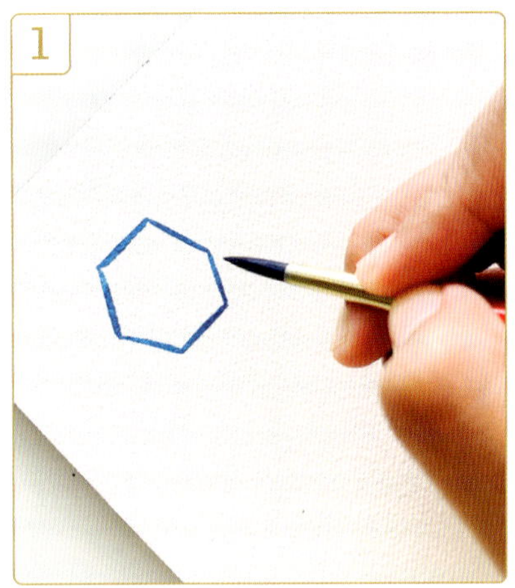

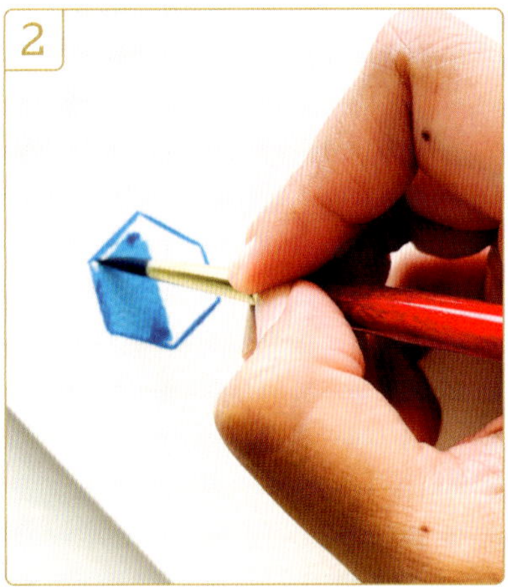

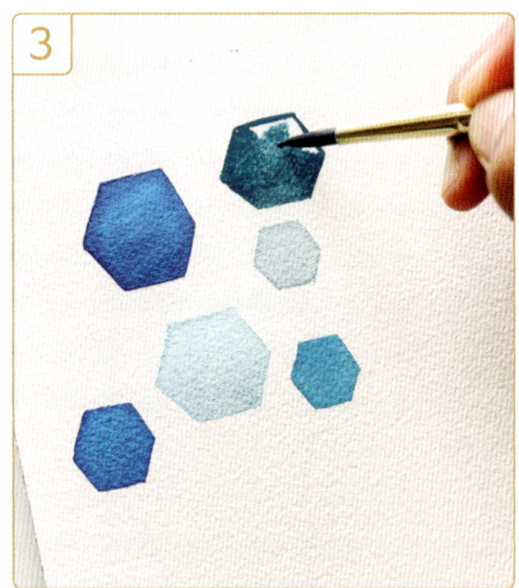

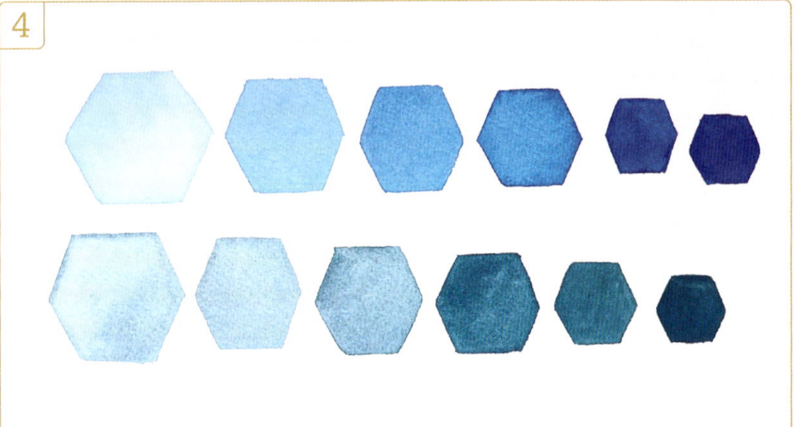

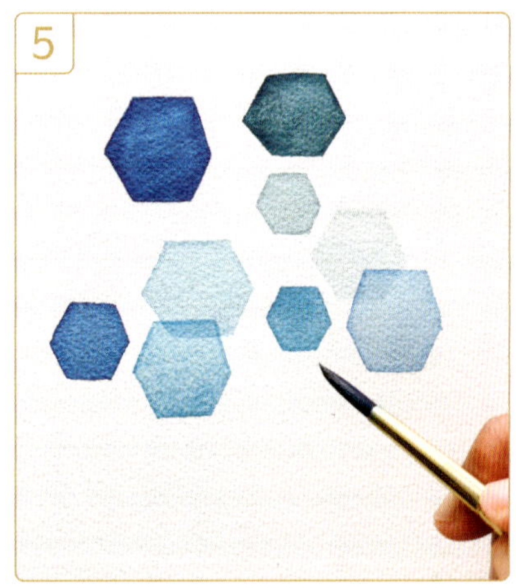

1 **Start the first hexagon.** Mix some paint in your palette that is fluid enough to paint lines. Hold the brush almost upright, perpendicular to the paper, so that the tip of the brush is touching the paper. Draw a hexagonal outline as shown.

2 **Fill the first hexagon.** Fill the hexagon you outlined with the same color. Make sure your brush is neither too dry nor dripping wet.

3 **Paint a few more hexagons.** Using other shades of blue, practice painting a few more hexagons in multiple sizes. Don't worry about symmetry or getting each side perfect. As long as you get the basic shape right, you are good to go.

4 **Work on painting subtly different color values.** Once you have the shape down, work on values. Start with the lightest value by adding lots of water to the paint, diluting it to an almost water-like consistency. Then add a bit more paint to create a slightly darker value. Continue to paint at least five or six values of the color until you are painting a "pure," very dark version of the color. To get a pure pigment color, you will need to add less water in order to maintain a high pigment ratio. Also try to paint hexagons in varying sizes from large to small.

5 **Practice layering.** Return to the assorted hexagons you painted earlier. Layer some new, darker hexagons on top of these. Make sure the first layer has dried completely—you do not want any bleeding.

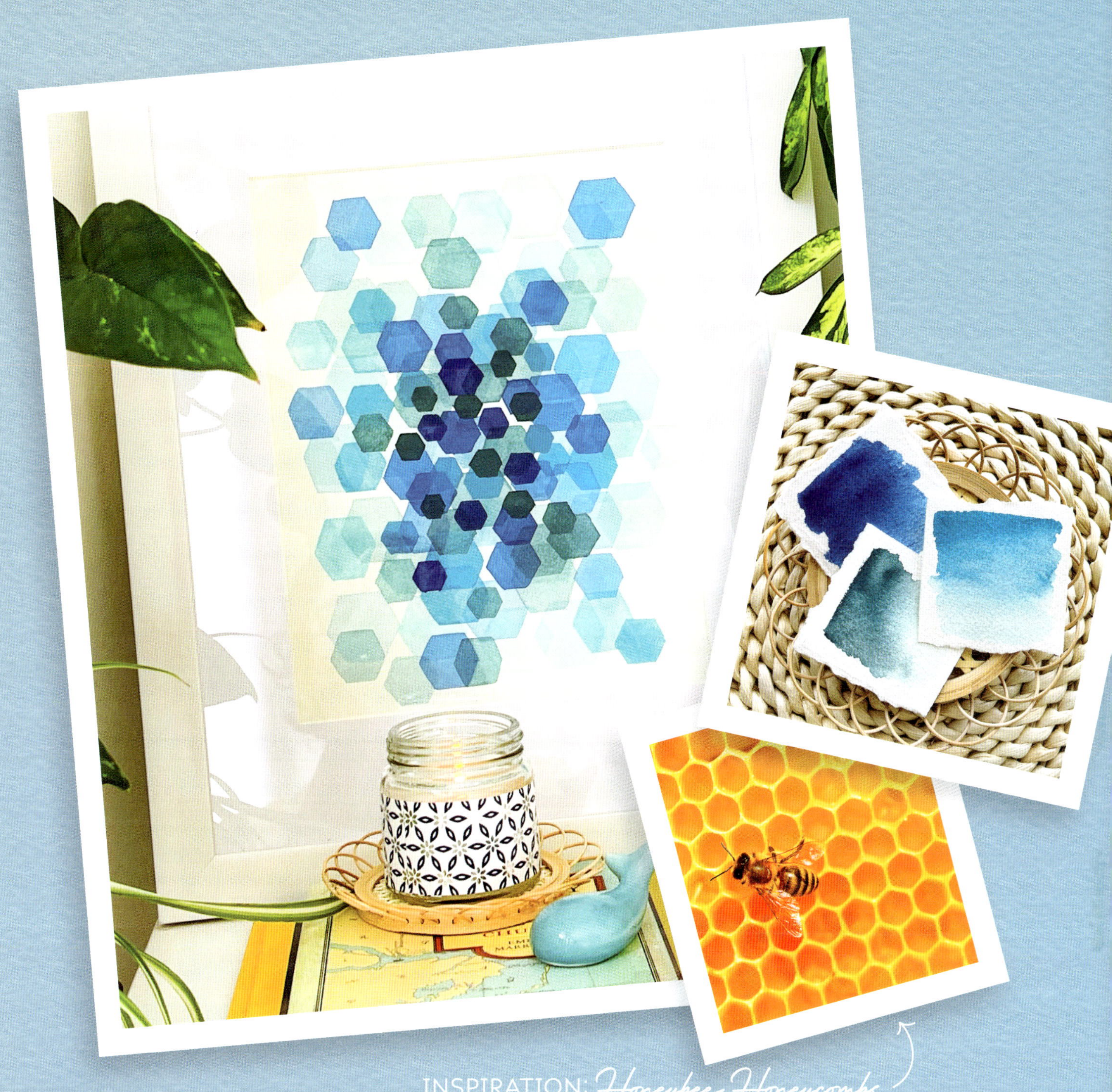

Let's Relax

This pattern is inspired by the beautiful hexagonal honeycombs that honeybees build using beeswax created by worker bees. I absolutely admire the perfection and efficiency with which bees create this structure. I am not a honeybee expert, so we will leave the "how" part of it for some other day. I am content just to use the natural honeycomb pattern as an inspiration for this piece! Think of all the man-made objects that have been inspired by the honeycomb pattern—I am sure you see this pattern every now and then in your daily life. As you build this pattern in layers, try to channel the confidence of a worker bee building a hive using its innate instincts.

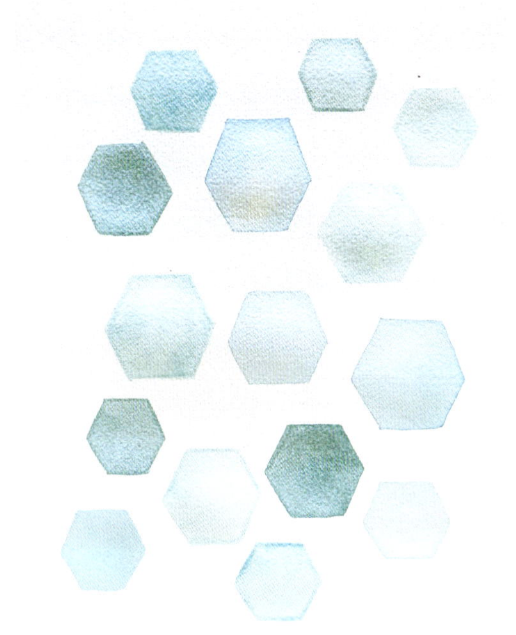

1 **Paint the first layer.** Mix the three paints. Dilute the colors heavily so that you are starting with the lightest shades. Start painting scattered, large, light hexagons one by one using each of the three colors.

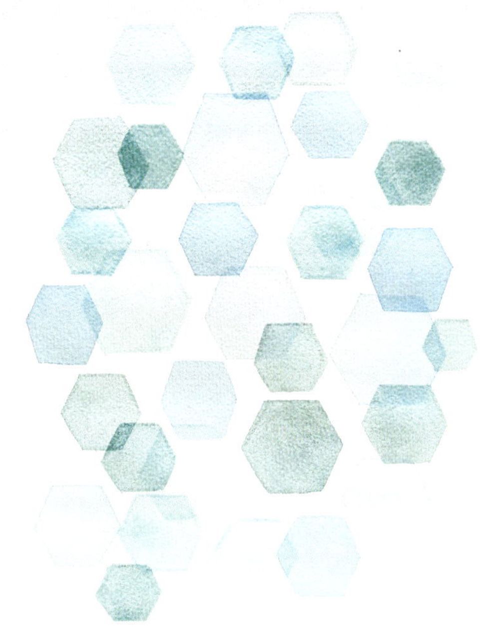

2 **Paint the second layer.** Now mix one shade darker than the previous shade for each of your three colors. Once the first layer has dried, paint some overlapping hexagons and begin to cover more of the page. Size the hexagons large to medium.

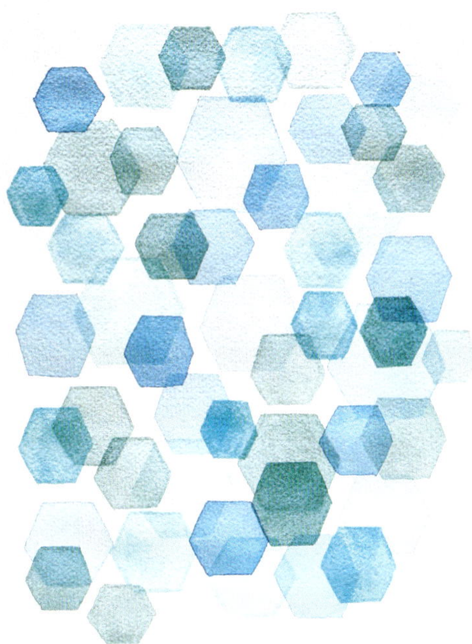

3 **Paint the third layer.** Again mix one shade darker than the previous shade for each of the three colors. Continue overlapping with new, medium hexagons. Be mindful not to completely cover the hexagons from the previous layers.

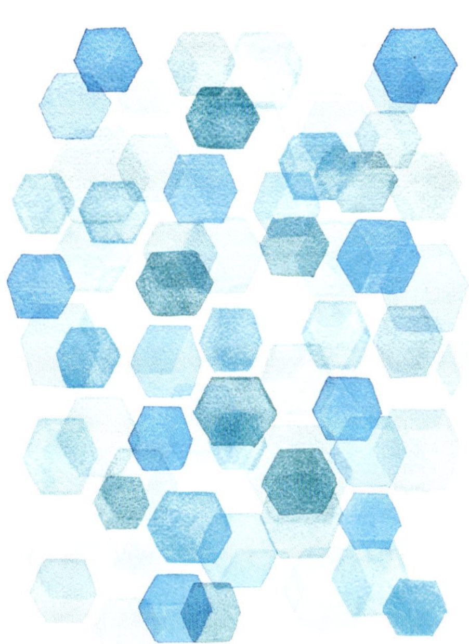

4 **Paint the fourth layer.** You know the drill—mix a darker shade of each color and add more, smaller hexagons. By this point, you will really start to see the layered effect. Don't stress too much—remember to have fun!

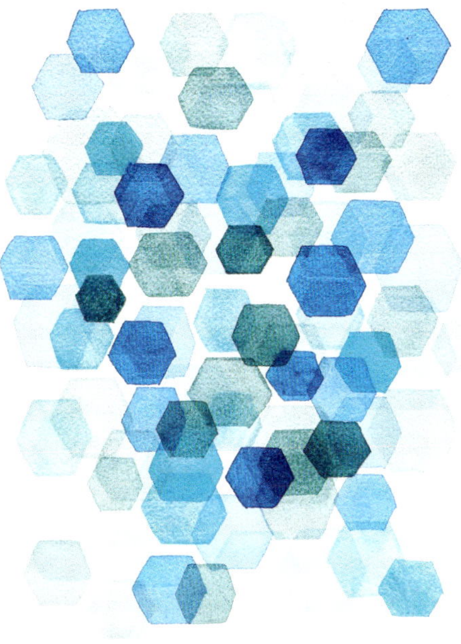

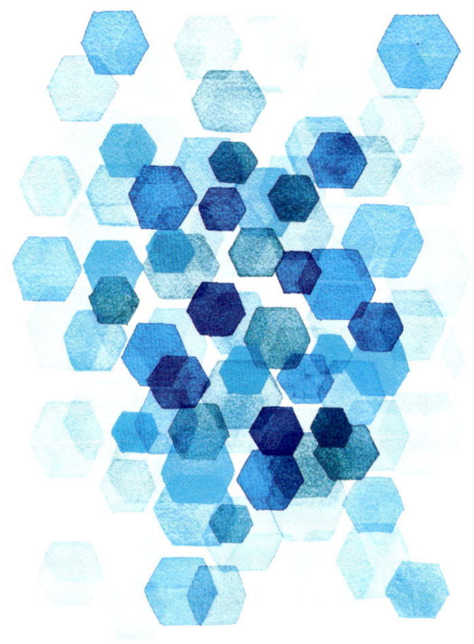

5 **Paint the fifth layer.** Keep on mixing gradually darker shades for each of the three colors. As you add to each layer, try to use each of the three colors equally. Be patient as everything comes together.

6 **Paint the sixth layer.** By this step, you should be about one shade away from the original value of all three colors. Carefully place small hexagons near the center of the page only to add depth and interest to the pattern and create a compact look.

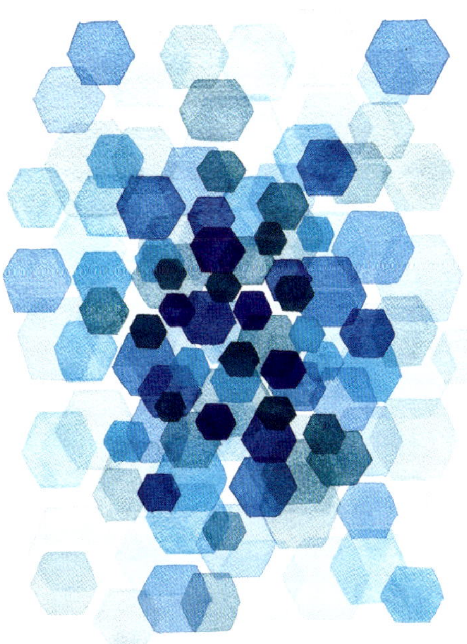

7 **Paint the seventh layer.** Use the darkest value of each color to paint a final set of small hexagons in the very center of the page. Take a step back and have a look from distance. If the pattern feels complete, stop adding hexagons.

Let's Paint

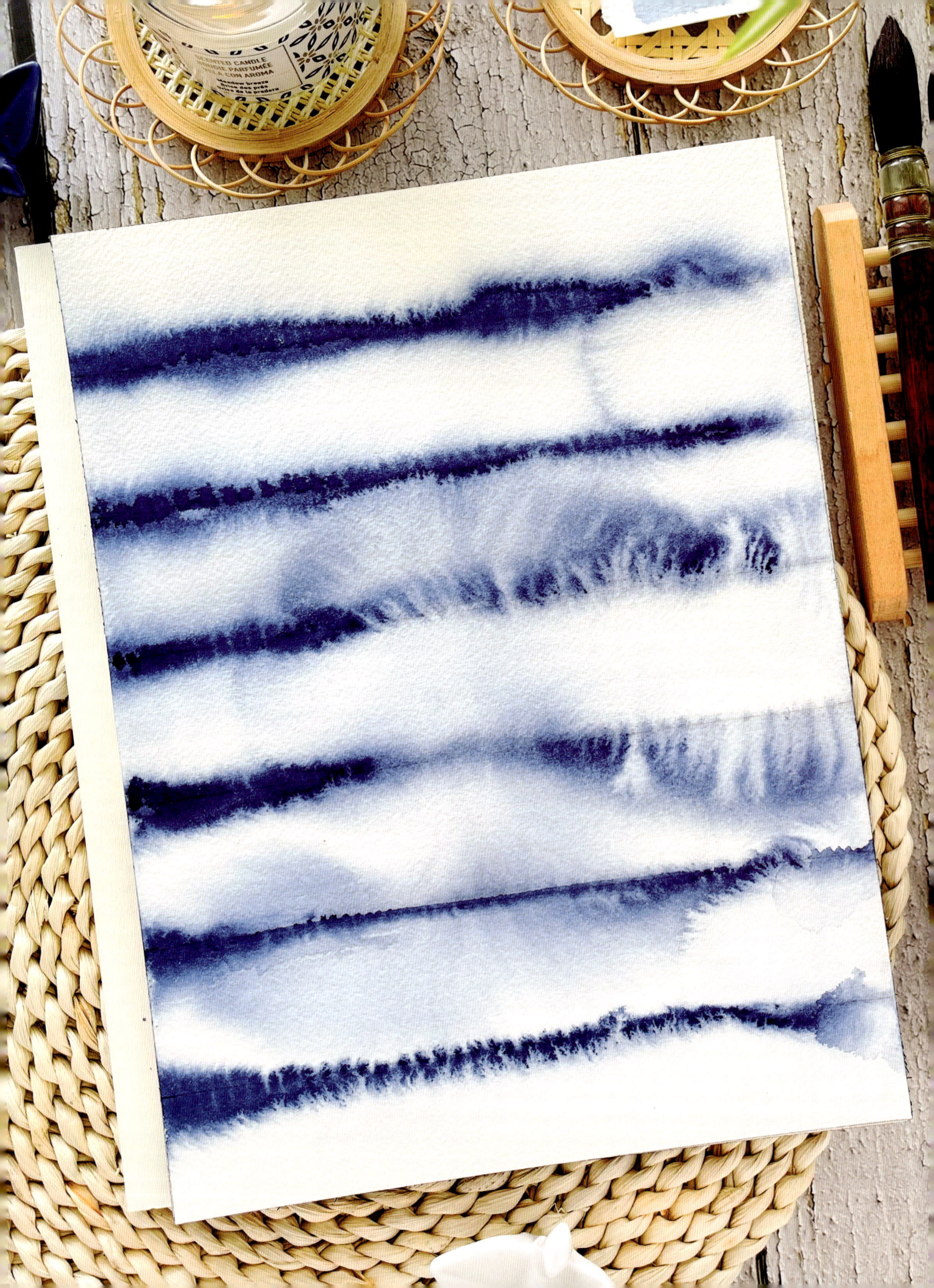

Shibori Stripes

This pattern is a perfect example of using the wet-on-wet technique to create abstract patterns that are totally unpredictable. It gives unique results every time you attempt it. You will enjoy the process of watching the color blend on its own. The use of a single pigment lets you be in a state of flow without worrying too much about color mixing and color arranging choices. It is a simple and quick pattern to paint.

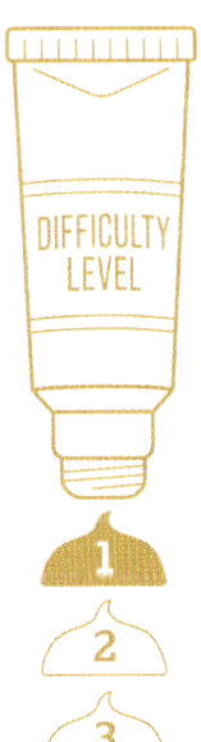

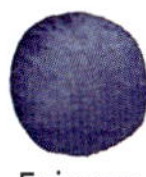

MATERIALS

BRUSHES: Size 6 round brush; size 3 round brush; size 6 quill brush or any other large round or flat brush for making the wash

PAPER: 8" x 10" (20 x 25 cm), cold pressed; or use a smaller size, such as 8" x 8" (20 x 20 cm) or 5" x 7" (13 x 18 cm), if you are short on time

OTHER: Pencil; ruler

COLORS:

Faience Blue*

***COLOR SUBSTITUTES:**
Faience Blue (any blue shade, such as Ultramarine, Prussian, or Indigo, could work)

TIP: Let the water do its thing and allow the color to blend the way it wants to. Letting go of control will give you organic and unpredictable results. Be ready to embrace the imperfections of watercolors and find joy in the process.

LET'S PRACTICE

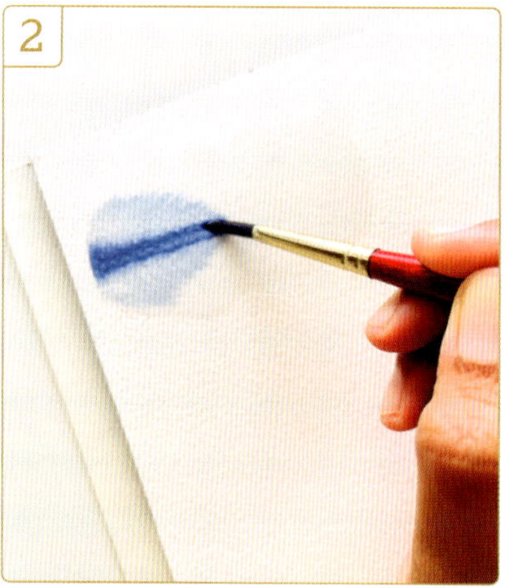

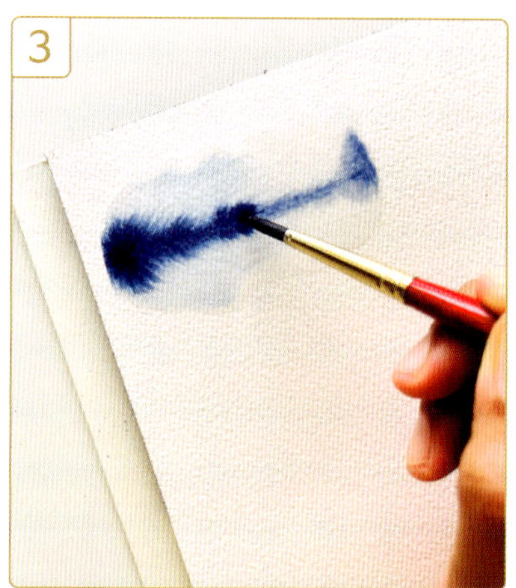

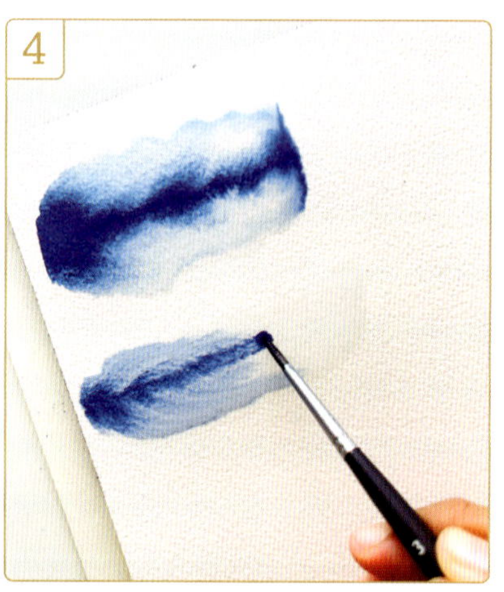

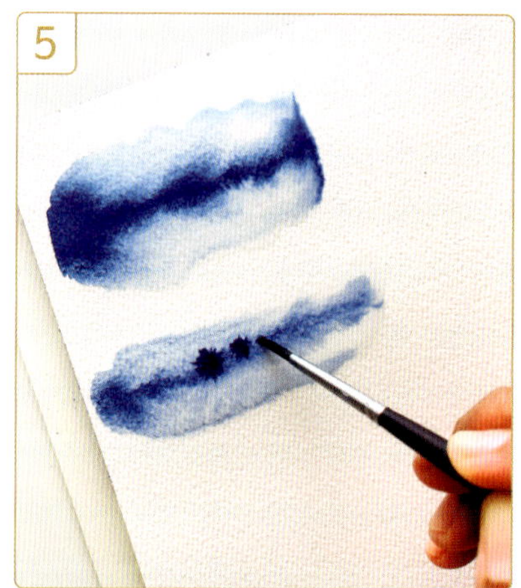

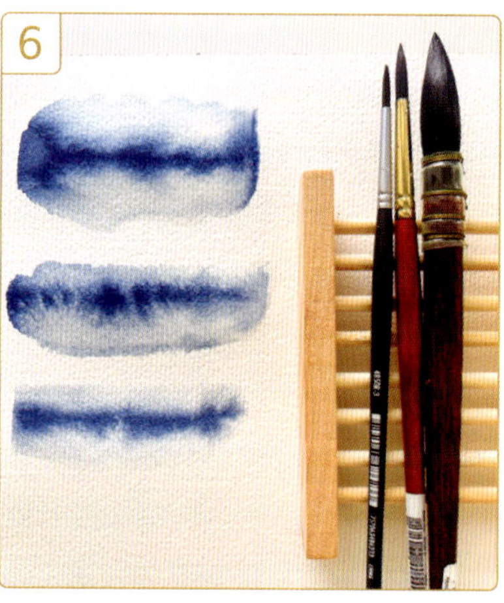

1 **Paint a water patch.** Mix some blue paint in your palette. Using a large round, flat, or quill brush, paint a patch of clean water. Make sure your brush is generously wet.

2 **Add some color.** Now switch to your size 6 round brush. Dip the brush in the blue paint and start dropping the color from left to right. Glide the brush smoothly toward the far end of the water patch. You will see the pigment bleed and flow rapidly.

3 **Add darker color.** Repeat, this time loading your brush with slightly creamier (less diluted) paint. Glide the brush again on top of the previous blue layer; the paint will continue to blend and run.

4 **Create a new patch.** Repeat the whole process with a fresh patch of water, this time using a small brush.

5 **Add paint dots.** Try placing some dots of color on top of the first layer to see how they disperse into the previous layer.

6 **Experiment.** Keep trying this wet-on-wet technique a few times until you start feeling comfortable. Try with smaller and bigger wet patches to see how the color blends.

Let's Relax

This pattern is inspired by the Japanese shibori method, which is a tie-dyeing technique that can result in all sorts of patterns. The word "shibori" comes from the verb "shiboru," which means to squeeze, press, and wring. Traditional shibori patterns come in an indigo color. There are different ways of tying and stitching the fabric to create the patterns. This painting project explores the shibori style using watercolors, where we will try to mimic the way the fabric looks after tying and dyeing to create a simple stripe pattern. You've probably tie-dyed a T-shirt before, which is somewhat similar to the shibori process—so as you paint, imagine how it feels to unravel your work and reveal the beautiful result!

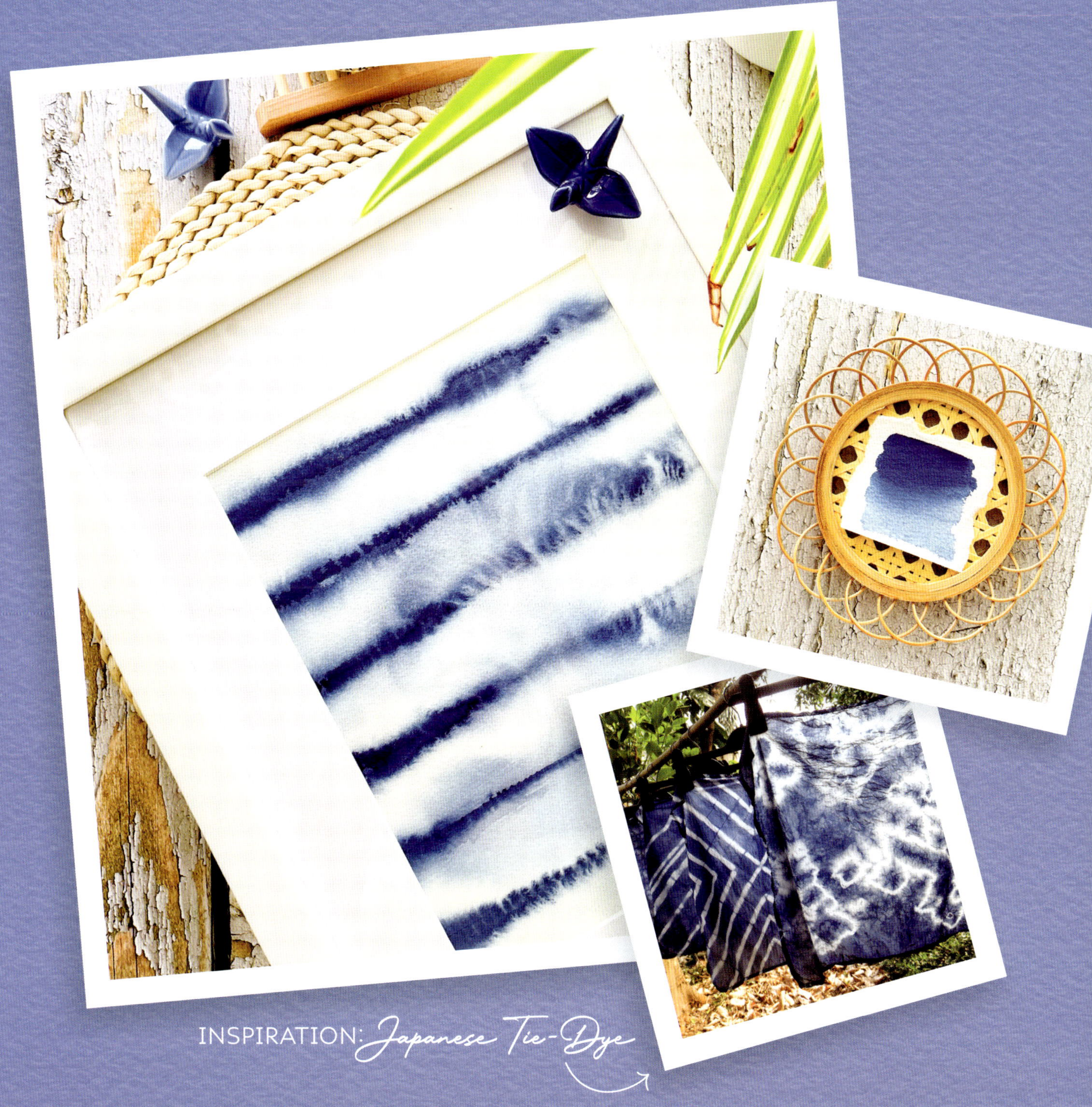

INSPIRATION: *Japanese Tie-Dye*

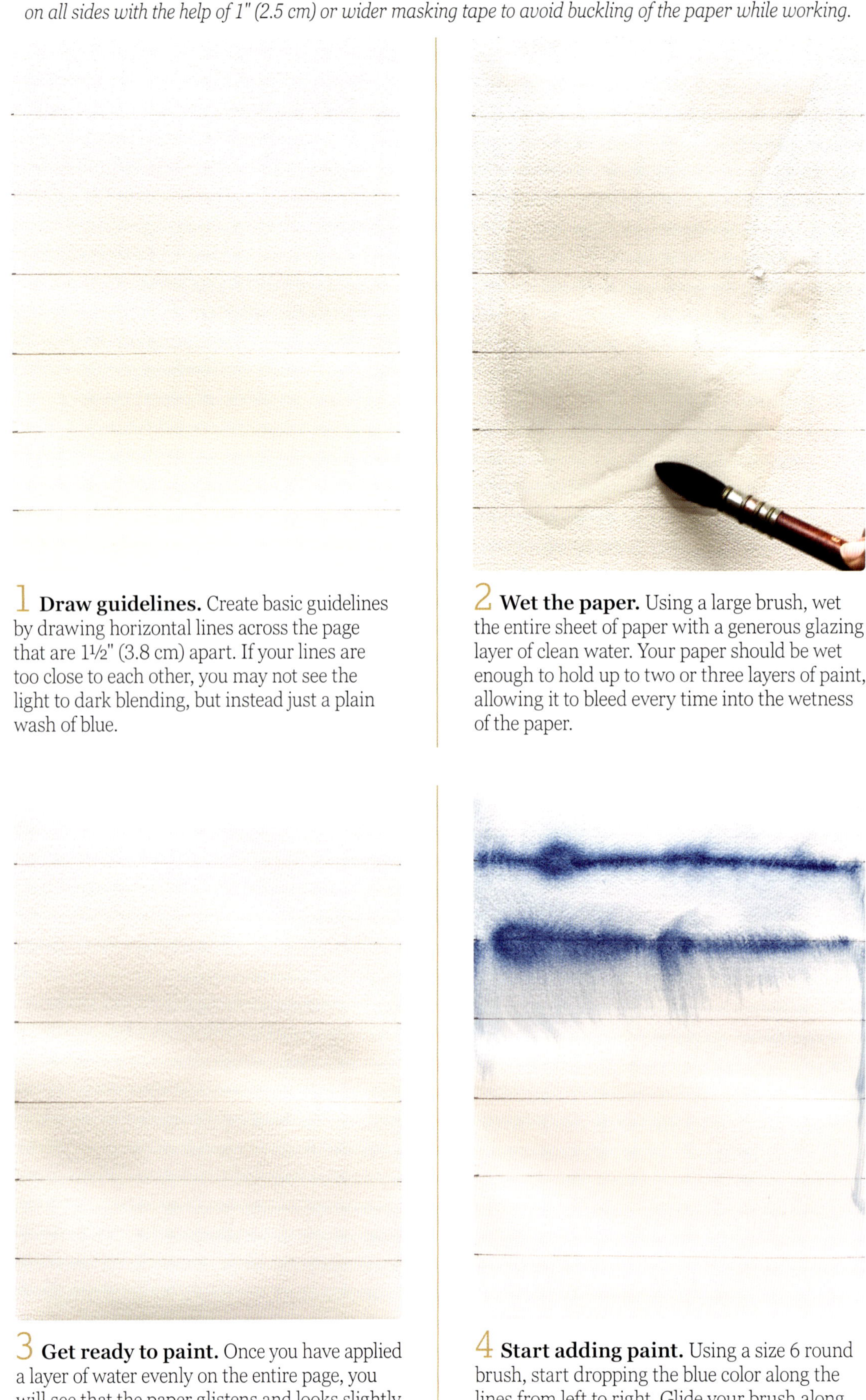

1 **Draw guidelines.** Create basic guidelines by drawing horizontal lines across the page that are 1½" (3.8 cm) apart. If your lines are too close to each other, you may not see the light to dark blending, but instead just a plain wash of blue.

2 **Wet the paper.** Using a large brush, wet the entire sheet of paper with a generous glazing layer of clean water. Your paper should be wet enough to hold up to two or three layers of paint, allowing it to bleed every time into the wetness of the paper.

3 **Get ready to paint.** Once you have applied a layer of water evenly on the entire page, you will see that the paper glistens and looks slightly bumpy. Prepare your blue paint now.

4 **Start adding paint.** Using a size 6 round brush, start dropping the blue color along the lines from left to right. Glide your brush along and watch the color spread on the wet paper. Allow it to go the way it wants to—simply keep dropping more paint along the lines.

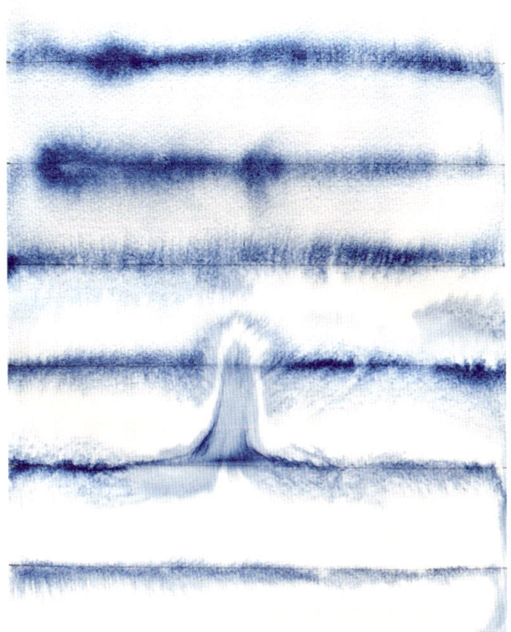

5 **Complete the first layer.** Finish dropping paint along each of the lines and observe the beautiful organic effects it starts to create. At some places, you will see the paint being pushed by the water.

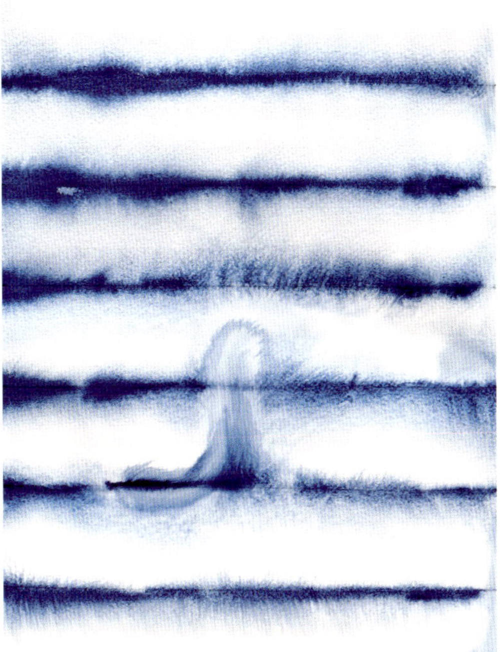

6 **Paint a second layer.** Mix some creamier (less diluted) blue paint that is darker in value than the previous layer. Start dropping color from the top again, this time using a small size 3 round brush. You will see the color spreads less, remaining more concentrated.

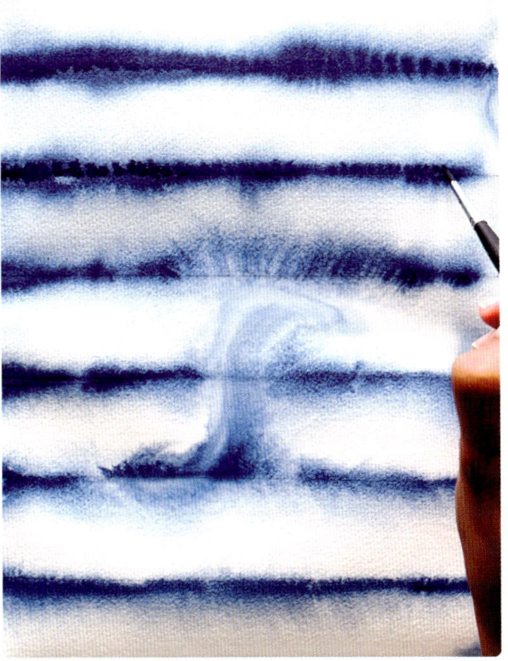

7 **Add a third layer.** If you are satisfied, feel free to stop here and enjoy the drying process— or you can add a third, darker layer and take the blending process further. I dropped in more pigment in a dotted fashion and let it blend.

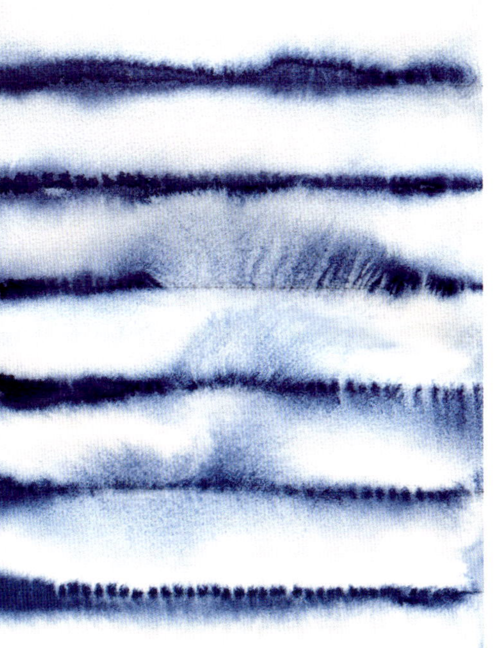

8 **Allow to dry.** Stop adding layers when your paper starts to dry. Let the paper and paint dry completely and enjoy the organic and satisfying color blends that result!

Let's Paint

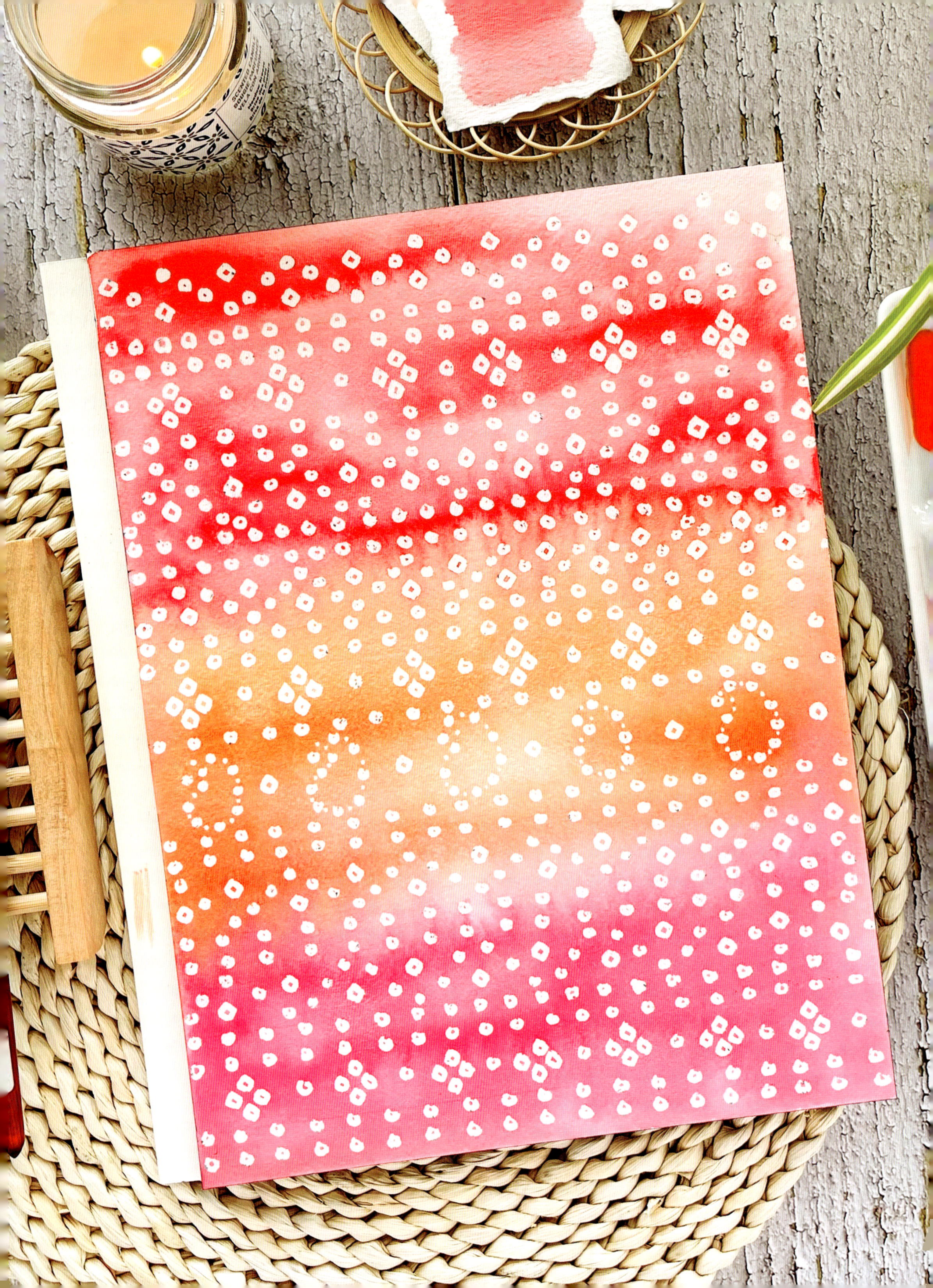

Indian Bandhani

For this piece, we will learn how to use marker-style masking liquid. Masking fluid repels water and paint, allowing you to paint right on top of it and then peel it away to reveal pristine white sections. Using masking fluid in a marker form is the best way to explore it for the first time. For this Indian Bandhani pattern, we will create our own design in pencil first and then trace over it using the masking fluid.

MATERIALS

BRUSH: Size 12 round brush

PAPER: 8" x 10" (20 x 25 cm), cold pressed; or use a smaller size, such as 8" x 8" (20 x 20 cm) or 5" x 7" (13 x 18 cm), if you are short on time

OTHER: Pencil; eraser; masking fluid pen

COLORS:

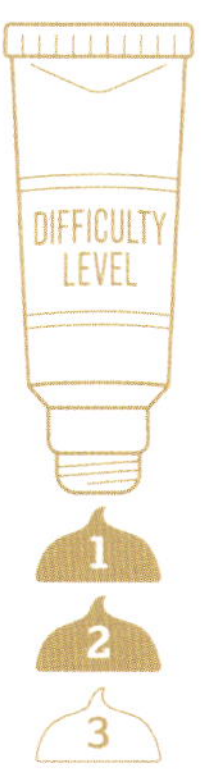

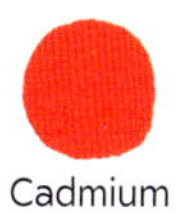
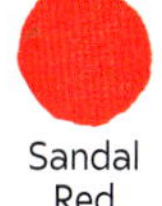
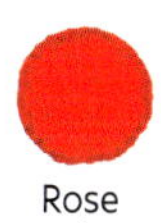

Cadmium Orange   Sandal Red   Rose Lake

TIP: Tracing over the pencil design using a masking fluid marker and later peeling it off are the two most important steps of this pattern. Both steps take a while, so be patient, especially if you are working on a paper size bigger than 5" x 5" (13 x 13 cm).

LET'S PRACTICE

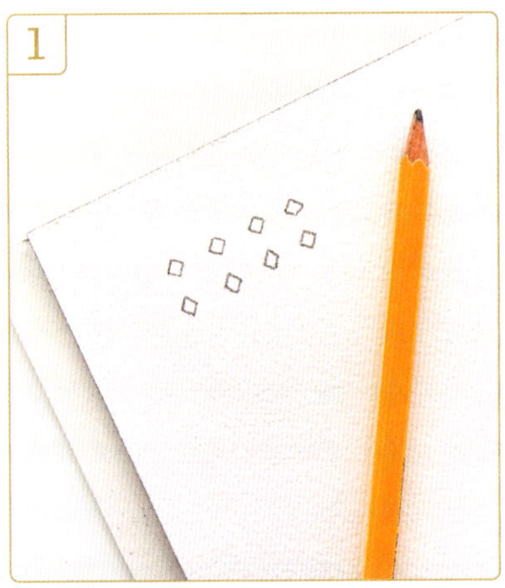

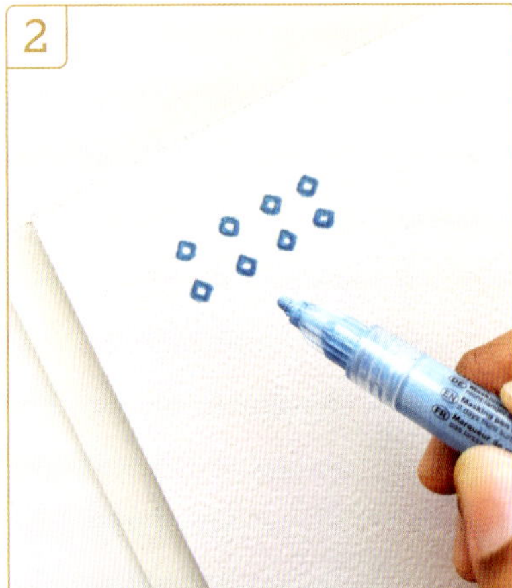

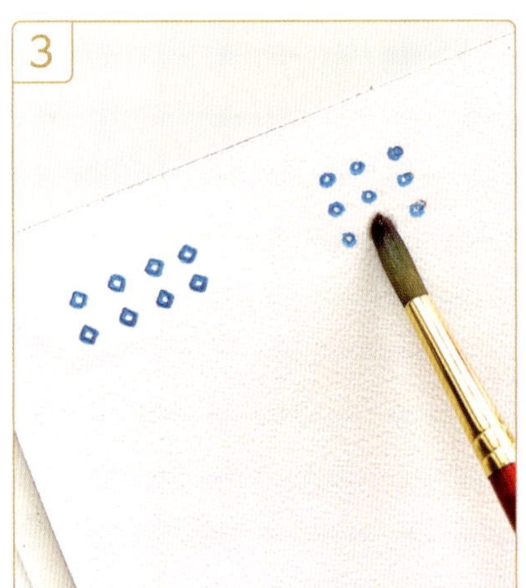

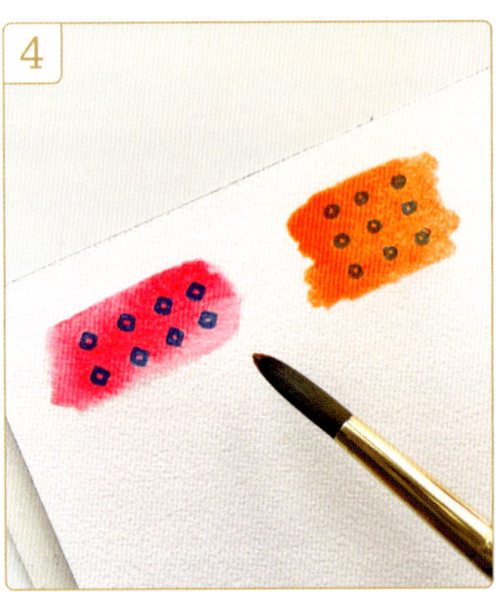

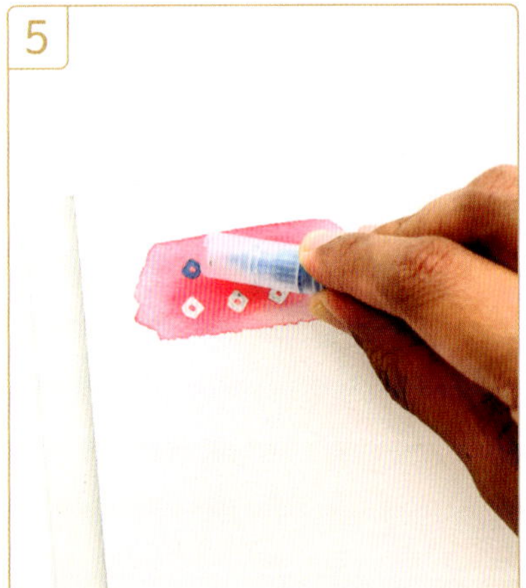

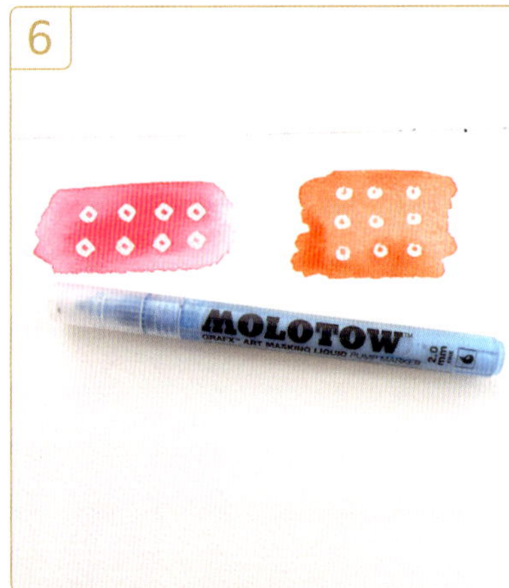

1 **Draw diamonds.** Using a pencil, draw a couple of small diamonds arranged in two rows.

2 **Mask the diamonds.** Use a masking fluid marker to carefully trace over the pencil marks, leaving the centers uncovered—you only want to cover the borders. Repeat this process to draw and trace a couple of rows of small circles separately.

3 **Add water.** Once the masking fluid is completely dry, apply a wash of clean water on the group of diamonds as well as on the group of circles, keeping the two water areas separate.

4 **Add paint.** Drop some pink paint onto the water layer over the diamonds. Drop some orange paint onto the water layer over the circles.

5 **Remove the masking fluid.** Once everything is dry, carefully peel off the masking fluid using an eraser, the lid of the pen, or any object that allows you to scratch the dried fluid away. Peel it carefully so as not to tear the paper underneath.

6 **Reveal your finished work.** Take your time to carefully remove each masked spot and reveal your finished pattern!

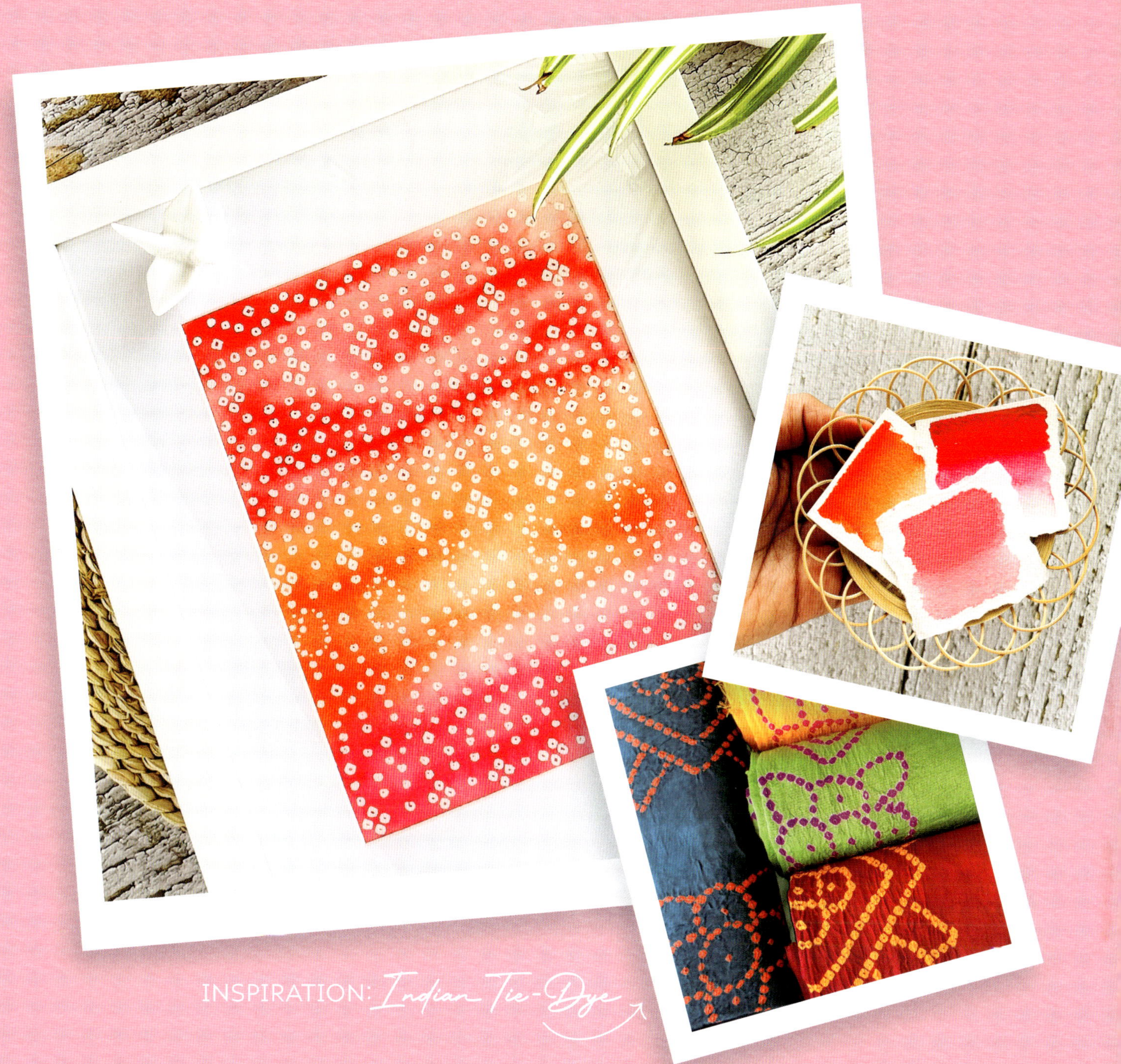

Let's Relax

This pattern is inspired by the Indian Bandhani technique, which is one of the oldest Indian tie-dye techniques used to create beautiful and intricate patterns. The word "Bandhani" is derived from the Sanskrit word "Bandhana," which means to tie. Small knots are tied across the fabric, which serve as resist points to prevent the dye from entering those areas, thereby creating a pattern. Once the fabric is knotted, it is dipped in one or more dyebaths. Artisans meticulously untie the desired knots at certain stages to achieve vibrant and colorful patterns. The most commonly used colors for Bandhani are red, yellow, orange, pink, blue, and green. The resulting fabrics are used to make a variety of traditional outfits, such as sarees, dresses, turbans, etc. Shall we try our hand at Bandhani as watercolor?

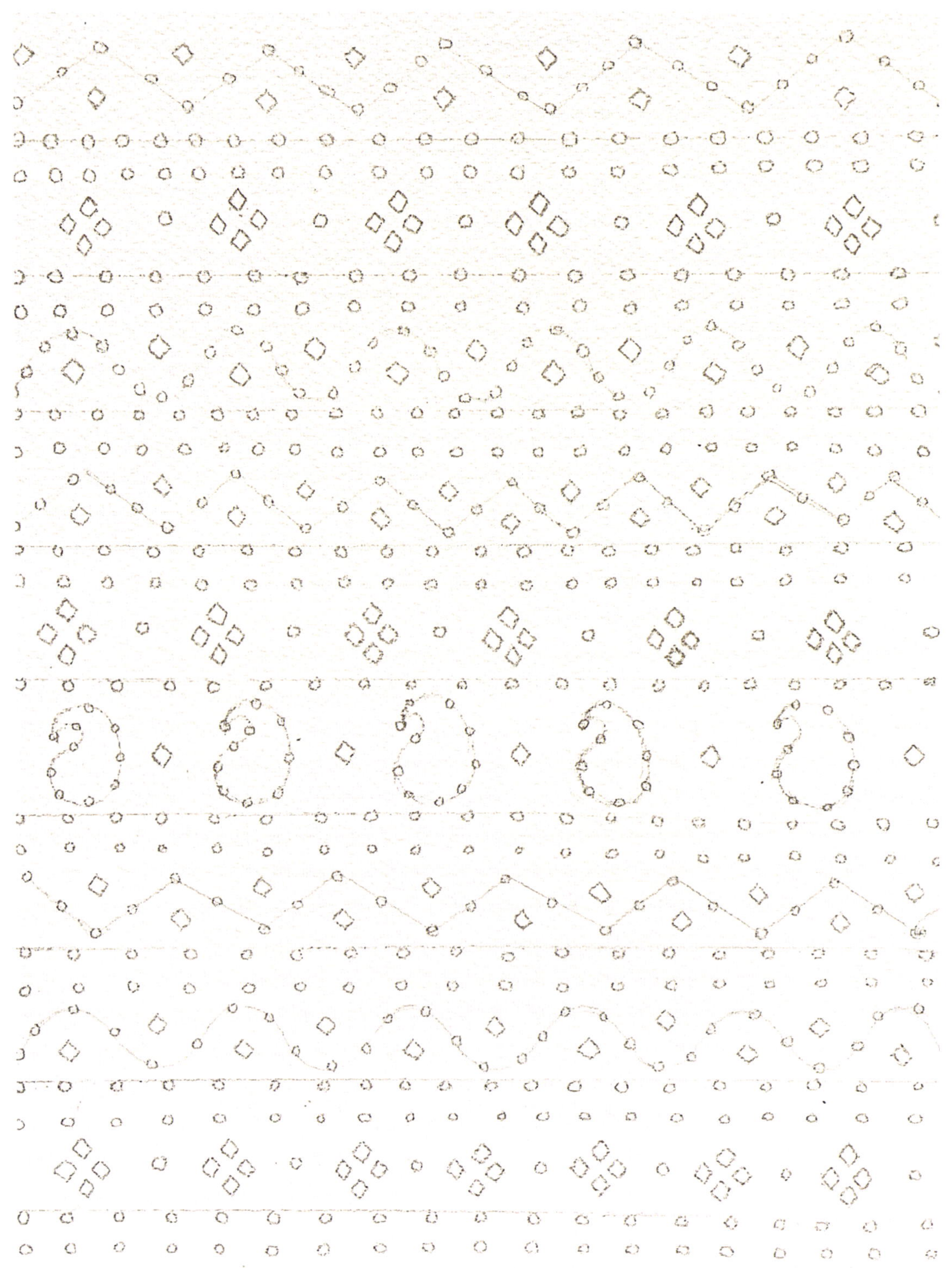

1 **Draw a pattern.** Using pencil, re-create the design shown; you can also refer to the full-page photo of the finished project and draw guidelines for yourself if it's helpful. Or feel free to create your own design!

NOTE: *If you are not using a block of watercolor paper as I am, I highly recommend taping down your paper on all sides with the help of 1" (2.5 cm) or wider masking tape to avoid buckling of the paper while working.*

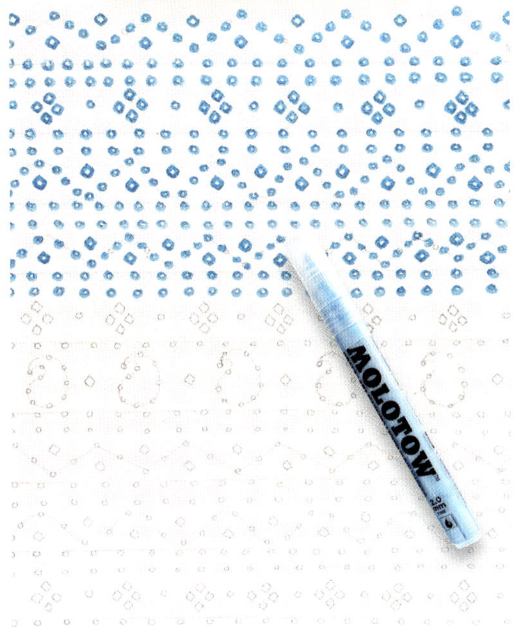

2 **Mask the design.** Start masking the pencil marks using the masking fluid. Go slowly and carefully over the entire design. If you happen to be using colorless masking fluid, be sure to not miss any spots. Then allow the fluid to dry completely.

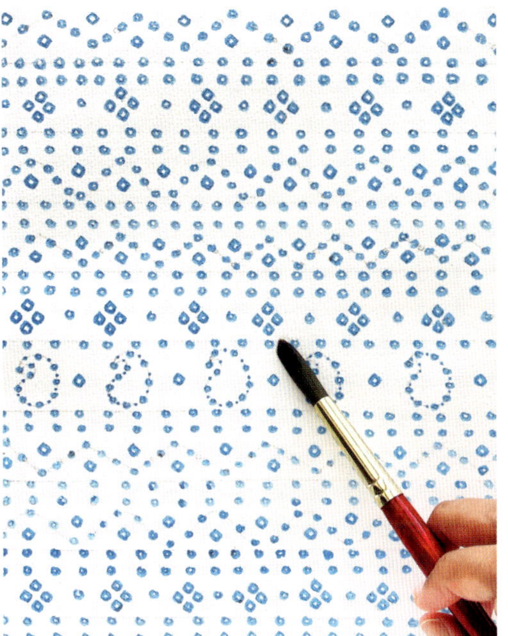

3 **Add water.** Once the masking fluid is dry, apply a wash of clean water all over the page. You want the entire page to be wet enough to apply a few layers of paint.

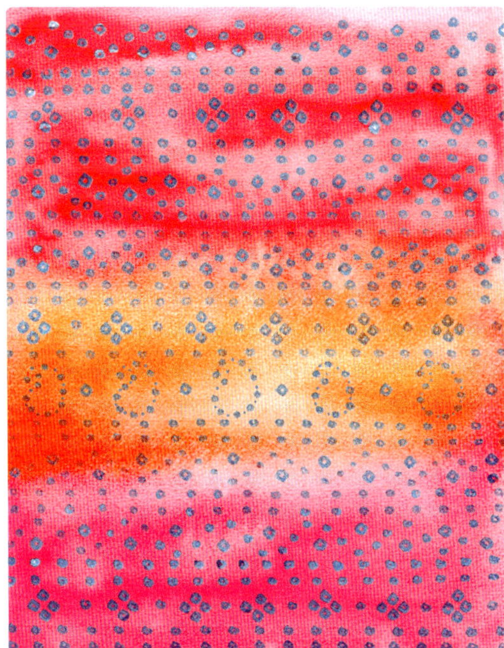

4 **Paint three rows of color.** Place some red color in the top third of the page. Spread it lightly and let the paint bleed on the wet surface. Next, apply orange color in the middle third, allowing it to blend with the red above. Finally, apply pink color in the bottom third. Make sure the three colors are applied in the form of imperfect washes—darker in places and lighter in others. You don't want even, flat wash of three colors.

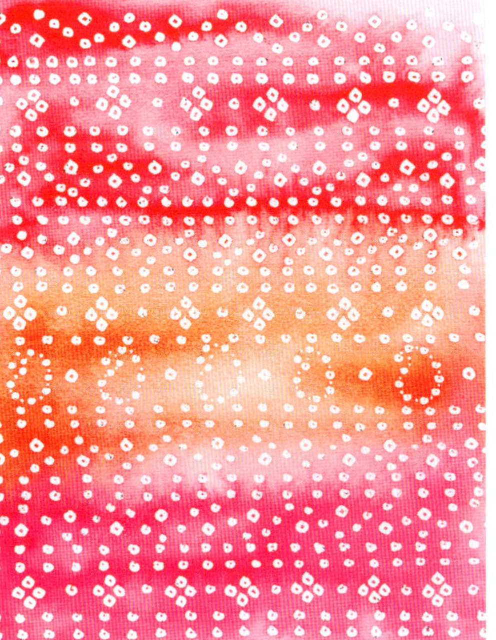

5 **Remove the masking fluid.** Wait for everything to completely dry, then start peeling off the masking fluid. This may take a while, but you will be satisfied to watch the pattern slowly become revealed!

Let's Paint

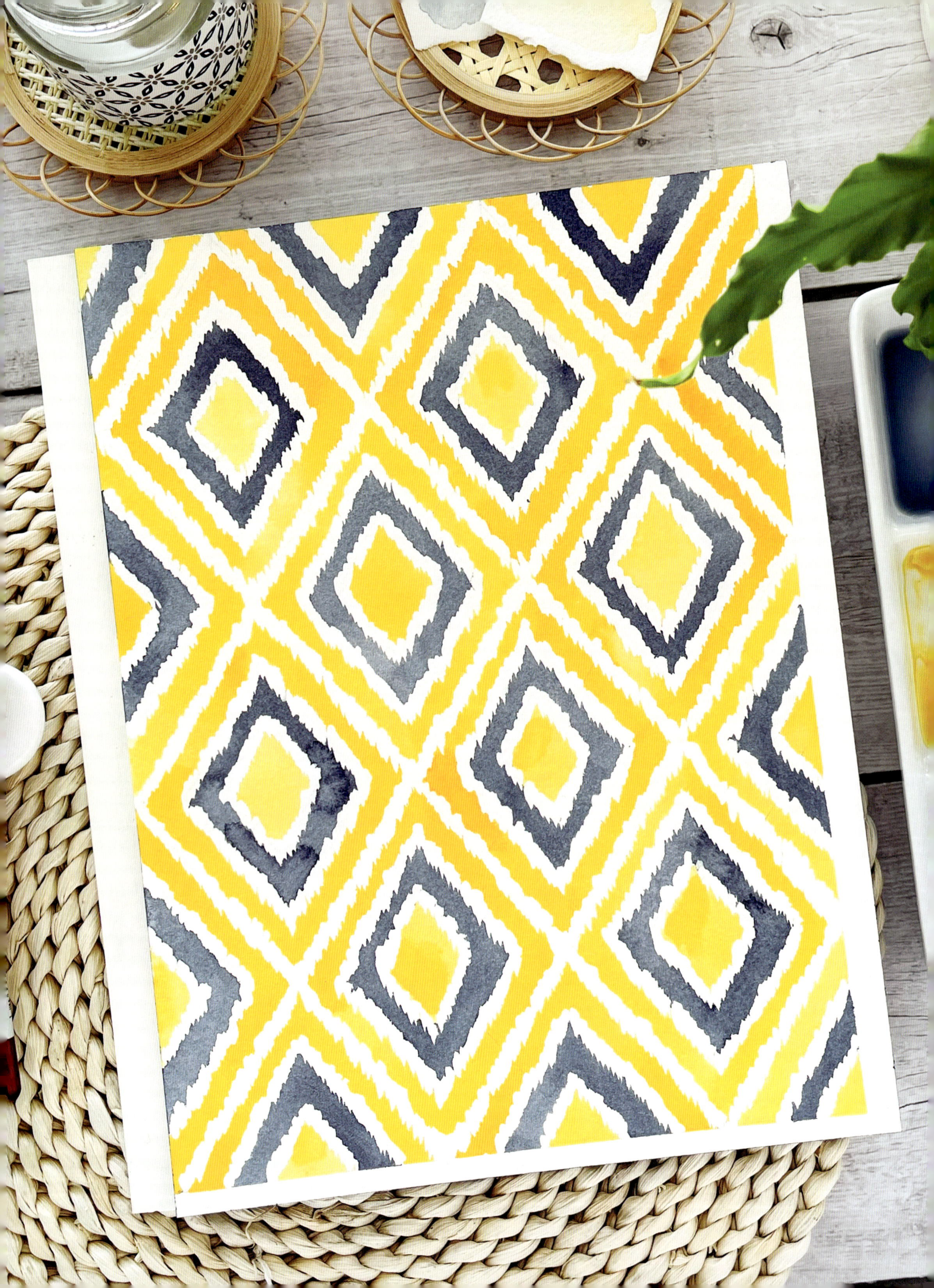

Indonesian Ikat

For this pattern, you will learn to use masking fluid with a more advanced technique. Unlike the masking fluid marker used in the previous pattern, for this pattern we will use bottled masking fluid, which can be applied using a brush. We will be carefully painting the lines using masking fluid in a specific way to mimic the Indonesian ikat design style.

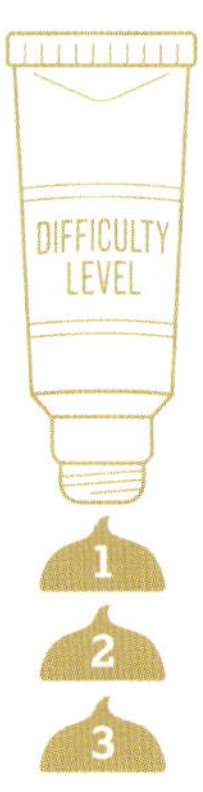

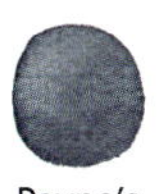
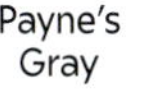

MATERIALS

BRUSHES: Size 6 round brush; in addition, choose an inexpensive small brush to use with masking fluid (the masking fluid may damage the bristles of your brush)

PAPER: 8" x 10" (20 x 25 cm), cold pressed; or use a smaller size, such as 8" x 8" (20 x 20 cm) or 5" x 7" (13 x 18 cm), if you are short on time

OTHER: Pencil; masking fluid (professional quality, peelable, liquid); ruler (optional)

COLORS:

Payne's Gray

Indian Yellow

TIP: The essence of this pattern is to be able to mimic the ikat style of vertical staggered lines or dyed threads that make ikat fabric appealing and unique. Pay close attention to getting it right.

This project's pattern is available as a bonus digital download! See page 14.

LET'S PRACTICE

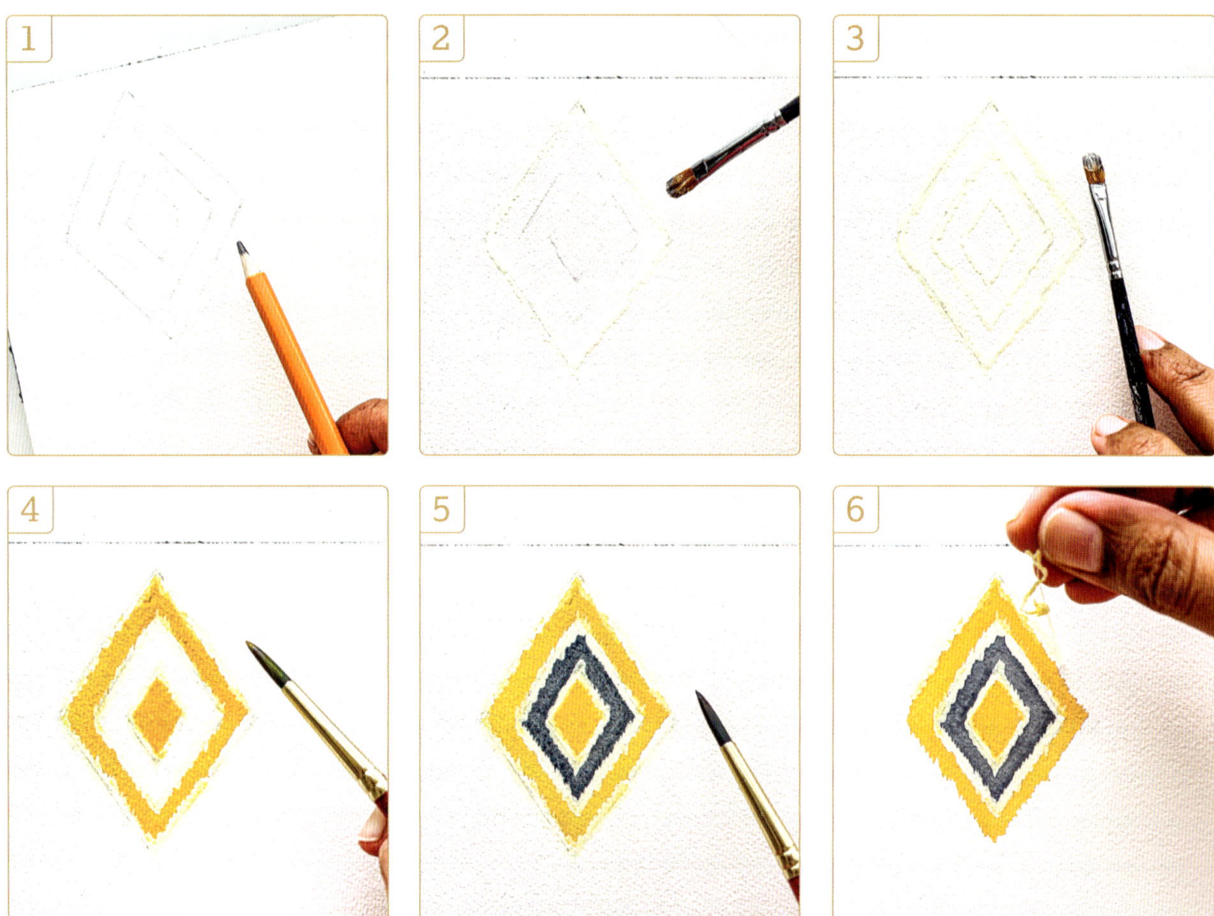

1 **Draw a set of nested diamonds.** Using a pencil, draw three nested diamonds in descending order of size. Make the space between them relatively consistent.

2 **Add masking fluid to the outermost diamond.** Dip a cheap brush into the masking liquid and cover the outline of the outermost diamond using staggered, vertical brushstrokes. For an authentic feel, make sure your lines are not too clean or straight.

3 **Mask the other diamonds.** Repeat for the middle diamond and the innermost diamond. Wait for the masking fluid to dry completely.

4 **Paint the yellow areas.** Paint the outermost diamond yellow, then the innermost diamond yellow. You will notice that the masking fluid repels the paint wherever you paint over it.

5 **Paint the gray area.** Paint the portion between the outermost diamond and innermost diamond gray.

6 **Remove the masking fluid.** Wait for the paint to completely dry, then carefully scratch and peel off the masking fluid. It is stretchy and easily comes off once you loosen an end. The final design is revealed!

Let's Relax

Ikat is a design created from threads that have been dyed before being woven into textiles. The word "ikat" comes from the Indonesian language, and, depending on context, it can mean thread, a knot, or even the finished ikat fabric. Unlike shibori or Bandhani, where the fabric itself is dyed, in ikat, dyed threads are used to weave patterns to form a patterned fabric. To show the ikat weaves in this piece, we will use masking fluid to mimic the staggered lines that go up and down toward the edge. There are so many different styles and techniques of ikat; the one that inspired this pattern is the most commonly seen pattern on textiles used for furnishings and clothing. Feel free to research other ikat patterns for inspiration!

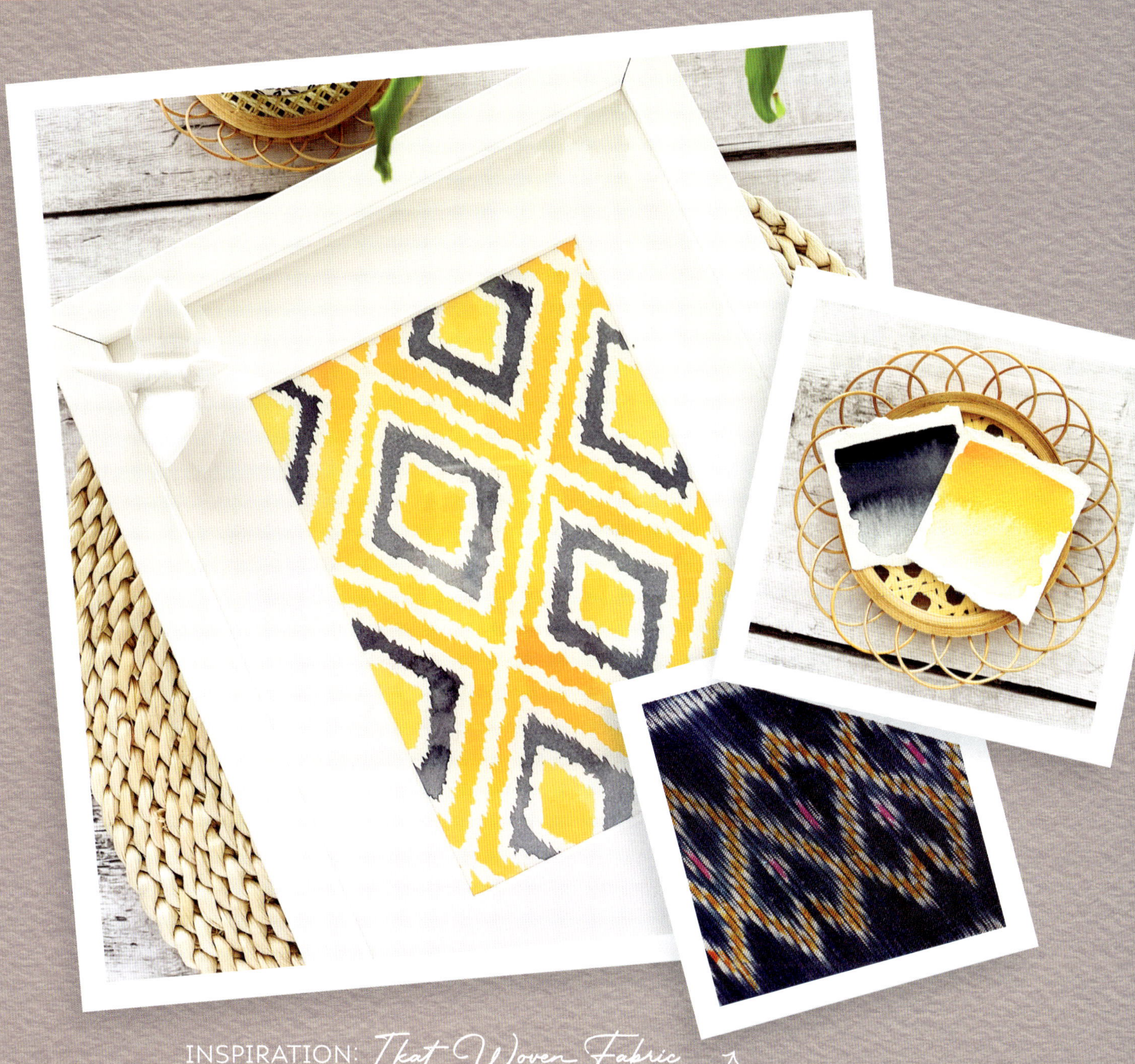

INSPIRATION: *Ikat Woven Fabric*

Let's Paint

1 Draw a pattern and mask the design.

Using pencil and a ruler, re-create the design shown, making sure that each guideline you draw is angled precisely parallel to the others so your diamonds come out neatly.

Here's one option for a precise method you could use: Cut a long, rectangular strip of paper that is 2⅜" (6 cm) wide, and use that as a spacer, along with a ruler, to ensure that your initial diagonal lines are evenly spaced and parallel. Then create a slightly less wide spacer for the medium diamonds and another even smaller spacer for the smallest

diamonds. Erase line segments as needed to create the final diamond grid.

You can also download the digital pattern linework and trace it on your paper (see page 14).

Once you have gotten the pattern down in pencil, dip your brush in the masking fluid and cover each of the pencil lines with staggered vertical strokes. Aim for imperfect and zigzagging vertical lines to get the blurred effect of ikat fabrics.

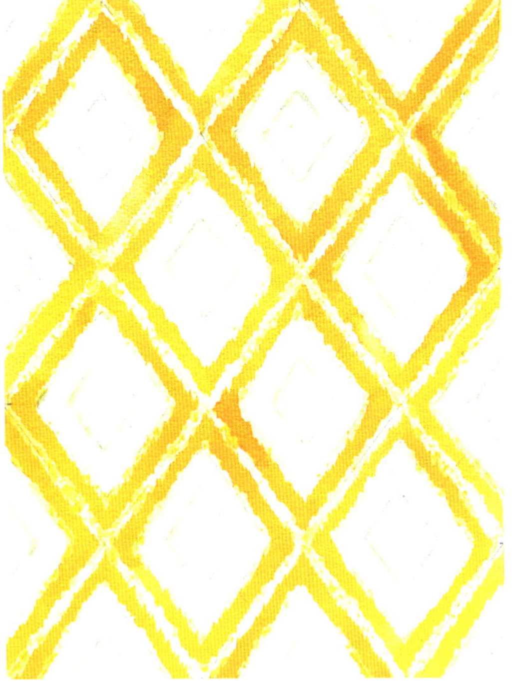

2 **Paint the large diamond outlines.**
Once the masking fluid is completely dry,
mix some yellow paint and start painting the
outermost diamonds, starting from the top of
the page. Carefully paint each such area until
you reach the end of the page.

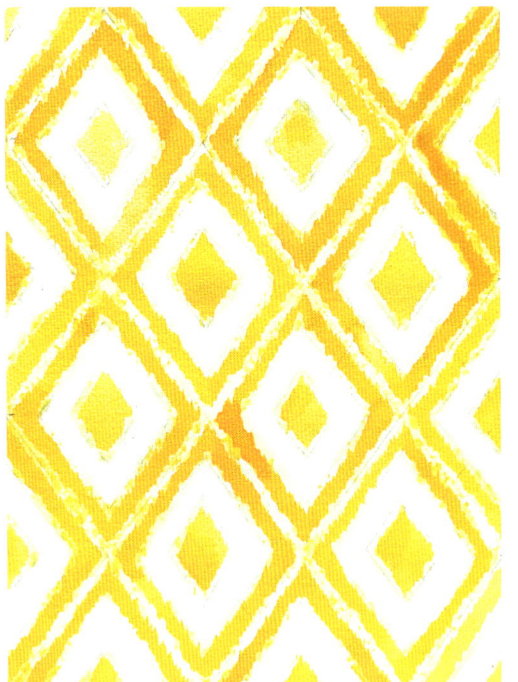

3 **Paint the innermost diamonds.** Using
the same shade of yellow, paint the smallest
diamonds in the center of each of the bigger
diamonds across the whole page.

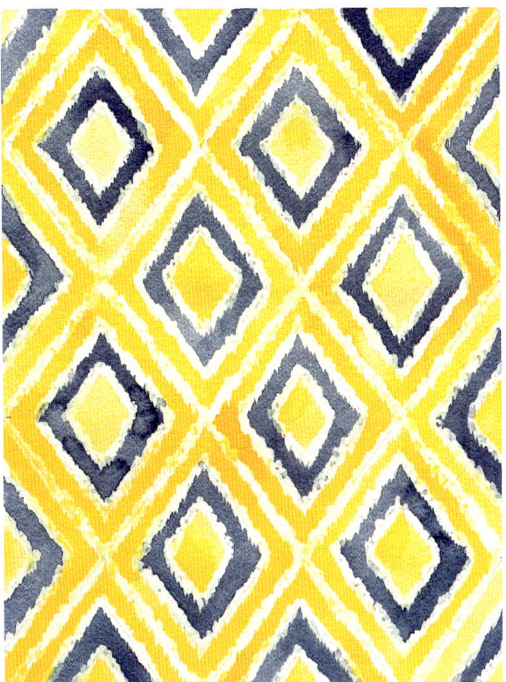

4 **Paint the gray areas.** In the remaining
spaces between the yellow areas, apply a layer
of gray paint. Don't worry if the paint slightly
spills over onto the masking fluid—it will be
cleaned up when the masking fluid is peeled off.

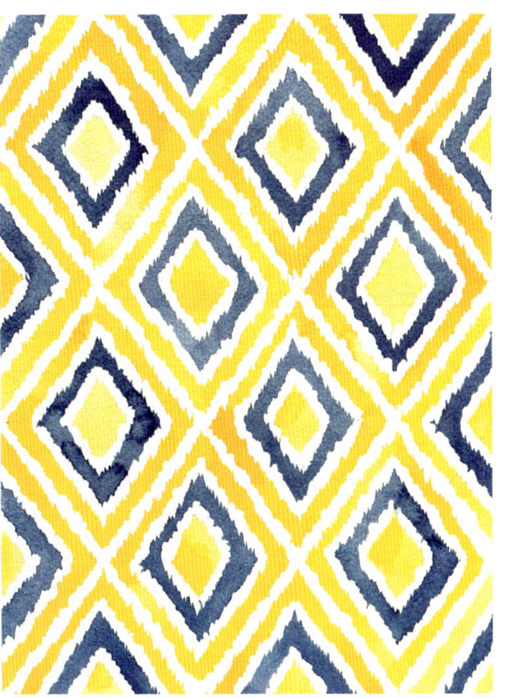

5 **Remove the masking fluid.** Wait for all
the layers of paint to dry, then start peeling off
the masking fluid. You may have to scratch at
an edge of it in the beginning. Keep peeling
away to slowly reveal the white paper beneath.

Let's Paint

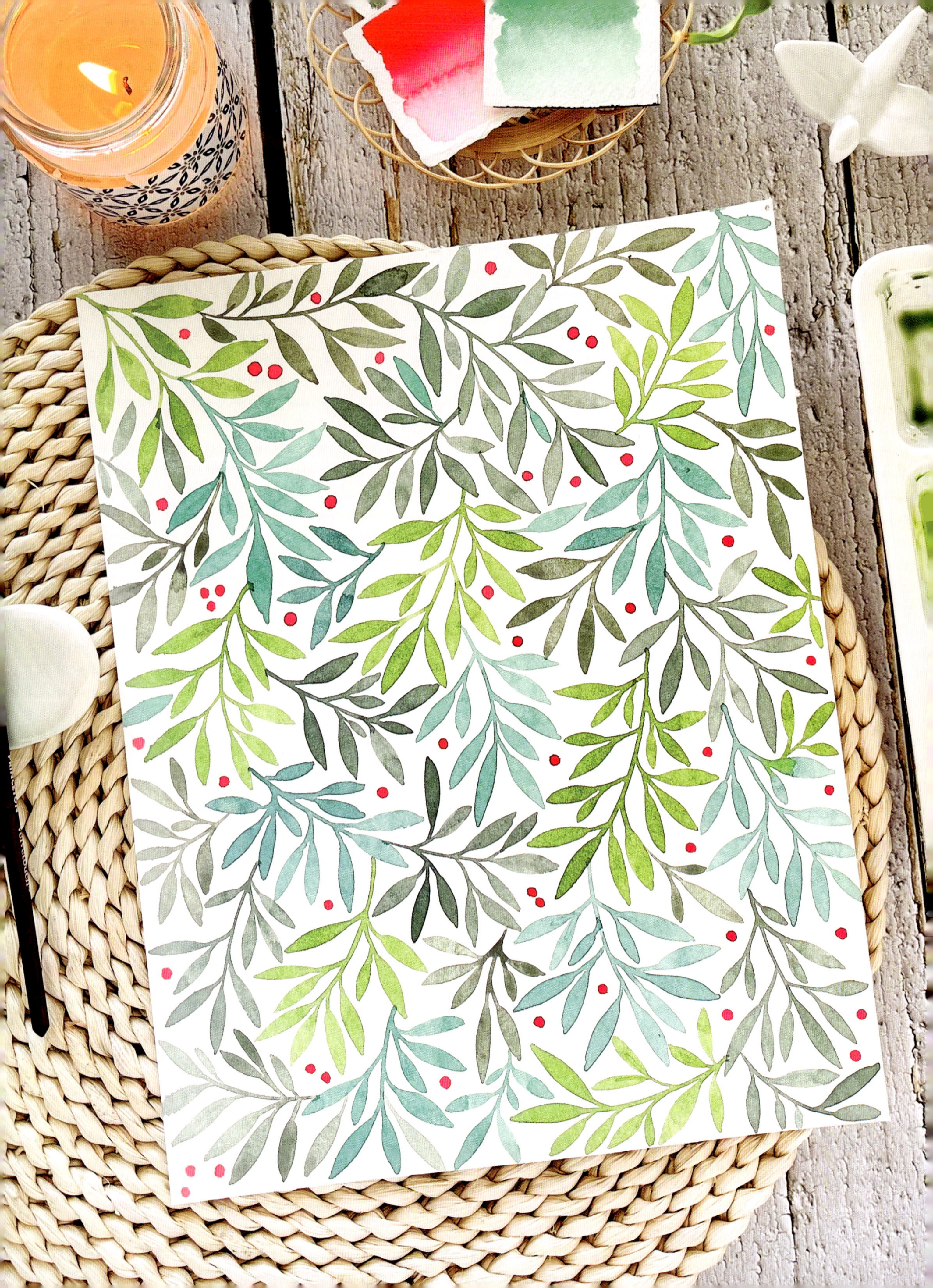

Therapeutic Leaves

We explored a lot of geometric patterns in the previous projects, so this project is a good break from those, since we will be exploring painting in a loose style using simplified leaves. We will arrange the leaves in a manner that looks almost like a repeat pattern to the eyes but that in fact is an abstract, asymmetric pattern. If you want, you could use a different color scheme for this piece, such as autumn-themed colors or a monochrome scheme like indigo or brown.

MATERIALS

BRUSH: Size 4 round brush

PAPER: 8" x 10" (20 x 25 cm), hot pressed; or use a smaller size, such as 8" x 8" (20 x 20 cm) or 5" x 7" (13 x 18 cm), if you are short on time

COLORS:

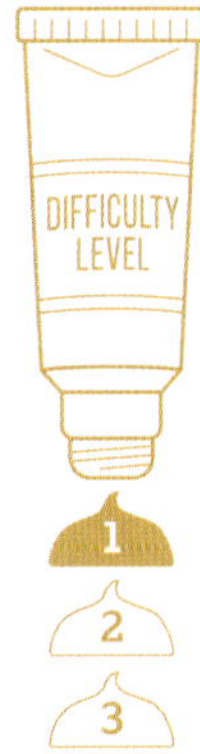

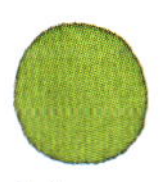
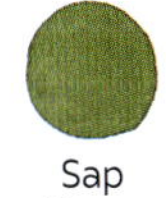
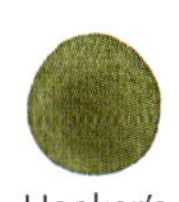
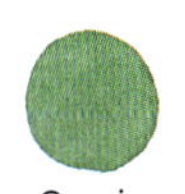
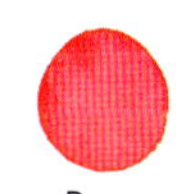

Faience Blue + Transparent Yellow*	Sap Green	Hooker's Green	Cupric Green Light + Payne's Gray*	Rose Lake

COLOR NOTE: You can use the greens you have in your palette or mix your own shades like I did. You may or may not have the exact shades that I have, so try to find the closest match you can.

***COLOR SUBSTITUTES:**

Faience Blue + Transparent Yellow
(try Ultramarine Blue or Prussian Blue instead of Faience Blue and Primary Yellow instead of Transparent Yellow)

Cupric Green Light + Payne's Gray
(try Viridian Green instead of Cupric Green Light)

TIP: Try to paint the leafy stems close to each other to have a repeating pattern-like feel. If you paint them too far apart, your pattern will end up with lots of white space that will be difficult to fill effectively later.

LET'S PRACTICE

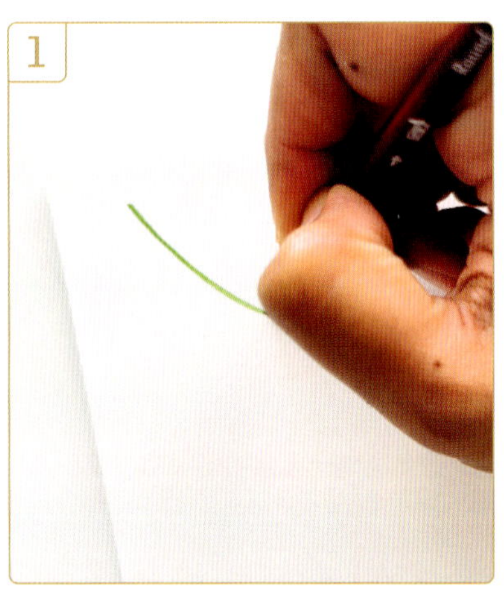 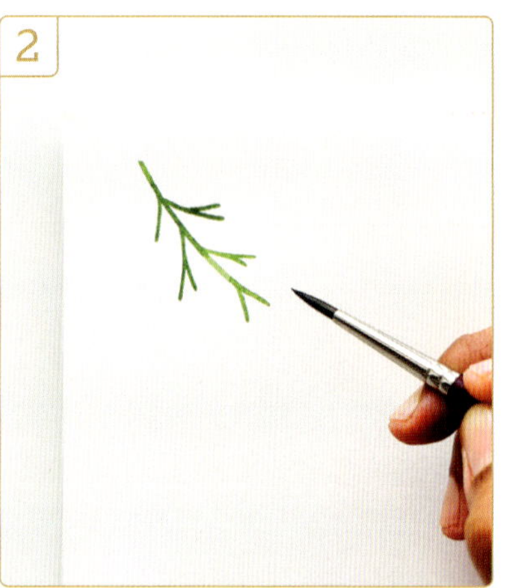 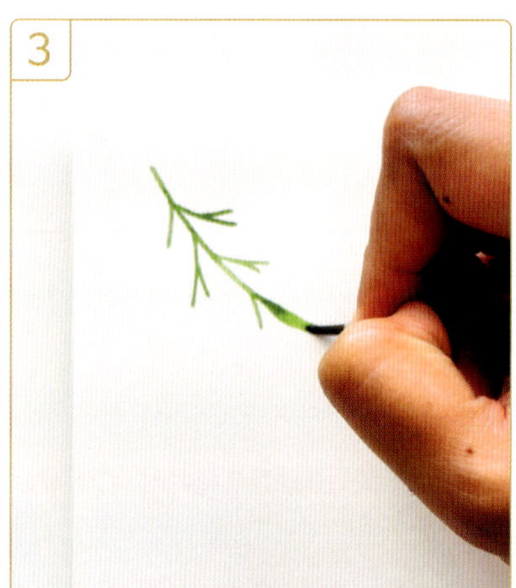

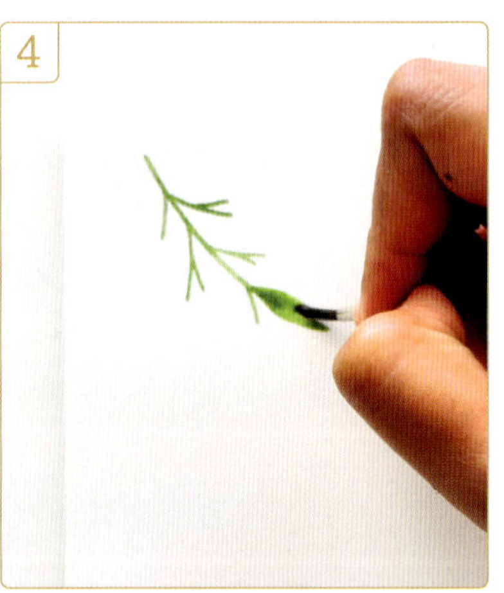 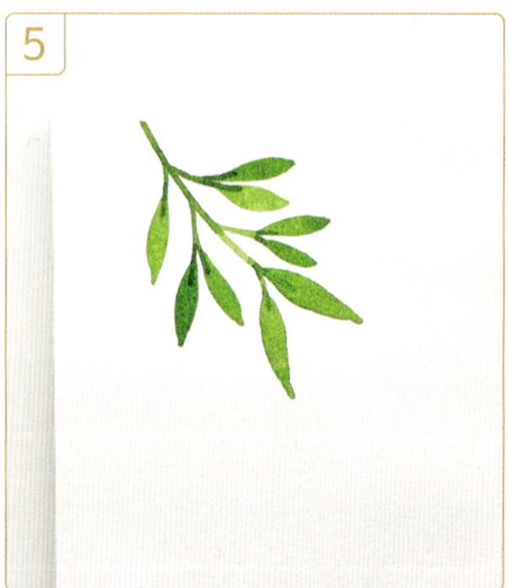 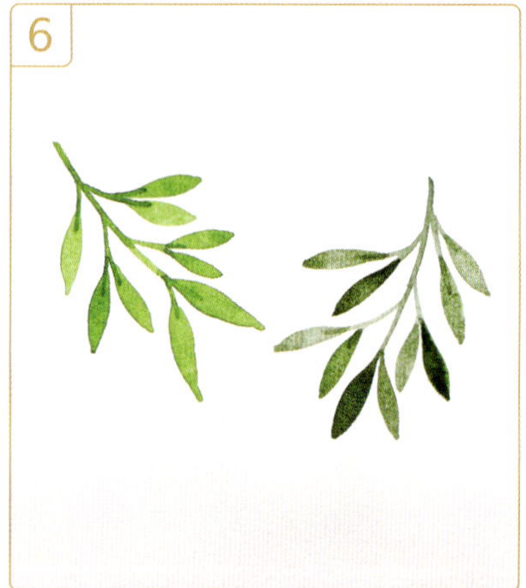

1 **Draw a branch.** Using any shade of green, draw a thin, curved stroke coming down. Don't press down on the tip of your brush too much or you will get a thick line. Try to hold the brush slightly upward instead of holding it slanted and close to the paper.

2 **Add stems to the branch.** From the sides of the main curve, paint small stems that sprout outward. Include single stems as well as some stems that split into two tiny stems.

3 **Start a leaf.** At the tip of the initial branch, press down on your brush and pull it downward to form one slightly curved half of a leaf. Lift the brush softly when you get the desired leaf length.

4 **Finish a leaf.** Repeat the same stroke but curved slightly to the other side to form the other half of the leaf, making sure this second half comes to a point with the first half. This completes one leaf.

5 **Fill the branch.** Now paint a leaf for every stem that you drew earlier. Vary the size of the leaves for diversity. By the end, your branch should look full and dense.

6 **Keep practicing.** Paint more branches using other shades of green. Try to paint your next branch facing a different direction. Continue to vary the leaf size, but don't change the leaf technique—you want the leaves to appear consistent.

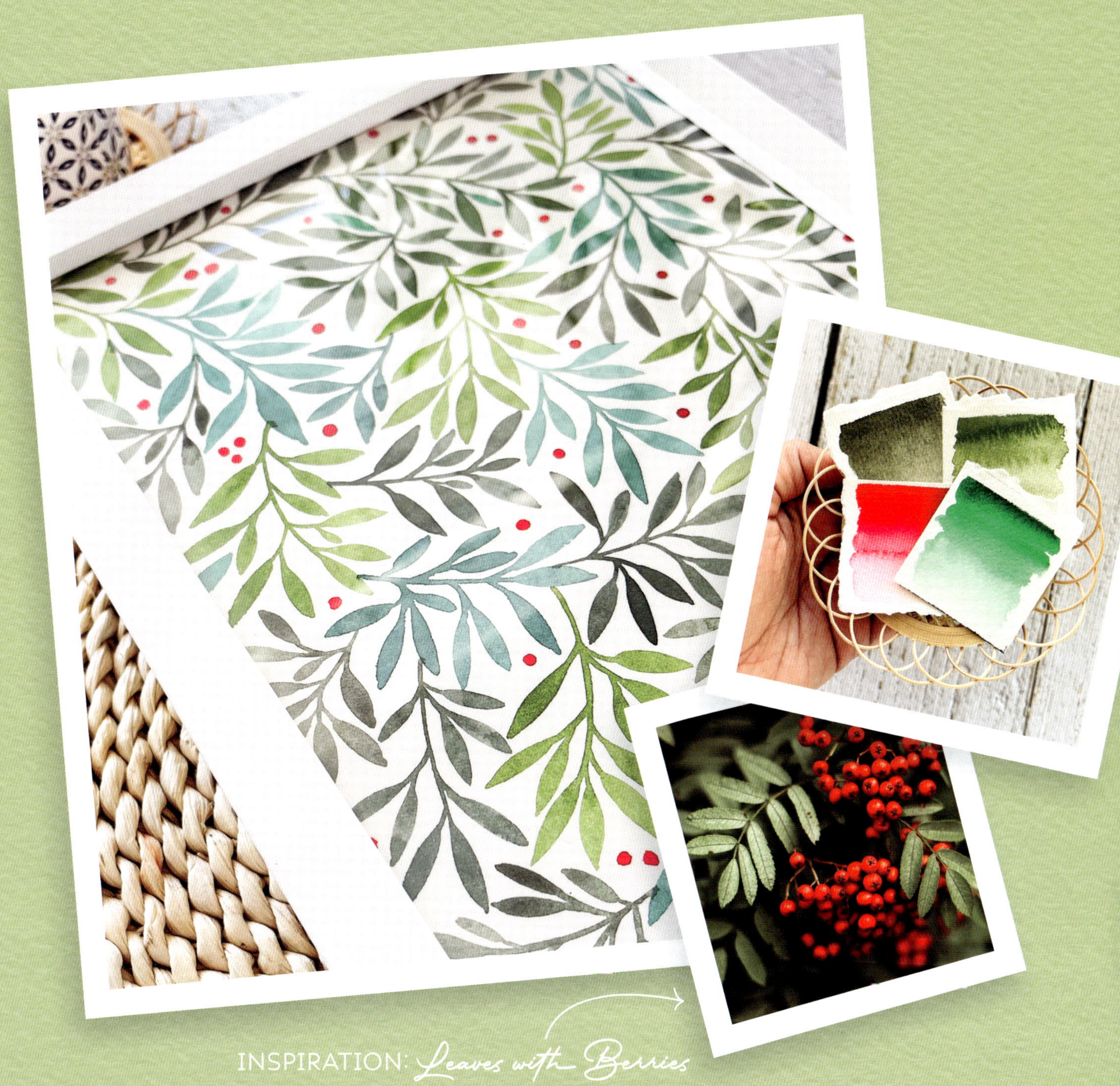

Let's Relax

I personally feel that painting leaves is a very relaxing and therapeutic process. I don't know if it is the calming green color or the repetitive technique for the leaves, which feels somewhat meditative. It's probably both! I could almost hear leaves rustling in a gentle breeze as I painted this piece. I hope that you will experience the same feeling while painting this pattern, or discover a new feeling of connection and comfort with your art. Either way, I am sure you will enjoy the process!

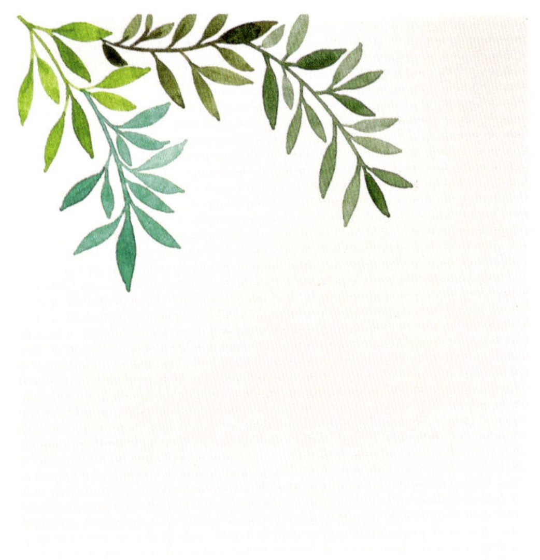

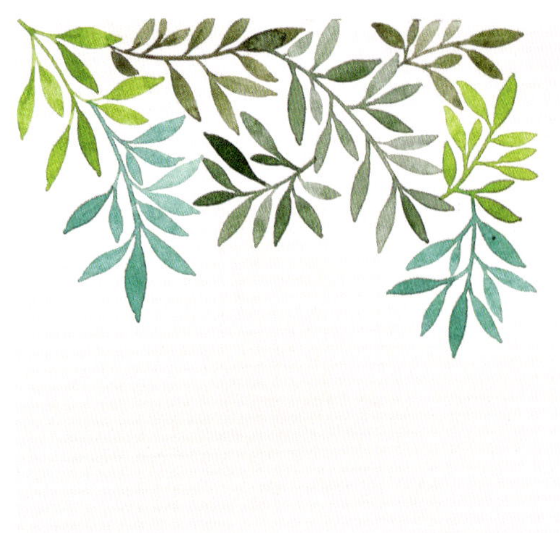

1 **Paint the first branches.** Mix each of the shades of green you are going to use. Start painting from the top left corner with your first shade. Then rinse your brush and move to the next shade, painting a branch that is connected to the first branch.

2 **Continue across the page.** Continue changing colors with every new branch and working your way across the paper. Try to paint branches and leaves going in different directions. Start filling the page from top to bottom.

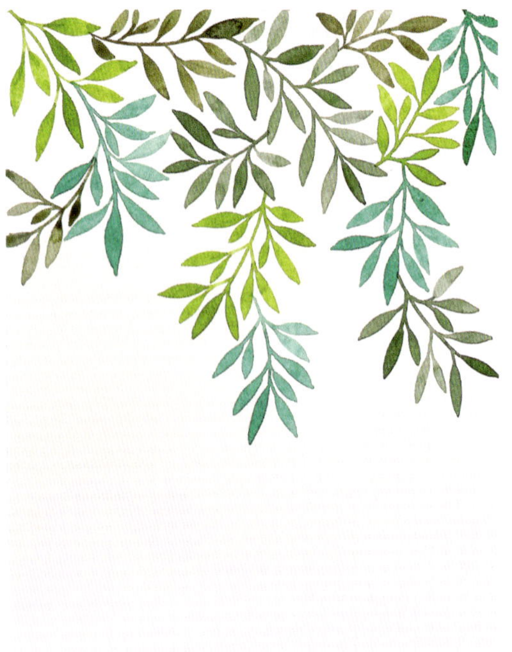

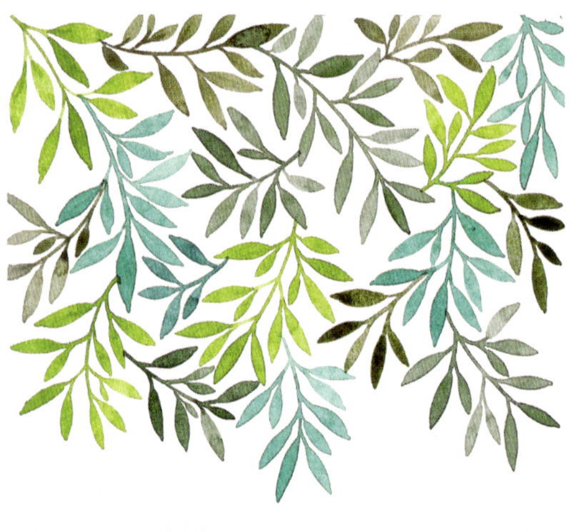

3 **Adjust size as needed.** Depending on the gaps, adjust the sizing of the leaves and the length of the stems and branches. Make sure that you don't crowd certain areas of the page and leave other spaces open and sparse.

4 **Keep working downward.** By now, you may have reached about halfway down the paper, and the different shades of green will start to look cohesive together.

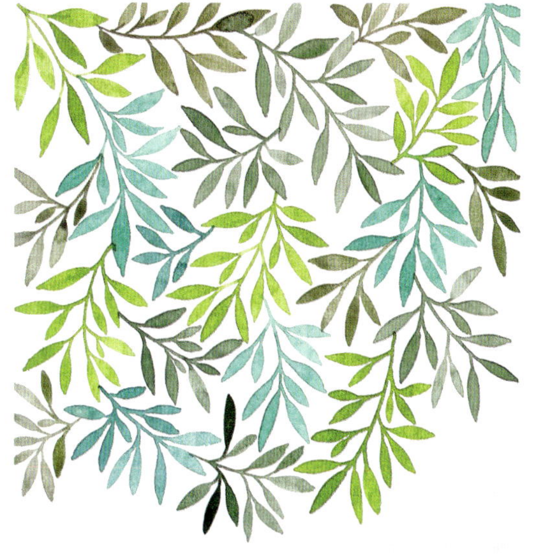

5 **Don't worry too much about exact colors.** Keep remixing the shades as needed as you go. It is fine to have a little bit of tonal variation within the same colors.

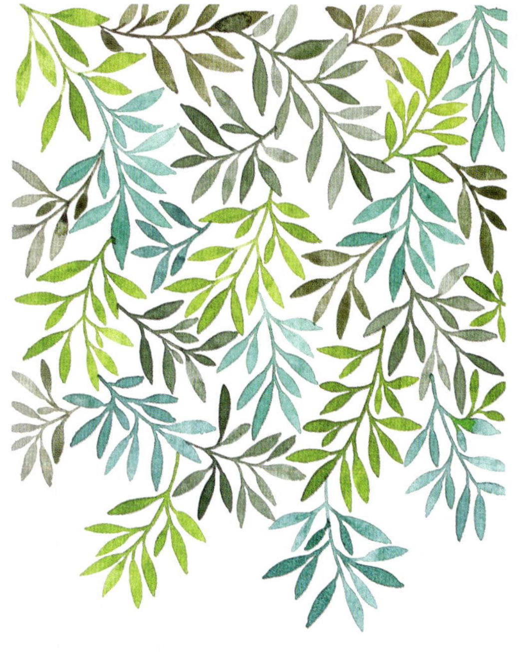

6 **Keep going.** Continue to add branches and leaves connecting everything together. You're almost at the bottom now.

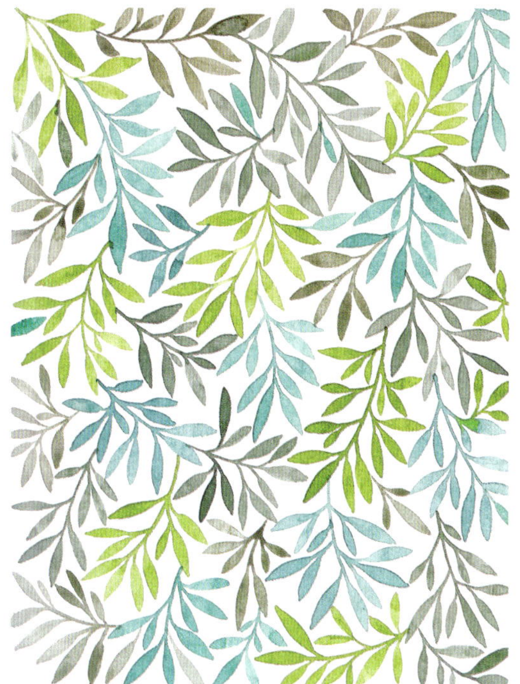

7 **Fill in empty spots.** Once you reach the bottom of the paper, take a step back to see if there are any obvious white spaces that you need to fill. Add leaves in those spaces by connecting them to existing branches or stems.

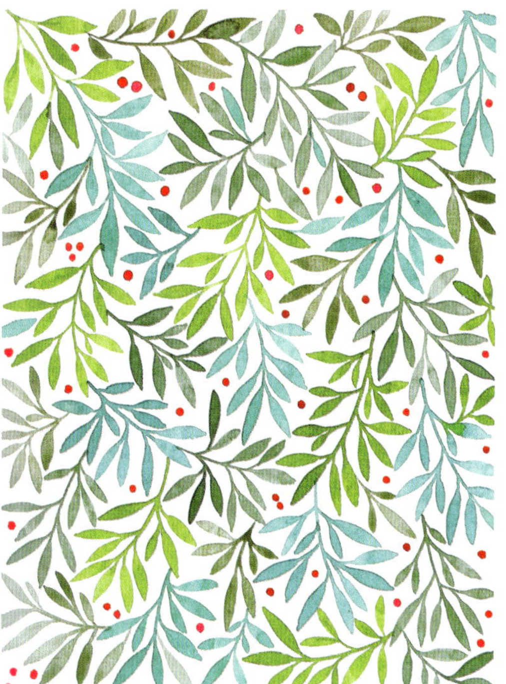

8 **Add berries.** Finally, add some pink dots, or berries, between the stems and leaves. This will add a nice sense of contrast and make the pattern more interesting with the added pop of color.

Let's Paint

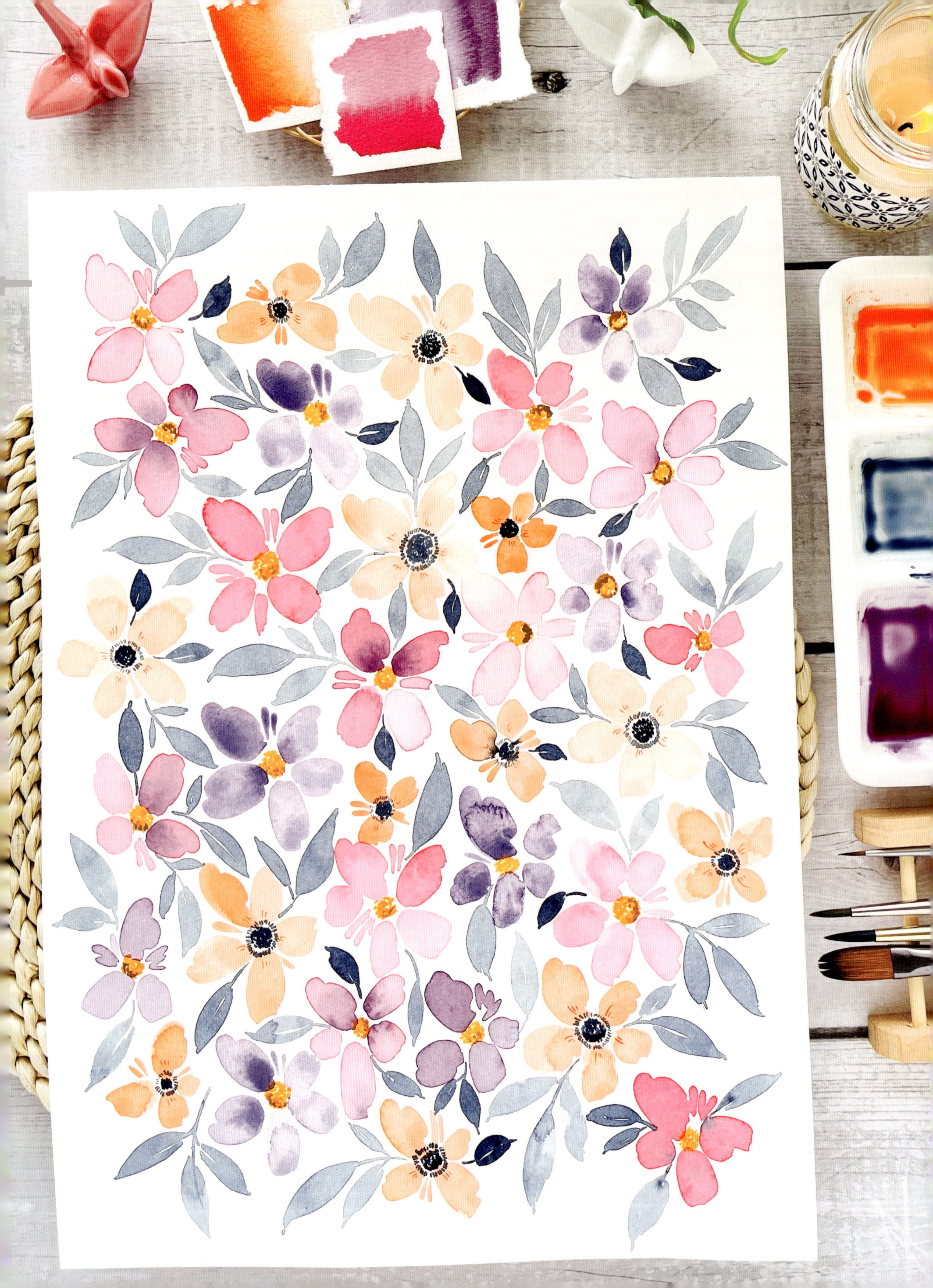

Pastel Florals

I had to include a floral pattern in this book! This piece is a perfect example of how anyone can turn simple, easy brushstrokes into soft, delicate, airy florals. The pattern will build your muscle memory for painting in a loose style that looks very modern. Painting basic floral shapes like these is a good skill to have in your repertoire. We will also paint basic leaves to support the soft florals, and together they will make a strong design. After you work on this piece, I'm sure you'll want to give it a go in a different color combination.

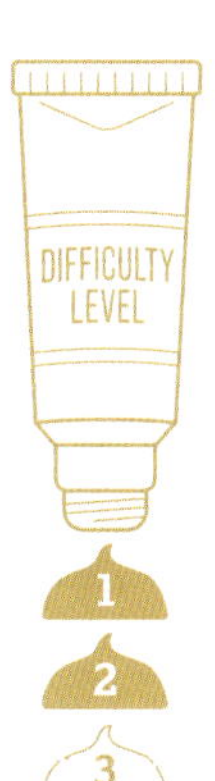

MATERIALS

BRUSHES: Size ½" (1.3 cm) oval or filbert brush for florals; size 6 round brush for leaves; size 4 round brush for small leaves; size 1 round brush for details

PAPER: 10" x 14" (25 x 35 cm), hot pressed; for this particular project, I chose a slightly bigger paper size since I wanted to accommodate many florals and leaves for a dense look

COLORS:

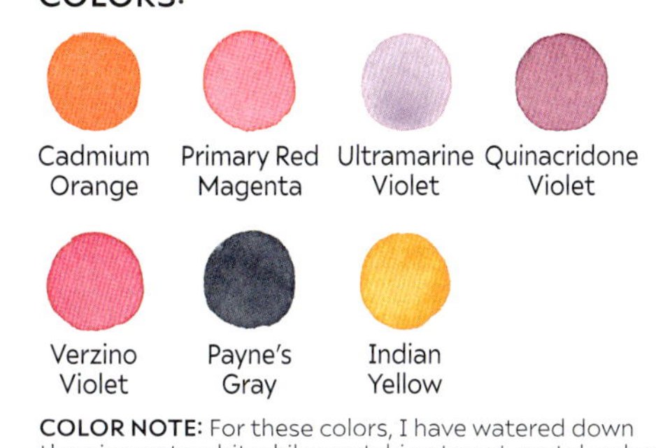

Cadmium Orange   Primary Red Magenta   Ultramarine Violet   Quinacridone Violet

Verzino Violet   Payne's Gray   Indian Yellow

COLOR NOTE: For these colors, I have watered down the pigments a bit while swatching to get pastel-y shades.

TIP: To get soft pastel florals, make sure to water down your pigments. I also suggest warming up your wrist by rotating it a couple times to loosen up the tight muscles before you begin painting. Trust me, it helps! Also, soft background music might help to calm you down and get you into the mood for painting soothing florals.

LET'S PRACTICE

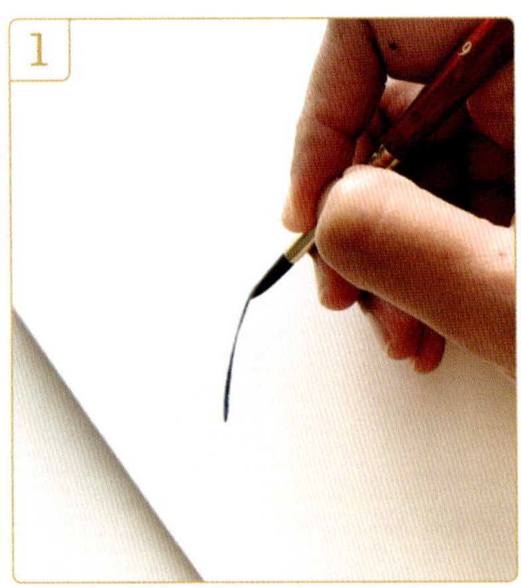  

 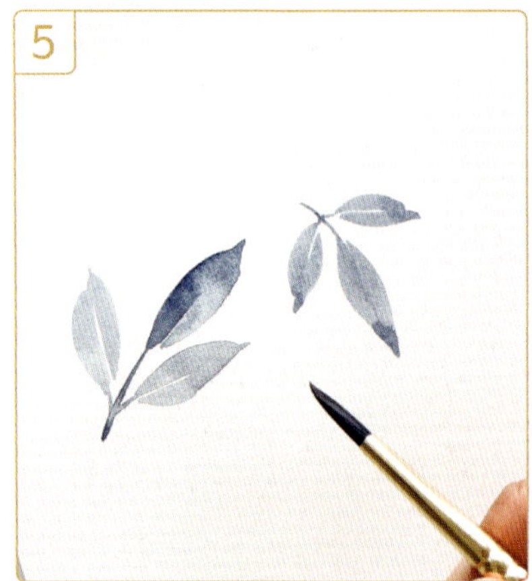 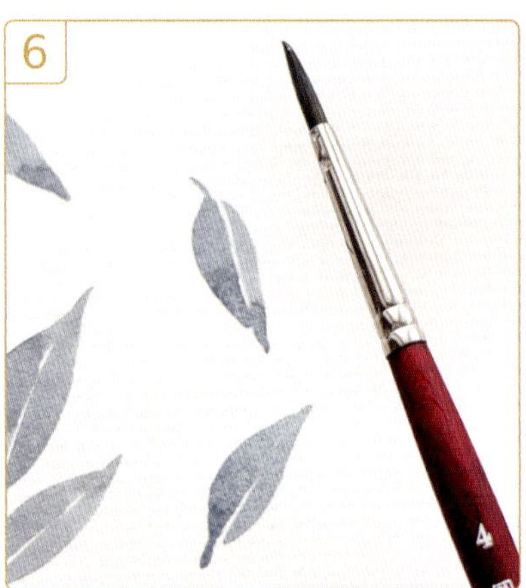

Leafy Branches

1 **Paint a stem.** Mix some gray color in your palette, neither too runny nor too dry. Using a size 6 round brush, draw a thin, curved line using the tip of the brush. Don't apply too much pressure.

2 **Paint half of a leaf.** Starting from the top tip of the curved line, draw a stroke by pressing the tip of the brush and dragging the brush by the belly. Lift the brush gently to create a pointed tip. This is one side of the leaf.

3 **Paint the other half of the leaf.** Repeat the same stroke next to the first. You may or may not leave a small white gap in the center between the halves.

4 **Add more leaves.** To add two more leaves sprouting out from the sides, first draw a tiny stem for each leaf, then draw the leaves using the two-stroke method.

5 **Keep practicing.** Try painting a few more leafy branches facing in different directions. Vary the leaf size slightly.

6 **Try a different brush.** Switch to a small round brush, such as a size 4, to see the difference in the resulting leaf size and shape. The method always remains the same!

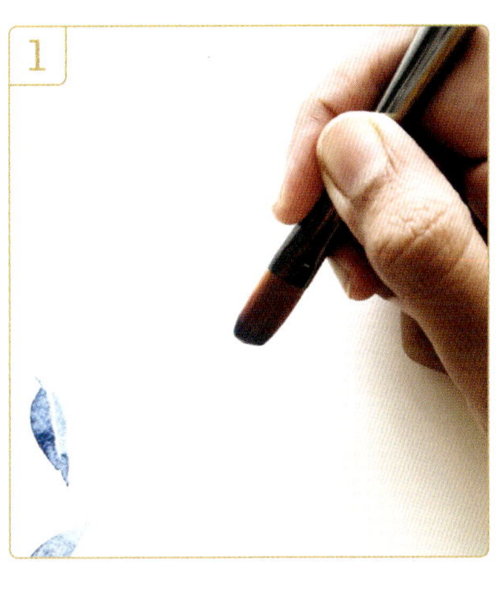
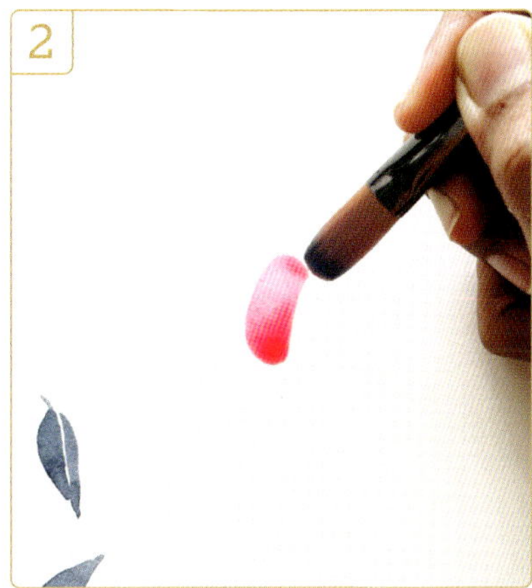
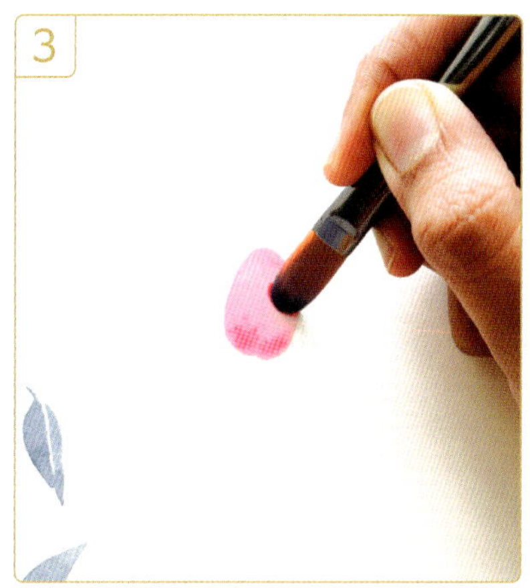
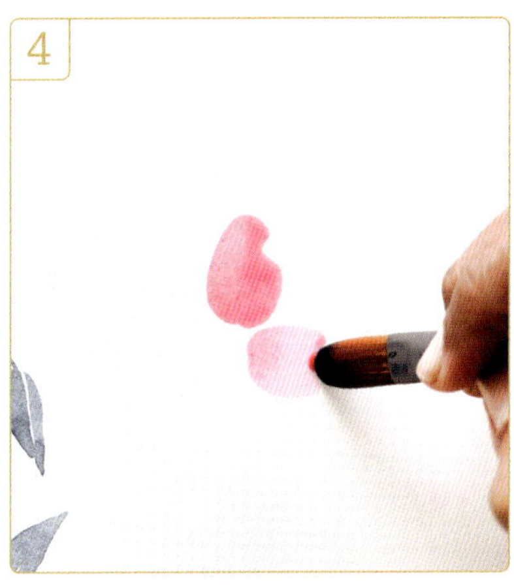
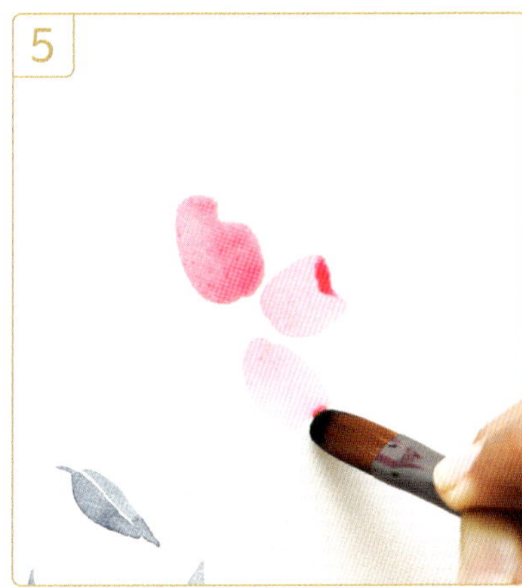

Flowers

1 **Prepare the brush.** We will use a ½" (1.3 cm) oval brush to paint the flowers. First, let's learn how to hold the oval brush correctly. Load the brush with the paint. Hold it slightly at an angle, with the broad tip of the brush ready to touch the paper.

2 **Make the first petal stroke.** Press down the broad side of the bristles and drag outward to create a small stroke. Lift the brush when the stroke is about 1" (2.5 cm) long. Don't stress about measuring— the goal is to learn to paint petals effortlessly.

3 **Make the second petal stroke.** Now paint another stroke to make the petal fluffier and bigger, combining two strokes to make one petal. This stroke can be longer or shorter than the first—each petal is unique and nonsymmetric.

4 **Paint a new petal.** Imagine you are going around an invisible center when you position your brush for the next petal. Leaving a small gap, paint the second petal using the same method as the first, but don't try to make it look identical.

5 **Paint a third petal.** Keep going around the imaginary center to paint one more completed petal using the same technique.

6 **Paint a tiny petal.** Now let's change the technique. Hold the brush sideways so the thinner part of the bristles touches the paper. Ever so lightly, press the thin part of the brush onto the paper and pull a stroke inward toward the imaginary center.

"Flowers" continues on next page.

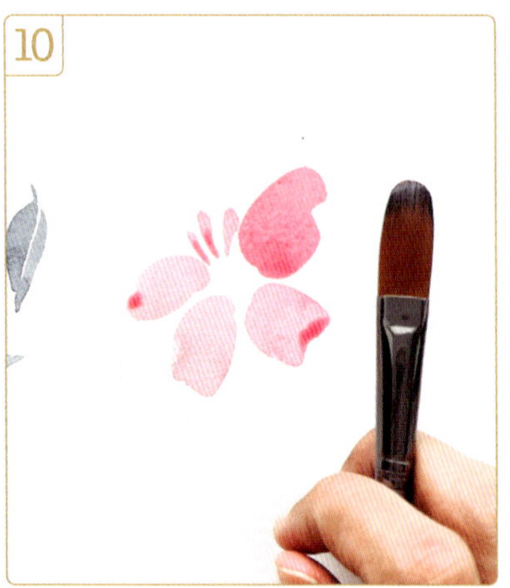
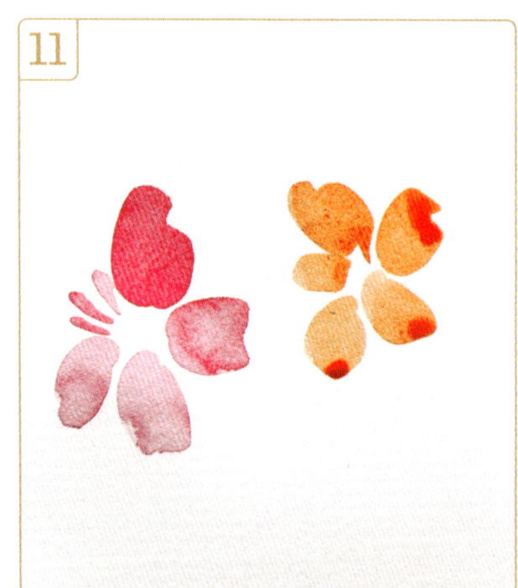
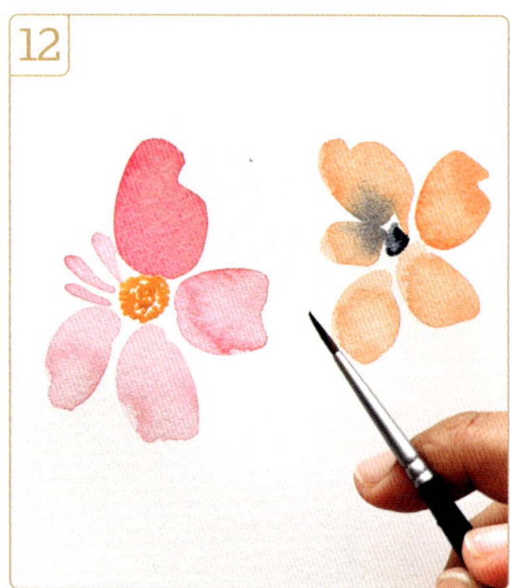

Flowers, continued

7 Paint a second tiny petal. Next to the previous stroke, add another skinny petal using the same technique. Adding such petals really adds character to the flower.

8 Paint another large petal. Continue around the imaginary center to add one more petal using the broad side of the bristles and the two-stroke technique.

9 Fill in the gaps. If you see big gaps between petals, you can simply add another skinny teardrop petal using the second technique.

10 Check your flower. Take a look at the petals together to see if your flower looks complete (the center is still to come). You are not aiming for perfect, symmetrical flowers. For a soft, breezy look, keep them perfectly imperfect!

11 Paint a second flower. Next to your first flower, paint a new flower in a different color, practicing your brushstrokes and petal techniques. Each flower should look similar yet unique.

12 Add the flower centers. Using a size 1 round brush, stipple yellow dots in the center of the pink flower and gray dots in the center of the orange flower. If your petals are still wet, it is fine if the dots bleed into the petals.

Let's Relax

Abstract, loose-style florals have always been one of the strongest parts of my portfolio. The idea of painting abstract florals is just very relaxing to me. The method removes any potential anxiety one might have related to painting something to perfection or with exact measurements. While painting these florals, surrender yourself to the flowy brush movements and enjoy every stroke that you make. Immerse yourself into the soft, pastel colors and have fun.

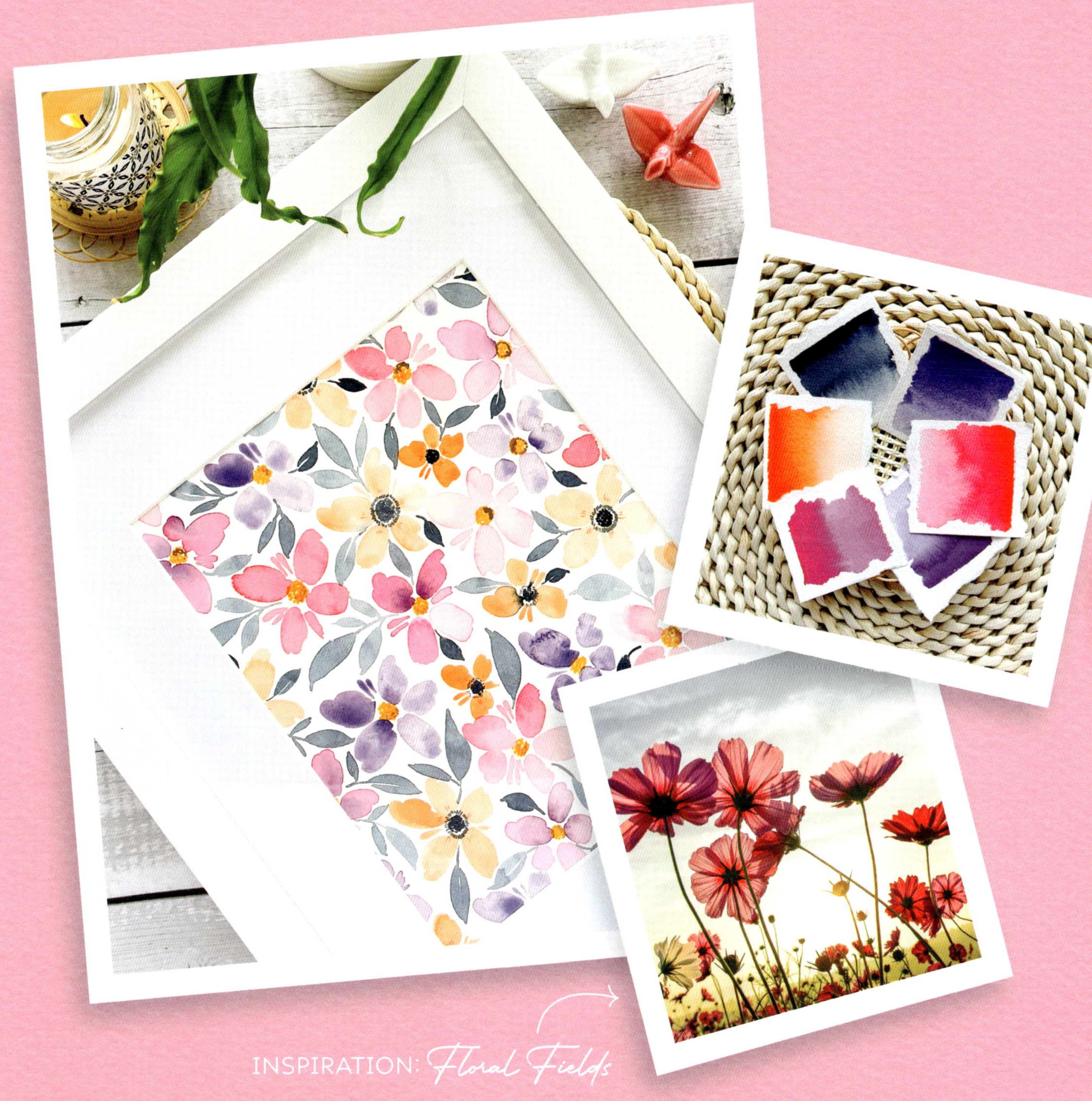

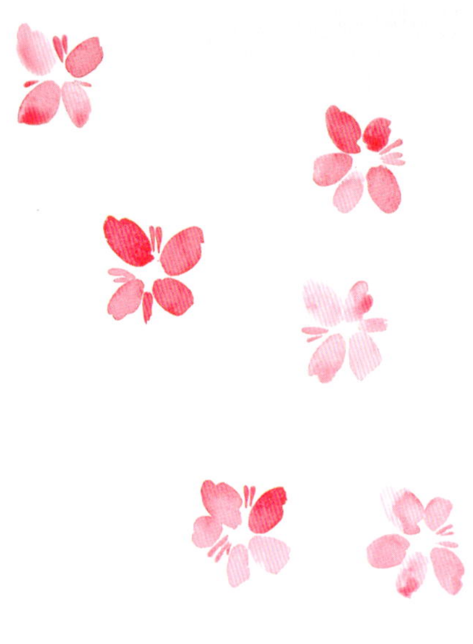

1 **Paint the pink flowers.** Mix your colors, diluting them to get soft pastel shades. Using your ½" (1.3 cm) oval or filbert brush, start by painting a couple of pink flowers scattered across the page. Keep each flower roughly the same size.

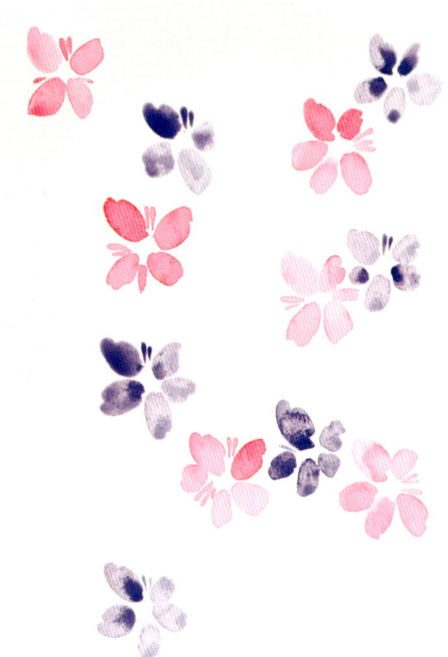

2 **Paint the purple flowers.** Up next, I chose Ultramarine Violet that is watered down to look like a soft pastel lavender color. Place a few lavender flowers around the pink flowers, roughly of the same size.

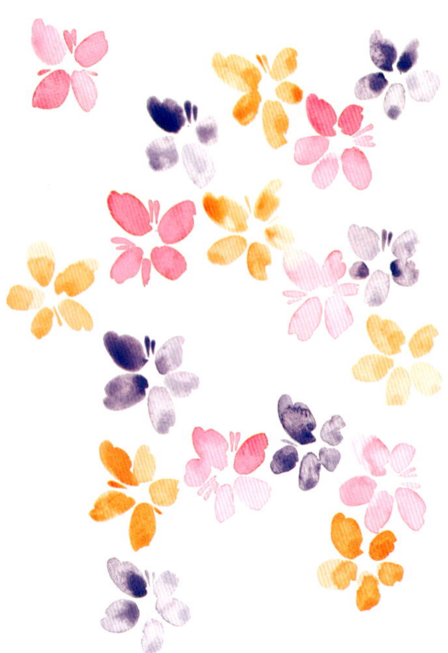

3 **Paint the orange flowers.** Let's go with a contrasting orange color next. Paint a few flowers in this color and start filling up open spaces. To make it easy to continue painting, rotate your paper to the ideal angle as you go.

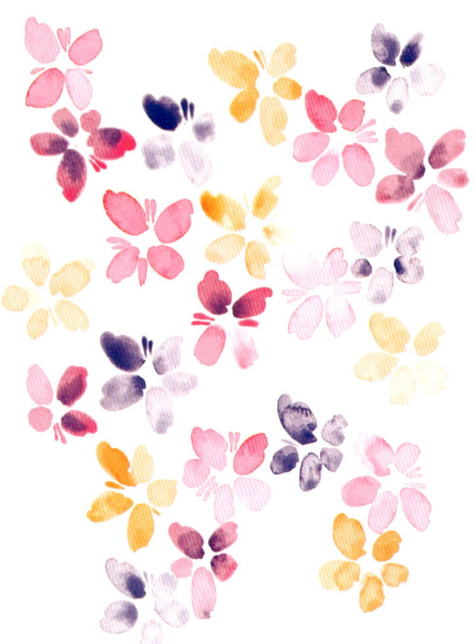

4 **Paint the magenta flowers.** Add some purply-pink flowers in the center and around the page to balance out the orange flowers. Add a slight color gradation by dropping in some Verzino Violet to the ends of some of the petals.

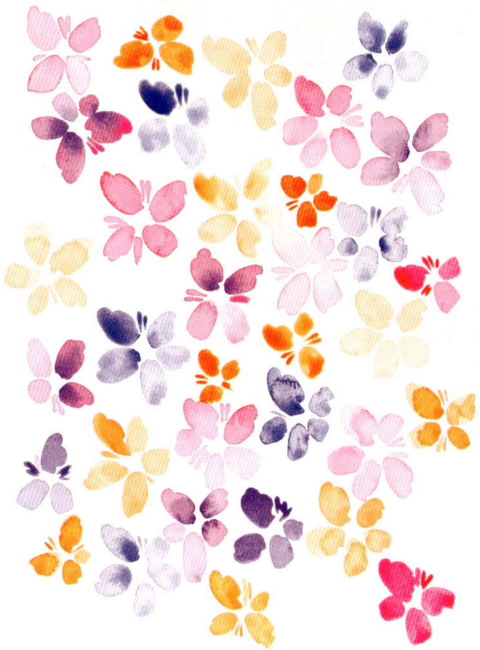

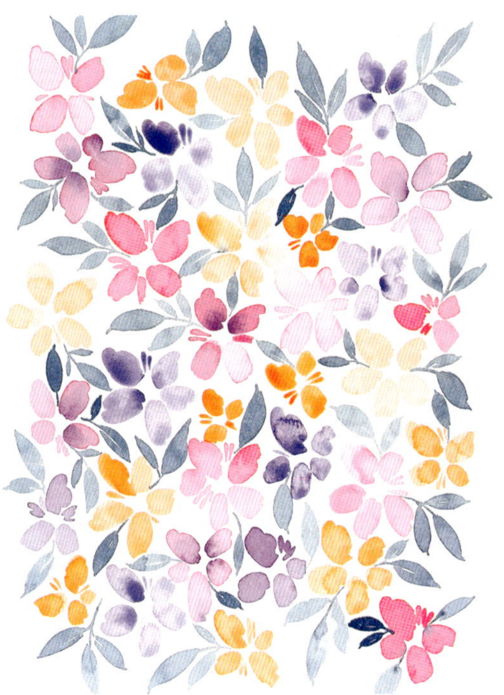

5 **Fill in with final flowers.** Now that you've used all the floral colors, appraise your work to see if you need to add more flowers. I added slightly darker but smaller orange and pink flowers in the gaps between bigger flowers.

6 **Add leaves.** Mix a light shade of gray and begin painting leaves between the flowers using a size 6 round brush. Aim to balance out all the white spaces, especially looking for chunky spaces. Adjust the sizes of the branches and leaves as needed.

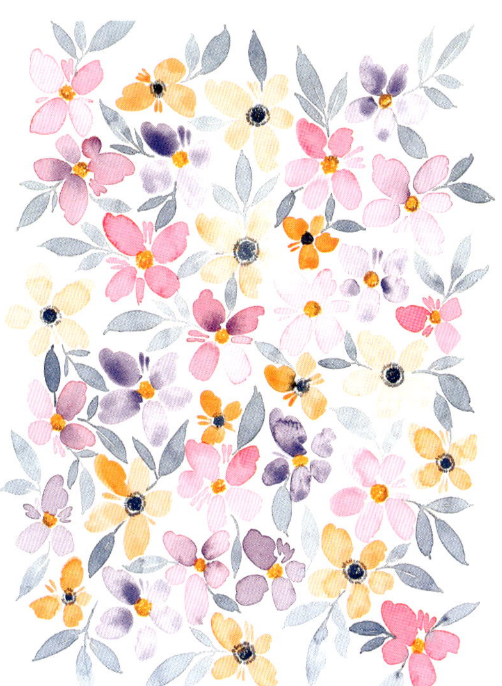

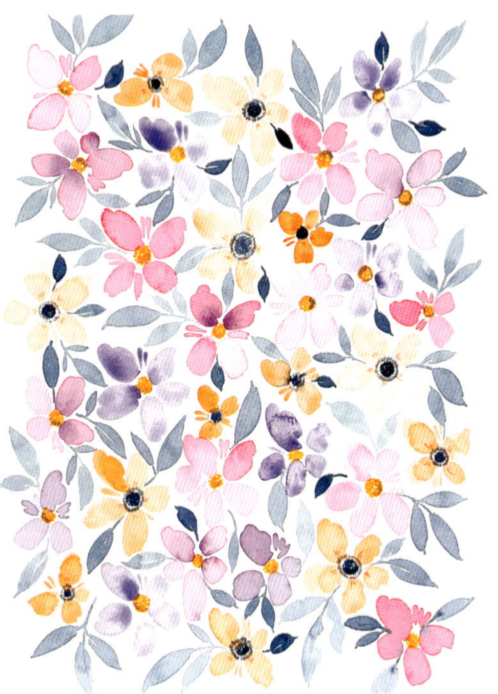

7 **Paint the flower centers.** Stipple some gray dots in the center of each of the orange flowers and some yellow dots in the center of each of the remaining flowers. For added detail, you can also paint a delicate ring of dots around the main center.

8 **Add final touches.** In any remaining gaps, add some tiny, dark-gray leaves. Stop filling space when you feel the piece is done. With a floral pattern like this, it can sometimes be tricky to know when to stop!

Let's Paint

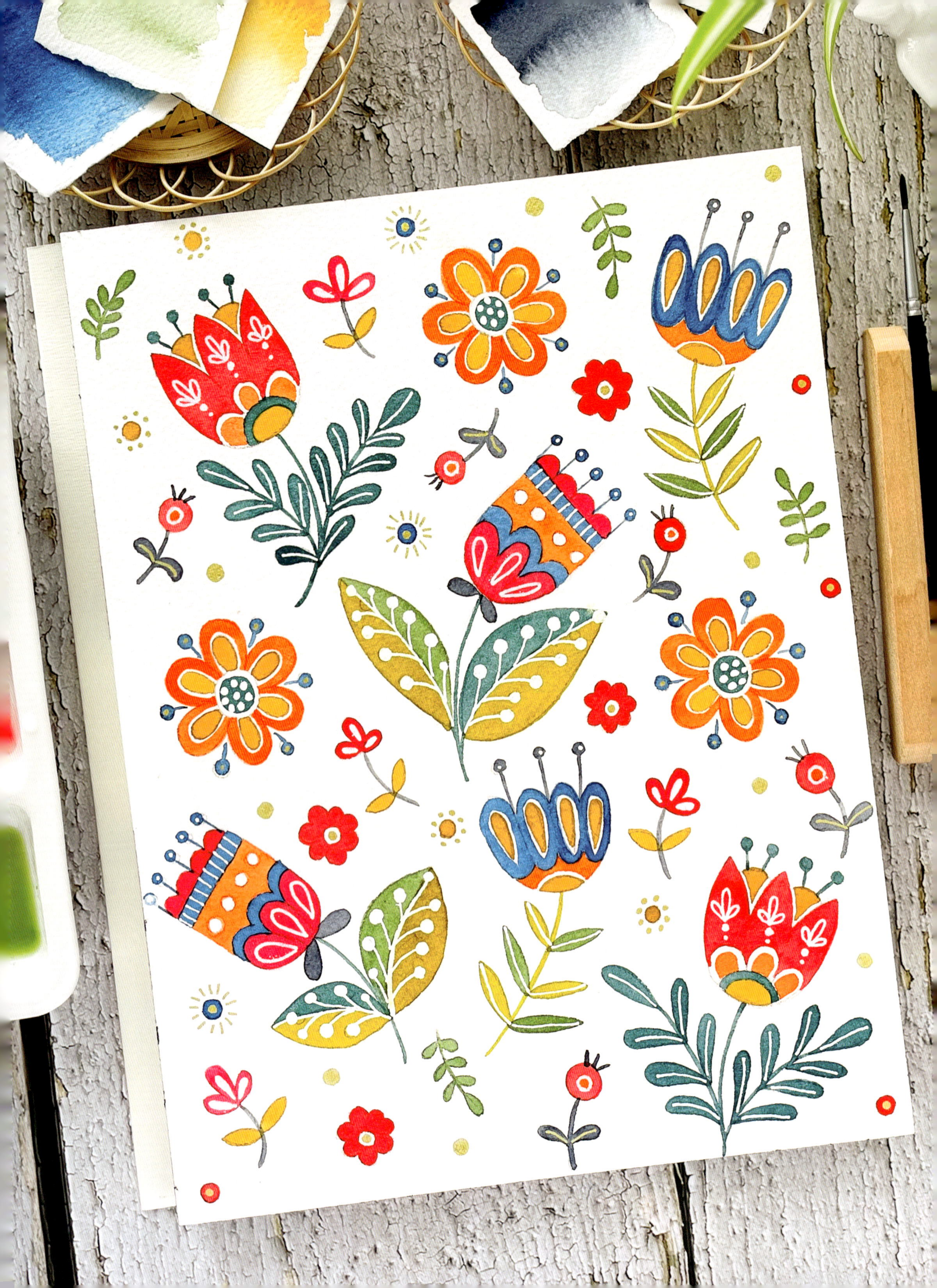

Folk Florals

In the previous project, we painted loose-style, contemporary florals, which helped you build muscle memory to paint the most-common petal styles. We will explore something quite the opposite in this project: painting florals in a more controlled and structured manner. Folk florals are ornate, bright, and detail-oriented designs that reflect the culture and particular artistic style of a region. For our folk florals, we will learn to paint inside lines just like in a coloring book! The idea is to explore multiple color combinations, especially bold and contrasting colors.

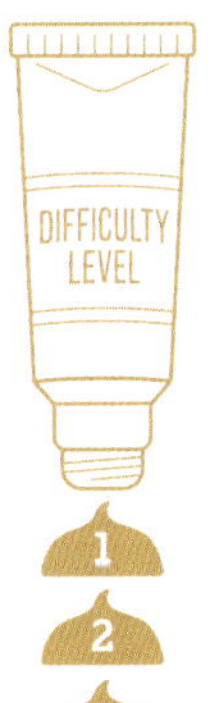

DIFFICULTY LEVEL

1
2
3

MATERIALS

BRUSHES: Size 4 round brush; size 2 round brush; size 1 round brush for details

PAPER: 8" x 10" (20 x 25 cm), cold pressed; smaller than this will be harder to use for this project

OTHER: Gel pens or paint pens (optional) in white and gold, 0.7 mm or thicker; pencil

COLORS:

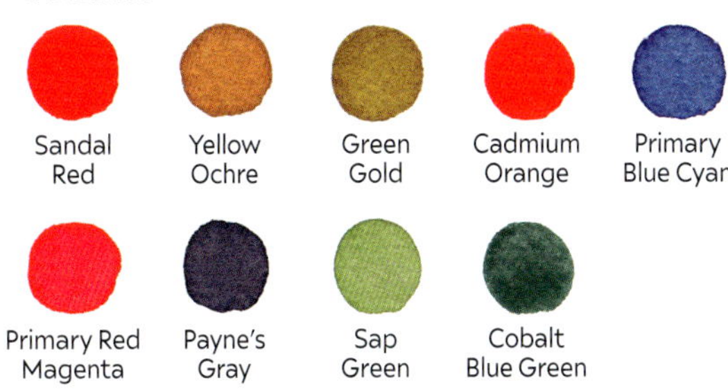

Sandal Red   Yellow Ochre   Green Gold   Cadmium Orange   Primary Blue Cyan

Primary Red Magenta   Payne's Gray   Sap Green   Cobalt Blue Green

TIP: To be able to paint small areas and details, try not to water down the paints too much. Keep them somewhat opaque to be able to spread the color evenly. This project is focused on color play rather than on wet-on-wet techniques as seen in previous projects, so enjoy the "coloring inside the lines" style!

This project's pattern is available as a bonus digital download! See page 14.

LET'S PRACTICE

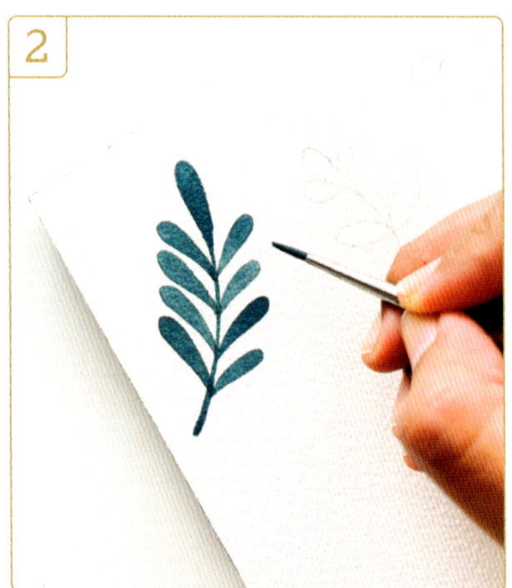

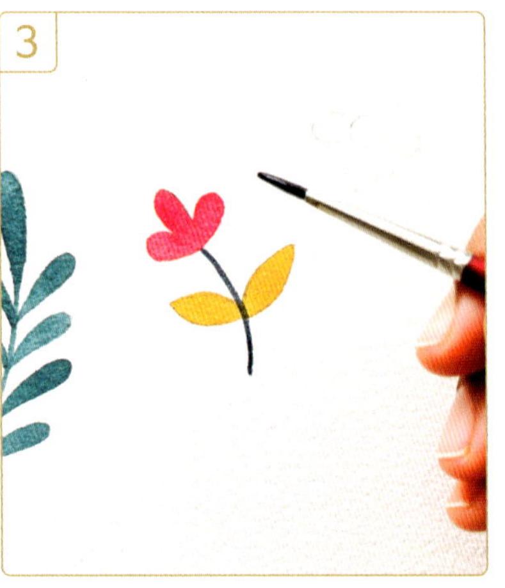

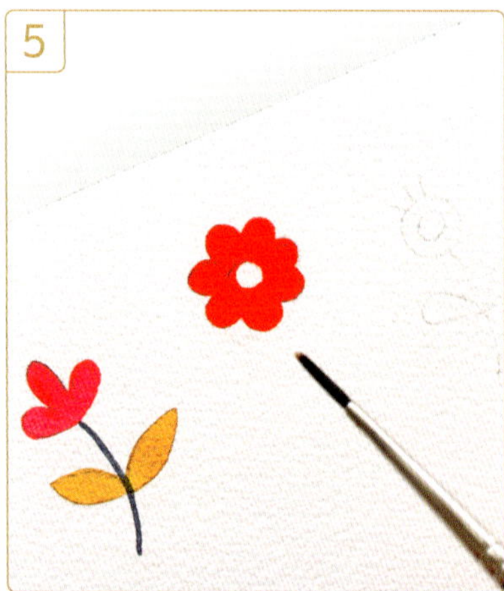

1 **Sketch flowers.** Using a pencil, draw some basic flower and greenery shapes as shown so that you can practice painting small shapes in a controlled manner. Lighten the pencil marks before you begin painting.

2 **Paint the leafy branch.** Pick a color and fill in the leafy branch shape using a small round brush. I used Cobalt Blue Green and a size 2 round brush here.

3 **Paint the first flower.** Let's paint the next shape using some different colors. I used Primary Red Magenta for the petals, Yellow Ochre for the leaves, and Payne's Gray for the stem. Make sure the paint is not too runny.

4 **Paint the floating flower outline.** Let's paint the next floral shape. Start by outlining the flower in Sandal Red. Hold the brush upright to be able to draw this thin outline.

5 **Finish the floating flower.** Now go ahead and fill in the flower with the red paint, leaving a small white circle open in the center.

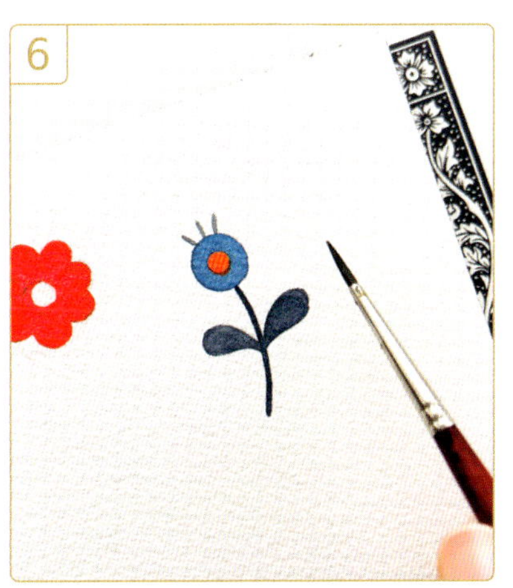

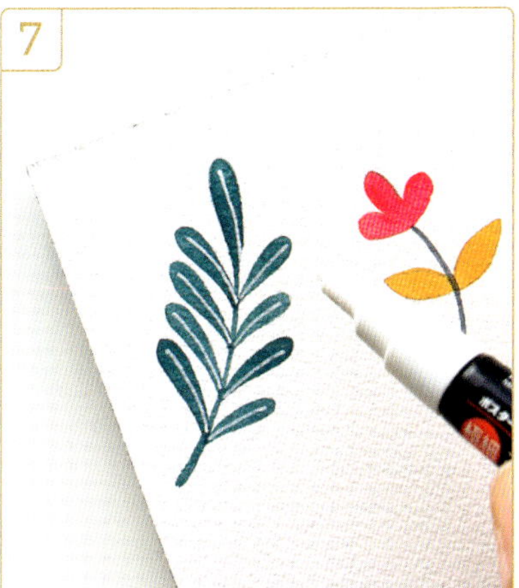

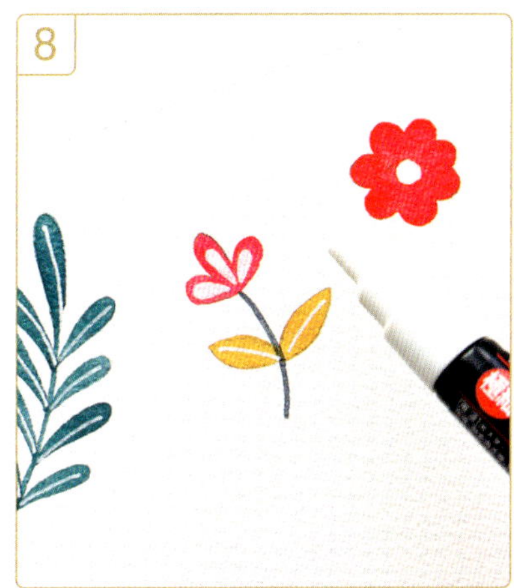

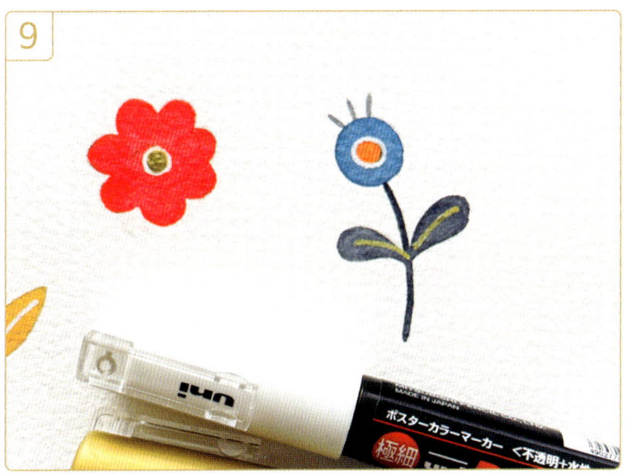

6 **Paint the final flower.** For this flower, use strongly contrasting colors—blue and orange—for the bud and gray for the stems and leaves. Wait to fill in the orange dot until after the blue layer has dried, to prevent the two colors from blending.

7 **Add white details.** Let all the shapes dry completely. Then it's time to draw some details using a white paint pen. Holding the pen upright, draw veins in the center of each of the leaves. The leafy branch instantly looks detailed and bold.

8 **Continue adding white details.** For the next shape, draw some layered white petals on top of the pink ones and a vein in the center of each of the leaves. Small details like these can instantly lift the mood of your designs.

9 **Add gold details.** Switch to a gold paint pen. Add details to the remaining flowers: gold in the center of the red flower and gold for leaf veins in the last flower.

10 **Freehand some more gold elements.** Try doodling a couple of filler shapes like these using the gold paint pen. These will be great for filling white gaps in the final piece.

Let's Relax

Let's talk a bit about folk florals. We are taking full liberty in this design to use bold and vibrant color combinations. We are focusing on enhancing small details using contrasting colors and then using pens to add additional intricate details without stressing your skills or your wrist. Simply filling in colors inside lines brings a different kind of joy. It is a relaxing process where you can completely get involved in the flow of choosing colors one after the other and forget about everything else!

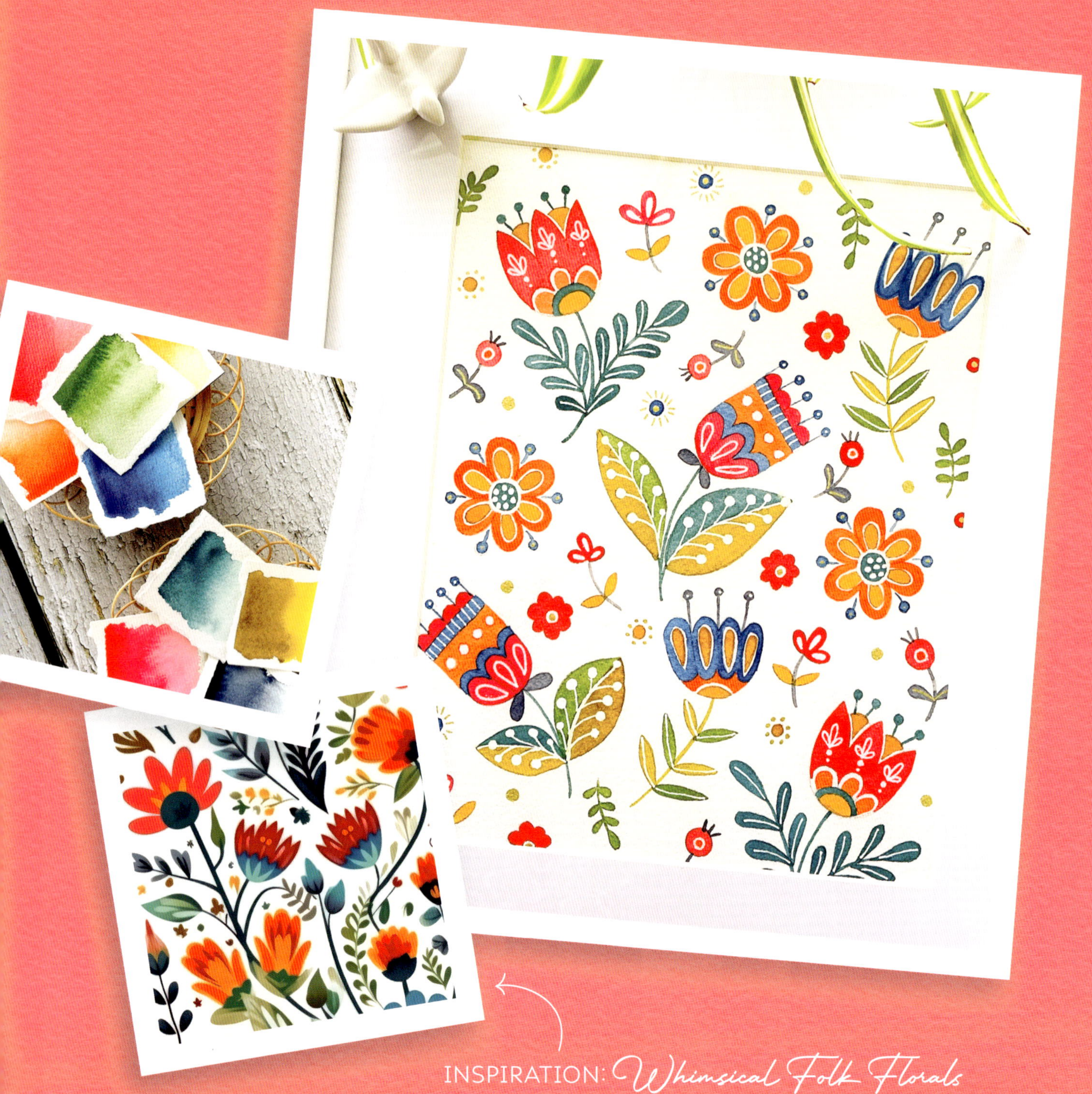

INSPIRATION: *Whimsical Folk Florals*

1 **Draw a pattern.** Re-create the sketch I have provided here, referring to the full-page photo of the finished project if you need to see the details larger. You can also download the digital pattern linework and trace it on your paper (see page 14).

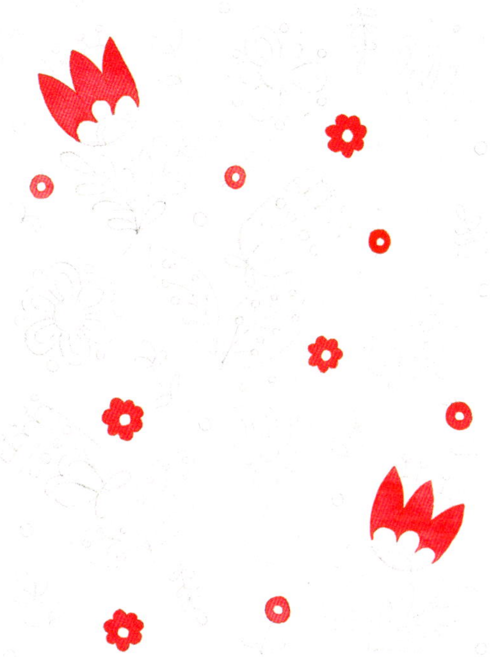

2 **Paint red sections.** Mix each color you'll be using. Don't water down the pigments too much. Start with red. Paint two big flowers and a few small ones to maintain the color balance. You can either paint the same flowers I did or something else of your choice.

3 **Paint blue-green sections.** Up next, I chose Cobalt Blue Green to paint the leaves of the big flowers. The idea is to start slowly and fill in colors one by one, evenly distributing them across the page.

4 **Paint yellow sections.** Use Yellow Ochre to paint some inside sections of certain flowers as well some small filler elements in between flowers.

Let's Paint

5 **Paint blue and orange sections.** Paint two big flowers blue and orange as shown. Also use this orange in smaller sections of the big red flowers.

6 **Paint green sections.** Let's bring in some green now and paint the small filler leafy branches and some leaves of the big blue-orange flowers.

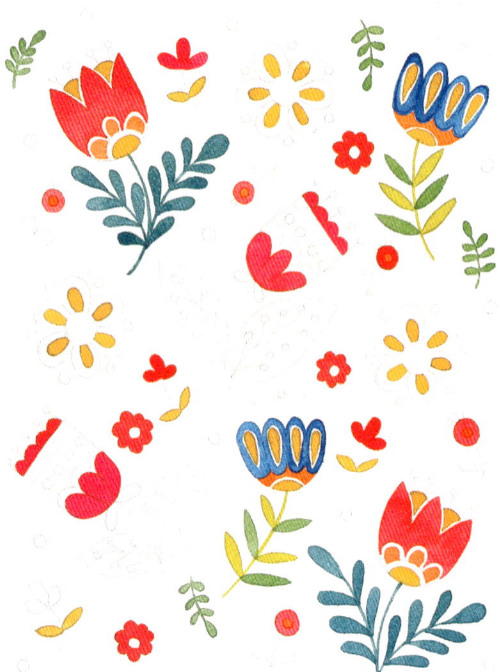

7 **Paint pink and green-gold sections.** Use Primary Red Magenta for some sections of the last two big flowers and filler buds and some Green Gold to fill in some leaves. Make sure that each of the six big flower motifs is painted using different color combinations.

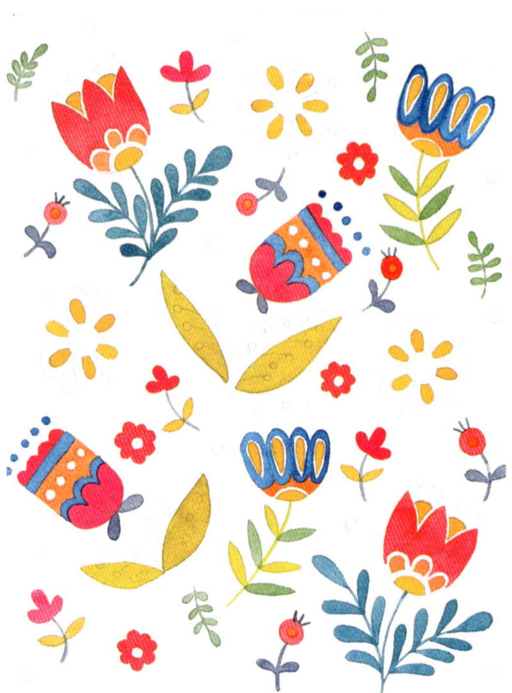

8 **Finish the last two big flowers.** Use orange, blue, and green shades to paint the remaining two big flowers. Don't forget to switch between brushes while painting bigger and smaller sections of the flowers. I have used sizes 1, 2, and 4 round brushes.

9 **Finish the remaining flowers and leaves.** Use orange for the remaining flowers and the remaining shades of green to paint the two big leaves. At this point, you will easily be able to identify colors that have been used enough and need to be balanced out.

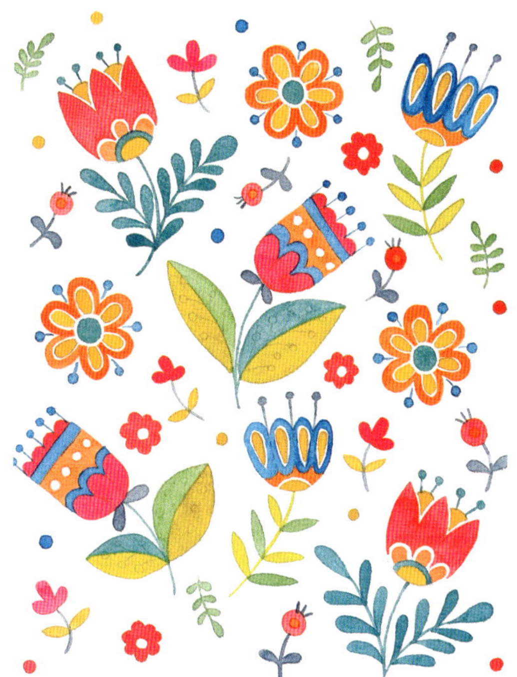

10 **Move on to the background.** Paint the filler background dots using yellow, blue, and red. Paint any other small sections inside the big flowers and finish filling up all the sections. Let everything dry before you proceed to the next step.

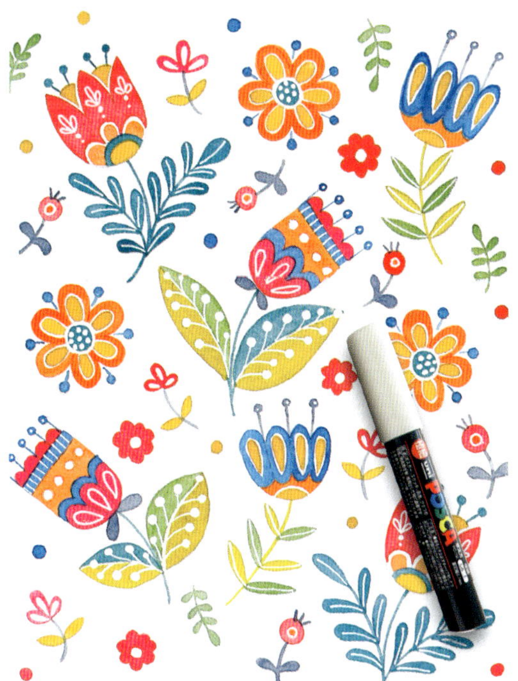

11 **Add white details.** Go through each motif, big and small, to re-create my doodles, or use your own creative ideas. I have added veins to leaves, added polka dots in the center of the orange flowers, overlapped petals with some white petals, and so on.

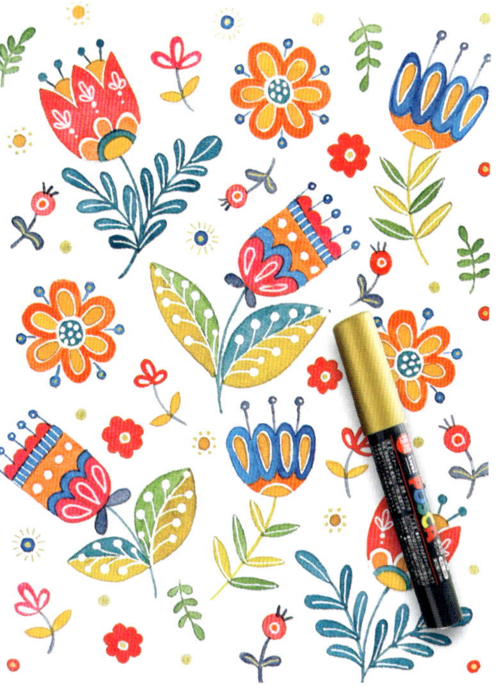

12 **Add gold details.** In any remaining big white gaps, add some freehand gold shapes. Incorporating these small elements instantly ties the pattern together and makes it look uniformly distributed across the page.

Let's Paint

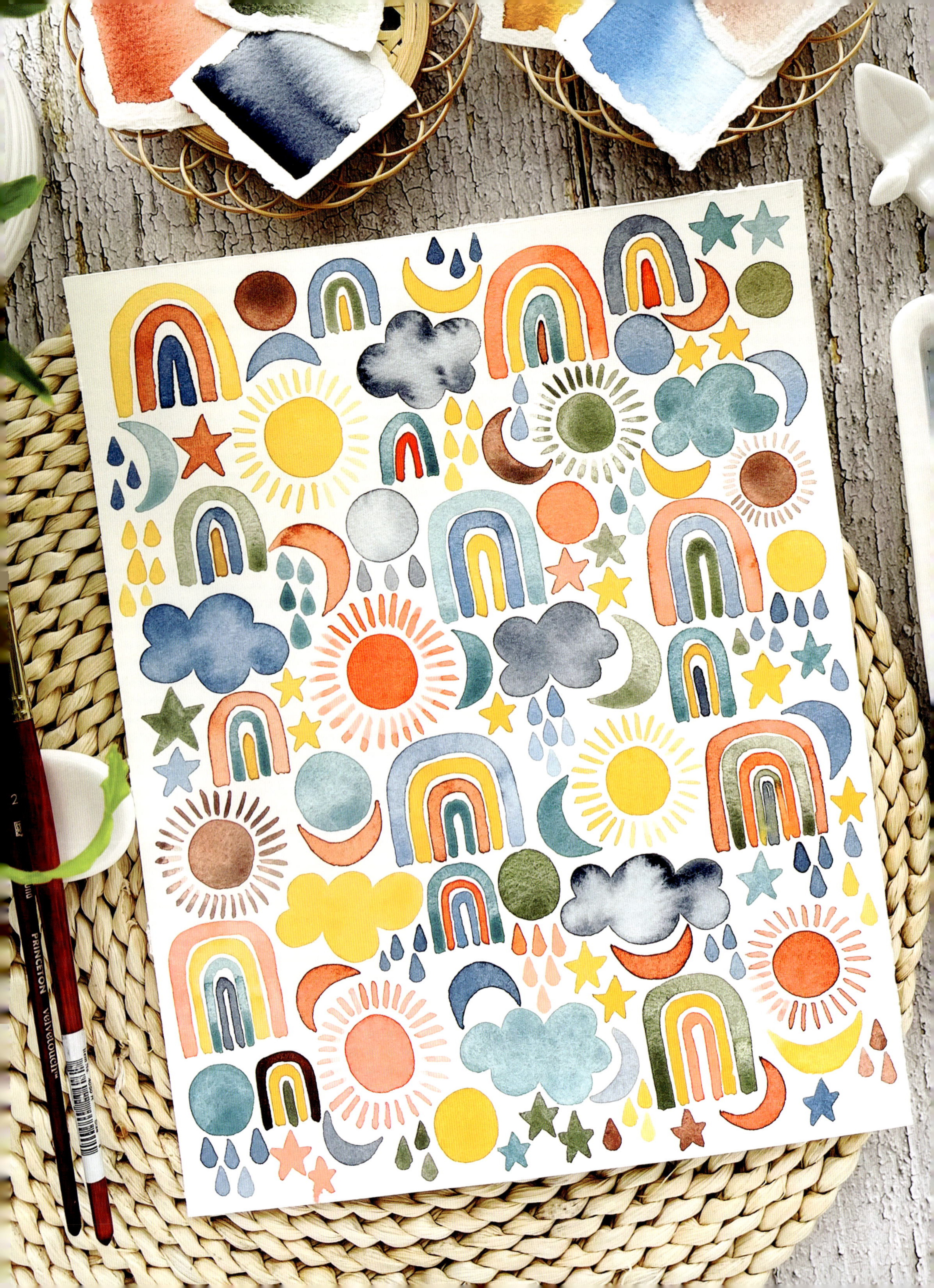

Boho Skies

In this project, we will use boho colors to paint some fun sky elements such as rainbows, clouds, stars, moons, suns, etc. Boho colors are a combination of earthy hues paired with neutral or warm colors and sometimes also combined with slightly neutral-toned cool colors such as greens and blues. This is a very interesting color pairing, and I am so excited to use this modern and contemporary color palette for this project. For this piece, we will focus on painting the individual shapes neatly rather than on the wet-on-wet technique or on blending colors.

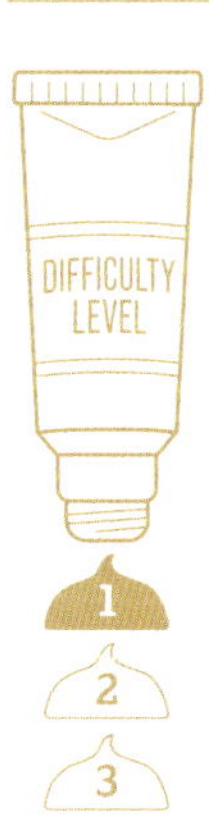

MATERIALS

BRUSHES: Size 6 round brush; size 2 round brush

PAPER: 8" x 10" (20 x 25 cm), hot pressed

COLORS:

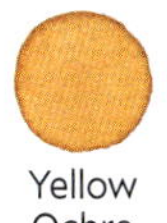 Yellow Ochre

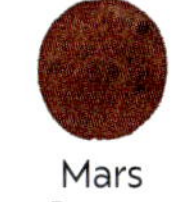 Mars Brown

 Payne's Gray

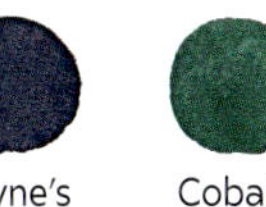 Cobalt Blue Green

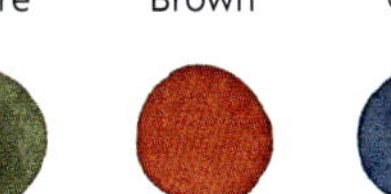 Hooker's Green

 Dragon's Blood

 Cerulean Blue + Payne's Gray*

Primary Red Magenta + Cadmium Orange + Yellow Ochre*

***COLOR NOTES:**

Cerulean Blue + Payne's Gray:
aim for a darker shade close to indigo

Primary Red Magenta + Cadmium Orange + Yellow Ochre:
aim for a shade similar to terra-cotta / peachy brown

TIP: We are going to paint this pattern without any prior pencil work, so use the practice session to build muscle memory. Remember that you can always move the paper around to deal with tricky spaces on the paper while drawing certain shapes.

143

LET'S PRACTICE

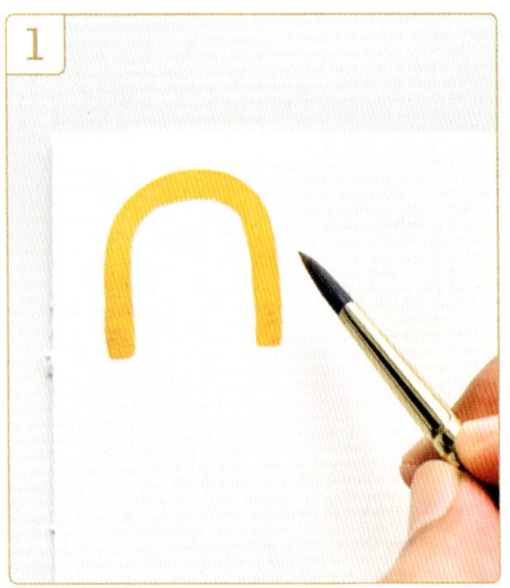

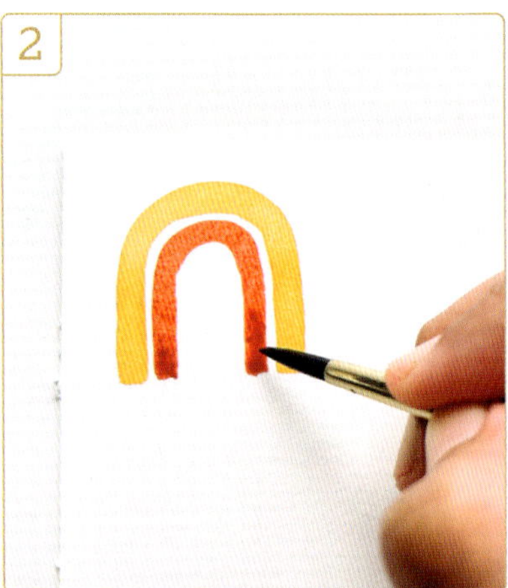

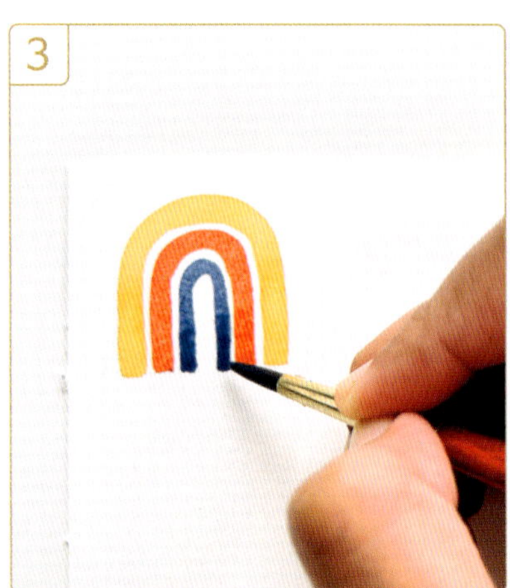

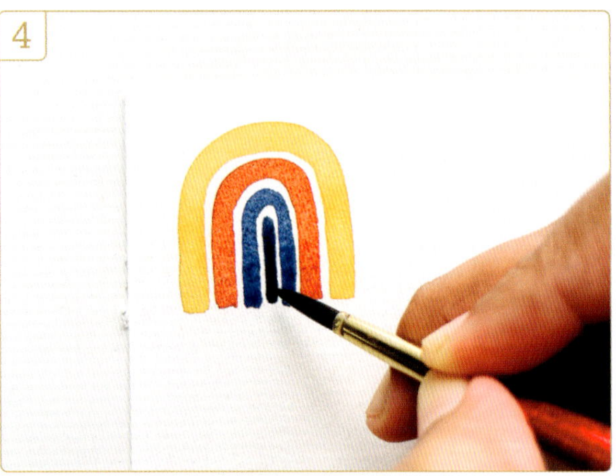

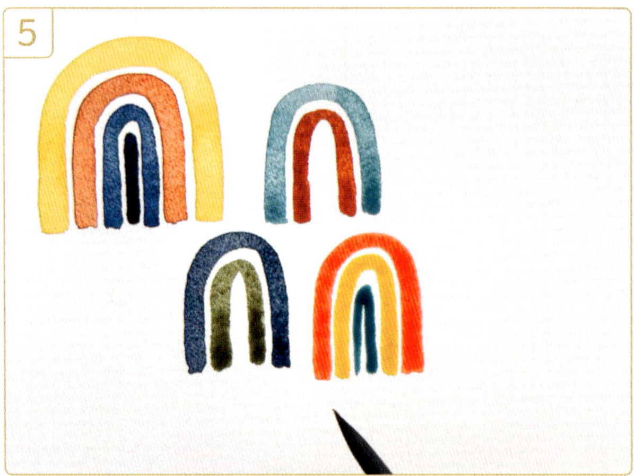

MODERN WATERCOLOR WORKSHOP

1 Start a rainbow. Using a size 6 round brush and a color of your choice, draw a tall semi-circle. If needed, even it out with the tip of the brush to make it uniformly thick.

2 Paint the second arc. Load your brush with the next color and, leaving a small white gap, draw another semi-circle within the first one.

3 Paint the third arc. Leaving another small white gap, draw one more semi-circle in a new color within the previous semi-circle.

4 Complete the rainbow. At this point you can either stop or choose to fill in the center with a small stroke using the next color from your palette.

5 Try different color combinations. Practice painting a few more rainbows using different colors from the palette. Paint small and big ones. You can continue using the size 6 round brush.

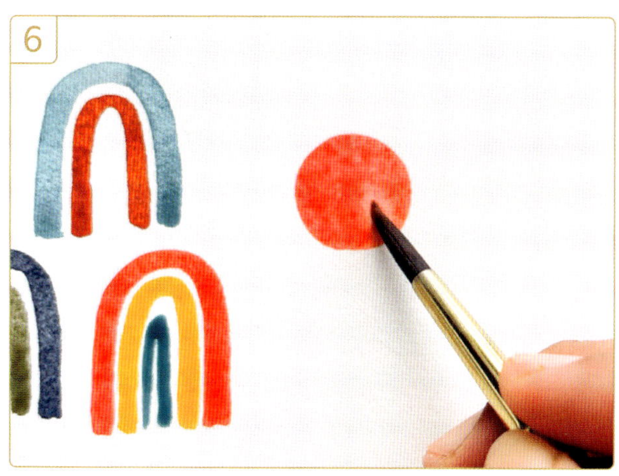 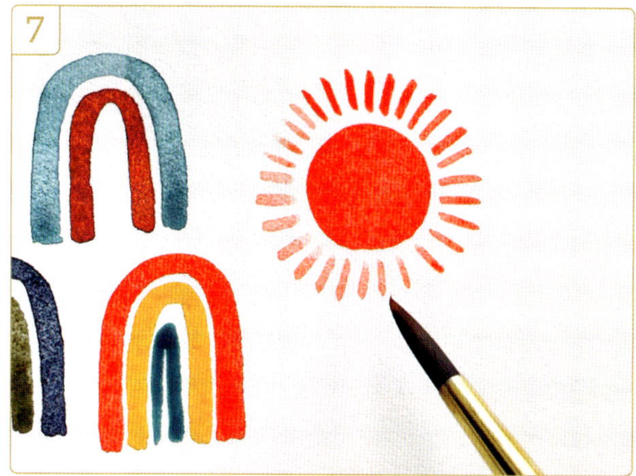

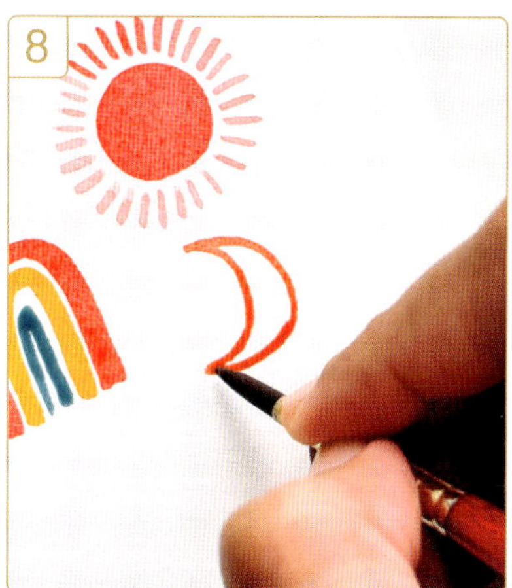  

6 **Start a sun.** Load your brush with a color of your choice and draw a medium-sized, filled-in circle.

7 **Add the rays.** Leaving a small white gap around the circle, draw short dash lines distributed around the circle to form the rays of the sun.

8 **Outline a moon.** Let's draw a crescent moon next. Start by drawing a C-shaped curve for the inner curve of the moon. Then join the first C-shaped curve with another C-shaped curve that is bigger and more curved.

9 **Fill in the moon.** Fill in the crescent shape with the same color.

10 **Draw a few more moons.** Draw a few more crescent moons at different angles using different colors.

Continues on next page.

LET'S PRACTICE

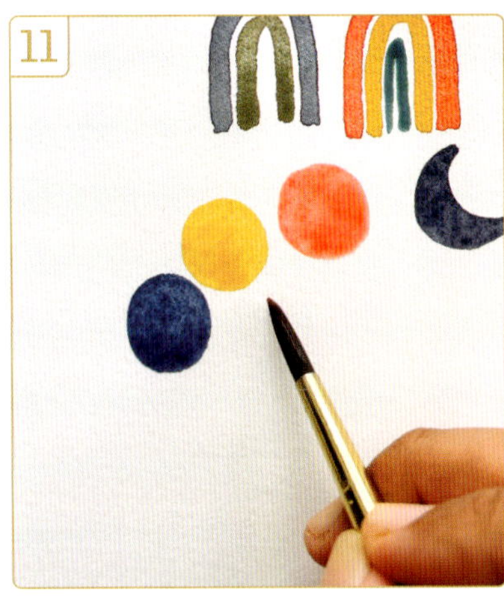

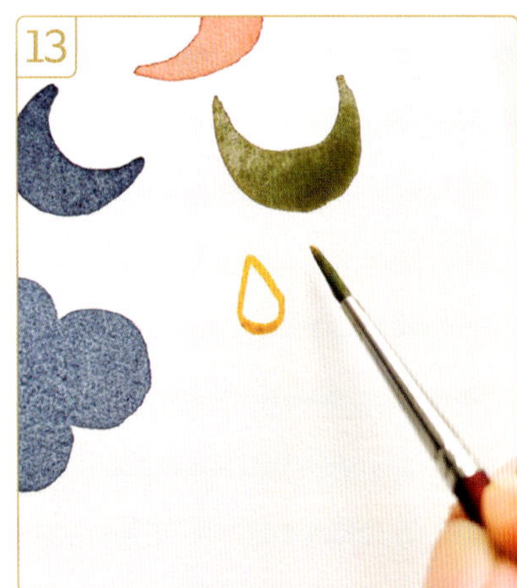

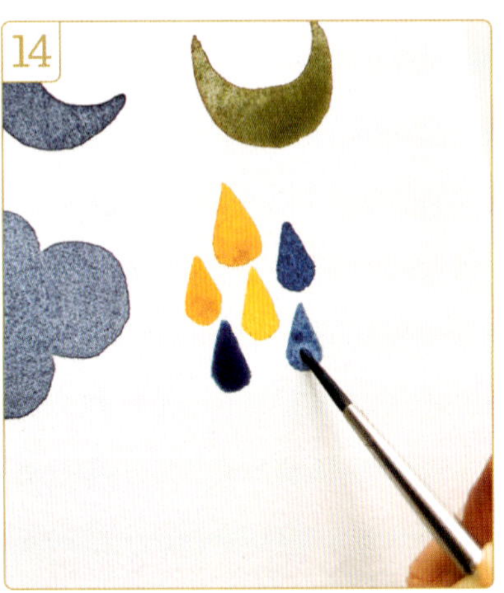

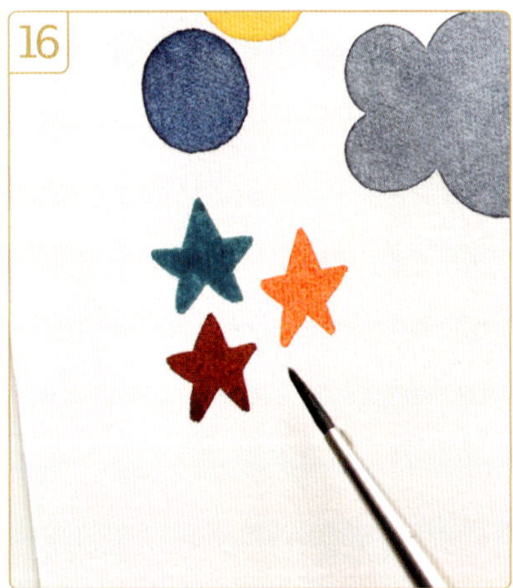

11 Practice drawing circles. We will also be using some circle shapes in the pattern, so paint a few circles using different shades to get the hang of them.

12 Paint a cloud. To paint a cloud, first outline it with C-shaped curves of various sizes all connected to form one fluffy cloud outline. Fill in the cloud with the same color. Keep the size of the cloud in proportion with the other elements.

13 Outline a teardrop. Switch to a small size 2 round brush to be able to draw this tiny shape. Outline a teardrop in your chosen color. Keep the size small compared to the other elements. This will be more of a filler shape to fill white space at the end.

14 Fill in the teardrop. Fill in the teardrop with the same color. Paint a few more teardrops using different colors. They look good if they are grouped together in a cluster.

15 Outline a star. Still using the size 2 round brush, draw a five-pointed star. It does not need to be perfect at all! Keep the size similar to that of the teardrops.

16 Fill in the star. Fill in the star with the same color, then paint a few more stars. You can paint scattered stars across the patterns to fill in small, empty spaces.

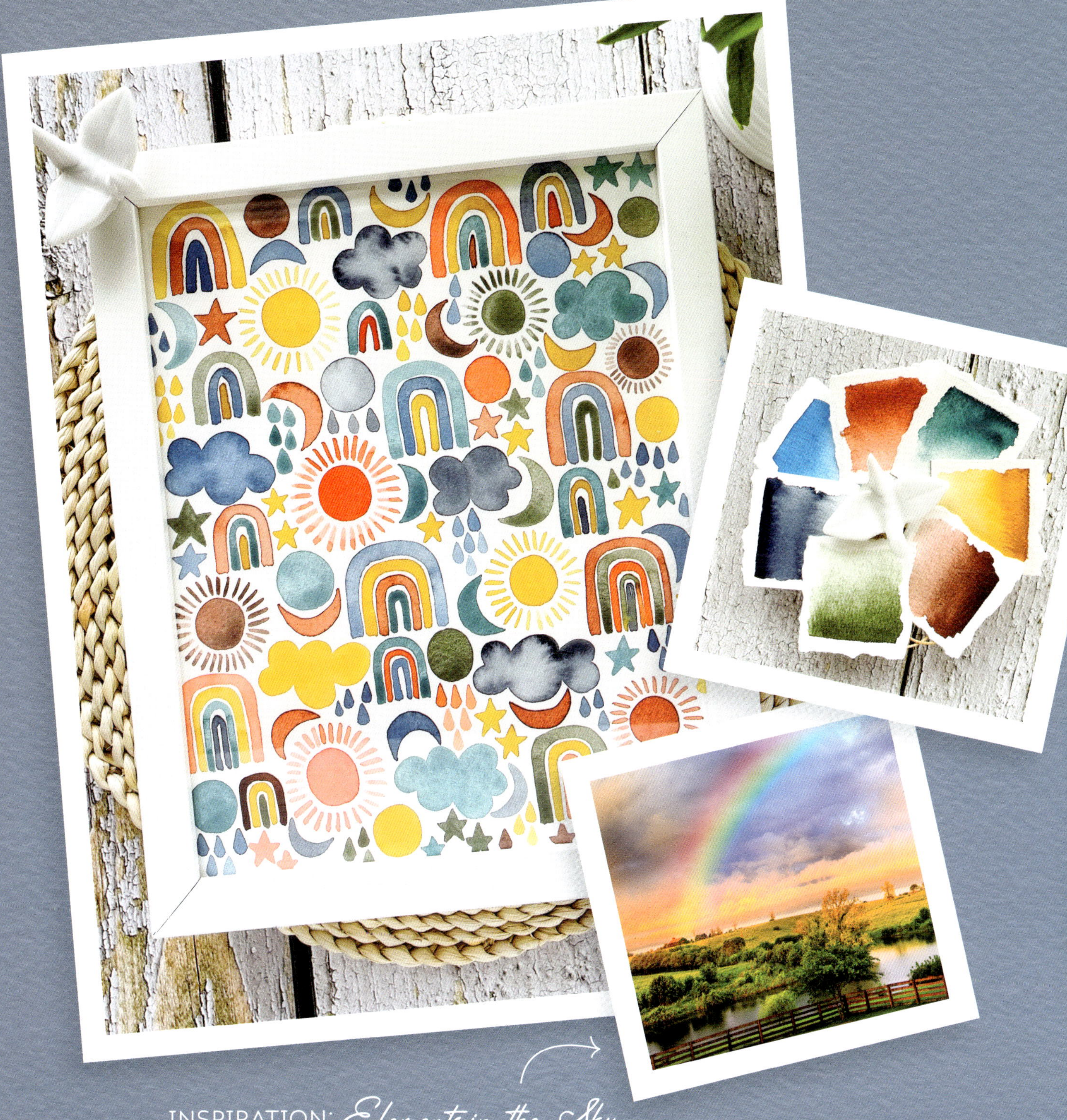

Let's Relax

The boho style has a relaxed, carefree, and minimalistic attitude through its simple use of earthy, warm colors. We will interpret the boho style in our way in this pattern to paint simple and easy shapes that still give the piece a defined theme—in this case, elements found in the sky. I can visualize this pattern being used in nurseries and on baby clothes; are there other applications you can think of for this pattern? I suggest putting on a soundtrack of rainfall or some kind of soothing music to inspire you as you paint this boho sky.

Let's Paint

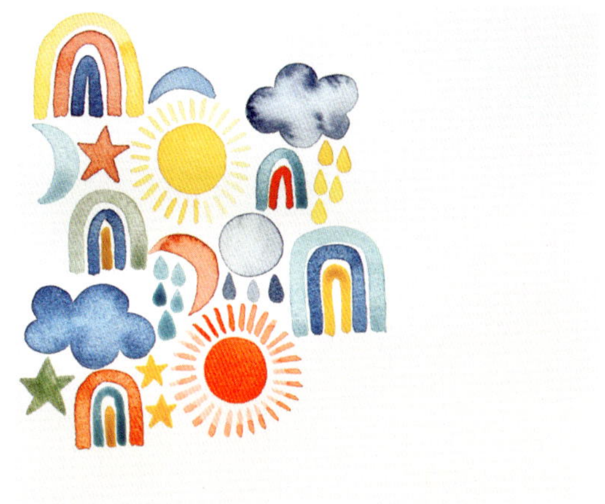

1 **Start placing elements.** Mix your colors. Begin painting from the top left, cycling through each of the elements covered in the practice session. Place them close to each other—ultimately, you want a compact, dense design.

2 **Switch up the colors.** Continue painting more of the same elements but use different colors and arrange them in a different order than the first time around. You can see here how each element looks unique because I switched colors. There is repetition of color and shape, but in a randomized way to add interest.

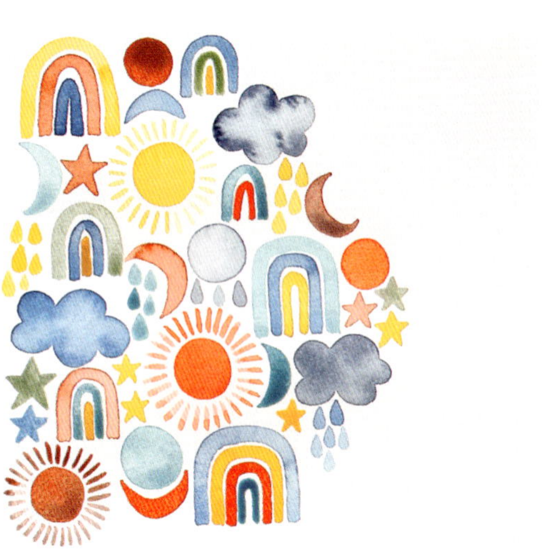

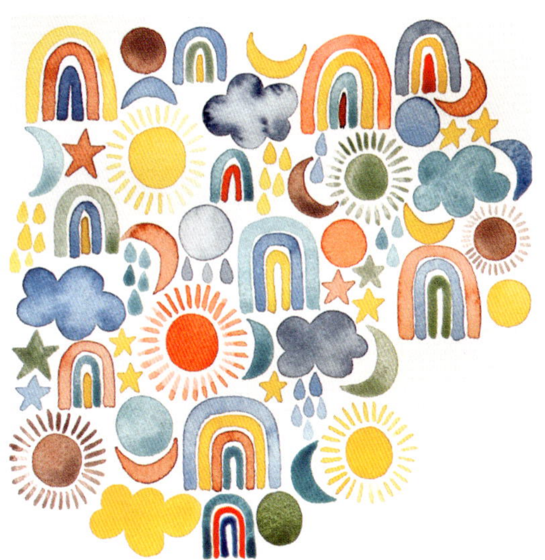

3 **Continue building.** Keep working diagonally down as you fill up the page. Try to balance the shapes by taking a step back after every few minutes to analyze your work. Remember to cycle through all the different shapes, colors, and sizes.

4 **Keep your shapes crisp.** As you come down diagonally, you also need to start filling up the right side of the page. Make sure that the shapes are not touching and blending into each other—for this piece, we want each shape to look sharp and crisp.

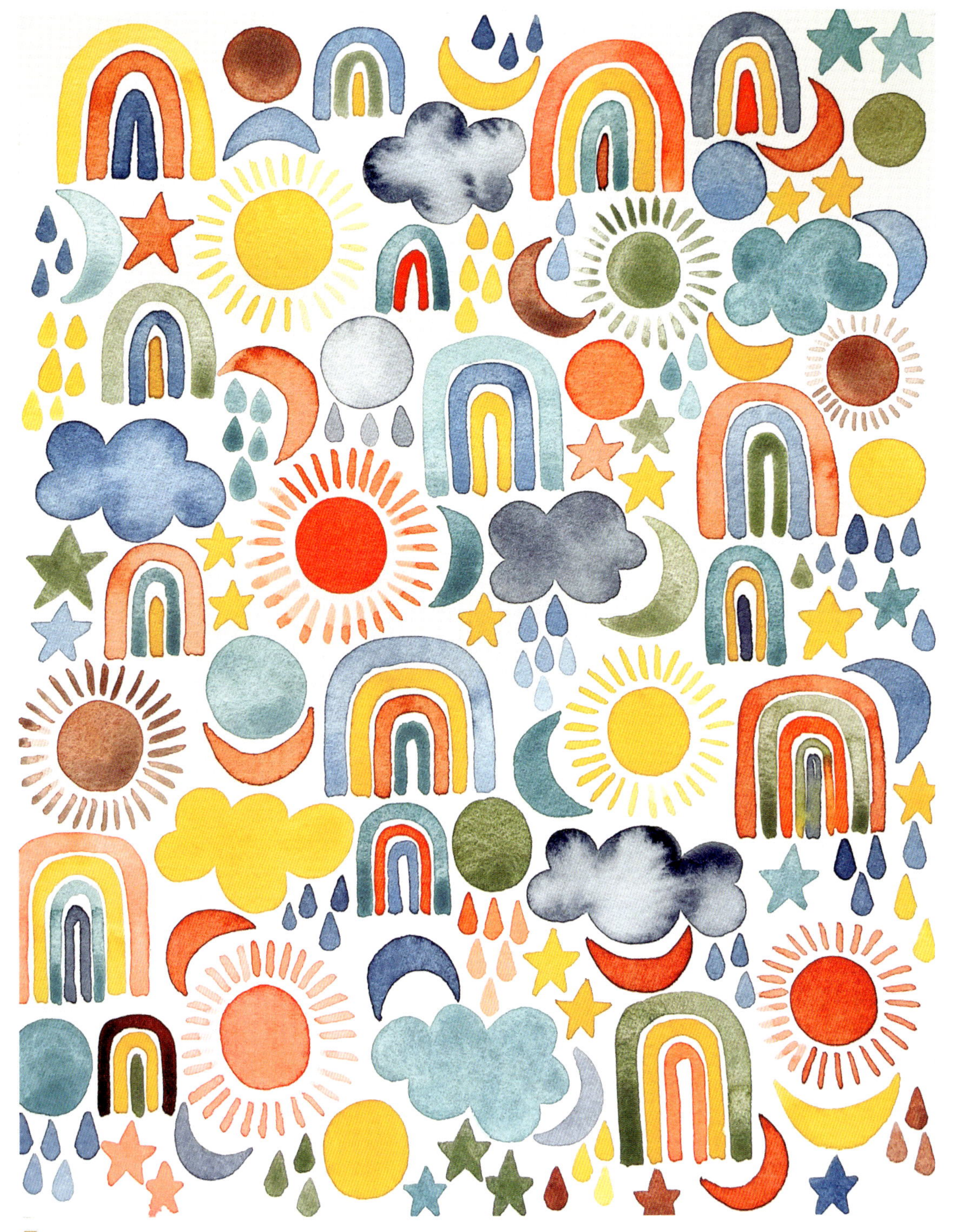

5 **Finish and fill in.** As you finish filling the page, you can go back in and fill any lingering white spaces with the smallest shapes, like teardrops and single stars. Enjoy getting into a meditative state as you finish this project!

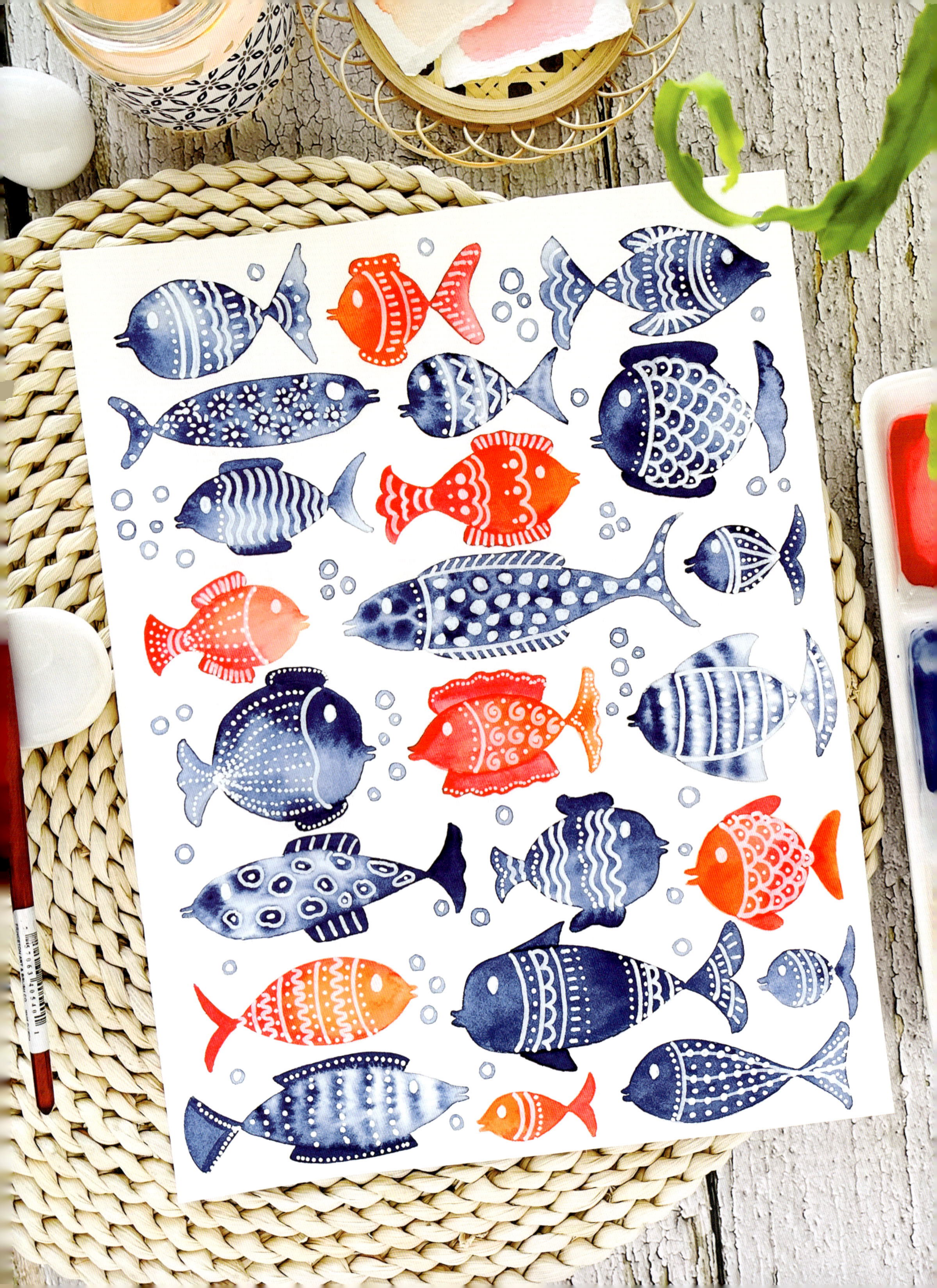

Gone Fishing

Since the emphasis of this set of projects is on exploring abstract, freehand shapes, I thought of these varied fish shapes, which are quite different from what we have explored so far in the previous projects. In this pattern, you'll learn to use watercolors as the base for painting the fish shapes and then to enhance them with fun doodles in white ink or paint.

151

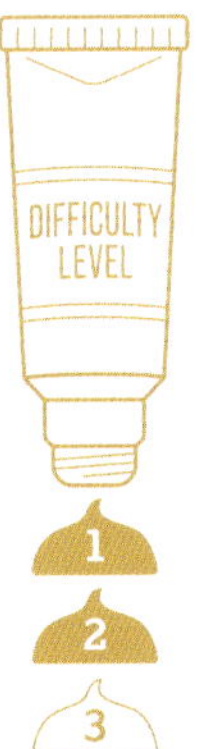

DIFFICULTY LEVEL

1
2
3

MATERIALS

BRUSH: Size 6 round brush

PAPER: 8" x 10" (20 x 25 cm), hot pressed

OTHER: Pencil; gel pens or paint pens in white, 0.7 mm or thicker; you could also use white gouache

COLORS:

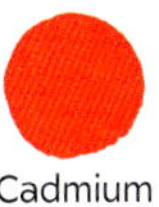

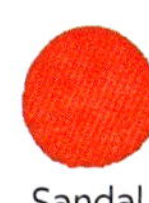

Faience Blue Cadmium Orange Sandal Red

TIP: Make sure to wait for the watercolor layers to dry completely before applying the white ink or paint. If you don't have white paint pens, you can use white gouache. Make sure your gouache is nice and creamy—don't water it down too much or you will end up mixing it with the underlying watercolor layer.

This project's pattern is available as a bonus digital download! See page 14.

LET'S PRACTICE

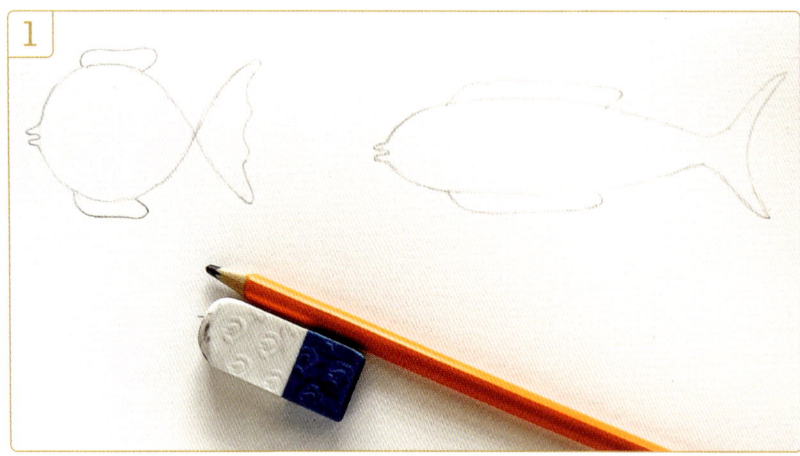

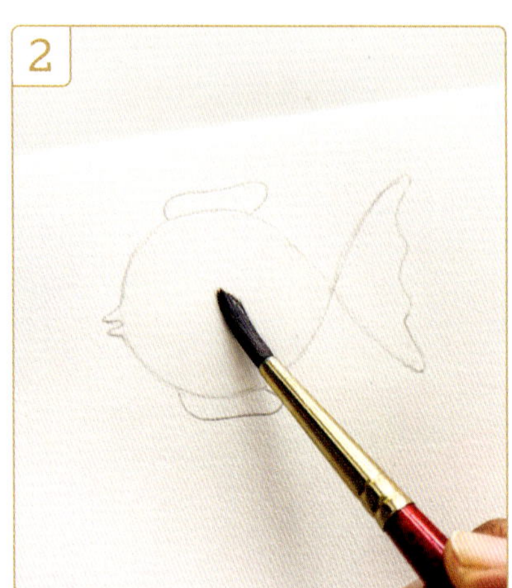

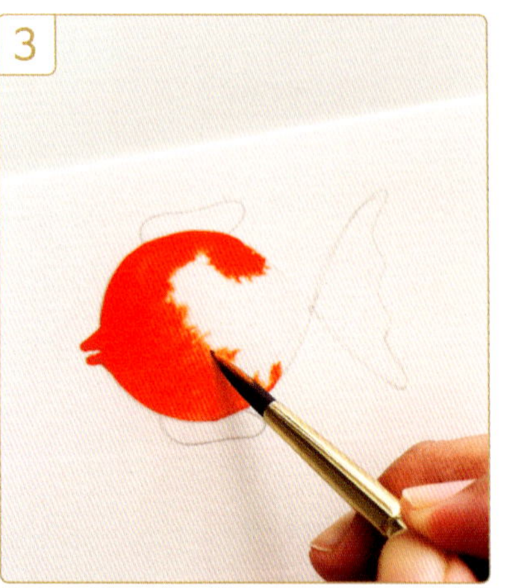

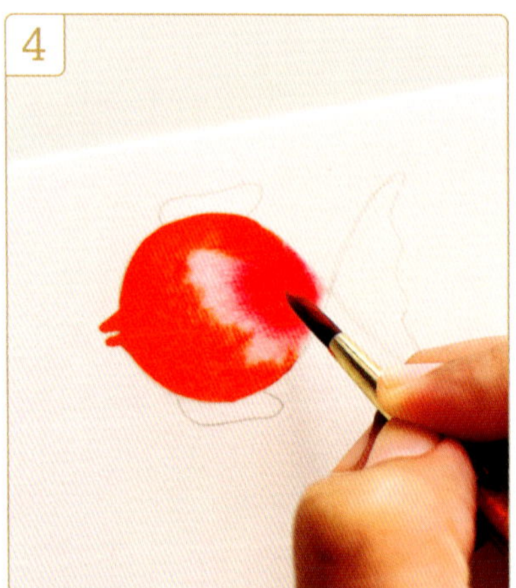

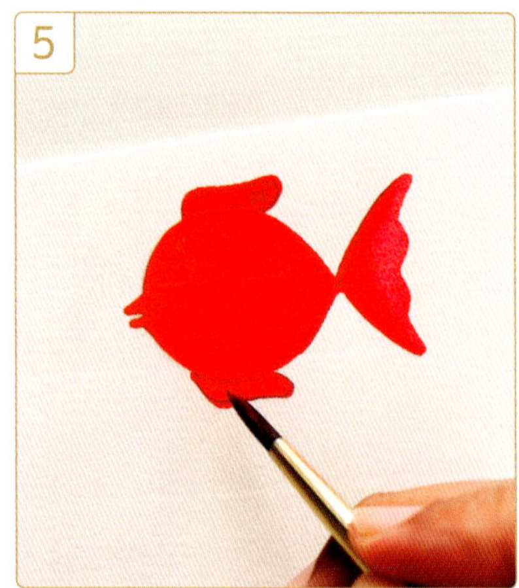

1 **Draw or trace some fish.** Use a pencil to freehand-draw two rough fish shapes as shown.

2 **Add a layer of water to one fish.** Load your brush with clean water and apply a thin layer on the leftmost fish's body only (not the fins or tail).

3 **Apply some color.** Load your brush with orange and apply it to half of the wet surface of the fish. The color will instantly start spreading across the wet area.

4 **Apply a second color.** Rinse your brush clean and load it with red. You can keep it slightly creamy to get a bright and saturated look. Apply the red on the other half of the fish and let the red bleed into the orange.

5 **Finish the fish.** Blend the two colors with a clean, moist brush. Don't use too much water while blending, to avoid making a wet puddle. You want a smooth, creamy blend. Paint the fins and tail using the same red color.

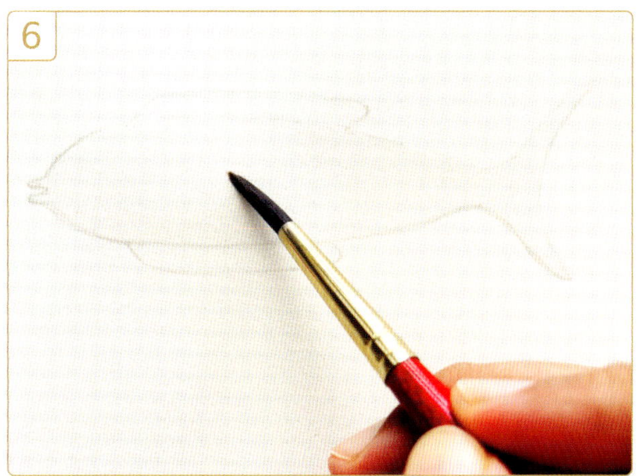

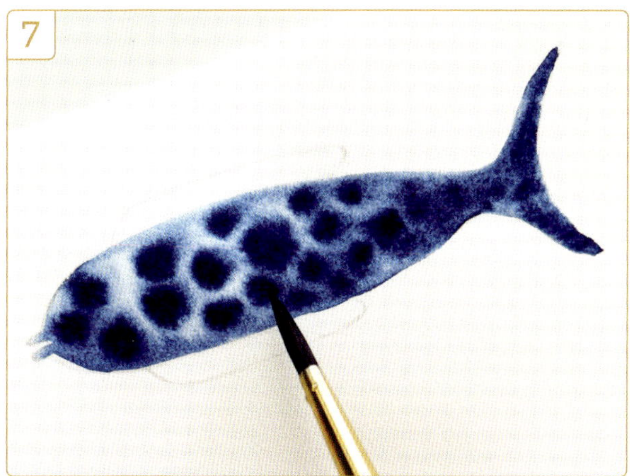

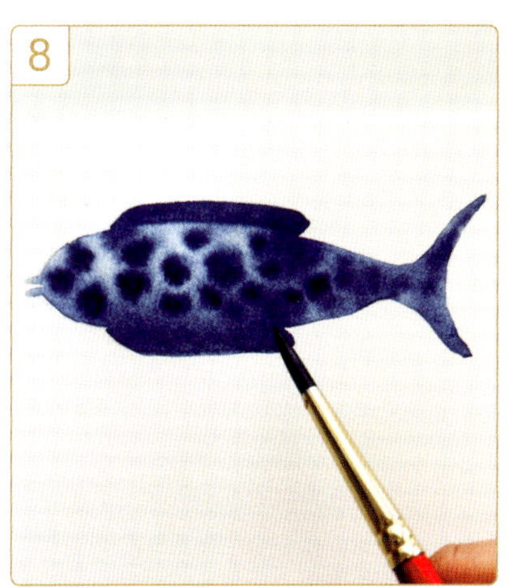

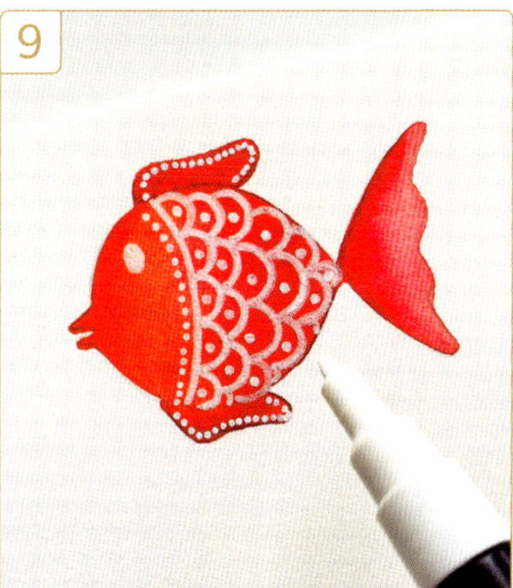

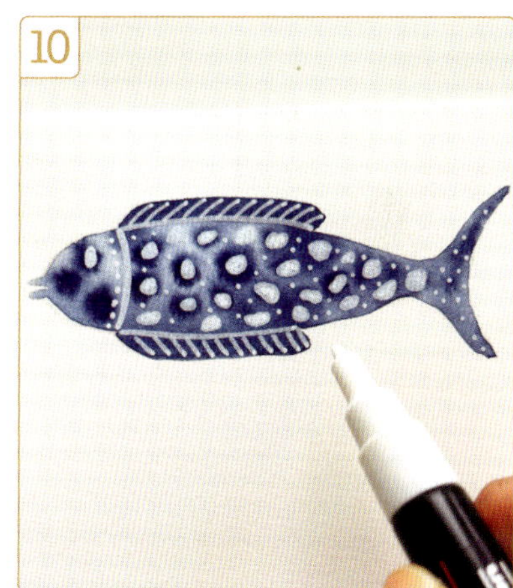

6 **Apply water to the second fish.** Move on to the other fish now. Load your brush with clean water and again apply it all over the fish's body (but not the fins).

7 **Apply color in dabs.** Load your brush with creamy (not too diluted) blue paint. Then apply the color in a dabbing fashion so that it creates blotches on the wet surface as you go. Leave space between the dots to create contrast as the color spreads.

8 **Paint the fins.** Wait for the body layer to dry at least partially, then go ahead and paint the fins using the same shade of blue.

9 **Add white details to the first fish.** Check to see if your first fish has completely dried. Once it has, use a white paint pen to doodle some designs on it as shown. I created fish scales and dots as well as an eye.

10 **Add white details to the second fish.** Once the second fish has completely dried, add details to it too. Experiment with different patterns. You can refer to my design or make up your own—there are tons of ways to decorate these fish shapes!

Let's Relax

To keep it easy and relaxing, this piece uses just three colors. Take your time painting each of the fish shapes and thoroughly enjoying the satisfying process of doodling at the end. For inspiration, you can look at pictures of beautiful fish found around the world and use those color combinations and designs in your own pattern. Have you ever been to an aquarium and watched all sorts of schools of fish that look so vibrant and colorful swimming in deep-blue waters? Their simple yet graceful movements in the water are calming and relaxing to view. Try to channel that soothing energy as you paint.

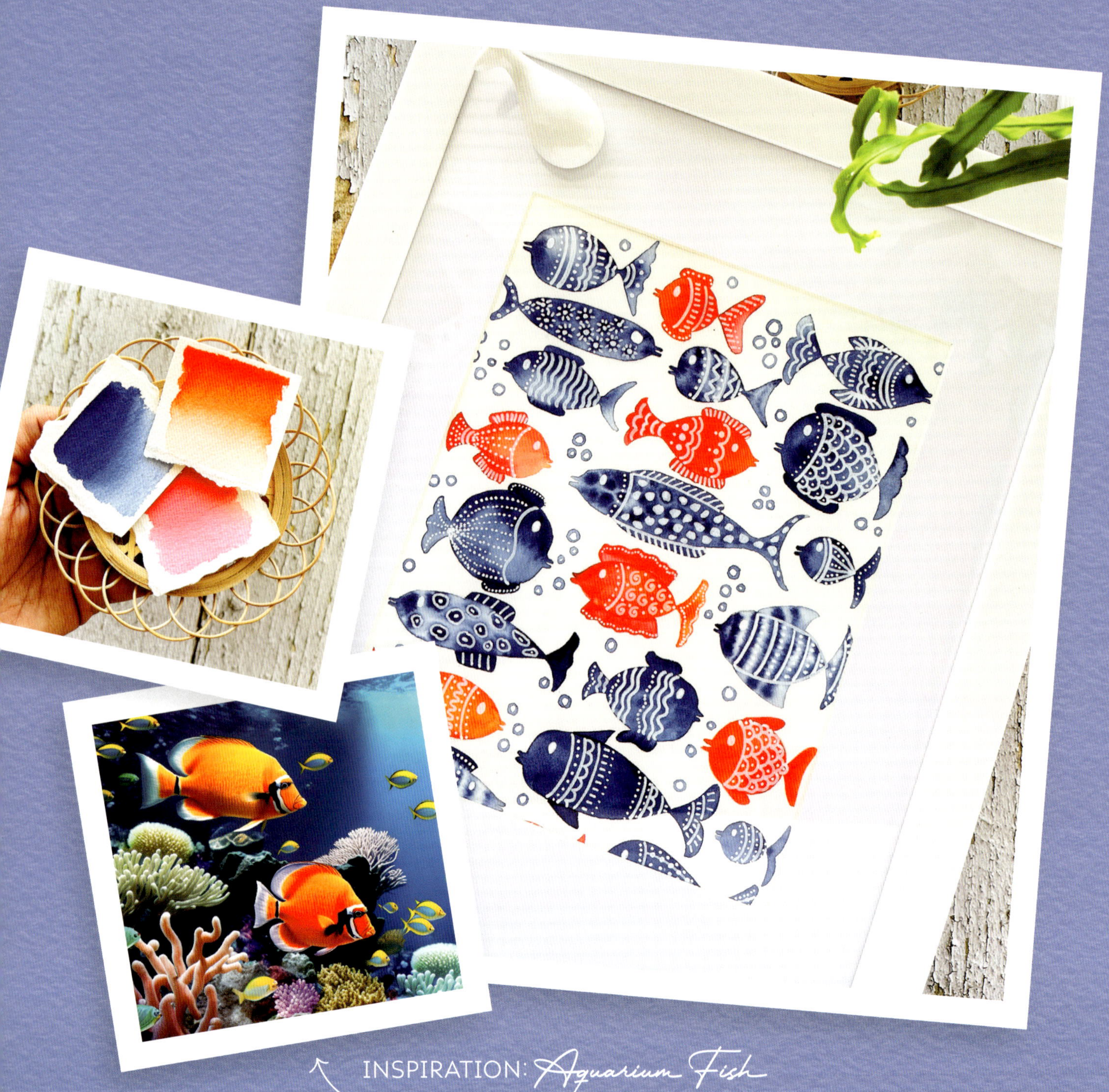

INSPIRATION: *Aquarium Fish*

1 **Draw a pattern.** Re-create the basic sketch I have provided here. You can also download the digital pattern linework and trace it on your paper (see page 14). Of course, you can also create your own composition using different fish shapes!

Let's Paint

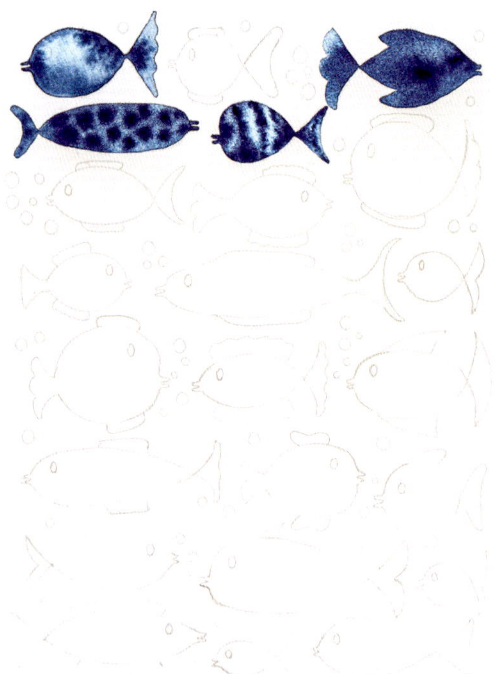

2 **Start painting the blue fish.** The plan for this piece is to include just one red fish in each row. Paint one fish at a time using the techniques you learned in the practice session. I used a saturated, deep shade of blue without watering it down too much.

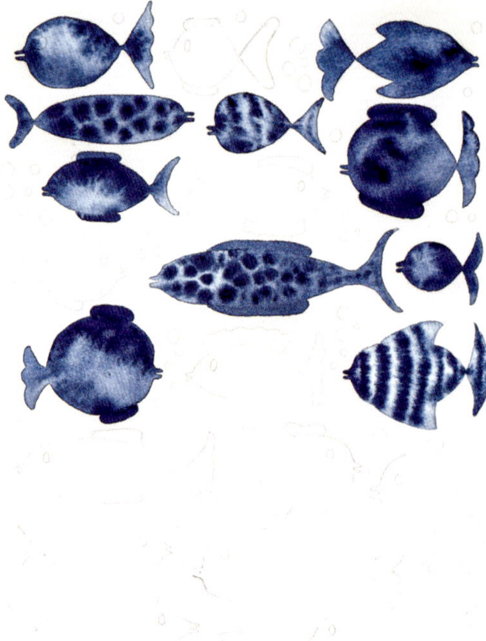

3 **Paint more blue fish.** Try a new technique: blue vertical stripes on a wet surface. Keep up the variety as you continue to paint the blue fish. That way, not all of them will look the same. Remember to leave some fish unpainted so they can be painted red later.

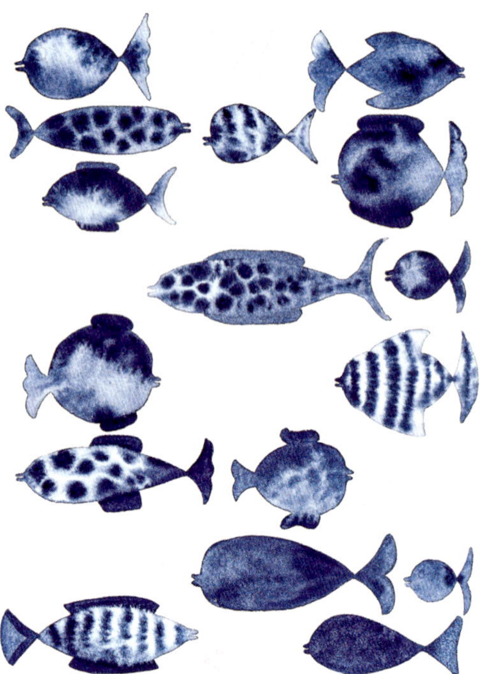

4 **Finish the blue fish.** Continue painting the blue fish until you reach the bottom of the page. Make sure to evenly distribute the different fish textures side to side and top to bottom—you don't want all stripes in one area and all spots in another!

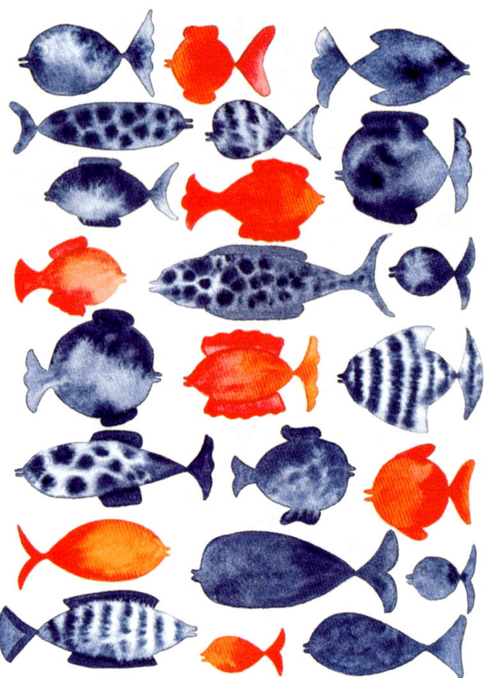

5 **Paint the red fish.** Make sure the blue fish are dry enough that you won't accidentally smear them as you go in to paint the red fish. For these, I didn't create any textures—I simply painted them in the ombré style with a graded wash of orange and red.

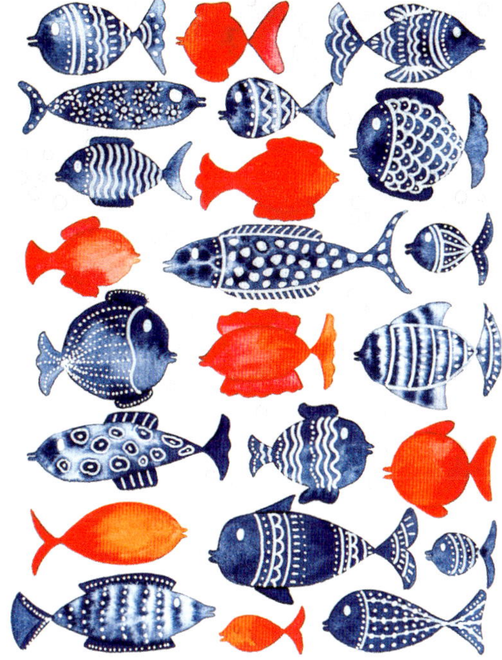

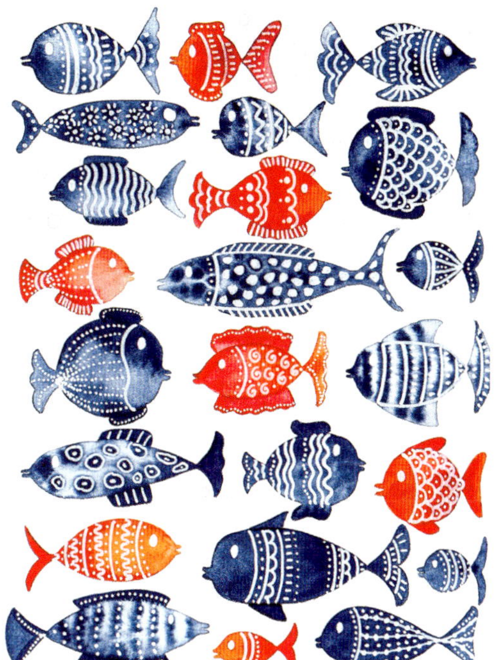

6 **Add white designs to the blue fish.**
When the blue fish are completely dry, use
your paint pen to add details. Make good use
of stripes, dots, curvy lines, dashed lines,
fish scales, and mosaic tiles to make intricate
patterns. Don't forget to mark each fish's eye!

7 **Add white designs to the red fish.**
Once they are completely dry, add white
detailing to the red fish too. You can keep the
design sparser to make sure the red color pops
out nicely.

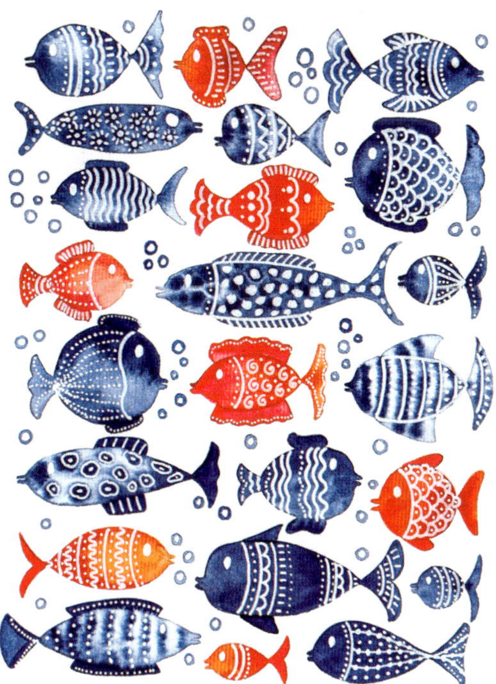

8 **Add filler bubbles.** Paint little bubbles
in the spaces between the fish using the same
shade of blue but more watered down. Adding
small details like these bubbles will instantly fill
up the page nicely.

Let's Paint

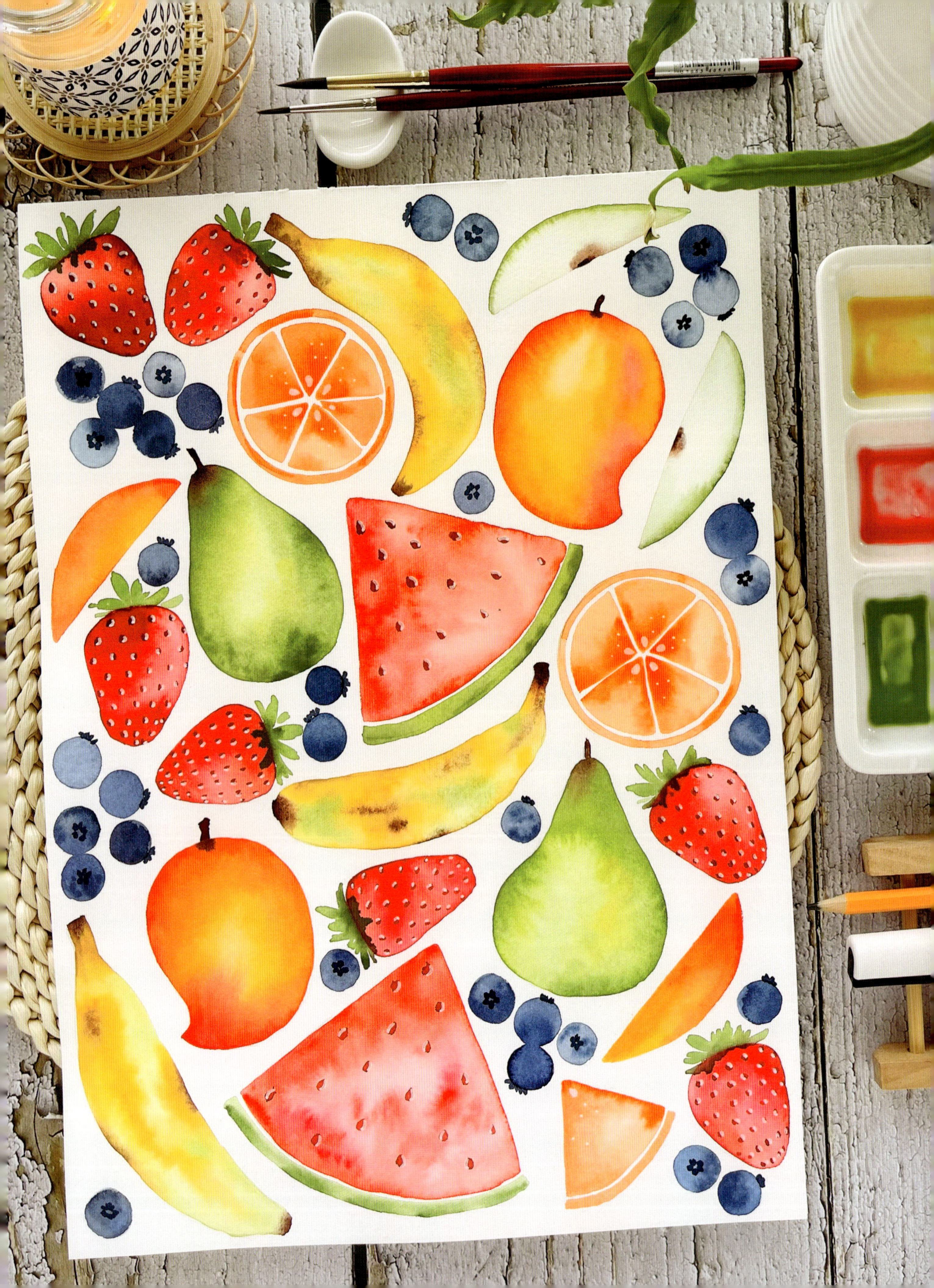

Fruitful Finds

How could we possibly skip painting fruits? Fruits come in a variety of shapes, so they provide a great opportunity for exploring color and shape through the process of learning watercolors. In this project, we are laying down fruits in a patterned manner. The final result looks absolutely sumptuous and mouthwatering in all its bright and vibrant colors.

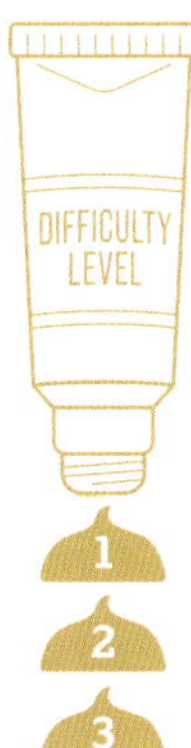

MATERIALS

BRUSHES: Size 6 round brush; size 2 round brush

PAPER: 10" x 14" (25 x 35 cm), hot pressed

OTHER: Gel pens or paint pens in white, 0.7 mm or thicker; you could also use white gouache

COLORS:

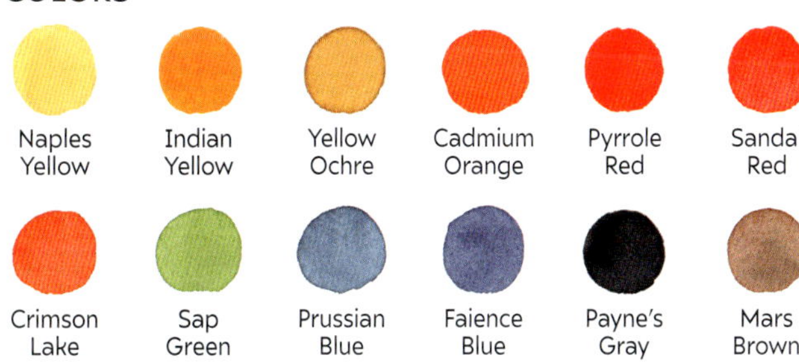

Naples Yellow	Indian Yellow	Yellow Ochre	Cadmium Orange	Pyrrole Red	Sandal Red
Crimson Lake	Sap Green	Prussian Blue	Faience Blue	Payne's Gray	Mars Brown

TIP: We will be using the wet-on-wet technique to the max for each of the fruits, so be sure to have a jar of clean water at the ready for laying down the initial washes. Blend the colors softly while they are wet to bring out the shadows and highlights on the surfaces of the fruits.

This project's pattern is available as a bonus digital download! See page 14.

LET'S PRACTICE

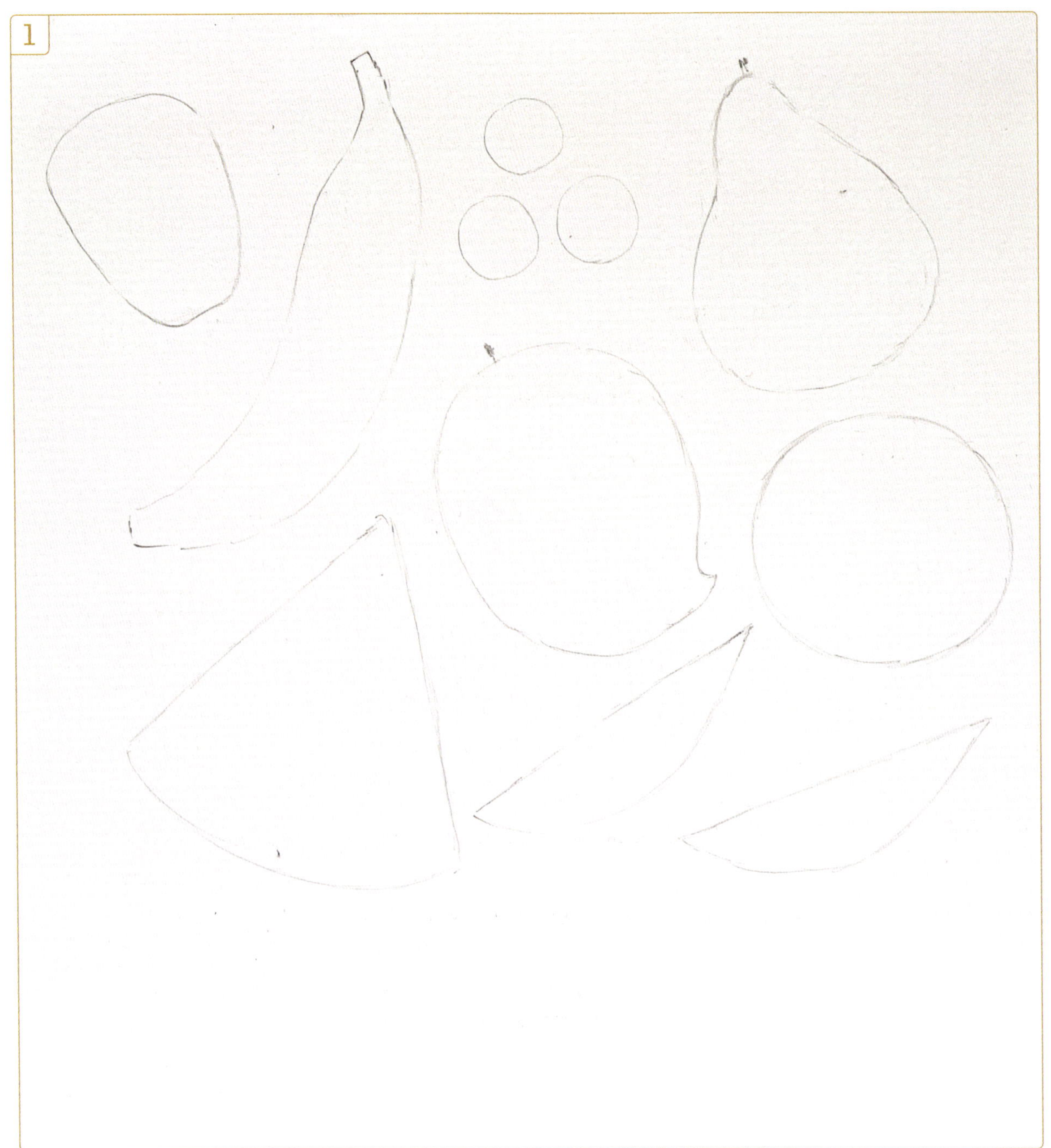

Before You Begin

1 **Sketch each fruit.** Sketch each of the fruits as shown here. Just draw the basic outline of each fruit; do not worry about realistic details. For each fruit except for the orange and the slices, always start with a clean water wash filling in the outline.

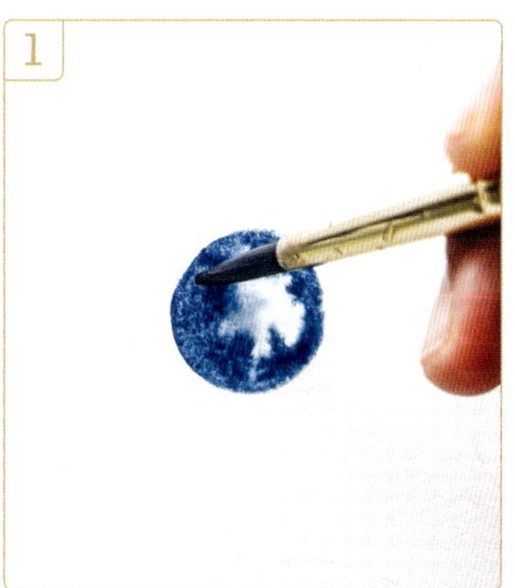

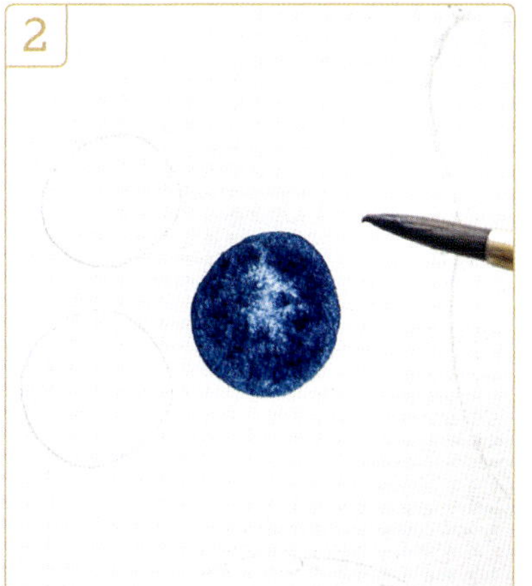

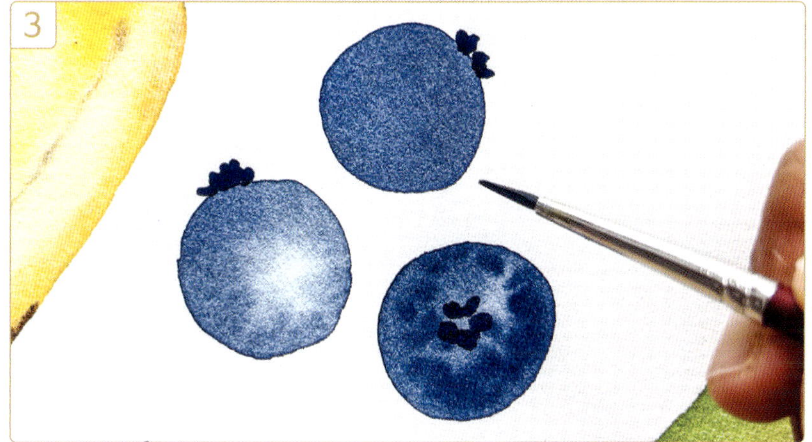

Blueberry

1 **Paint around the edges.** Fill the shape with a water wash. Mix some Prussian Blue or any other dark shade of blue and Payne's Gray to form a dull bluish shade. Apply this on the wet surface of the blueberry around the circumference.

2 **Add a darker blue.** Blend the existing paint softly with a darker shade of blue, being sure to retain the dotted texture on the surface.

Paint the other blueberries too, a few dark and a few light, making each blueberry a bit different.

3 **Add details.** Once the blueberries have dried, mix a dark shade of blue and draw the center (or the calyx) for each one. For some, draw it on the circumference to indicate a side angle; for others, draw it in the center to make the blueberry front-facing.

LET'S PRACTICE

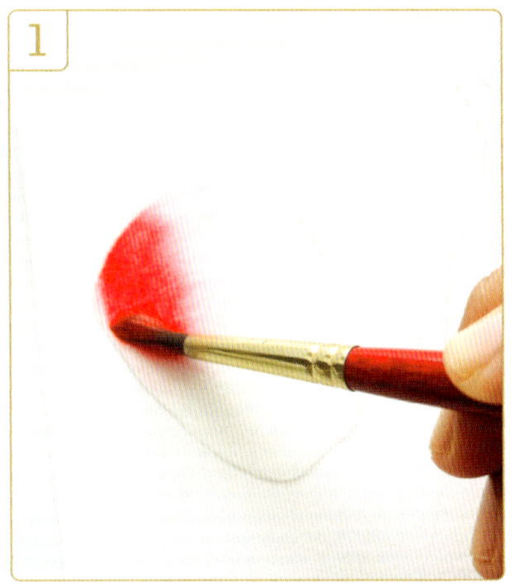

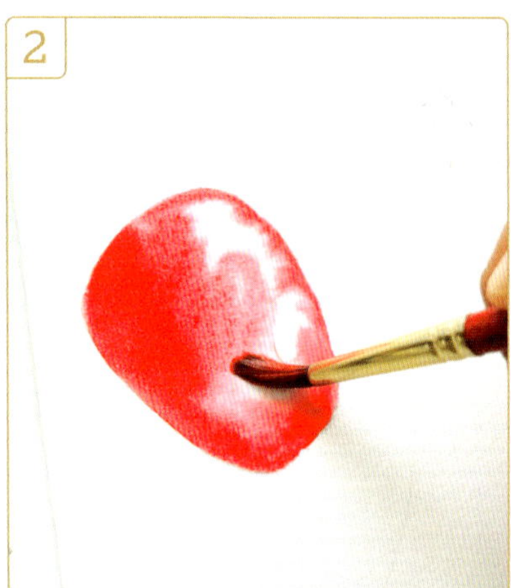

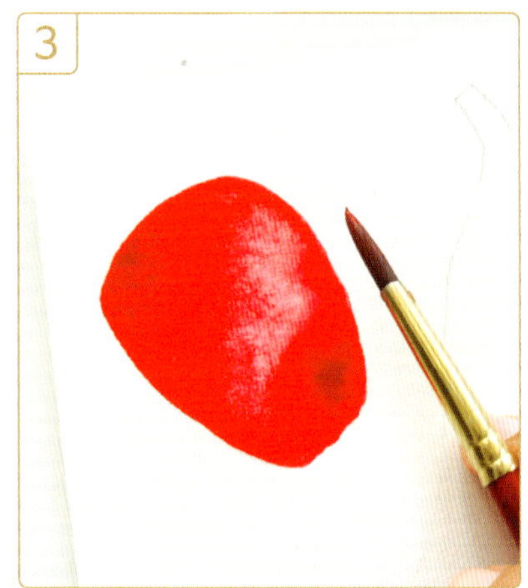

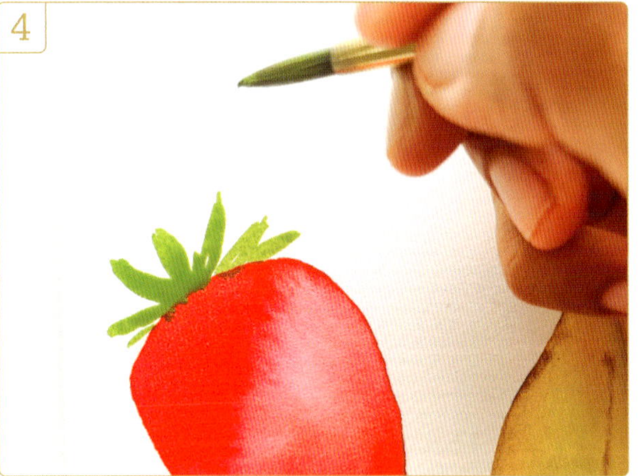

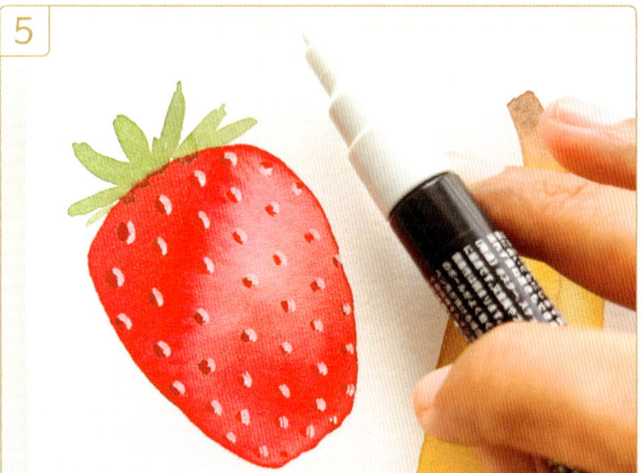

Strawberry

1 **Start painting with red.** Fill the shape with a water wash. Using a size 6 round brush, mix a shade of red without watering it down too much. Load your brush with the red paint and start laying down the color from the top.

2 **Leave the center open.** As you lay down the paint from the right side, leave a small gap in the center as a highlight—you don't want to paint the entire strawberry in flat red. Blend the red color softly to help it spread naturally.

3 **Add darker red.** Rinse your brush clean and load it with a darker shade of red. You can either add a bit of Crimson Lake or a brown color to the red to mix a slightly maroon shade. Apply this on the top and bottom of the strawberry and let it blend naturally.

4 **Add leaves.** Let the red portion completely dry. Then mix some Sap Green and yellow to get a shade of fresh green. Using your size 6 round brush, paint some small leaves to form the crown of the strawberry.

5 **Add seeds.** Use the shade of maroon color you mixed earlier to paint tiny dots on the surface of strawberry using a size 2 round brush. Once the dots have dried, use a white paint marker to add some depth to the seeds by making marks right next to each dot.

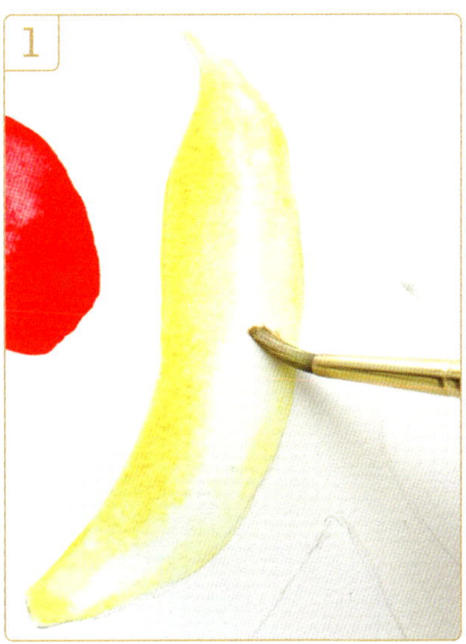

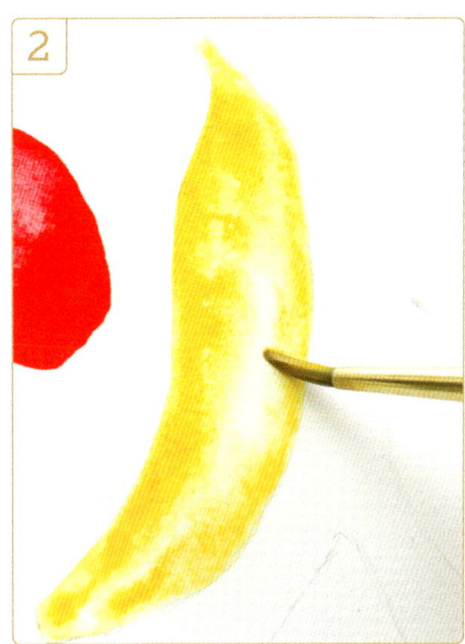

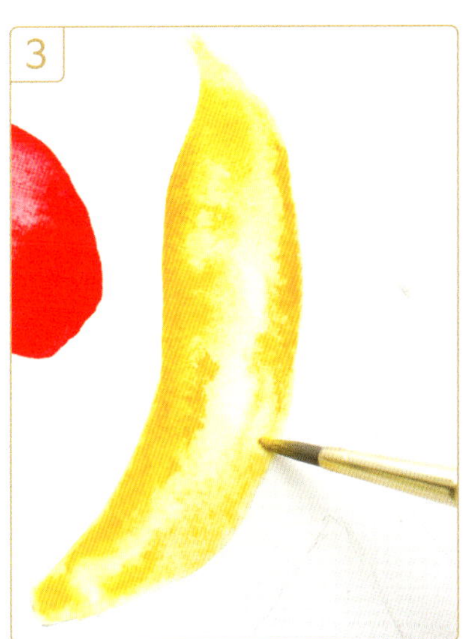

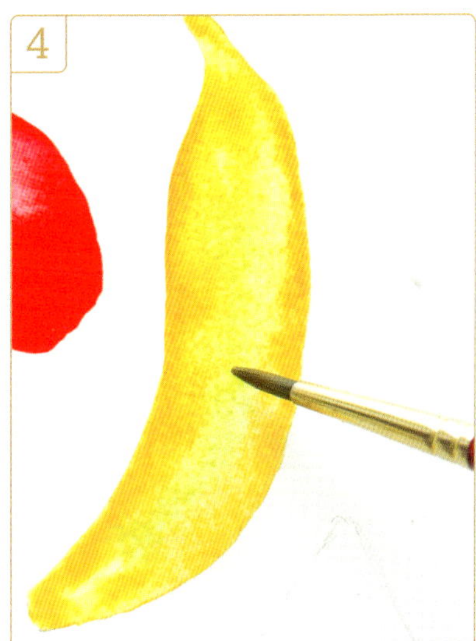

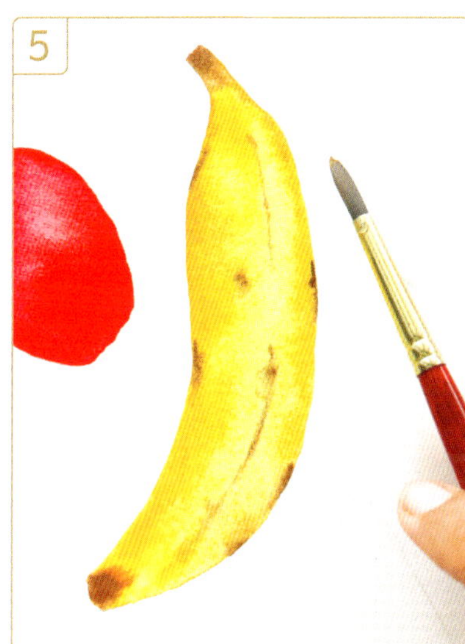

Banana

1 **Start painting with yellow.** Fill the shape with a water wash. While the surface is wet, lay down any light shade of yellow or Naples Yellow from both sides of the banana. Leave an open highlight in the center.

2 **Add a darker yellow.** Load the brush with a slightly darker shade of yellow such as Cadmium Yellow or Indian Yellow. Lay it down on top of the previous shade of yellow. Blend the two colors ever so gently without gliding the brush harshly.

3 **Add another yellow.** Next, mix some Yellow Ochre and lay it down on top of the previous two layers. Make sure that all the shades of yellow are visible and you don't cover up everything underneath. Maintain that soft, empty highlight in the center.

4 **Paint the center.** Blend a very light, watery mix of Sap Green and gently apply it in the center portion, in the highlight.

5 **Add details.** Rinse your brush and load it with a shade of not-too-watery dark brown. Apply it gently on just a few spots near the top stem and bottom portion of the banana. With a soft hand, add a few dots on the surface to represent the ripe black spots on the peel. Gently glide the brush to make one or two soft brown lines. Don't overdo it!

LET'S PRACTICE

Watermelon

1 **Start with red.** Fill the shape with a water wash. Apply red paint from one side first, making sure your paint is not too watery. Blend in red paint from the far side next, leaving a soft highlight in the middle.

2 **Add darker red.** Mix a darker shade of red by adding some brown, black, or gray. Layer this on top of the existing red color and merge the two colors just a little.

3 **Paint the rind.** Mix some Sap Green and paint the rind along the bottom of the slice. Leave a tiny white gap between the red and green.

4 **Add seeds.** After the red layer has dried, paint some small teardrops on the slice. For this, add some more black or brown to your red to darken it. Once the seeds have dried, use a white paint pen to add a highlight to each seed.

Orange

1 **Paint the rind.** For this fruit, do NOT use a water wash! Instead, use slightly runny orange paint to paint a thick outer rind using a size 6 round brush.

2 **Paint the inside.** Paint the triangular sections of the orange one by one, keeping an imaginary center in your mind. Add a darker shade of orange near the center of each section. Once dry, add small white seeds with a white paint pen.

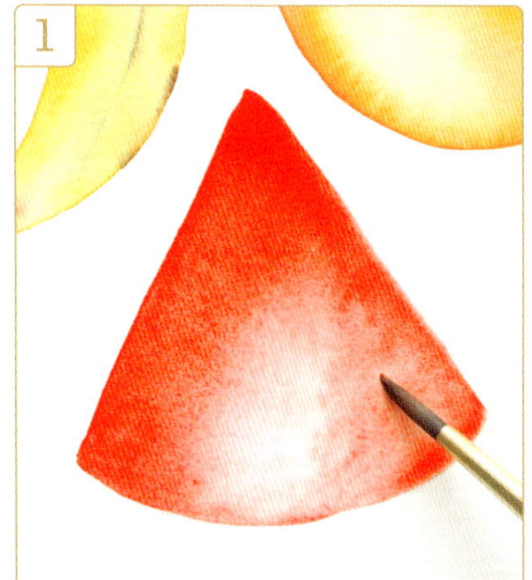

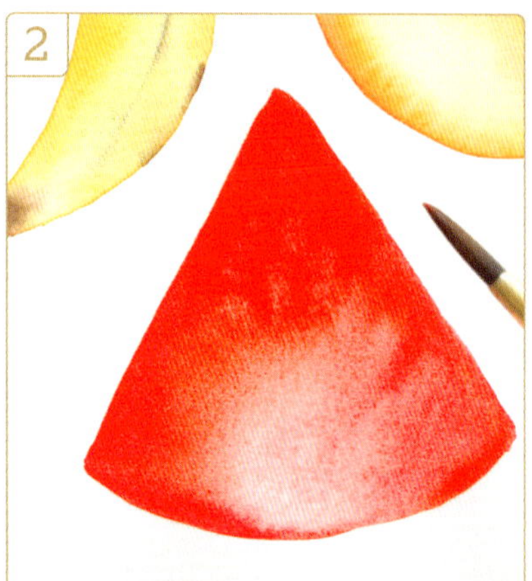

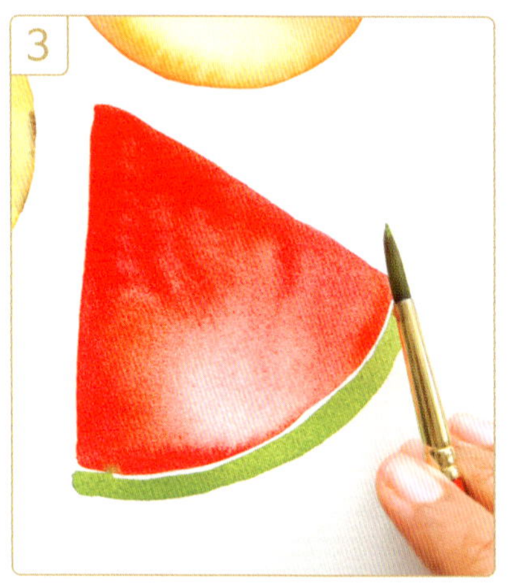

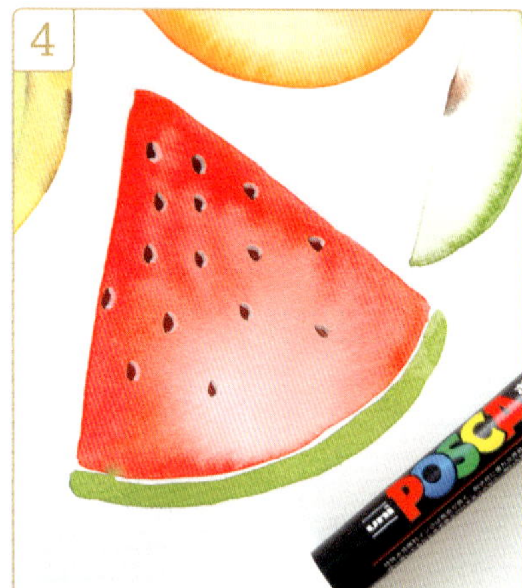

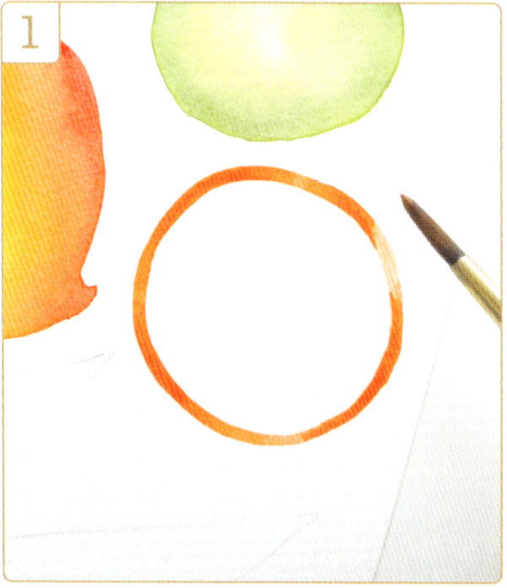

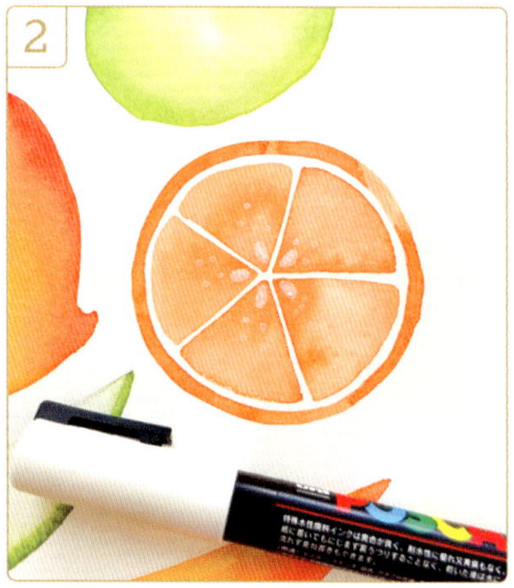

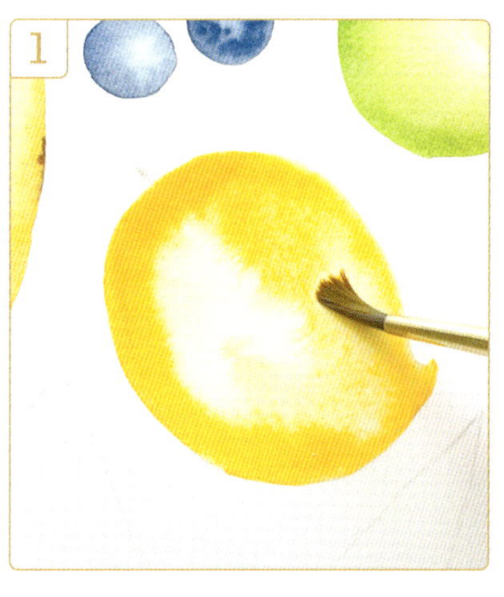

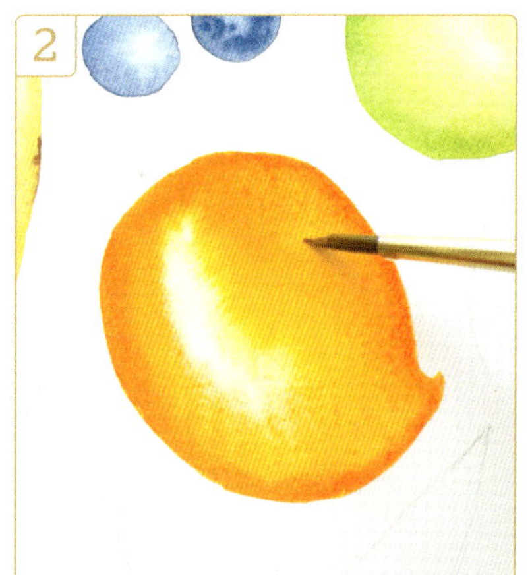

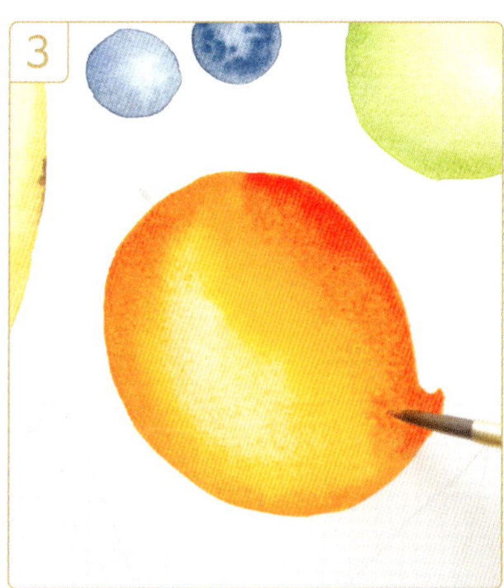

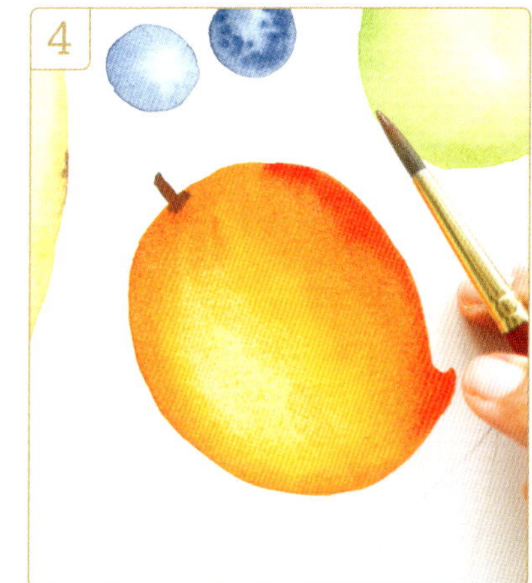

Mango

1 Start with yellow edges.
Fill the shape with a water wash.
Load the brush with a deep shade
of yellow such as Cadmium Yellow
or Indian Yellow. Glide your brush
around the surface of the mango,
leaving a highlight in the middle.

2 Add orange. Next, load your
brush with orange paint. Add the
orange layer on top of the yellow
layer and allow the two colors
to blend into each other without
totally losing the yellow.

3 Add red. Mix some red paint
on your palette. Drop in the red
paint ever so lightly on the outer
edges. Don't hide the yellow and
orange layers completely. Blend
harsh edges smooth with a
moist brush.

4 Add details. Once you are
happy with your blending, add a
small brown stem on top of
the mango.

LET'S PRACTICE

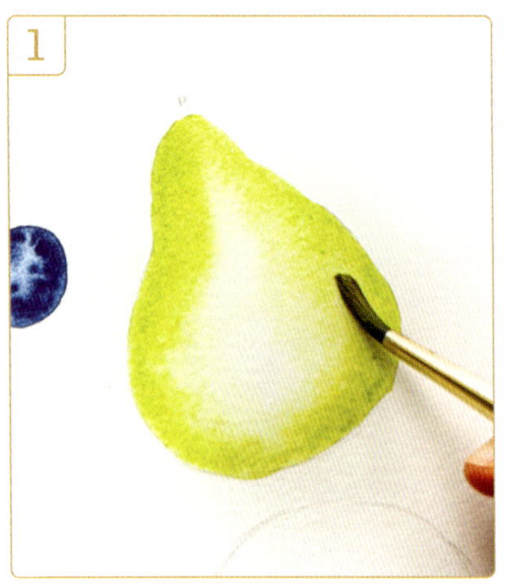

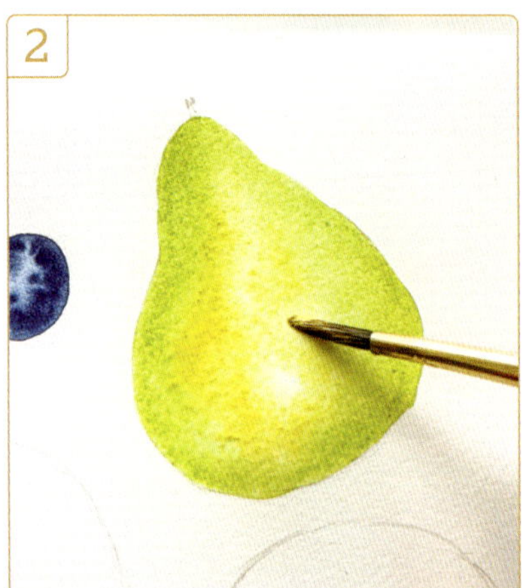

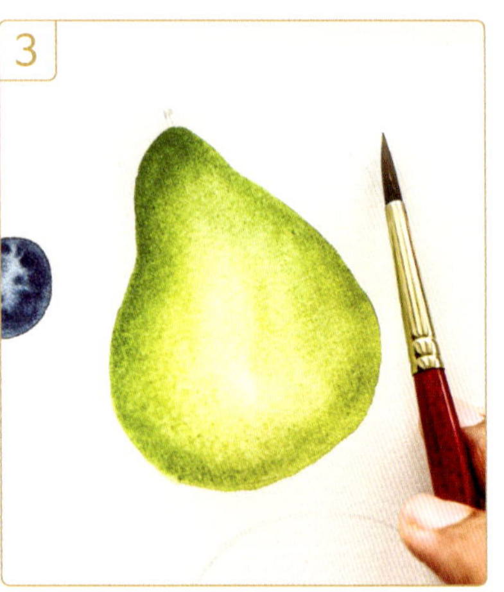

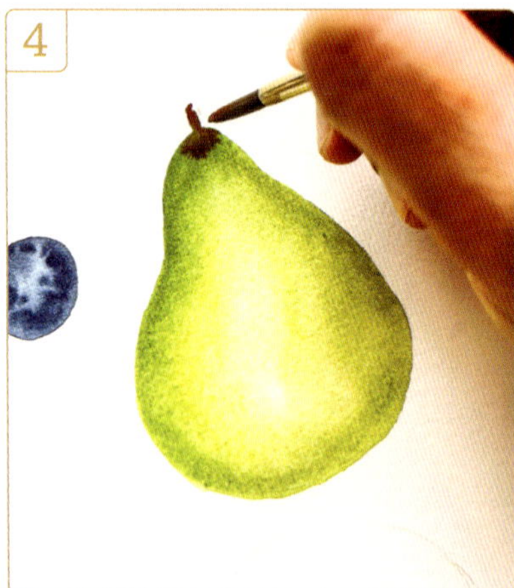

Pear

1 **Start at the edges.** Fill the shape with a water wash. Mix a soft shade of green by including lots of Lemon Yellow. Apply this green on the sides of the pear, leaving a highlight in the center.

2 **Paint the middle.** Apply a soft shade of slightly watered-down yellow in the middle of the pear. Blend the green and the yellow slightly—don't move the colors around too much.

3 **Add a darker edge.** Apply a slightly darker shade of Sap Green around the outer surface of the pear. Using a moist brush that is not overloaded with water, blend all the color slowly and gently. Aim for a soft gradient as shown.

4 **Add final details.** Load a brush with a creamy shade of dark brown. Paint a small brown stem on the top, allowing the brown to blend just a little bit into the green portion.

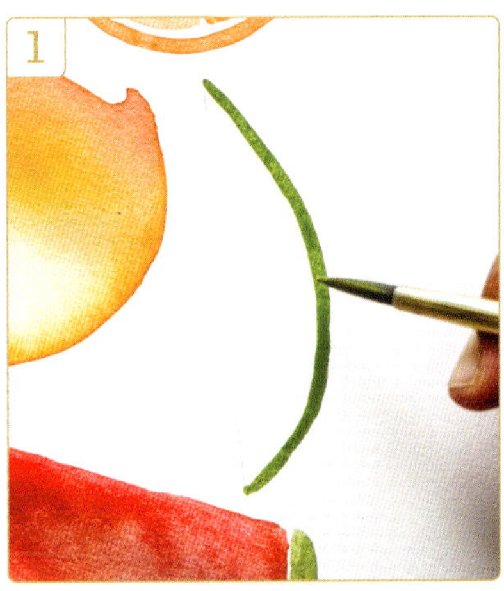

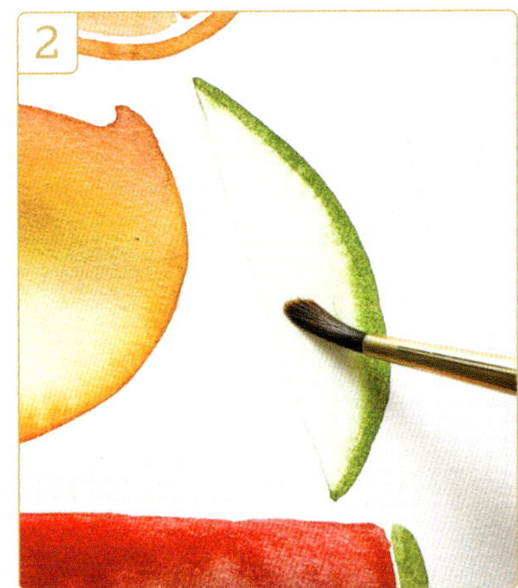

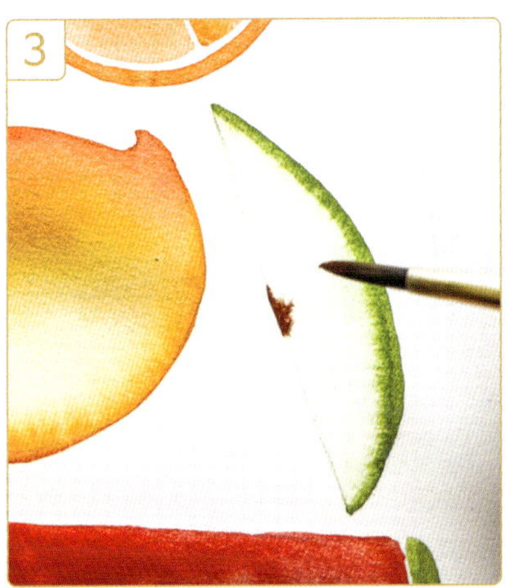

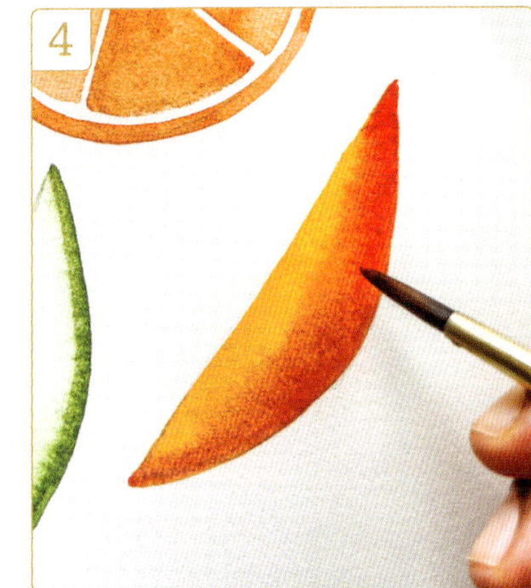

Pear and Mango Slices

1 **Paint the pear rind.** For these fruit slices, do NOT use a water wash! To paint the pear slice, start by painting the outer skin layer using Sap Green.

2 **Paint the pear flesh.** Rinse your brush. Using a moist brush, wet the inside portion, letting your brush slightly touch the outer rind. The green color will instantly bleed into the wet area. Keep the blending to minimum—you want most of the slice to be white.

3 **Add a seed.** While the slice portion is still drying, apply a small brown dot on the edge to create a single seed.

4 **Paint the mango.** Apply a layer of yellow on the surface of the slice, then blend orange and red paints on that base layer one at a time.

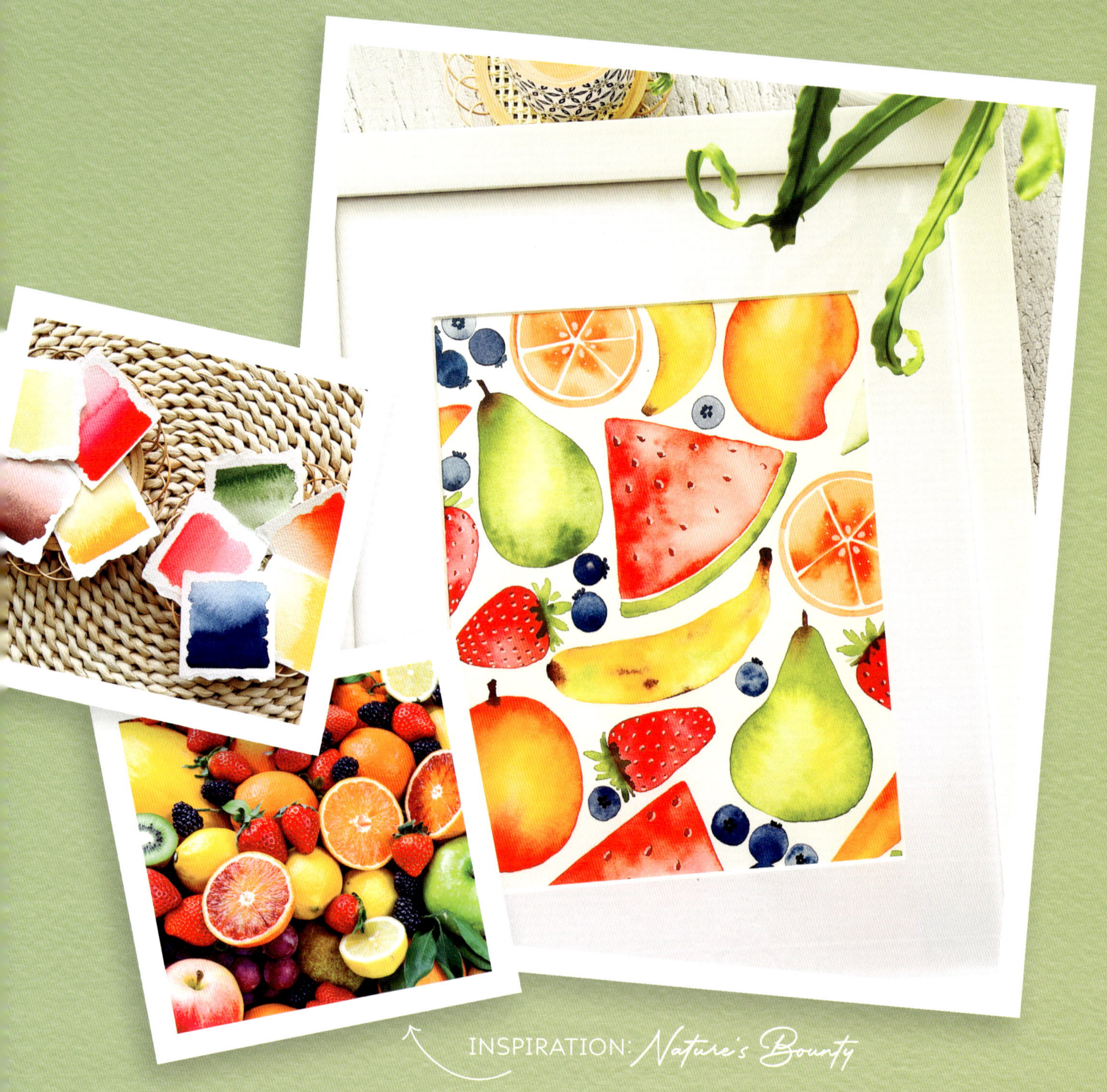

Let's Relax

After practicing all the fruits, I am sure you must be excited to now paint the final pattern. You may have noticed that the method for painting each fruit is pretty much the same—you are simply switching colors depending on the fruit! Don't let the number of colors you need for this project overwhelm you. Think of this as an opportunity to work with a wide color palette, which will strengthen your skills in incorporating multiple colors in a piece. Focus on the color play and enjoy every aspect of the color blending. As I painted this pattern, I not only craved eating fresh, bountiful fruits but also felt grateful to Mother Nature for providing us with such beautiful, natural, and delicious food options to relish!

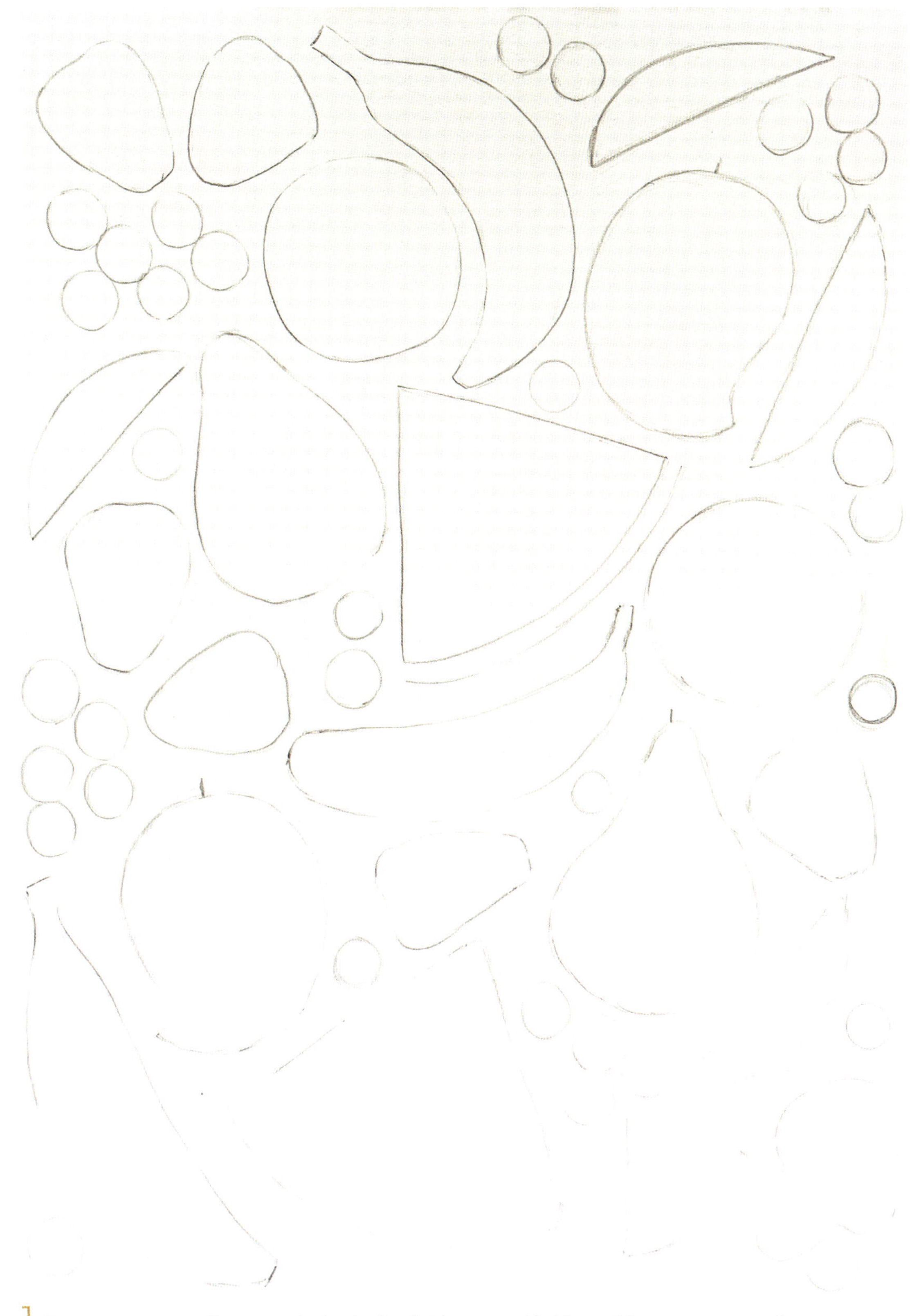

Let's Paint

1 **Draw a pattern.** Re-create the basic sketch I have provided here. Of course, you can also create your own composition using the different fruit shapes you've learned! You can also download the digital pattern linework and trace it on your paper (see page 14). To complete this project, we are going to paint all the fruits of one kind one at a time, then add the details at the very end.

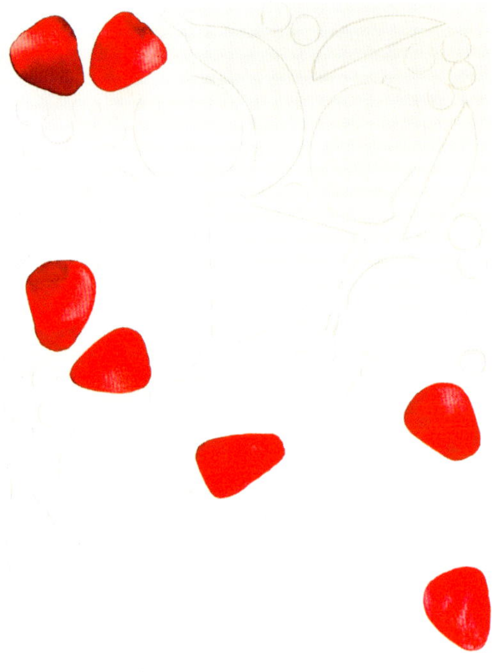

2 **Paint the strawberries.** Make sure to leave some soft highlights and strategically place the darker hues while maintaining soft color blends. Be mindful about your hand placement—go from top to bottom and left to right. Hold off on the seeds for now.

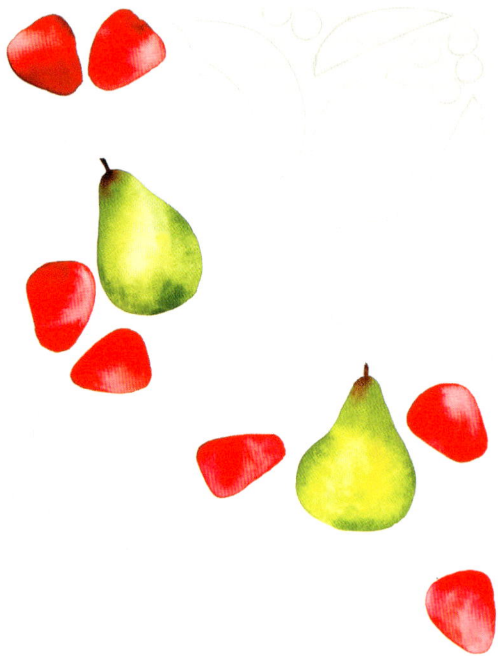

3 **Paint the pears.** Paint the full pears one at a time. Make sure the surrounding strawberries are dry enough that you won't risk smearing them as you work on the pears. Rotate the page as needed.

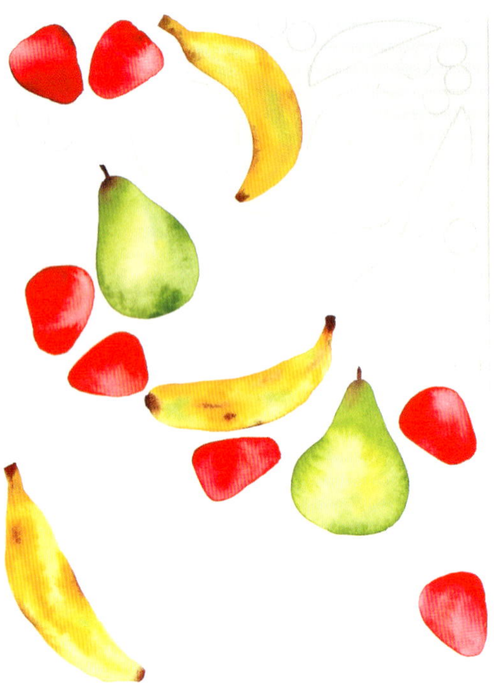

4 **Paint the bananas.** Mix the colors you need to paint the bananas and then paint them one at a time, making each one a bit different. For some, keep more yellow and less green, and vice versa; for others, show more brown texture or use just minimal brown.

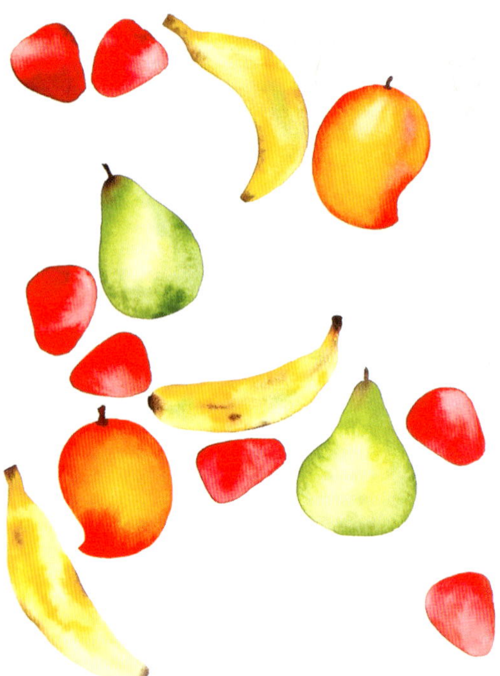

5 **Paint the mangoes.** Let's paint the mangoes next. Lay down the three colors—yellow, orange, and red—one by one as explained in the practice session, blending them to form smooth ombré layers. Don't forget the stems!

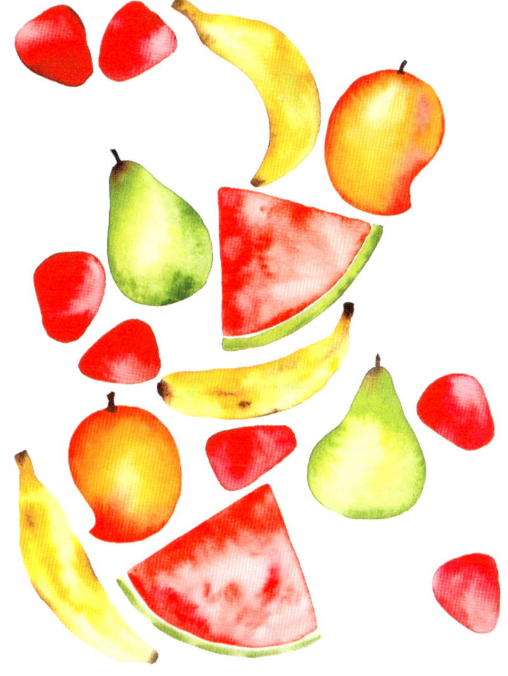

6 **Paint the watermelons.** Paint the watermelon slices next. Place your wrist carefully to avoid smudging the wet areas. Hold off on the seeds for now—those will come later.

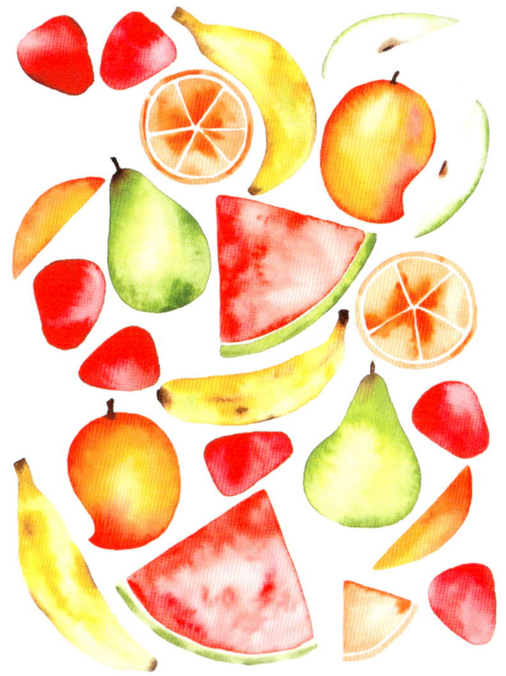

7 **Paint the oranges and pear and mango slices.** Unlike the other fruits, the oranges and the slices do not start with a water wash layer. Make the slices around the top right mango into pear slices, and the ones around the two pears into mango slices.

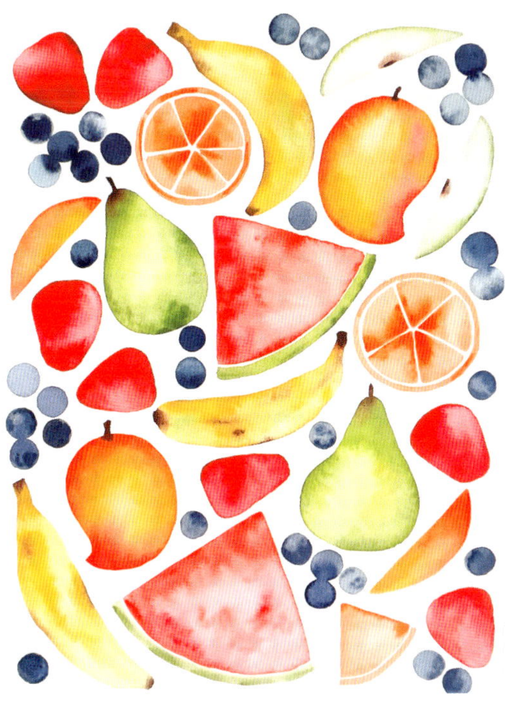

8 **Paint the blueberries.** Paint the blueberries in varying shades of blue as shown. Hold off on painting their details until the final step. Adding the cool-toned blueberries will instantly make your warm-toned pattern look balanced and vibrant.

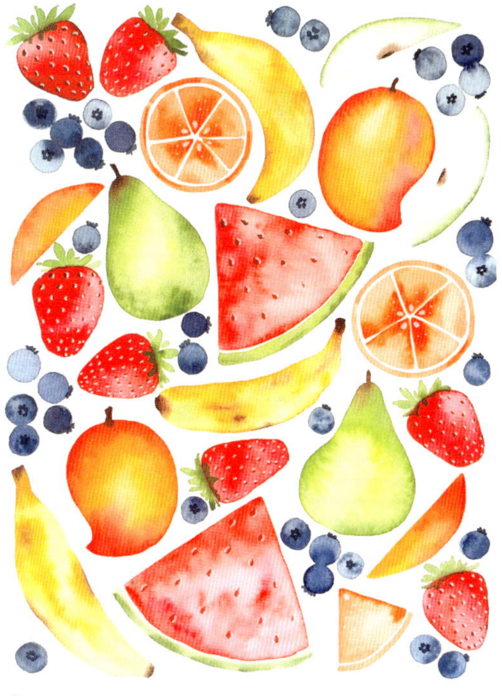

9 **Add all the details.** Once all the fruits are completely dry, add the details on the strawberries, watermelons, blueberries, and orange slices.

Let's Paint

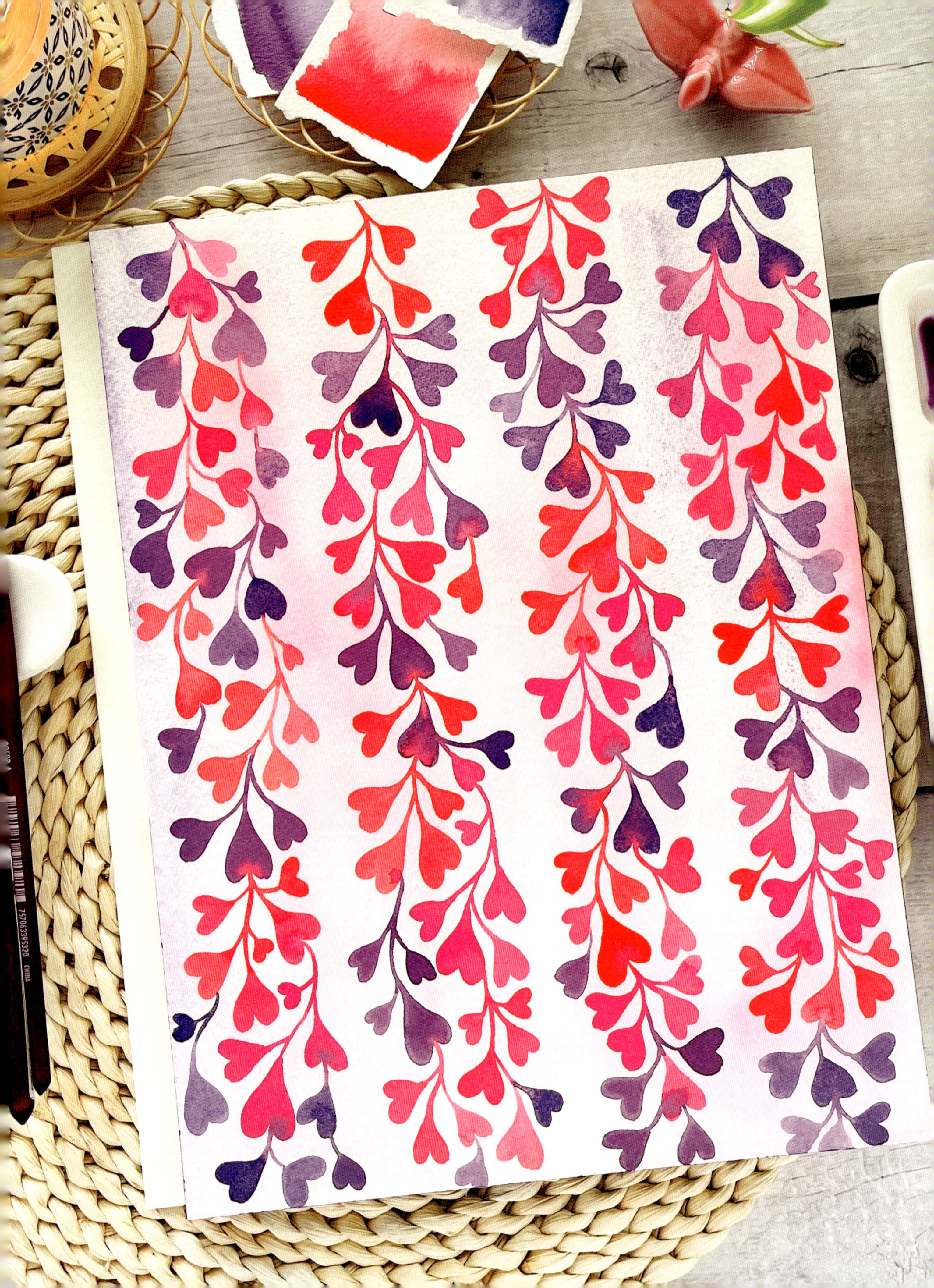

String of Hearts

Whether it is Valentine's Day or not, painting hearts with watercolors is always fun! You will see a lot of artists out there painting heart patterns, so it was an obvious choice for me to include at least one heart-focused pattern in this book. In this project, you will learn how to add a background wash, which lends a totally different texture and feel to the pattern.

173

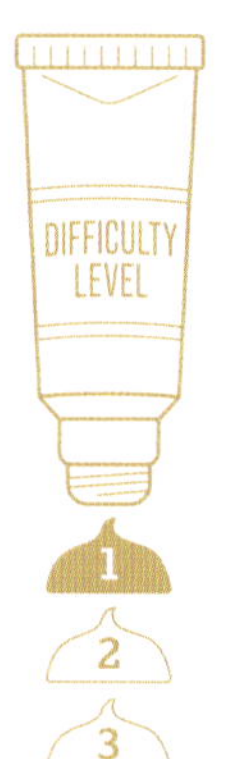

DIFFICULTY
LEVEL

1
2
3

MATERIALS

BRUSHES: Size 4 round brush; size 6 quill round brush

PAPER: 8" x 10" (20 x 25 cm), cold pressed

COLORS:

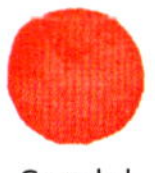
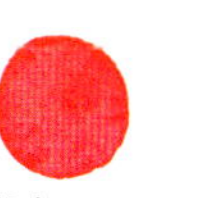

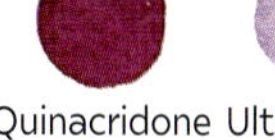

Sandal Red   Primary Red Magenta   Verzino Violet   Quinacridone Violet   Ultramarine Violet

TIP: We are using a soft background wash for this pattern. Make sure to use clean water and a clean brush to apply the watery wash. If either of the two are not clean, your design will look dull and the pattern will lose its brightness.

LET'S PRACTICE

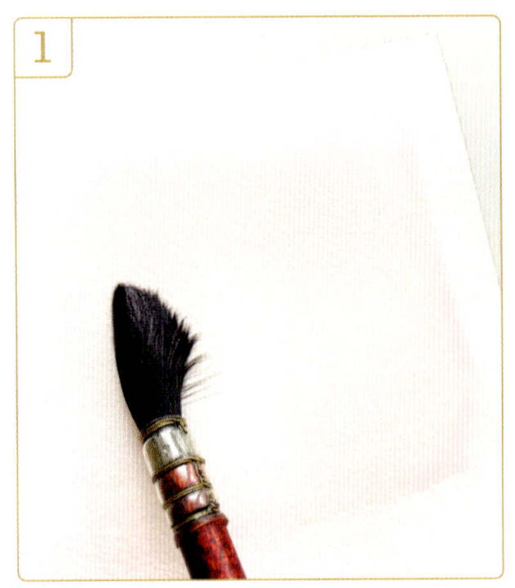

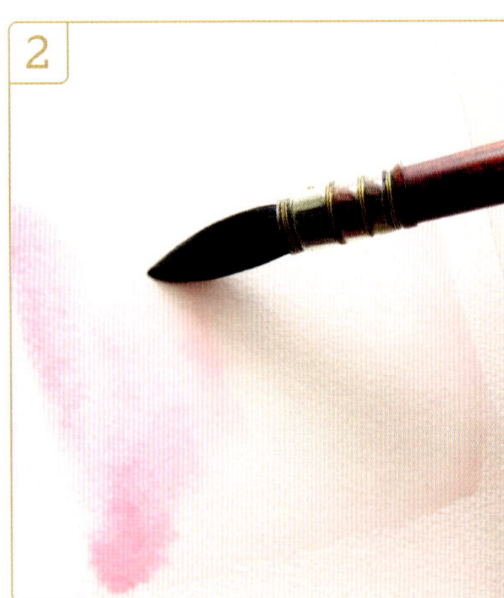

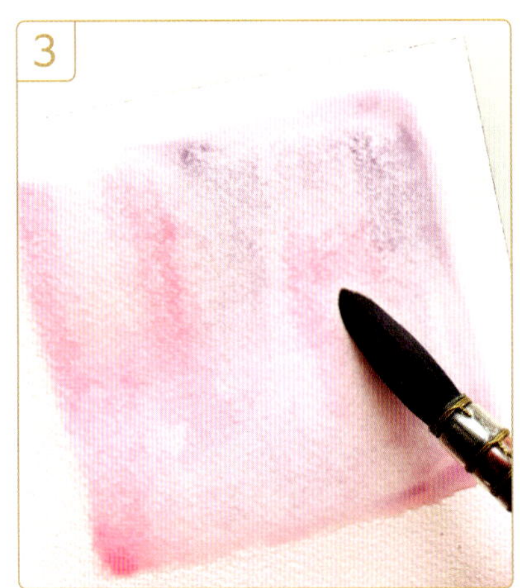

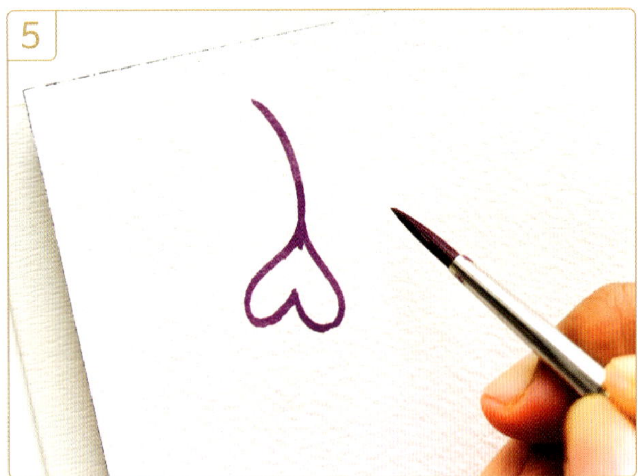

1 Prepare a water wash. Using a large round brush, apply a layer of clean water on a small area of your practice sheet. Make sure not to leave any dry spots within your chosen area.

2 Add pink to the wash. Mix an extremely light, watered-down pink shade. Load your brush with this pink and lay it down in the wet area. The paint will instantly start spreading on the surface. Glide your brush smoothly to help it move.

3 Add purple to the wash. Mix a just-as-watery violet shade and load your brush with it. Apply it on the remaining wet area, allowing the new color to spread and merge into the existing pink. Try to keep it light and soft.

4 Draw the first stem. Move to a fresh area of your practice sheet. Mix your chosen paints. Don't make them too watery. Using a size 4 round brush, draw a small string or stem coming down. Hold your brush a bit upright to get a delicate curve.

5 Draw the first heart. Starting from the bottom end of the stem, draw an upside-down heart using the same color.

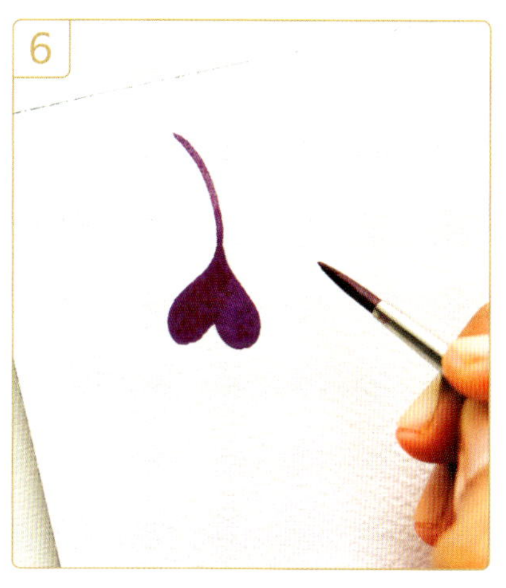

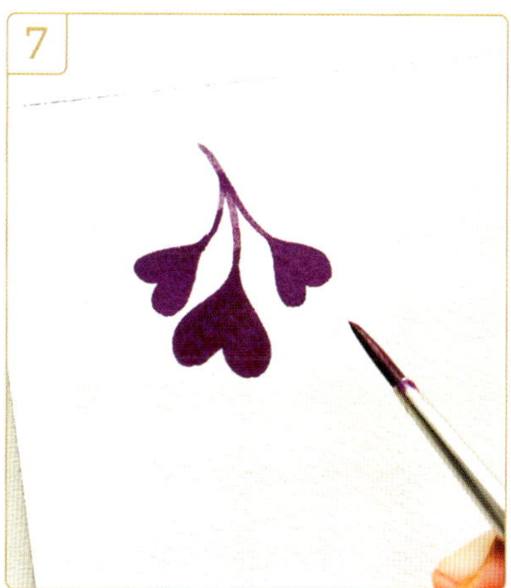

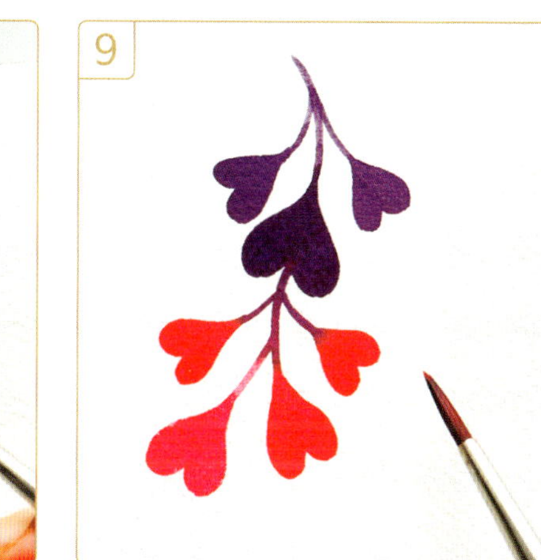

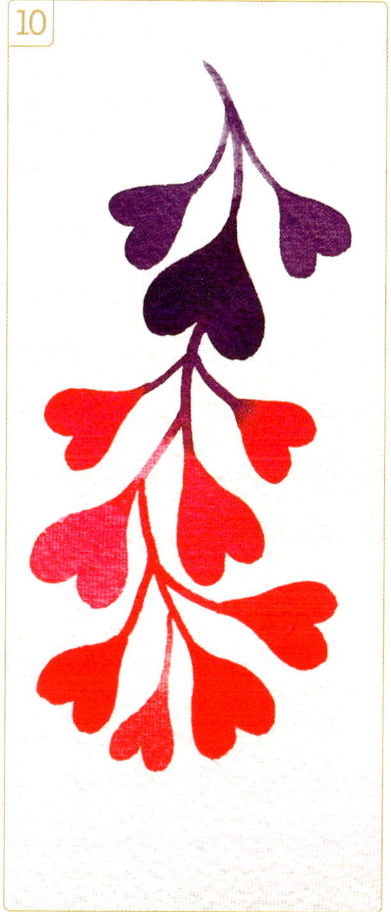

6 **Fill in the heart.** Fill the heart in with the same color.

7 **Add two more hearts.** On either side of the main stem, draw two more small stems and add hearts at the tips. It is okay to vary the sizes of the hearts to create visual interest.

8 **Change to a new color.** Rinse your brush and load it with the next color you wish to use. Continuing from the previous set of stems, draw a new stem sprouting from one of the previous hearts. There will be a bit of color blending.

9 **Add hearts in the new color.** Paint some more stems and hearts on both sides and the end of this new stem to complete this color section.

10 **Change to a third color.** Rinse your brush and load it with the next color. This time, draw a stem sprouting from an earlier stem (instead of from an earlier heart). From this new stem, continue painting hearts in the new color. Always move downward.

Let's Relax

My goal with this design was to paint a Valentine's Day pattern that was not quite literal. That's why I decided to draw inspiration from the plant named string of hearts. I tried to paint a few hearts strung together on stems and came up with a few options. Upon painting the hearts upside down, it instantly felt unique and like something I had not tried before. I continued to paint these strings of hearts and started weaving them together, and thus this pattern came to life! Always try to find inspiration around you—you never know what might strike a chord and be turned into something beautiful.

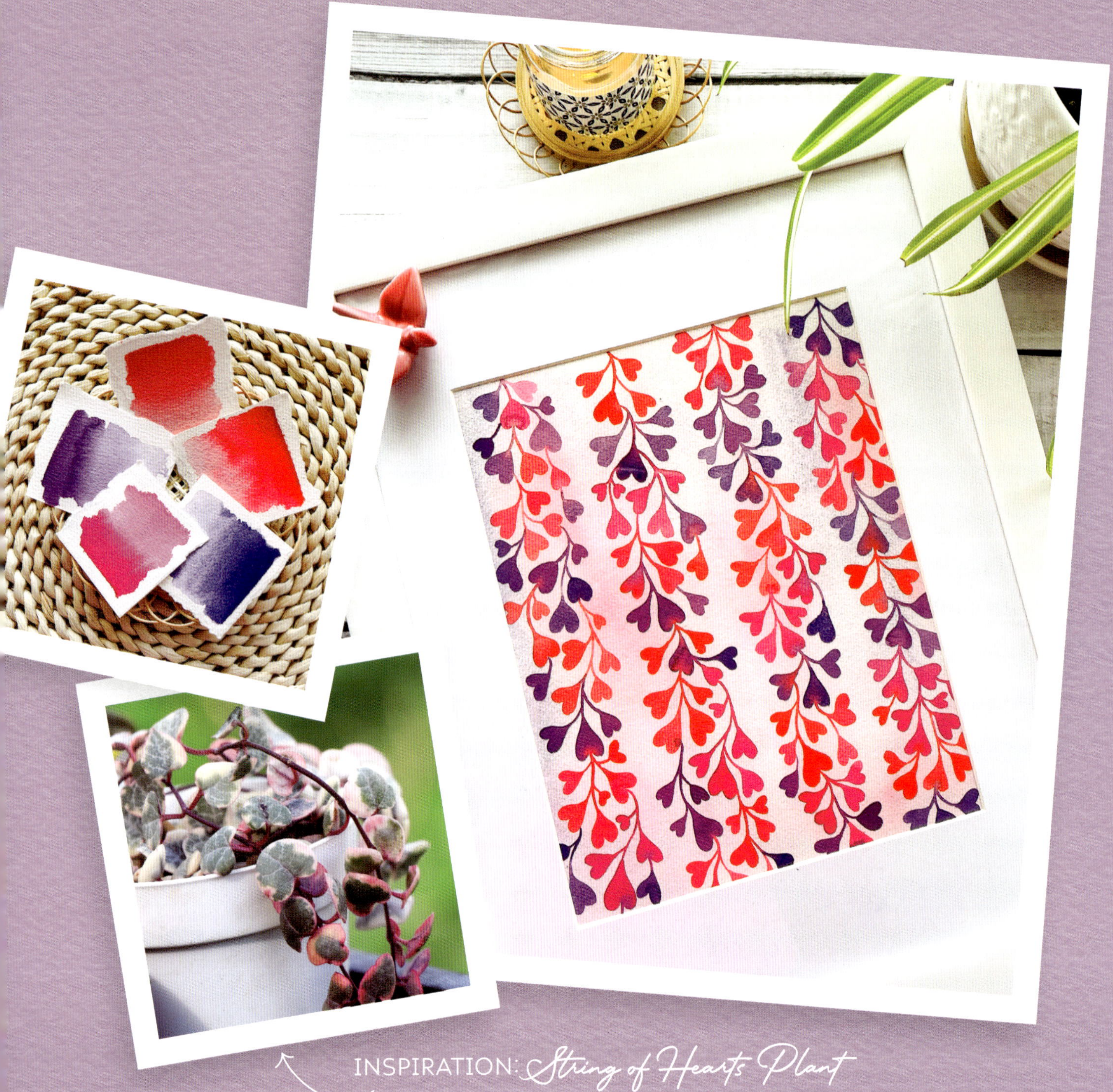

INSPIRATION: *String of Hearts Plant*

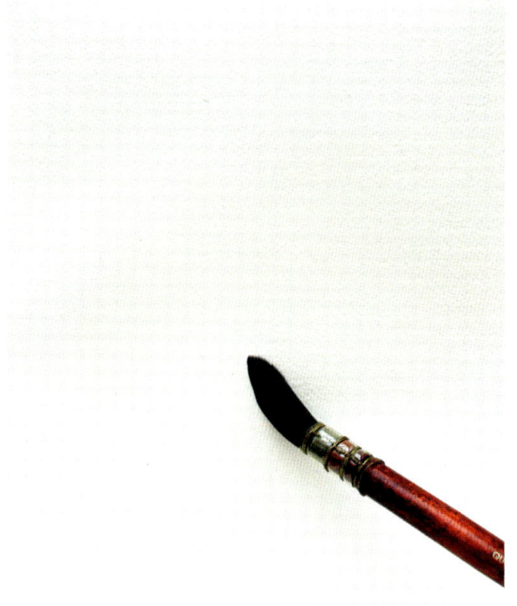

1 **Cover the paper with a water wash.**
With a large, clean round brush, apply a wash
of clean water all over the page. Make sure
the paper is moist, with no dry patches. If the
paper is not wet enough, you will have trouble
spreading the paint wash over it.

2 **Add purple to the wash.** Mix an
extremely watery, soft shade of Ultramarine
Violet. Using the same large round brush, start
spreading this color on the wet page. It's fine to
apply it in some areas darker than others, but
make sure it is overall very light.

3 **Add pink to the wash.** Mix an extremely
watery, soft shade of pink and apply it around
the violet areas. Blend the two colors very softly
so that both shades remain visible. Now wait
for everything to completely dry—it may take
a while, so be patient!

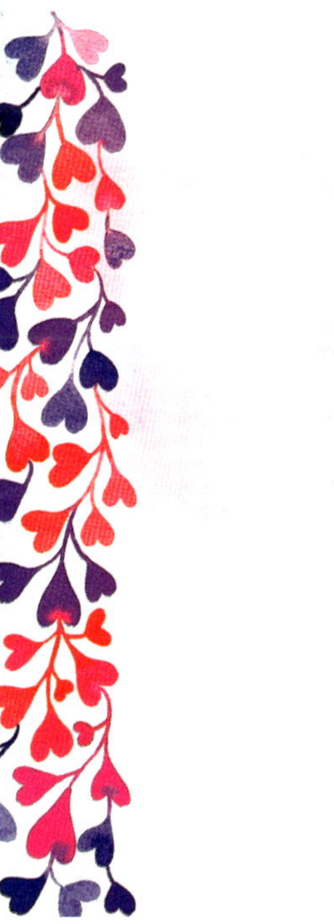

4 **Paint the first column.** Mix all the colors
you need for your design. Divide your page into
four or five columns (in your head or with a
pencil). Aim to paint your hearts with a small
empty gap between each column. Then grab
your size 4 round brush and start painting!

Let's Paint

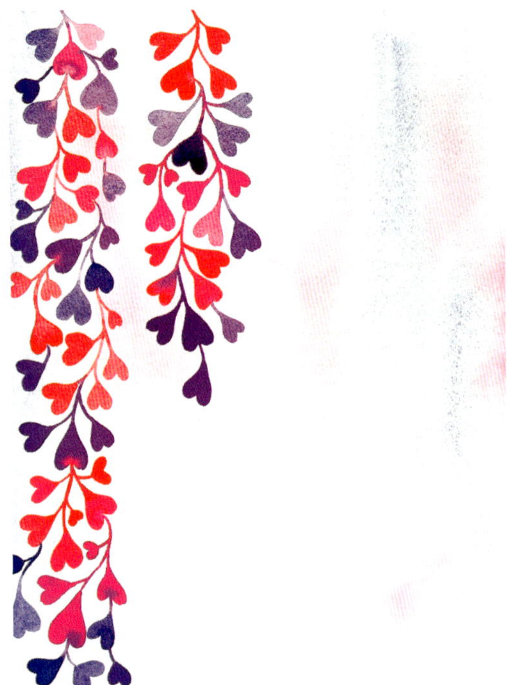

5 Continue on to the second column.

Once you finish the first column, leave a small gap and start painting the hearts again from the top of the second column. Keep color balance in mind—don't start the new column with the same color you started the first column.

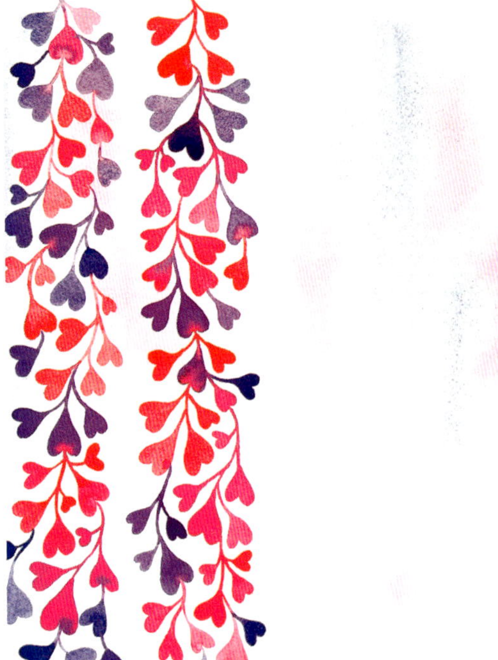

6 Get into a good flow.

At the start, it may take a while to choose colors and place stems and hearts, but as you sink into the process, the hearts will start falling into place naturally. Keep the stems curved at all times to make them look graceful.

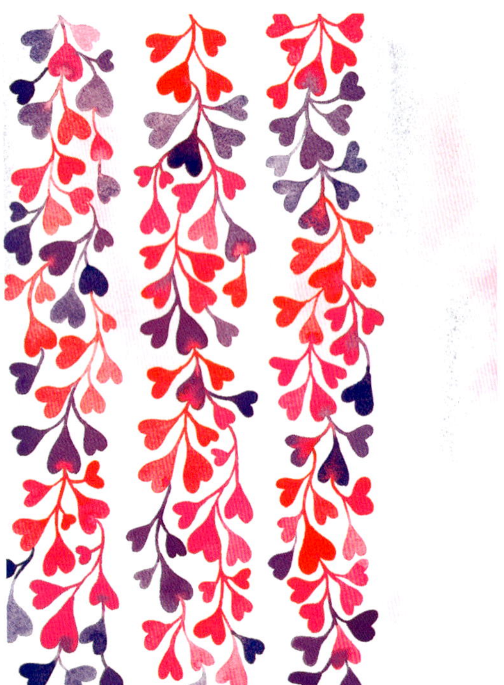

7 Paint the third column.

Move on to the next column and repeat the process. Be careful to keep the sizes of your hearts consistent between the three columns and not to make one column more densely packed than another.

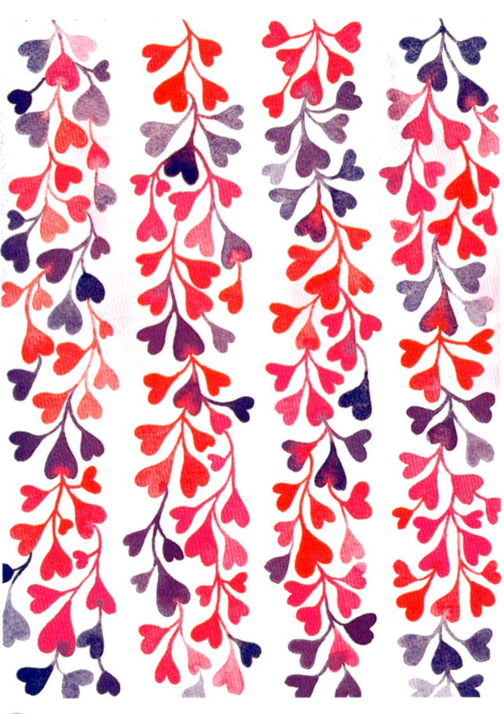

8 Paint the final column.

If you are using a sheet of paper with columns like mine, this will probably be your last column. As I reached the end of this piece, I thought I had a good mix of all the colors and that the pattern looked bold and vibrant.

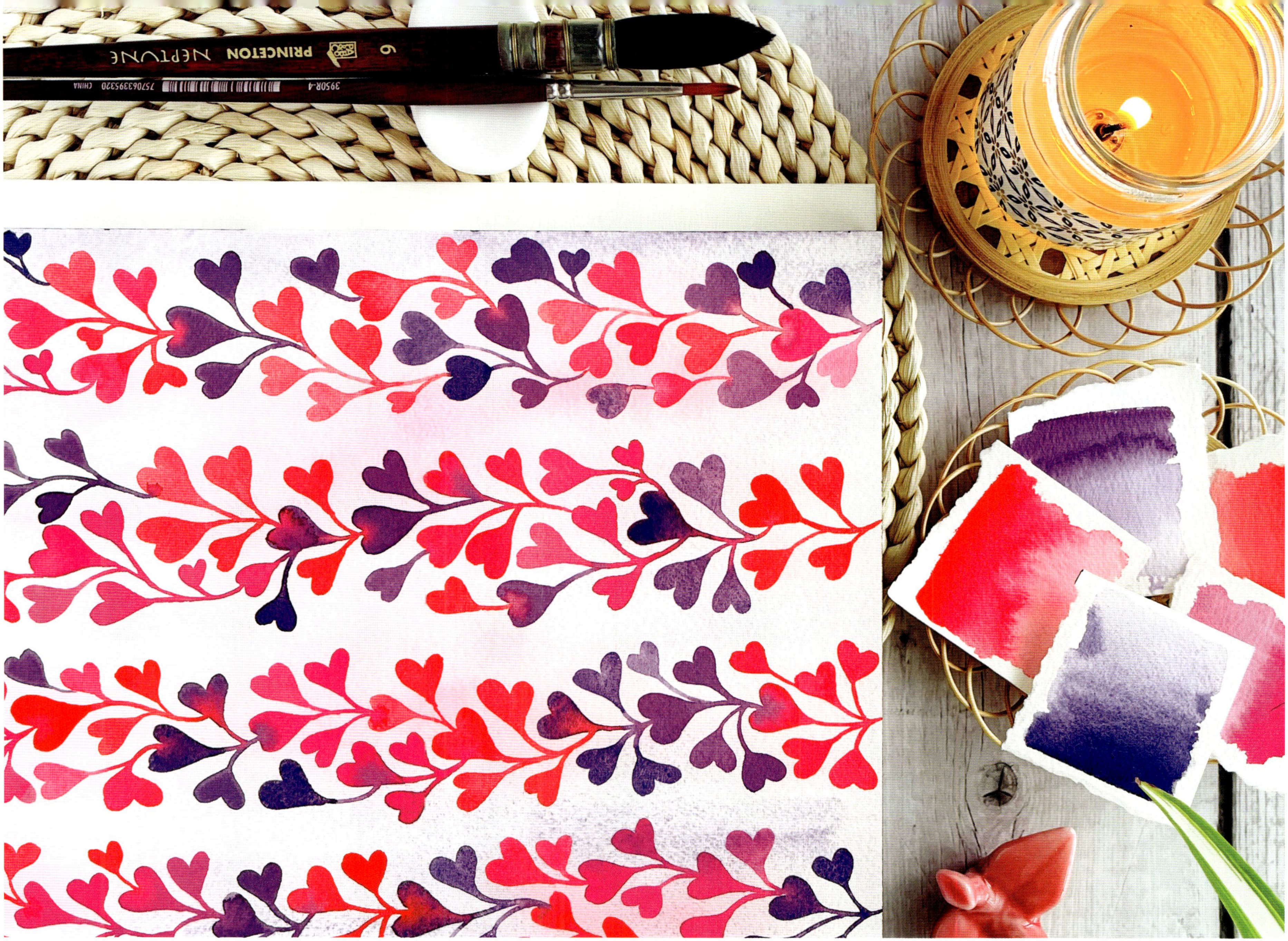

String of Hearts

Let's Paint

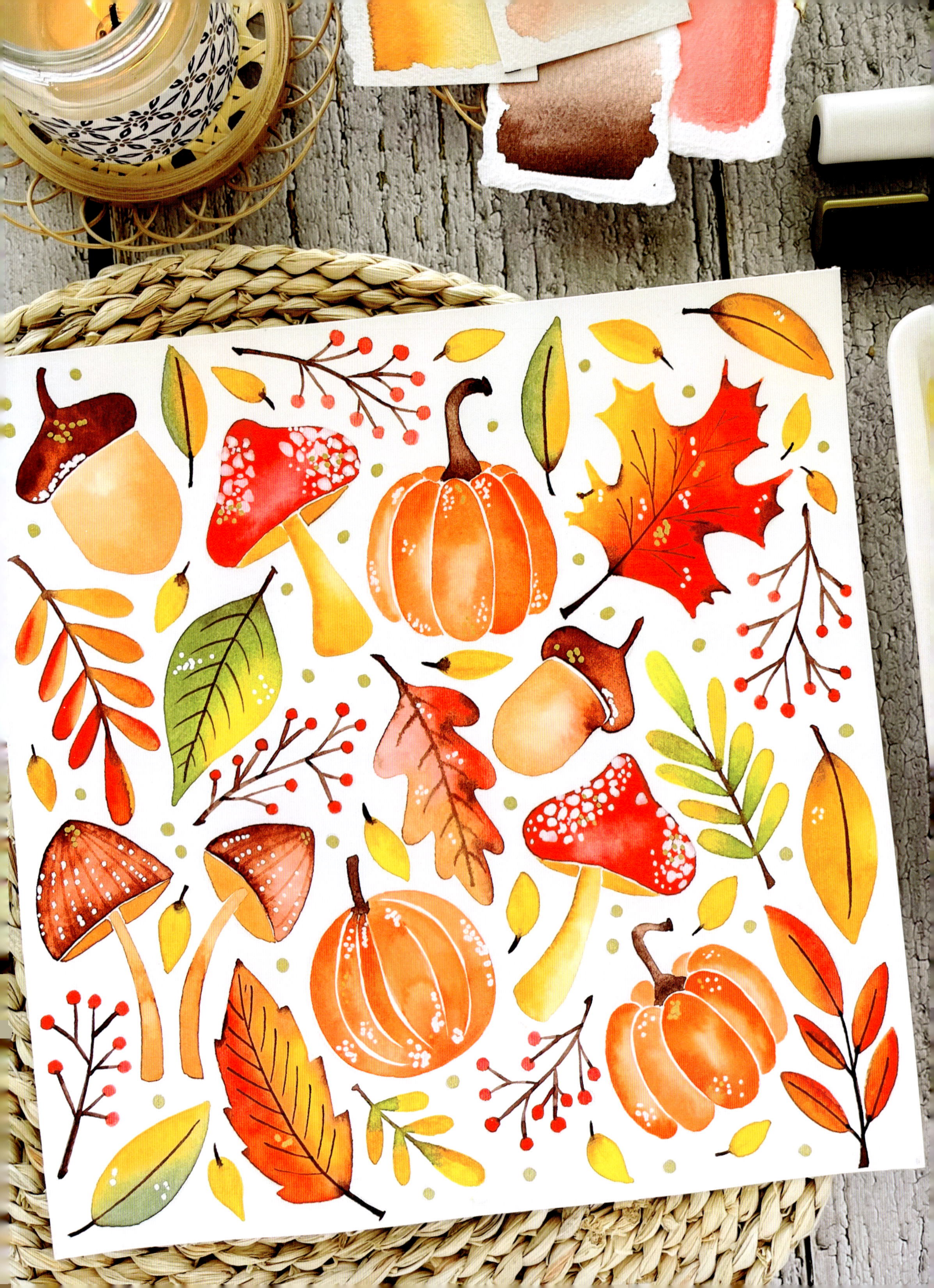

Fall into Autumn

This cozy autumn pattern is a perfect seasonal design for us to explore some of the most iconic fall elements, such as mushrooms, fiery leaves, pumpkins, and berries. We will use textures as an added step to bring out the boldness of the autumn colors and aim for great color vibrancy to reflect the moody warmth of the season!

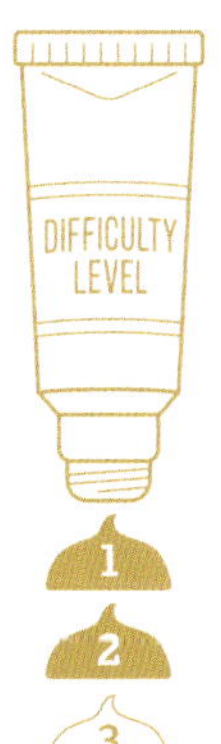

MATERIALS

BRUSHES: Size 6 round brush; size 1 round brush for details

PAPER: 9" x 9" (23 x 23 cm), hot pressed

OTHER: Gel pens or paint pens (optional) in white and gold, 0.7 mm or thicker; you could also use white gouache

COLORS:

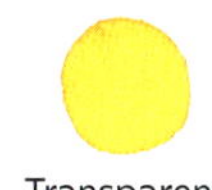 Transparent Yellow or Lemon Yellow

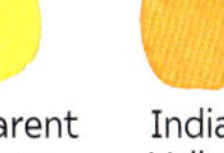 Indian Yellow

 Yellow Ochre

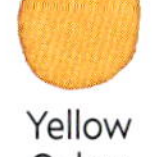 Cadmium Orange

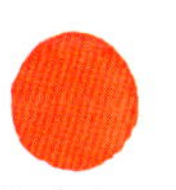 Sandal Red

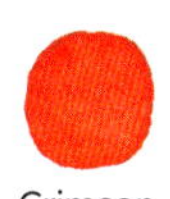 Crimson Lake

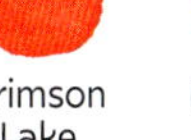 Dragon's Blood

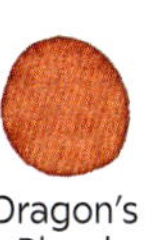 Mars Brown

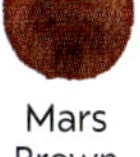 Sap Green

TIP: We are using a warm color palette for this pattern, so try to blend the colors in such a way that you play with light and dark contrast while placing the colors next to each other. For instance, try not to put two orange elements right next to each other. Break the colors down by using different proportions of reds, browns, yellows, and greens.

This project's pattern is available as a bonus digital download! See page 14.

LET'S PRACTICE

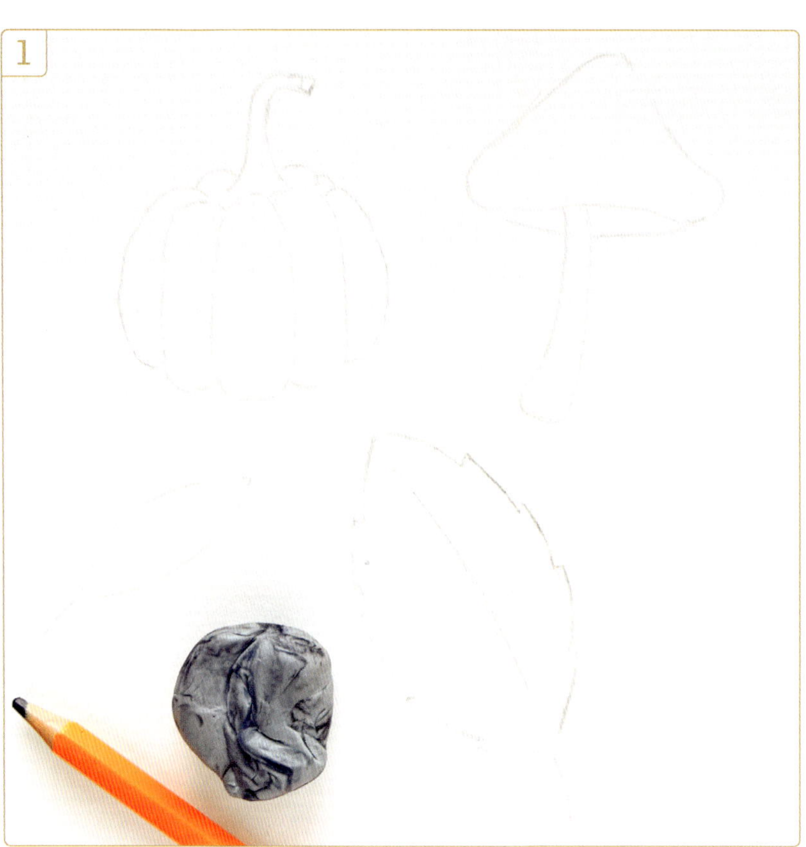

Before You Begin

1 **Sketch each element.** Sketch each of the elements that we will be using in the final pattern as shown here. Just draw the basic outline of each element; do not worry about realistic details.

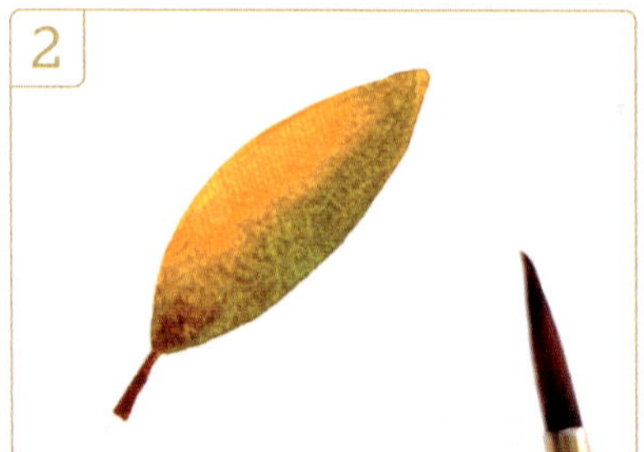

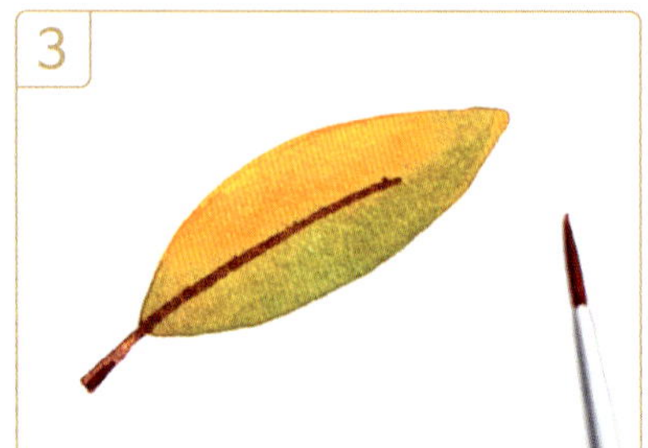

Small Leaf

1 **Paint half of the leaf.** We'll paint the small leaf using yellow and green. Start by applying a shade of yellow to one half of the leaf using a size 6 round brush.

2 **Paint the second half and the stem.** Next apply a green on the other side of the leaf, blending it nicely with the yellow without using too much water. Then rinse your brush and paint a small brown stem on the leaf, letting the stem blend a bit with the other colors.

3 **Add the central vein.** Once the leaf is dry, use a size 1 round brush to paint on a vein using the same brown color you used for the stem. These little leaves are good filler between the bigger elements of the pattern.

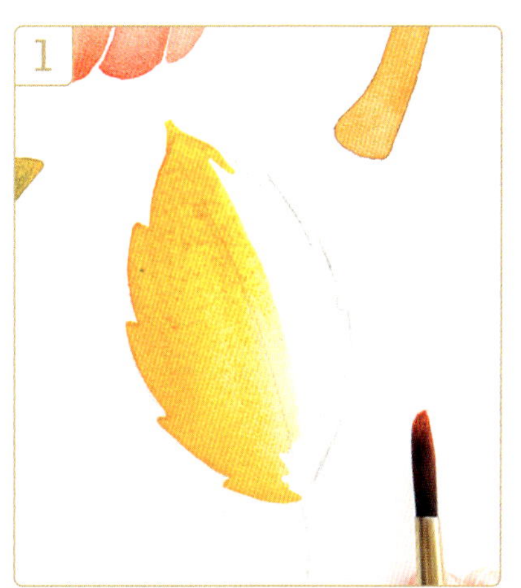
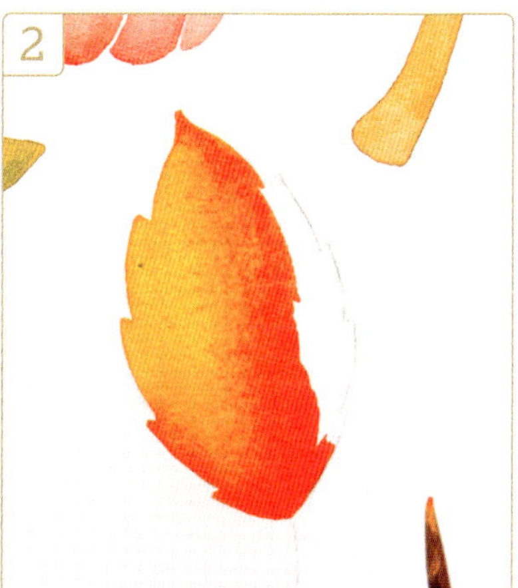
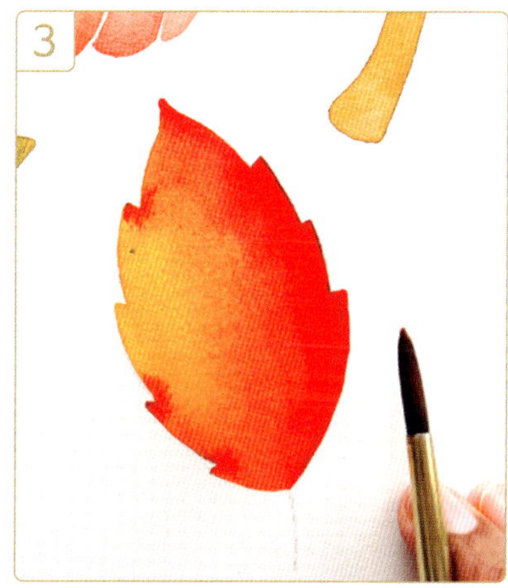
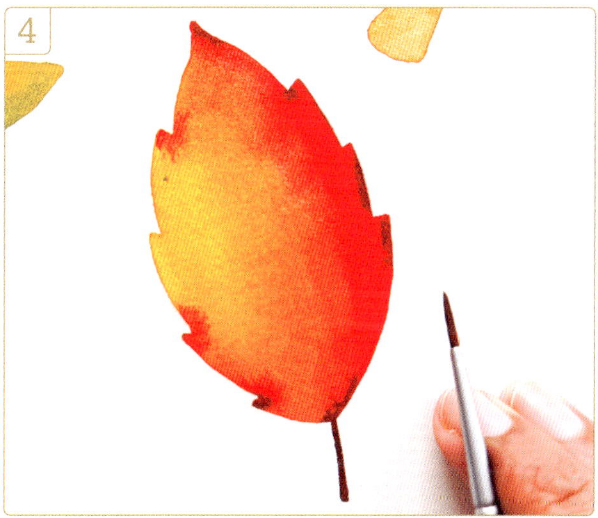
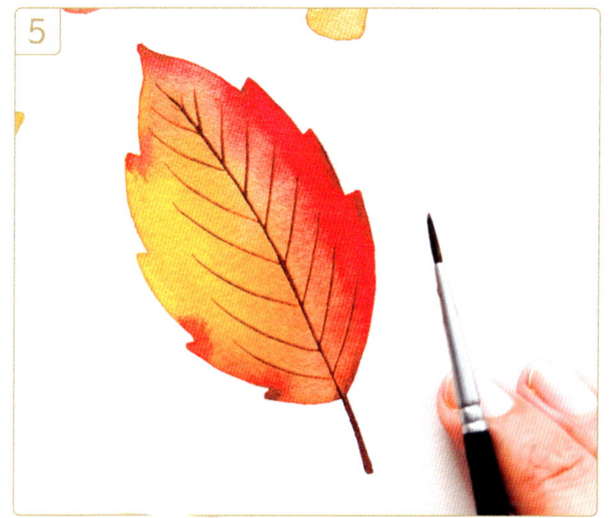

Big Leaf

1 **Paint the first color.** Now for the big leaf! Using your size 6 round brush, apply a layer of Indian Yellow or any other yellow on one half of the leaf. Keep the yellow a bit watery so it can be blended smoothly.

2 **Paint the second color.** Rinse your brush and load it with orange. Apply this color on the middle portion of the leaf. Allow the orange to overlap and blend into the yellow.

3 **Paint the third color.** Rinse your brush, mix some red, and apply it on the remaining edge of the leaf, blending it a bit with the orange. Also add some red spots on the left ridges of the leaf. If the colors look patchy, even them out with a clean, moist brush.

4 **Paint a stem.** Switch to a size 1 round brush and add a brown stem at the base of the leaf. You can also add some brown spots on the leaf to indicate wear while the colors underneath are still wet.

5 **Paint veins.** Allow the leaf to completely dry. Then draw veins on top of it using the same brown color and the size 1 round brush.

LET'S PRACTICE

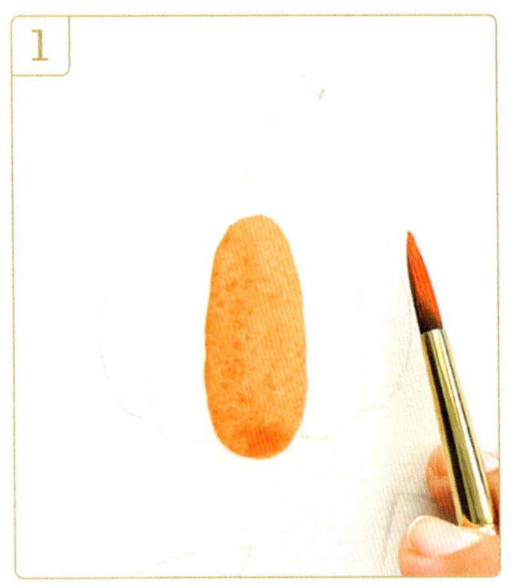
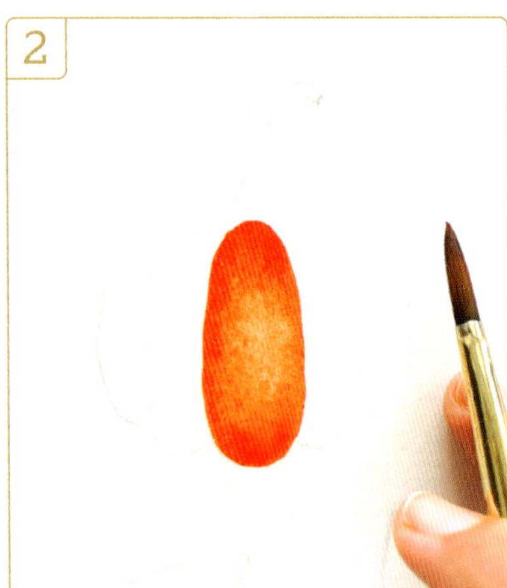
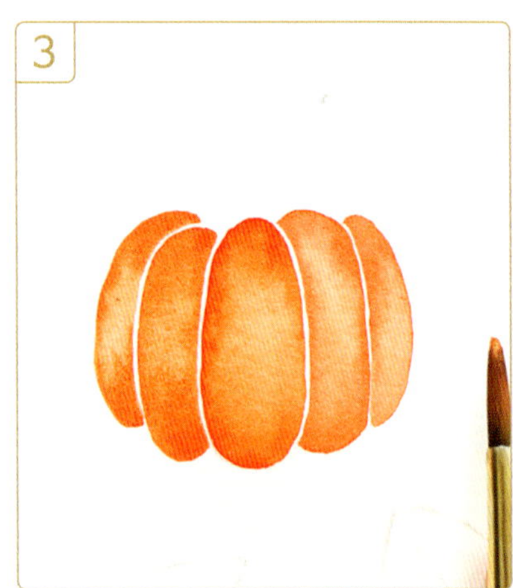
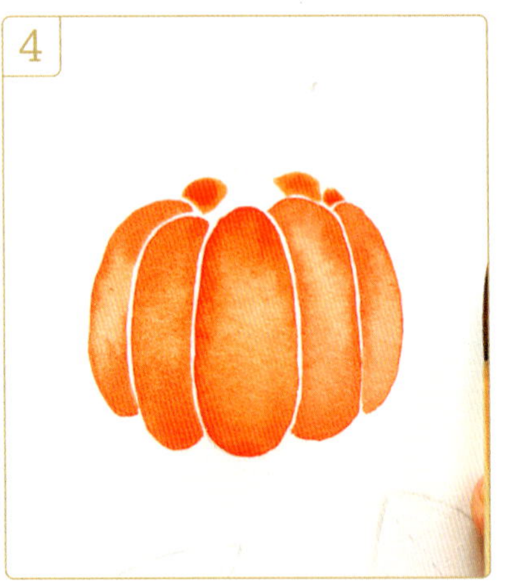
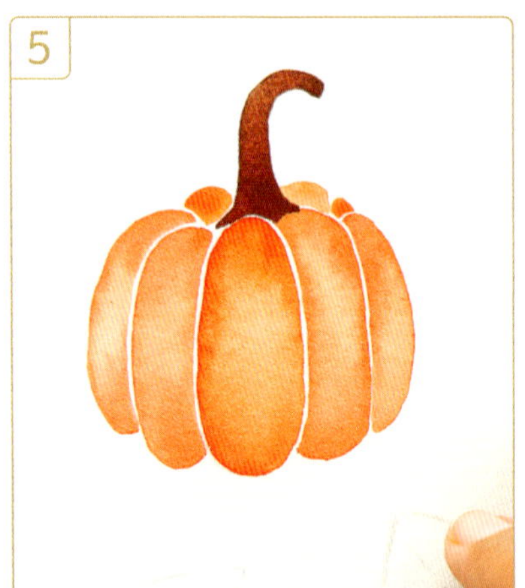
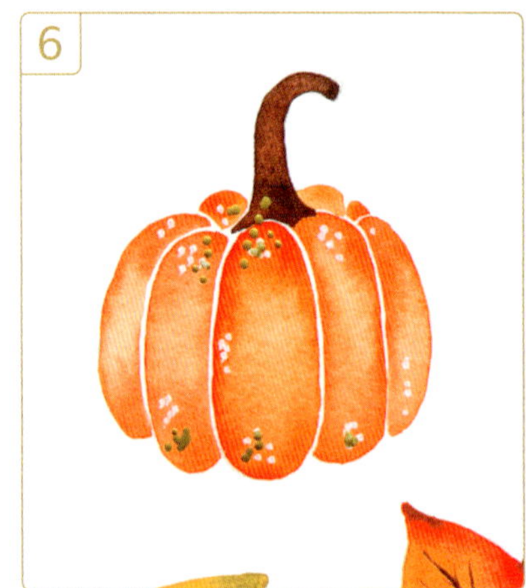

Pumpkin

1 **Start painting with the first section.** We will paint the pumpkin in sections. Start with the centermost section of the pumpkin. Fill it with a soft layer of orange color using a size 6 round brush.

2 **Add a darker color.** Mix a slightly darker shade of orange by either making it more saturated or by adding a tinge of red or brown to it. Apply this color on top of the first orange layer just around the edges, leaving a highlight in the center.

3 **Move on to the remaining sections.** As you apply the first layer of each new section, leave a small white gap between it and the surrounding sections. This white space creates contrast and definition. Finish each section using two colors.

4 **Paint the tiny sections.** Don't forget to paint the very back sections of the pumpkin that look hidden from the front. Don't worry about including a highlight in these small sections.

5 **Paint the stem.** Once the orange layer is completely dry, paint the stem of the pumpkin using a dark shade of brown.

6 **Add texture and detail.** Once the stem has dried, add some white and gold dots across the surface of the pumpkin to make it look interesting and textured.

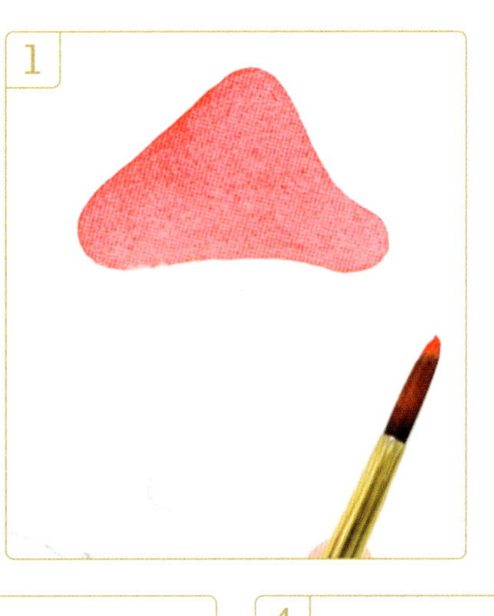
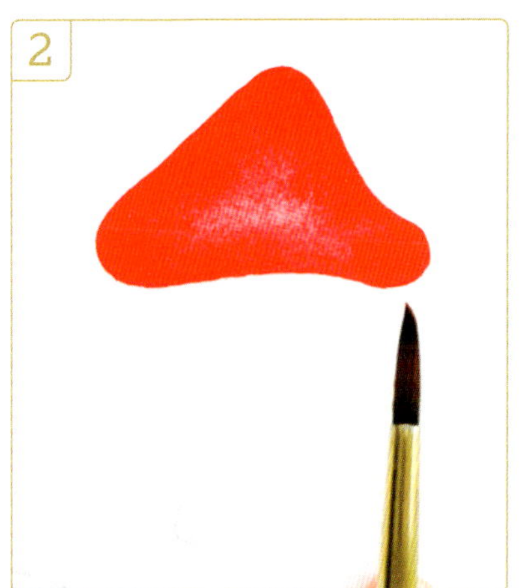
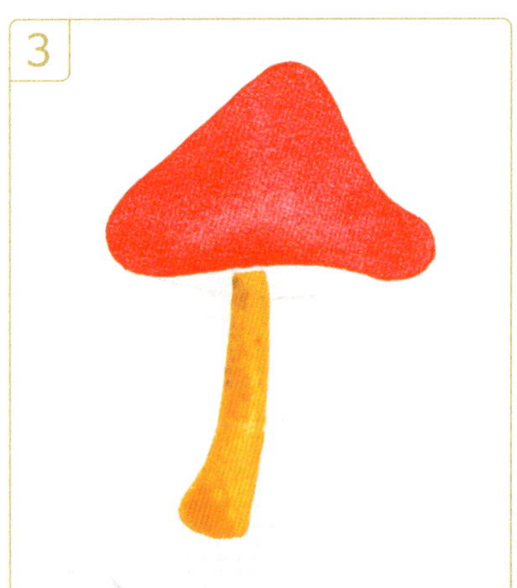
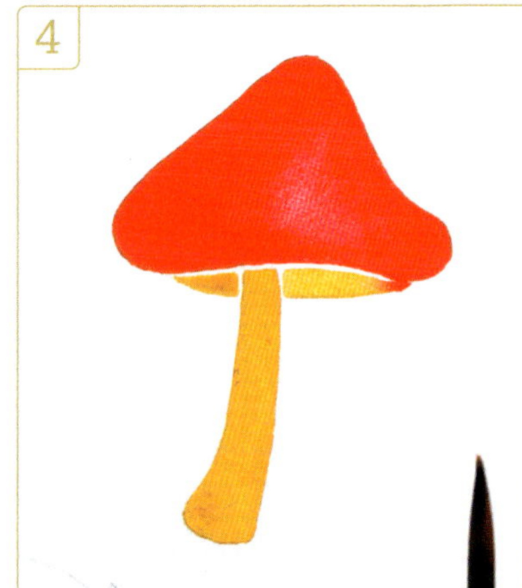
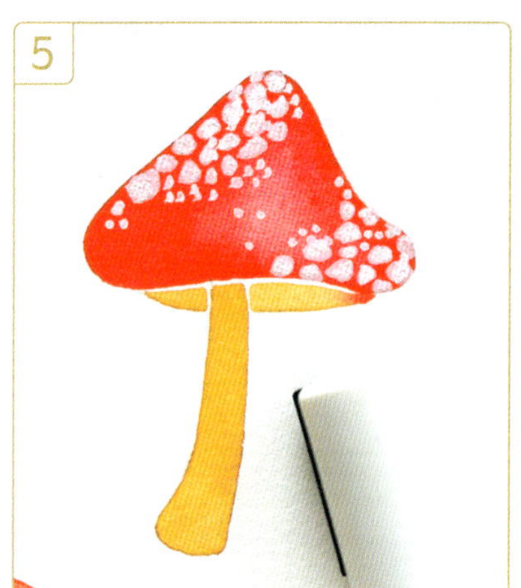

Mushroom

1 **Start painting the top.** Apply a soft wash of red color on the head of the mushroom. These will be the popular mushroom that many people don't know the name of: they're called fly agaric mushrooms!

2 **Add a darker red.** Mix a darker shade of red and apply it as a second layer on top of the initial soft red. Leave a small highlight in the center.

3 **Paint the stem.** Mix some Yellow Ochre and apply it in layers to paint the stem. Leave a small white gap between the stem and the head for definition and to avoid bleeding between the two.

4 **Paint the underside.** Then paint the underside of the mushroom around the stem area using the same yellow. Again, leave a white gap around the edges for definition and to prevent bleeding.

5 **Add details.** Once the mushroom is completely dry, add some uneven white spots on the surface of the head using a white paint pen or gouache.

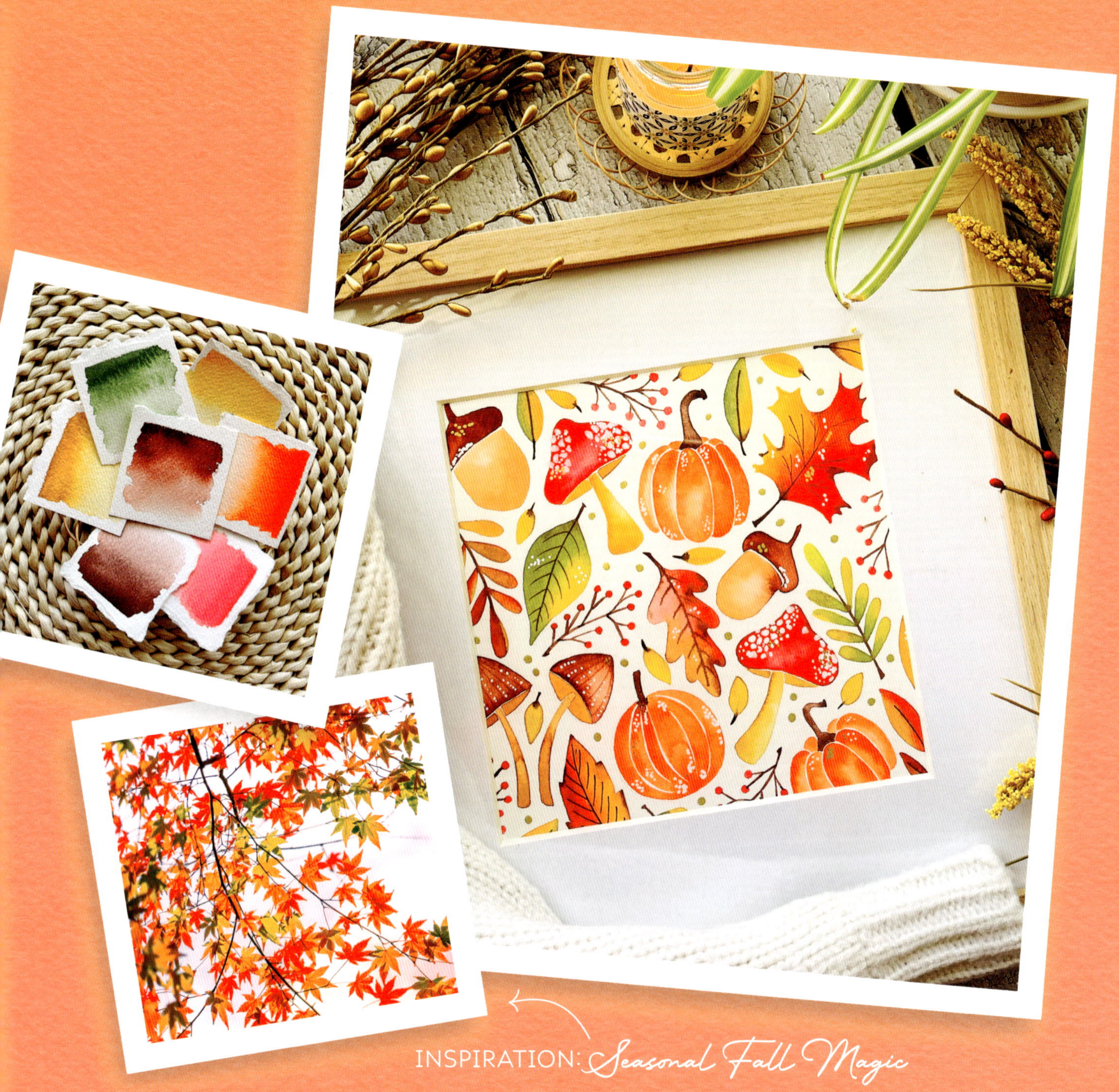

Let's Relax

Though I am not originally from North America, I have been living here for a while now, and autumn is by far the most beautiful time of year. The sight of magical fall leaves in glistening shades of yellow, gold, orange, and red never gets old. The transition from summer to autumn is a spectacular sight; all the positive quotes and sayings out there about autumn are absolutely no exaggeration, in my opinion! With this pattern, I want you to enjoy painting the autumn season with a beautiful warm color palette that makes you feel both crisp and cozy. Get a warm cup of tea or coffee and dive in!

1 **Draw a pattern.** Re-create the basic sketch I have provided here. Of course, you can also create your own composition using the different elements you've learned! You can also download the digital pattern linework and trace it on your paper (see page 14). The process for this piece is to paint the like elements in batches—so, all the pumpkins, then all the mushrooms, etc.

188

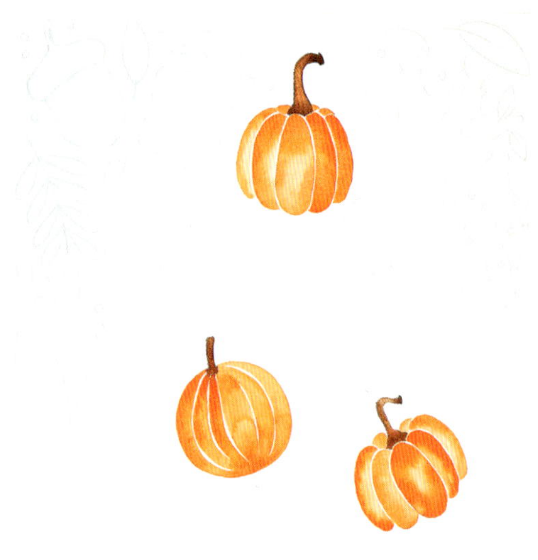

2 Paint the pumpkins. Mix two shades of orange: a lighter orange and a darker one with a small amount of red or maroon added. Don't make them too watery. Paint the pumpkins section by section, then paint the stems brown after the pumpkin bodies have dried.

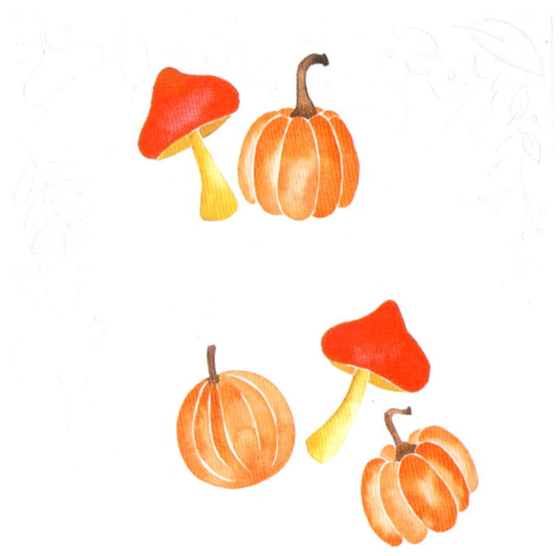

3 Paint the red mushrooms. Let's paint the two fly agaric mushrooms in red and yellow next. Paint these using two shades of red for the caps and Yellow Ochre for the stems. Remember to leave a small white gap between the individual sections.

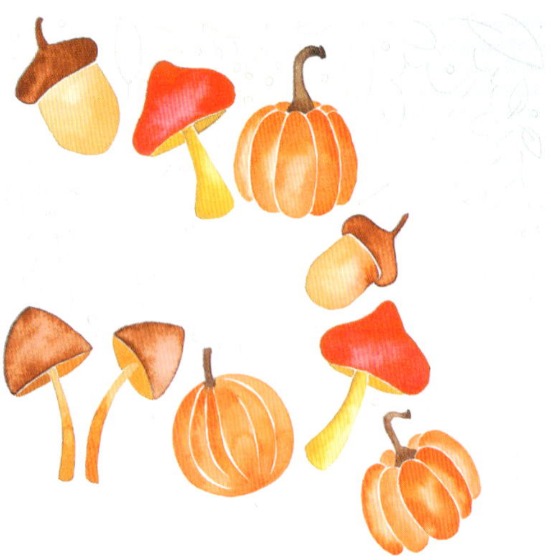

4 Paint the brown mushrooms and acorns. These were not covered in the practice session, but they're easy! For the acorn and mushroom heads, use a dark brown; for the mushroom stems and the acorn bodies, use a soft mix of Yellow Ochre. Wet each section before laying down the color.

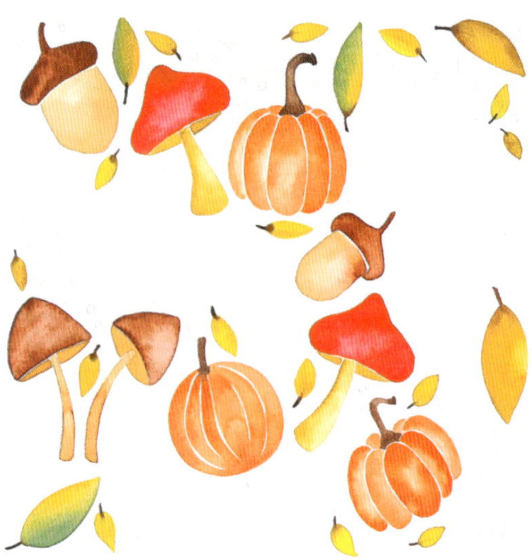

5 Paint the small leaves. Layer each small leaf using two sets of colors: Indian Yellow and Sap Green for some, and Indian Yellow and Yellow Ochre for others. Use a dark shade of brown to paint each stem while the leaves are still wet.

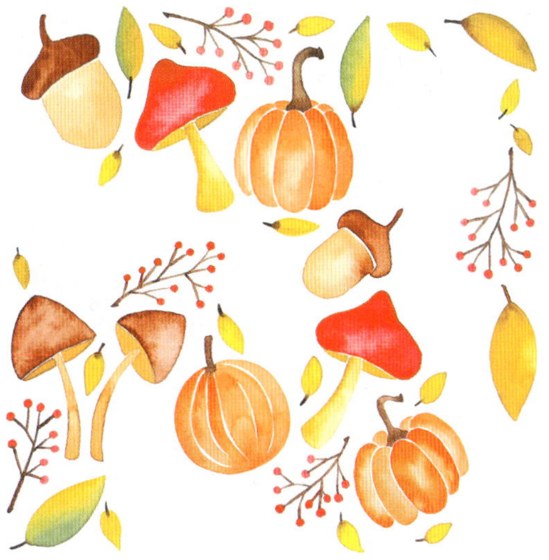

6 **Paint the berries.** The red berry stems were also not covered in the practice session, but they are quite straightforward! First use a size 1 round brush to paint the stems brown, then switch to red for the berries.

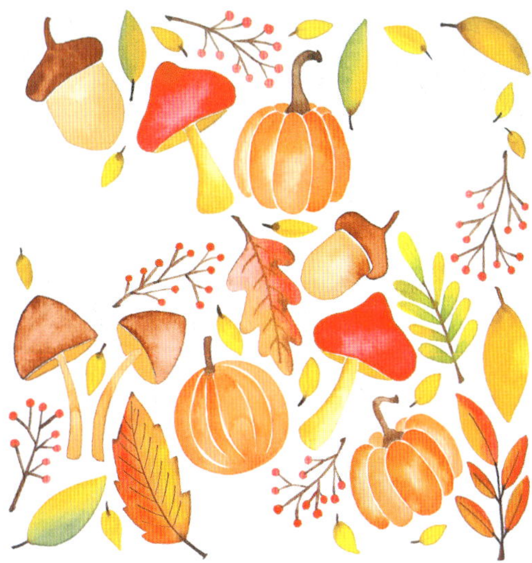

7 **Paint some of the big leaves.** Use combinations like Crimson and Yellow Ochre, any yellow and any orange, and any yellow and any green. Balance the colors so that no same-colored elements are right next to each other. Once the leaves are dry, add brown stems and veins.

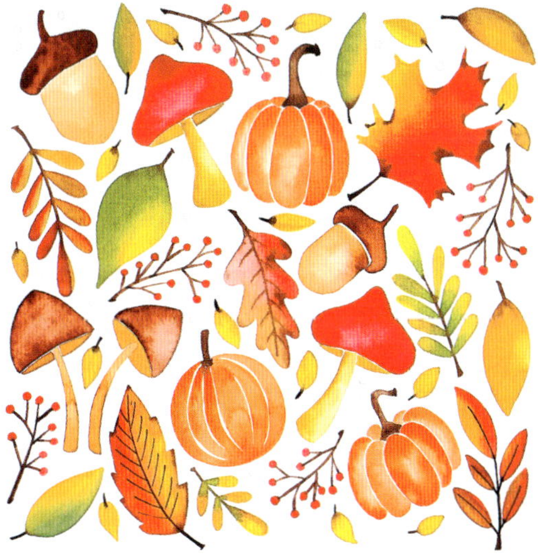

8 **Finish the remaining big leaves.** Finish the remaining three big leaves in a variety of color combinations. To paint the maple leaf, use a color gradation of Indian Yellow, orange, and red. If you missed any leaves at this point, go ahead and paint them now.

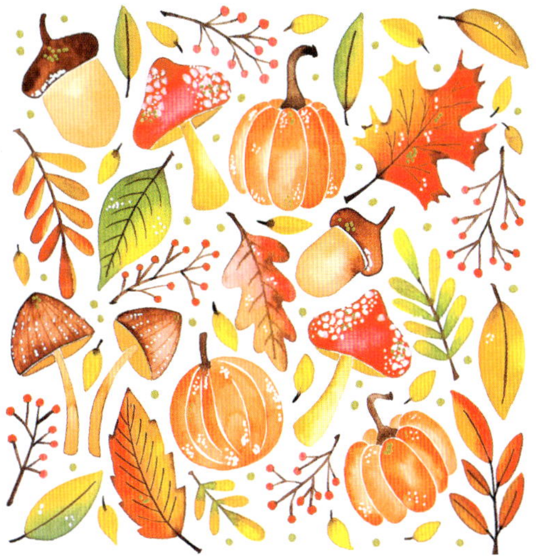

9 **Add the final details.** Color in all the background dots using a gold paint pen or gold watercolor. Add veins to the last few leaves and a varying white and gold dotted texture to the mushrooms, the pumpkins, and some leaves. For this, use whatever tools you have, such as paint markers or gouache.

Let's Paint

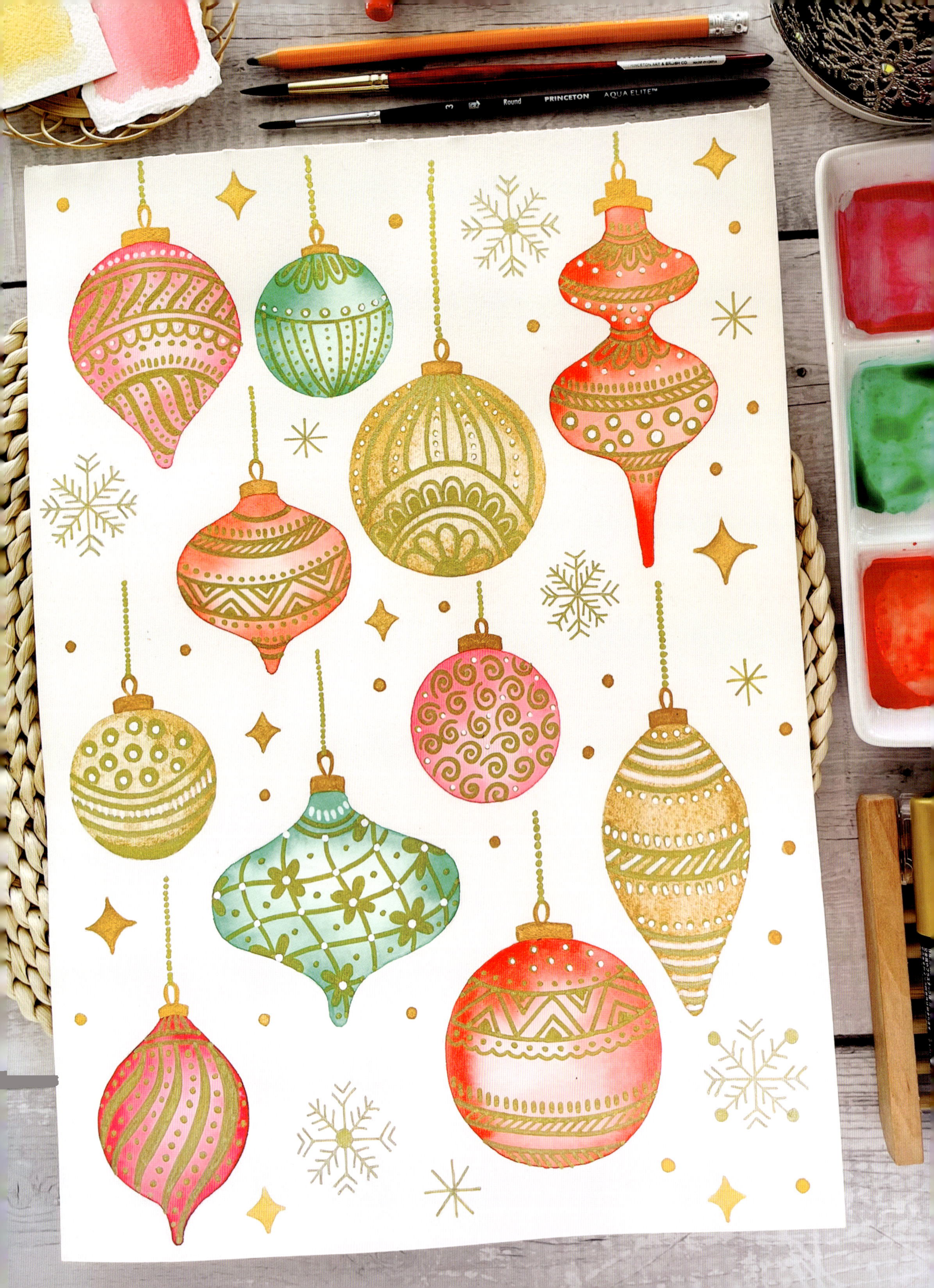

Ornate Christmas

How could we possibly not include a Christmas-inspired pattern to round out this final set of seasonal patterns? This design includes delightful hanging Christmas ornaments with ornate filigree decoration. We will be painting all the ornaments using watercolors as a base, and then work on the intricate designs using gold watercolor or a gold paint pen. Using special accents like gold can greatly benefit your watercolor work with its added detail and uniqueness.

191

MATERIALS

BRUSHES: Size 6 round brush; size 1 round brush for details

PAPER: 11" x 14" (28 x 35 cm), hot pressed

OTHER: Pencil; compass; gel pens or paint pens (optional) in white and gold, 0.7 mm or thicker; you could also use white gouache

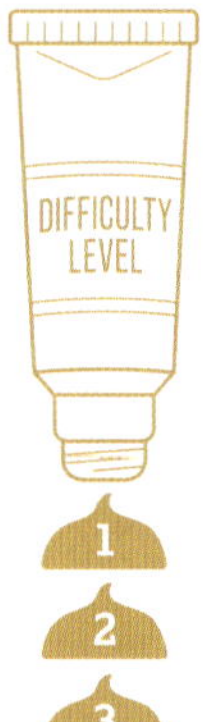

COLORS:

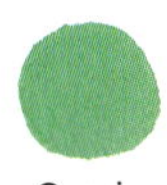 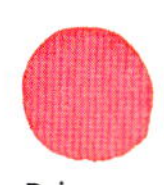 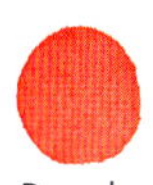 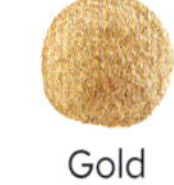

Cupric Green Light Primary Red Magenta Pyrrole Red Gold Watercolor or Yellow Ochre

TIP: Do not hesitate to use a pencil to draw the ornate filigree designs on the ornaments before tracing them with a gold paint marker. Take your time figuring out (or carefully copying) the designs. This pattern is meant to be highly decorative, so the detail is part of the spirit.

This project's pattern is available as a bonus digital download! See page 14.

LET'S PRACTICE

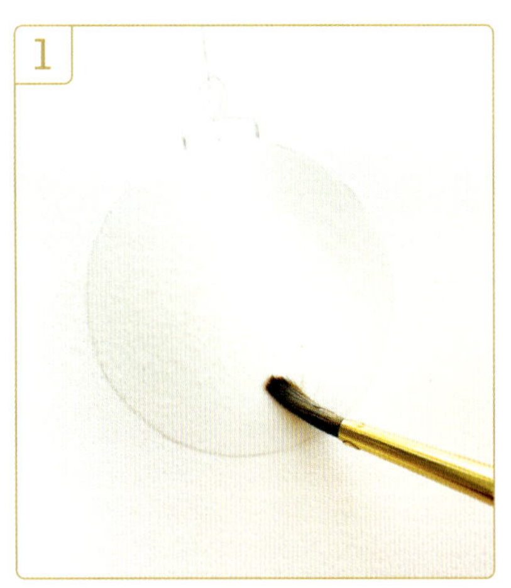

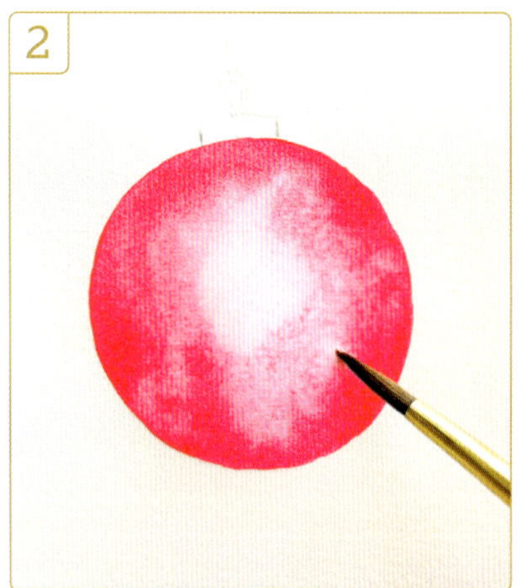

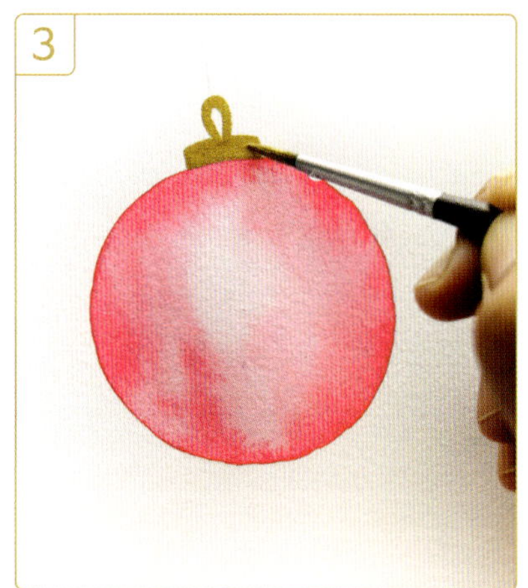

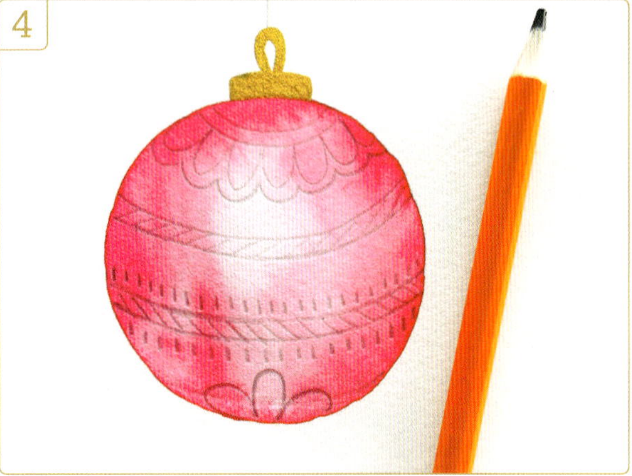

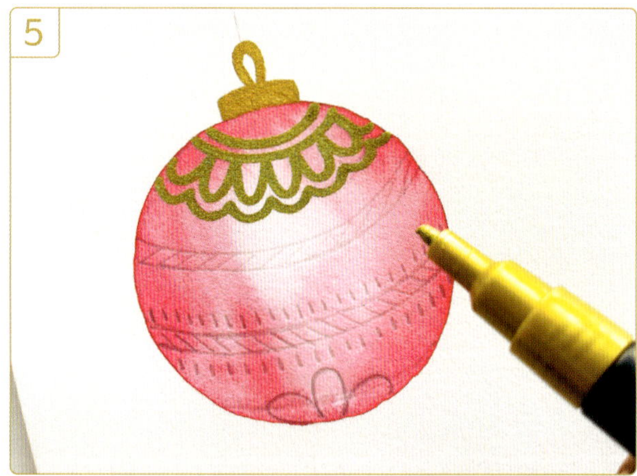

1 **Draw an ornament and add a water wash.** Draw a medium-sized circle using a compass or a lid. Then draw a cap and a string coming out from the top. Keep all the pencil lines light. Apply a layer of clean water on the circle portion using a size 6 round brush.

2 **Color the ornament ball.** Mix a shade of pink, then start applying it on the wet surface of the circle. Start by placing it on the outer edge, leaving a soft highlight in the center. Help the color to move around using gentle brushstrokes.

3 **Paint the cap.** Wait for the pink ball to dry. Then mix some gold watercolor in your palette and paint the cap using a small round brush. If you don't have gold watercolor, you could use Yellow Ochre instead.

4 **Draw the filigree.** On the dry surface of the ball, doodle some designs using a pencil. Include circular lines, dots, rounded loops, and stripes. Keep the linework slightly curved to add some visual depth to the ornament.

5 **Trace your designs.** Using a gold paint pen or gold watercolor and a small round brush, begin tracing your linework, starting from the top of the ornament.

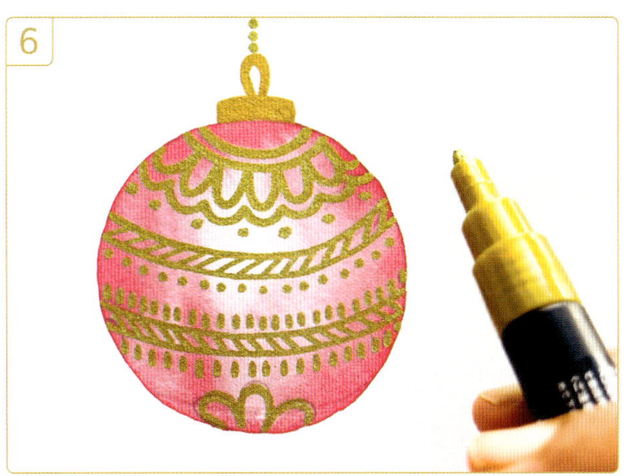

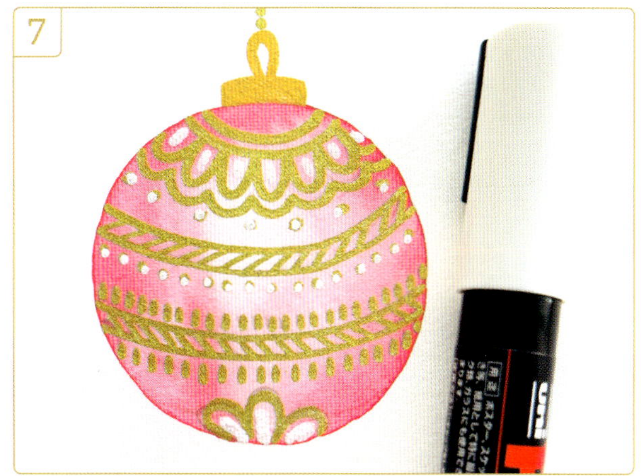

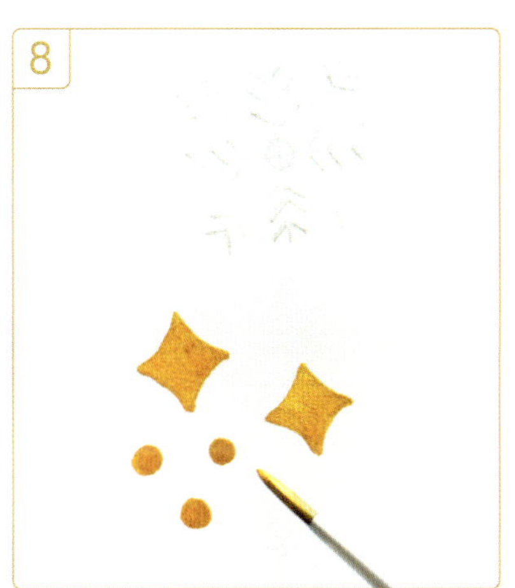

6 **Detail the string.** Finish tracing all the gold linework. Allow it to dry for a few moments. Then, using the same gold, create a beaded string by covering the hanging line with small dots placed very close to one another.

7 **Add white details.** This step is completely optional. Using a white paint pen, layer some of the gold dots with white for added boldness and texture. You could also use white gouache for this.

8 **Practice small details.** Now let's move on to the background filler for the final project, which includes four-pointed stars and scattered dots. Using a small round brush, paint these as shown using gold watercolor or Yellow Ochre.

9 **Practice creating large snowflakes.** Sketch a snowflake like the one shown, then trace over it with a gold paint pen. You can use a ruler to draw the pencil lines or simply draw it freehand. You will include one or two variations of such a snowflake in the final piece.

10 **Practice small snowflakes.** To add even more variety to the background motifs, practice drawing one more simple intersecting-line snowflake as shown. It should be a bit smaller than the large decorative snowflake you just practiced.

Let's Relax

Every Christmas season, I get to see some amazing Christmas ornaments in all the home décor stores around me, and each one is equally beautiful, dazzling, and special. They are all so festive, and the sparkly designs in gold, silver, and champagne colors have always been my favorites! The ornaments that we will be painting in this pattern are inspired by all the ornaments I have seen over the years. Honestly, I couldn't think of a better ending for this book than this festive Christmas design, which comes at the end just like the holiday comes at the end of the year. Let's paint together one last time.

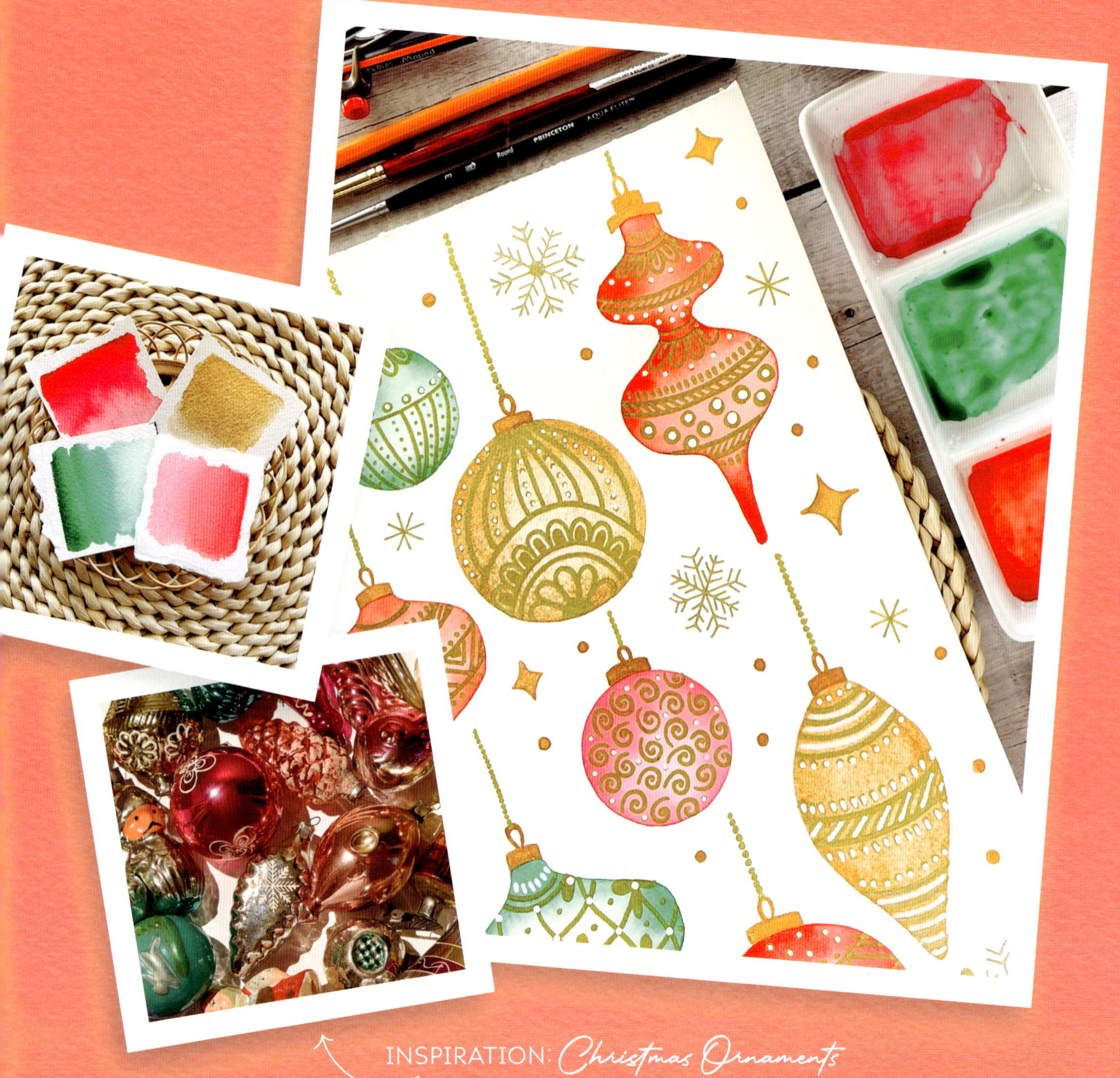

INSPIRATION: *Christmas Ornaments*

1 **Draw a pattern.** Re-create the basic sketch I have provided here. Of course, you can also create your own composition using different ornament shapes! You can also download the digital pattern linework and trace it on your paper (see page 14). The process for this piece is to paint all the basic ornaments, then move on to the details.

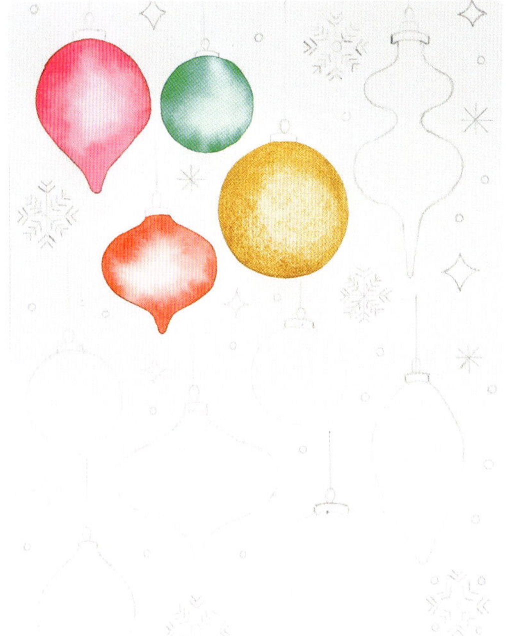

2 **Paint the base colors of the first few ornaments.** Start with the four ornaments in the top left. Paint each one using one of the four palette colors. Start with a layer of clean water and then drop in the paint, remembering to leave a soft highlight in the center.

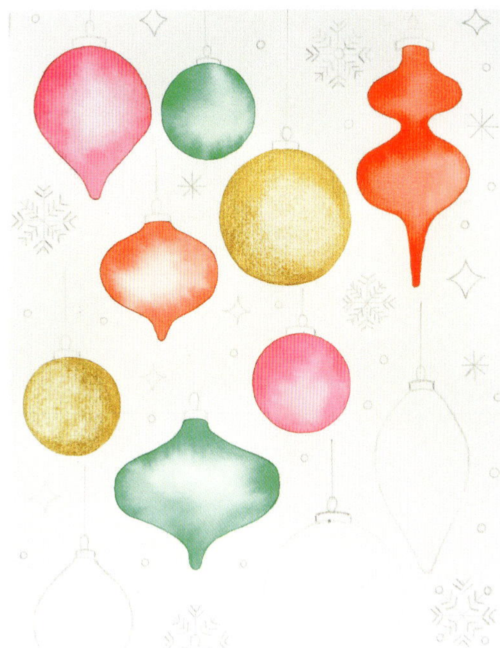

3 **Paint the next four ornaments.** Paint the four ornaments next to the first four by choosing colors appropriately to balance out the composition. Make sure that no two ornaments next to each other are the same color.

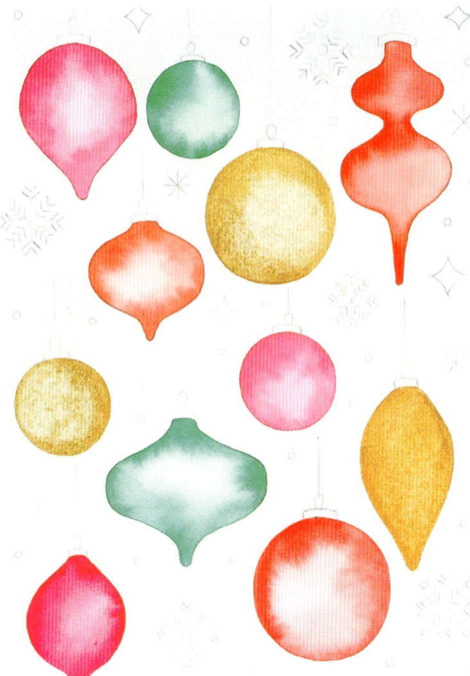

4 **Finish up the last three ornaments.** Tackle the last three ornaments now, again making sure to place different colors next to one another. I liked how the colors ended up being distributed across the page in this piece!

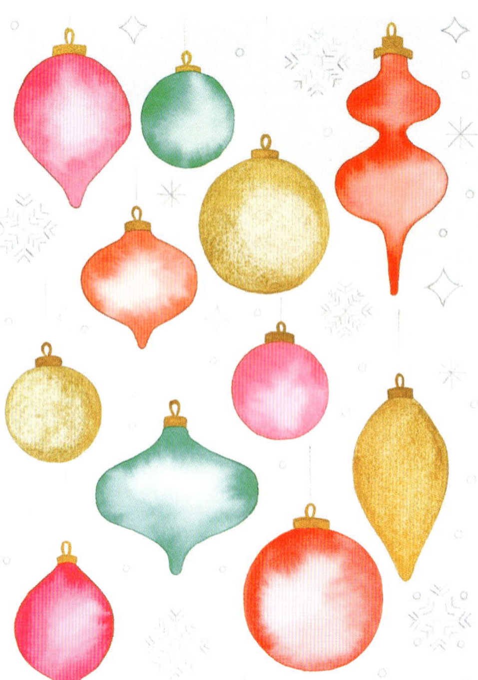

5 **Paint the caps.** Once all the ornaments are dry, paint the cap of each one using gold watercolor (or Yellow Ochre).

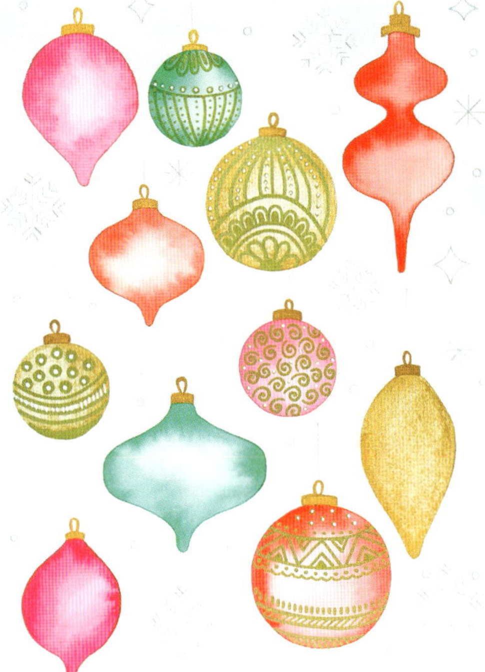

6 **Add filigree to the round ornaments.** It's time for the fun part! Start drawing intricate designs on each of the round ornaments using a pencil. Then, using a gold paint pen or gold watercolor, trace your marks on one ornament at a time.

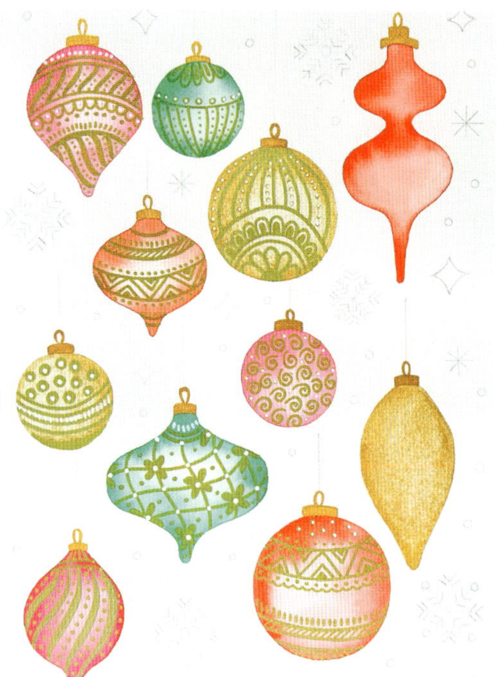

7 **Add filigree to more ornaments.** Next work on the oddly shaped ornaments on the left half of the page. Try to make every ornament at least a little different. Add white detail once the gold has dried—I had already added some in the previous step.

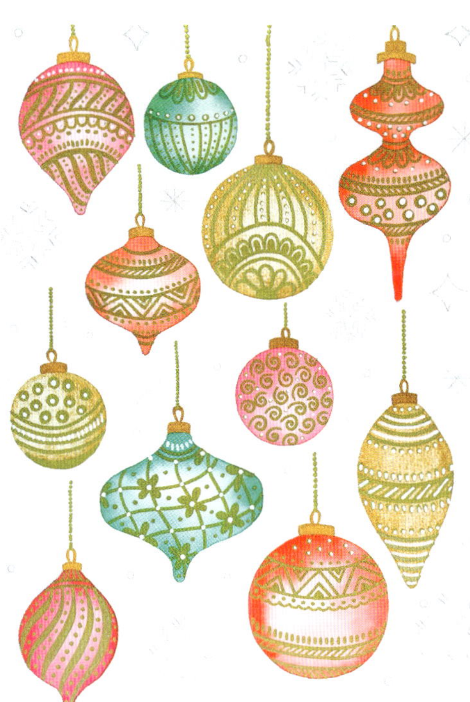

8 **Finish the filigree and detail the strings.** Wrap up the remaining ornaments. Once you are done with the filigree designs throughout, finish by covering the hanging strings with tightly placed dots. These look so intricate and pretty!

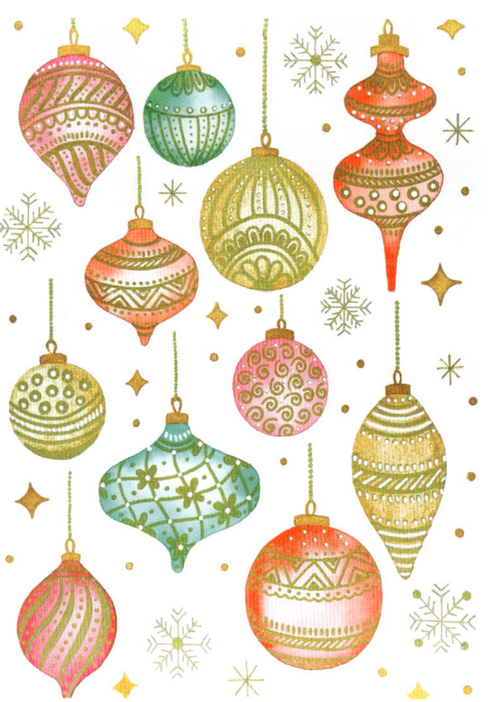

9 **Add final filler details.** Now you can paint the stars, snowflakes, and dots throughout the background, as explained in the practice session. I painted the dots and the four-pointed stars using gold watercolor, then used a gold paint pen for the remaining stars and snowflakes.

Let's Paint

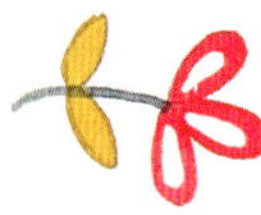

ACKNOWLEDGMENTS

I cannot call this book done without thanking all those who have contributed directly or indirectly to it and to my art journey through today. Thank you to:

My publisher, Peg, and editor, Colleen, for bringing out the best in me and encouraging me with kind words every time I sent in new artwork. It kept me going and pushed me to make great art for the book. Thanks also to the book's splendid designer, Michael Douglas. Thank you for the opportunity, BDB. It means so much!

My entire big Indian family—especially Prakash, Nandini, Abhijit, Vandita, Sonali, and Anika—for always rooting for me and for being there for me. They are my loyal brand ambassadors who share my work with utmost pride and enthusiasm every time I do something new.

My friends, Instagram followers, and students on Skillshare, for always showering love and sweet comments on my work. It only helps me to do better and better.

My licensing agency, MHS Licensing, for being ever so supportive of my personal project and giving me all the time I needed to finish this book peacefully. I appreciate it so much.

FILA Group (Arches, Canson, Daler-Rowney, Lyra, Maimeri, Princeton, St Cuthberts Mill, Strathmore), for supporting me through their high-quality art supplies.

Last but not the least, thank you, dear reader, for choosing to buy this book over many other equally good ones!

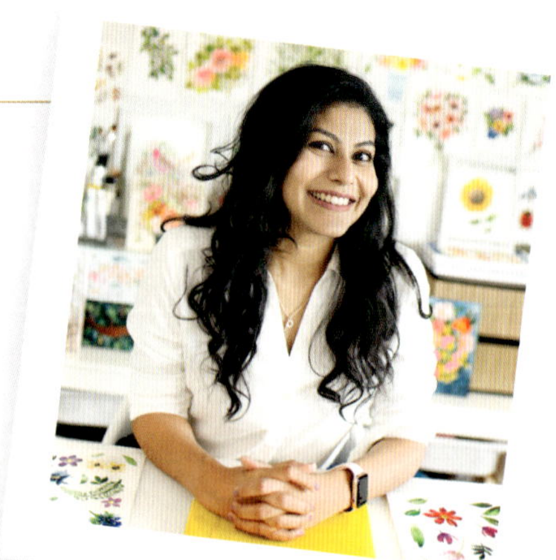

Pooja Kenjale-Umrani is a self-taught watercolor artist with a drive to become a successful entrepreneur in the creative world. After studying computer engineering and working in IT for seven years, she quit her tech career to follow her dream of establishing a successful art business.

Pooja was always inclined toward art, but her real art journey began at the end of 2016, when she started painting and posting pictures of her daily watercolor practice on social media. She inspired her followers to paint with her and formed a close-knit community, never expecting that art would become her career within three years. Pooja is now a self-employed, full-time surface designer and a licensed artist with MHS Licensing. She absolutely loves creating designs that bring joy.

Pooja has conducted online and in-person watercolor workshops across Canada, India, and the US and has taught more than 20,000 students worldwide via Skillshare. With a growing fan base of 125K on Instagram and as a brand ambassador of the FILA Group, Pooja shares easy how-to-watercolor tutorials for her followers almost every day on social media.

Learn more at www.bythelakesideartstudio.com and on Instagram @by_the_lakeside.

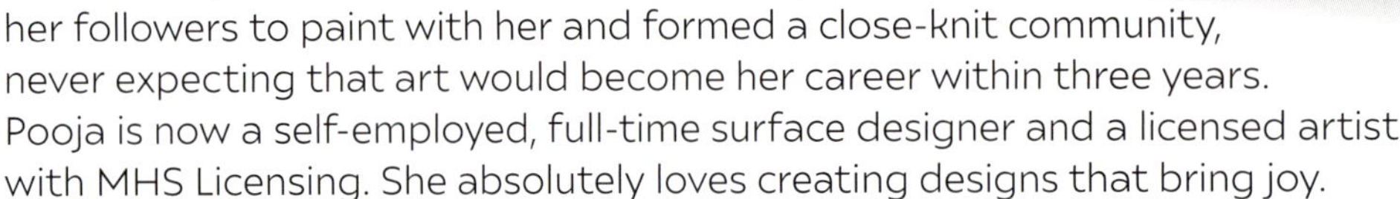

Index

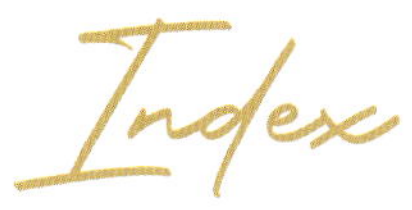

Note: Page numbers in *italics* indicate projects.

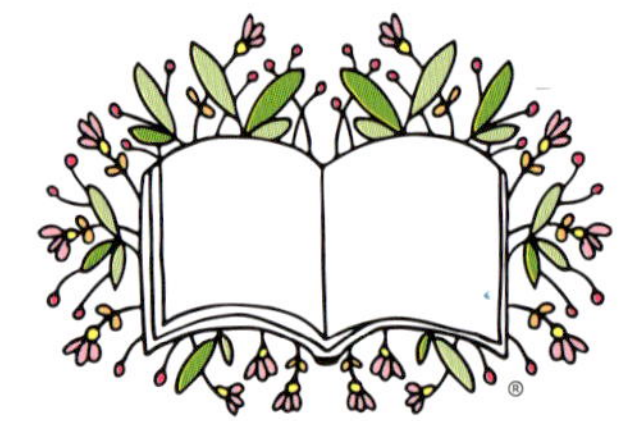

BETTER DAY BOOKS®

HAPPY • CREATIVE • CURATED

Business is personal at Better Day Books. We were founded on the belief that all people are creative and that making things by hand is inherently good for us. It's important to us that you know how much we appreciate your support. The book you are holding in your hands was crafted with the artistic passion of the author and brought to life by a team of wildly enthusiastic creatives who believed it could inspire you. If it did, please drop us a line and let us know about it. Connect with us on Instagram, post a photo of your art, and let us know what other creative pursuits you are interested in learning about. It all matters to us. You're kind of a big deal.

it's a good day to have a better day!®

www.betterdaybooks.com

better_day_books